MW00778141

RETURN TO THE MOTHERLAND

A volume in the series

Battlegrounds: Cornell Studies in Military History

Edited by David J. Silbey

Editorial Board: Petra Goedde, Wayne E. Lee, Brian McAllister Linn, and Lien-Hang T. Nguyen

A list of titles in this series is available at cornellpress.cornell.edu.

RETURN TO THE MOTHERLAND

Displaced Soviets in World War II and the Cold War

Seth Bernstein

CORNELL UNIVERSITY PRESS **ITHACA AND LONDON**

First published 2023 by Cornell University Press

Library of Congress Cataloging-in-Publication Data

Names: Bernstein, Seth, author.
Title: Return to the motherland : displaced Soviets in WWII and the Cold War /
    Seth Bernstein.
Description: Ithaca : Cornell University Press, 2023. | Series: Battlegrounds:
    Cornell studies in military history | Includes bibliographical references and
    index.
Identifiers: LCCN 2022013957 (print) | LCCN 2022013958 (ebook) |
    ISBN 9781501767395 (hardcover) | ISBN 9781501767401 (epub) |
    ISBN 9781501767418 (pdf)
Subjects: LCSH: Return migrants—Soviet Union—Social conditions—
    20th century. | Return migration—Social aspects—Soviet Union. |
    Cold War—Social aspects—Soviet Union. | World War, 1939–1945—
    Forced repatriation.
Classification: LCC JV8186 .B47 2023 (print) | LCC JV8186 (ebook) |
    DDC 305.9/069120947—dc23/eng/20220715
LC record available at https://lccn.loc.gov/2022013957
LC ebook record available at https://lccn.loc.gov/2022013958

Contents

Acknowledgments

This book must begin with my acknowledgement of something that is missing: Russia's war on Ukraine. I am adding this paragraph in April 2022. It is unusual when an event reframes history as dramatically as the Russian invasion has. Much of this book takes place in Ukraine, and it uses Ukrainian archives extensively. Some of these materials have been destroyed in the war. Other files in Ukraine and Russia will be difficult or impossible to access in the future. I recognize that this book could have spent more time on specifically Ukrainian aspects of the story. The war has also highlighted patterns in the treatment of refugees and in the actions of the displaced. I hope to return to these themes in future work. In the meantime, I believe that this study will contribute to discussions about the historical precedents of the war and the Soviet legacies of displacement.

I began this book in Moscow in 2014 and finished it as a repatriate to the United States in Gainesville, Florida. It is a project I began at a time of increasing instability in Eastern Europe and finished during the COVID-19 pandemic. As for many of us, events conspired to separate me physically from colleagues, friends, and family during this period, but the shared effort of writing this book brought us closer in other ways.

A group of mentors played an important role in this work. Lynne Viola has been a model of intellectual rigor, collegiality, and support throughout my career. I am grateful to Oleg Khlevniuk for his advice and insightful reading of a draft of the full manuscript. I benefited from the environment and resources of the International Center for the History and Sociology of World War II and Its Consequences at the Higher School of Economics (HSE) and from continuing discussions with Oleg Budnitskii, Michael David-Fox, and Liudmila Novikova. I would also like to thank Aleksandr Kamenskii, my chair at HSE, and Elizabeth Dale and Jon Sensbach, my chairs at the University of Florida, for their support of the project.

I relied on many colleagues' readings of chapters in this book and related work. Their number is so large that I worry I have missed some. They include Rachel Applebaum, Alan Barenberg, Wilson Bell, Jon Brunstedt, Diana Dumitru, Geoff Eley, Alice Freifeld, Norm Goda, Anna Hajkova, Sam Hirst, Artem Latyshev, Vojin Majstorovic, Irina Makhalova, Tracy McDonald, Alex Melnyk, Dan Newman, Liudmila Novikova, Anatoly Pinsky, Maris Rowe-McCulloch, Erik Scott, David Shearer, Lewis Siegelbaum, Vladimir Solonari, Lynne Viola, Alex Voronovici,

Zbig Wojnowski, and Katherine Zubovich. A special thanks is due to Susan Grant, who read nearly the entire book as I produced chapters. I also would like to thank Natalie Belsky, Florin Curta, Franziska Exeler, Krista Goff, Michael Gorham, Aaron Hale-Dorrell, Kristy Ironside, Andy Janco, Sheryl Kroen, Ilya Kukulin, Matt Lenoe, Mike Loader, Thom Loyd, Angelina Lucento, Steve Maddox, Laurie Manchester, Jared McBride, Alison Smith, Jessica Werneke, and Beate Winzer for suggestions and discussions that informed the work. The members of my student research group at HSE provided valuable help processing data and discussing their meaning with me: Irina Makhalova, Anastasia Zaplatina, Vasilina Chernysheva, Vladislav Iakovenko, Dmitrii Kotilevich, Sofia Filina, Nelli Gasimova, Valeria Pleshkova, Aleksandra Riabichenko, Maria Satyeva, Elizaveta Solodovnikova, Liza Stovba, and Vladislav Tiurin.

The research for this book brought me to archives in Russia, Ukraine, the United Kingdom, and the United States. I owe much to Maria Panova of Ukraine's secret police archive, who has instructed me on its workings since 2014 and has always found materials for me, even if I did not know what I was looking for. I also thank Vadim Altskan, Jürgen Matthäus, and others at the United States Holocaust Memorial Museum, who helped me navigate the museum's extensive holdings. Anne Friebel of the Leipzig Nazi Forced Labor Memorial went to extraordinary lengths to track down information on members of Leipzig resistance groups. Alena Kozlova at Memorial in Moscow, closed by the Russian government in 2022, gave me early access to interviews with former forced laborers that would become part of the wonderful site Ta storona (The Other Side, http://www.tastorona.su).

It has been a pleasure to work with Cornell University Press. Emily Andrew organized an insightful review of my manuscript. I thank Mark Edele, who unmasked himself as a reviewer, and the two reviewers who remain cloaked as the book goes to press for their generous comments on my work. Bethany Wasik has been a model of responsive editing since she took over the project in its middle stages. David Silbey, the series editor for Battlegrounds, has buoyed this work with unflinching enthusiasm. Susan Ecklund of Westchester Publishing Services ironed out the text and caught most of my typos.

My family has endured separations that we anticipated and those we did not. My parents, Jim Bernstein and Lynn Franklin, made many trips across the Atlantic to visit while I worked on this book from Moscow. My sister, Miranda Bernstein, made two trips, which is also pretty good. Liubov Glakhova, Andrei Kuzmin, Andrei Glakhov, and Alesia Glakhova provided food, company, and daycare while I wrote in Smolensk. My job took me away from Tanya and Teo for hours, days, weeks, and, unexpectedly, more than a year in 2020–21. And then once we were reunited, I made Tanya help me with the maps over the holidays at the end of 2021 instead of letting her drink eggnog and relax. This book is also a product of their sacrifices.

This work received financial support from the Russian Academic Excellence Project "5–100." I also benefited from my time as the Pearl Resnick Fellow at the Jack, Joseph and Morton Mandel Center for Advanced Holocaust Studies, United States Holocaust Memorial Museum. The University of Florida sponsored my final research trips for the project. Funding toward publication was provided by the University of Florida College of Liberal Arts and Sciences and the Center for the Humanities and the Public Sphere (Rothman Endowment and Humanities Fund in Honor of Dr. Bonnie Effros, founding director). An earlier version of chapter 5 appeared in the article "Ambiguous Homecoming: Retribution, Exploitation and Social Tensions during Repatriation to the USSR, 1944–1946," *Past & Present*, no. 242 (2019): 193–226.

Note on Transliteration and Conventions

This book uses a modified version of the Library of Congress (LOC) transliteration conventions. Citations adhere to unmodified LOC transliteration. Within the text, I have used the commonly accepted spelling of well-known places and people (e.g., Moscow, Dnepr River, Trotsky). I have also converted names and places with "iia" endings to "ia" and dropped the soft sign mark ('). For example, the Eastern Workers Natal'ia Berkun and Efrosiniia Usenko in this book are Natalia and Efrosinia. People's names I have given as transliterated from the language of the source document, except in cases where the original as rendered in Latin characters was clear. For example, the French name Claude is rendered as such rather than Klod, which a direct transliteration from documents in Russian would produce.

Navigating the various languages of the region presents a difficulty for giving place-names. The people in this book understood and used multiple languages depending on the context, time, and place. Place-names also changed depending on which power ruled the area. To streamline the work, I have attempted to call place-names by their official designation at the time in the official language of the region. Ukraine's capital is Kyiv (Ukrainian) rather than Kiev (Russian).

Post-Soviet countries like Ukraine have declassified Soviet police records based on a commitment to transparency about the past, even painful questions like wartime collaboration, and do not require anonymization of the subjects of these files. It is in this spirit of clarity, both historical and narrative, that I give full names of people in this work except as required by repositories.

Repositories

AUSBU ChO   Arkhiv Upravlinnia Sluzhby Bezpeky Ukrainy Cherkas'koi Oblasti (Archive of the Administration of the Security Service of Ukraine in Cherkasy Province)

AUSBU MO   Arkhiv Upravlinnia Sluzhby Bezpeky Ukrainy Mykolaivs'koi Oblasti (Archive of the Administration of the Security Service of Ukraine in Mykolaiv Province)

AUSBU ZO   Arkhiv Upravlinnia Sluzhby Bezpeky Ukrainy Zakarpats'koi Oblasti (Archive of the Administration of the Security Service of Ukraine in Zakarpattia Province)

DAKO   Derzhavnyi Arkhiv Kyivs'koi Oblasti (State Archive of Kyiv Province)

FO   Foreign Office, National Archives (UK)

GARF   Gosudarstvennyi Arkhiv Rossiiskoi Federatsii (State Archive of the Russian Federation)

GAUMO   Glavnoe Arkhivnoe Upravlenie Moskovskoi Oblasti (Main Archival Administration of Moscow Province)

HDASBU   Haluzevyi Derzhavnyi Arkhiv Sluzhby Bezpeky Ukrainy (Sectoral State Archive of Security Service of Ukraine)

NA IRI RAN   Natsional'nyi Arkhiv Institut Rossiiskoi Istorii Rossiiskoi Akademii Nauk (National Archive, Institute of Russian History, Russian Academy of Sciences)

NACP   National Archives Building, College Park, Maryland

RGASPI   Rossiiskii Gosudarstvennyi Arkhiv Sotsial'no-Politicheskoi Istorii (Russian State Archive of Social-Political History)

RGVA   Rossiiskii Gosudarstvennyi Voennyi Arkhiv (Russian State Military Archive)

TsDAHO   Tsentral'nyi Derzhavnyi Arkhiv Hromads'kykh Ob"iednan' Ukrainy (Central State Archive of Public Organizations of Ukraine)

TsDAVO   Tsentral'nyi Derzhavnyi Arkhiv Vyshchykh Organiv Vlady Ta Upravlinnia Ukrainy (Central State Archive of Higher Organs of Power and Government of Ukraine)

USHMM   United States Holocaust Memorial Museum
ZA   Zwangsarbeit Archiv (Archive "Forced Labor 1939–1945,"
           © Freie Universität Berlin)

Record Listing Abbreviations

ark.   *arkush* (folio) (Ukrainian)
d.   *delo* (file) (Russian)
f.   *fond* (collection) (Russian/Ukrainian)
l./ll. *list/listy* (folio) (Russian)
ob.   *oborot* (Russian)/*obert* (Ukrainian) (reverse)
op.   *opis'* (Russian)/*opis* (Ukrainian) (box)
r.   *razdel* (section) (Russian)
RG   Record Group
spr.   *sprava* (file) (Ukrainian)
t.   *tom* (volume) (Russian/Ukrainian)

BSV	Bratskii Soiuz Voennoplennykh (Brotherly Union of Prisoners of War)
CIC	Counter Intelligence Corps
GlavPUR	Glavnoe Politicheskoe Upravlenie Raboche-krest'ianskoi Krasnoi Armii (Chief Political Administration of the Red Army)
IRO	International Refugee Organization
KGB	Komitet Gosudarstvennoi Bezopasnosti (Committee for State Security (secret police, 1954–91))
Komsomol	Kommunisticheskii Soiuz Molodezhi (Communist League of Youth)
KONR	Komitet Osvobozhdeniia Narodov Rossii (Committee for the Liberation of the Peoples of Russia)
MGB	Ministerstvo Gosudarstvennoi Bezopasnosti (Ministry for State Security (secret police, 1946–53))
MVD	Ministerstvo Vnutrennikh Del (Ministry for Internal Affairs (criminal police, 1946–53; secret police and criminal police, 1953–54))
NKGB	Narodnyi Komissariat Gosudarstvennoi Bezopasnosti (People's Commissariat for State Security (secret police, 1941, 1943–46))
NKVD	Narodnyi Komissariat Vnutrennikh Del (People's Commissariat for Internal Affairs (secret police and criminal police, 1934–41, 1941–43; criminal police 1943–46))
NTS	Narodno-Trudovoi Soiuz Rossiiskikh Solidaristov (National Alliance of Russian Solidarists)
ROA	Russkaia Osvoboditel'naia Armiia (Russian Liberation Army)
RROK	Russkii Rabochii Osvoboditel'nyi Komitet (Russian Workers Liberation Committee)
SD	Sicherheitsdienst des Reichsführers-SS (German security agency)
SMERSH	Smert' Shpionam (Death to Spies (military counterintelligence, 1943–46))
UNRRA	United Nations Relief and Rehabilitation Administration
UPVI	Upravlenie Po Delam Voennoplennykh i Internirovannykh (Administration for Prisoners of War and Internees)

Recurring Personages

This book follows people and groups whose names recur across chapters. For reference, I list the most important here:

Petr Astakhov: Prisoner of war and trainee at the Wustrau propagandist camp.

Natalia Berkun: Eastern Worker from Pavlohrad (Dnipropetrovsk province, Ukraine) sent to work in Leipzig. A member of the Russian Workers Liberation Committee (RROK) who married a fellow member, Aleksandr Kuprii.

Efim Brodskii: Political officer and historian researching the history of resistance among prisoners of war and forced laborers in Germany.

Aleksei Dunchevskii: Prisoner of war and trainee at the Wustrau camp.

Aleksandr Dzadzamia: Physician and prisoner of war recruited for training as a pro-German propagandist at the Wustrau camp. Member of the Wustrau Georgian choir. Later a camp physician for forced laborers in Leipzig and a member of RROK.

Aleksandr Kashia: Engineer and prisoner of war who became a Georgian barracks head at the Wustrau camp.

Evgenii Kiselev (pronounced *Kiselyov*): Technician from Mykolaiv (Ukraine) sent to the Buchenwald concentration camp. Displaced person camp leader in Leipzig and RROK member.

Aleksandr Kuprii: Eastern Worker from Pavlohrad sent to work in Leipzig. Member of RROK and postwar husband of Natalia Berkun.

Prokofii Lesnichenko: Activist from Pavlohrad sent to forced labor in Leipzig. Leader of RROK.

Aleksandra Mikhaleva (pronounced *Mikhalyova*): Eastern Worker from Kursk (Russia) sent to factory work in Waltershausen with her cousin in 1942.

Antonina S.: Eastern Worker who hid that her mother was Jewish and married a French laborer in Germany.

Nadezhda Severilova: Eastern Worker who traveled to Italy after World War II under the name Nella Antilucci.

Ilia Sherstiuk: Prisoner of war and trainee at the Wustrau propagandist camp.

Nikolai Shevchenko: Eastern Worker deported from Ukraine to Bavaria and leader of the Central Committee for Struggle, a resistance group. Museum worker after the war.

Mikhail Sinitsyn: Eastern Worker deported from Ukraine to Bamberg (Bavaria). Arrested for poetry writing in Germany and member of the Central Committee for Struggle.

Efrosinia Usenko: Eastern Worker from Pavlohrad deported to Leipzig. Member of RROK.

MAP 1. Soviet annexations 1939–45, with notable locations. Prepared by the author and Tanya Glakhova.

Austria
Poland
Germany

MAP 2. Division of postwar Germany, with notable locations. Prepared by the author and Tanya Glakhova.

DISPLACED IN WAR AND PEACE

Aleksandra Mikhaleva returned to her parents in Kursk in September 1945. The last time she had seen them was in 1942, when she was just eighteen years old. German forces had deported Mikhaleva, her cousin Galina, and dozens of other teenagers from Kursk to the Third Reich. These young people were to be forced laborers who would produce arms for Germany's struggle against the Soviet Union. For three years Mikhaleva toiled for meager rations, scavenging and working odd jobs for Germans to get extra food. She also found boyfriends among relatively privileged non-Soviet forced laborers from Poland, the Czech lands, and Italy, who helped her with gifts of food and clothes.

Liberation by American forces in April 1945 was a joyous moment. Mikhaleva spent two months in a scenic German town under Allied rule with her Italian boyfriend, Ugo. She briefly considered marriage to him but knew she could not live without her family in Kursk. Her journey back to the USSR lasted another two months and was filled with new dangers: the search for transport and shelter, sexual predation by Red Army soldiers, and verification (so-called filtration) by Iosif Stalin's secret police. Despite the adversity she faced during her return, Mikhaleva arrived at her home safely. She was one of 5.4 million returnees, a figure that included people displaced within Soviet borders, former prisoners of war returning from abroad, and former Eastern Workers like Mikhaleva. Like most returnees, she was not sent to the Gulag by the secret police. Her reunion with her family did not end her troubles, though. Constant suspicion from neighbors and Soviet authorities cost her friends and jobs. Her wartime tribulations were over, but the ordeal of return had only begun.[1]

This book explores the lives of people like Mikhaleva. They were more than seven million civilian forced laborers and POWs deported to work for the Germans and their allies (table I.1). In Nazi Germany they were Eastern Workers (Ostarbeiter) and POWs. In postwar Europe they were displaced persons. Those who returned to the Soviet Union became repatriates (*repatrianty*). Those who refused to come to the USSR became nonreturners in Allied-occupied Europe. Many of these Soviet-claimed people had lived in the country only from 1939, when the USSR annexed the western areas of contemporary Belarus, Moldova, Ukraine, and the three Baltic republics. Soviet accounts put the number of nonreturners at 450,000, but they were possibly more numerous.[2] Forced labor, displacement, and

TABLE I.1   Repatriation Administration assessment of dislocation of Soviet displaced persons, December 1, 1946

CATEGORY	NUMBER*
1. Registered as taken from the USSR	6,834,708
Civilians	4,829,060
Former POWs**	2,005,648
2. Found after liberation	5,715,162
Civilians	3,709,514
Former POWs	2,005,648
3. Returned to Soviet control	5,415,925
Civilians	3,582,358
Former POWs	1,833,567
4. Sent to next disposition***	5,382,990
Civilians	3,551,324
Former POWs	1,831,666
5. In occupied areas ("former front")	32,935
Civilians	31,034
Former POWs	1,901
6. Subject to repatriation (i.e., nonreturners)	299,237
Civilians	127,156
Former POWs	172,081
7. Presumed dead (i.e., missing)	1,119,546

Source: GARF, f. 9526, op. 6, d. 235, ll. 21–22.

*Totals include so-called internally displaced people, those who were deported within Soviet borders, and those who lived beyond Soviet borders.

**Former POWs registered as taken from the USSR include only those prisoners registered as alive after liberation and do not include the significant number of POWs who died during the war.

***The designation in the original document is "sent to place of residence," which is inaccurate. This category includes people who passed through filtration, regardless of whether they faced repression, were sent to the army or labor battalions, were sent to exile, or went to their prewar residences.

repatriation all entailed deprivation and peril. Yet the period in Europe was also a moment of new experiences. For many it was the first time they had lived outside of Stalin's rule, albeit as oppressed people in Adolf Hitler's forced labor empire. After the USSR's victory over Germany, Stalinist leaders were determined to return them to the motherland physically and spiritually.

Repatriation became a shameful chapter in the history of the USSR that raised uncomfortable questions about the Soviet experience of World War II. How had the Soviet Union allowed so many of its people to be taken as forced laborers and POWs? Was it only force that brought people to Germany? Through intimidation and arrest, Stalin's regime suppressed repatriates' story of the war. In the West, Soviet repatriation became known as a notorious moment of Allied complicity with Stalin's regime. At the Yalta Conference in February 1945, as victory over Germany neared, Winston Churchill, Franklin Roosevelt, and Iosif Stalin agreed to the compulsory repatriation of all Allied citizens. The Allies would transfer millions of liberated civilians and former POWs back to the USSR. The decision became a source of controversy in the Cold War, when commentators presumed that the returnees went against their will to their arrest and perhaps execution.[3] The loudest critic, Nikolai Tolstoy, scion of the Russian noble family in emigration, lost a libel suit and was ordered to pay 1.5 million British pounds for accusations he made against a politician who had participated in the decision to repatriate.[4] During the peak of anticommunism in the Thatcherite 1980s, Britain's Parliament authorized a monument to the "countless innocent men, women, and children from the Soviet Union and other East European states who were imprisoned and died at the hands of Communist governments after being repatriated" (figure I.1). Despite the outcry over repatriation in the West, what happened after return to the USSR was largely unknown, obscured by the Iron Curtain.

Popular and scholarly notions of repression after repatriation have persisted, but works based on declassified post-Soviet archives have contained revelations about this story. On the eve of the USSR's collapse, the historian Viktor Zemskov published evidence showing that far from all repatriates faced arrest at the time of their filtration. Among the 4.2 million returnees arriving from beyond Soviet borders, the secret police arrested 6.5 percent (table I.2). Stalin's regime pressed approximately 35 percent of returnees into service in the army or labor battalions, and, as this book suggests, 1 to 2 percent of repatriates faced arrest after filtration as well.[5] Arrest was hardly a guarantee, and more than half simply went home, but these homebound returnees also faced discrimination. Pavel Polian's mammoth *Victims of Two Dictatorships* followed Soviet people to Germany and back to condemn Stalin's regime as using discriminatory and exploitative practices that mirrored those Nazi Germany had used against Eastern Workers.[6] Other scholars

FIGURE I.1.   *Twelve Responses to Tragedy*, London, Angela Conner, 1986. Photograph by the author.

have presented more moderate findings than Polian, using regional state archives to reveal the connections and tensions between the Soviet state's goals to root out wartime traitors and its aim to reintegrate returnees.[7]

The work of Polian and others owed much to increased German interest in the history of POWs and forced laborers during World War II. Many of these

TABLE I.2   Dislocation of Soviet displaced persons returning from outside Soviet borders, March 1, 1946

CATEGORY	CIVILIANS	%	MILITARY	%	TOTAL	%
Sent to place of residence (to the USSR)*	2,146,126	80.68	281,780	18.30	2,427,906	57.81
Conscripted in army	141,962	5.34	659,190	42.82	801,152	19.08
Labor battalions	263,647	9.91	344,448	22.37	608,095	14.48
Sent to the NKVD ("special contingent")	46,740	1.76	226,127	14.69	272,867	6.50
Located in the collecting points and working in Soviet Military units abroad	61,538	2.31	27,930	1.81	89,468	2.13
Total	2,660,013		1,539,475		4,199,488	

Source: Viktor Zemskov, *Vozvrashchenie sovetskikh peremeshchennykh lits v SSSR. 1944–1952 gg.* (Moscow: Institut rossiiskoi istorii, 2016), 127.

*Includes groups like ethnic Germans, whom Soviet authorities subsequently sent to exile.

works, like Christian Streit's monograph on Soviet POWs and Ulrich Herbert's on foreign laborers, focused on German responsibility for wartime atrocities and exploitation.[8] In the 1990s, debates in Germany over the state's culpability for wartime forced labor culminated in compensation for the survivors and motivated a new focus on understanding their experience through oral history.[9] A related historiography grew in the wake of international trials of former Soviet POWs like John Demjanjuk, who worked in German death camps. Scholars took advantage of the declassification of war crimes investigations in the USSR and Germany to consider the motivations of Soviet people who collaborated and their complicity in Nazi genocide.[10]

This book uses new archival evidence released in the 2010s in Russia and Ukraine to validate these findings and move beyond them. I use these materials, especially secret police investigations of repatriates from Ukraine, to employ a cast of figures to humanize the experience of forced labor and repatriation.[11] Biographical depth provides a fresh understanding of wartime displacement and its aftermath. The writing about Soviet forced laborers and repatriates has mostly adopted the perspective of the state—how Nazi Germany or the Soviet Union attempted to control and exploit migrants and laborers. Insofar as it has been a social history, it has been the history of state-society relations, with most of the agency resting in officialdom. The war and the subsequent occupations, however, marked a chaotic period when states, stretching their resources to the limits, competed to mobilize contested populations. The end of the war in 1945 resulted in a vacuum of state control across Europe. The tumultuous postwar situation allowed individuals and groups to cultivate new identities—or to exclude others from adopting them—according to notions of national belonging, wartime guilt and victimhood, and anticommunism.

The first theme of *Return to the Motherland* connects Soviet displacement to the history of Europe's war and postwar, in which violence and turmoil created fluid identities and, at times, agency in society.[12] Although this argument appears throughout the book, it emerges most strongly in the first five chapters, covering the period of World War II and its immediate aftermath. As forced laborers in the Third Reich, Eastern Workers faced the worst conditions of any group outside of concentration and death camps. Uprooted from their homes, they forged new communities in the barracks and among people from their home regions. Gender defined this experience in important ways. Eastern Worker women typically received better treatment than men, and far better than Soviet POWs. Women were the objects of sexual coercion by Germans and foreign workers from Western Europe, but their recourse to sexual barter—the trade of sexual attention for goods or favors—simultaneously increased the danger to them while providing opportunities to improve their situation.[13]

Men, especially POWs, and a smaller number of women became targets for recruitment for formal service in pro-German military formations and as camp personnel. Some became death camp guards, the people directly responsible for mass murder in the Holocaust. Before casting judgment on these men and others, though, it is critical to remember that Soviet prisoners faced brutal conditions in POW camps. Collaboration probably saved many from death by starvation—the fate of no fewer than 2.6 million of their comrades.[14] A minority may have seen collaboration with Hitler's regime as a path to oppose Stalinism.[15] At the same time, as this book shows, some who collaborated in pro-German units simultaneously resisted their German superiors.

Those writing about collaboration have wrestled with morally charged questions: Were these people criminals who deserved righteous judgment and often received it at the hands of Stalin's police? Or were they victims of the war, forced to cooperate with Nazi Germany against their will?[16] This book avoids a categorical verdict but instead views these cases as an opportunity to explore wartime agency.[17] Insofar as individual cases demand an assessment, it is necessary to consider the range of action a person had, their intentions, and the impact of their deeds. In general, the political scientist Stathis Kalyvas's arguments about agency in civil war fit Soviet collaboration well: people confronted with conflicting powers tend to do what is necessary to ensure survival and material comfort regardless of individual ideological preferences.[18] The most obvious pattern that emerges from the lives of Soviet-born people in Germany is that the demands and privations of war gave advantages—from food that allowed them to survive to positions of relative comfort and privilege—to people with a range of attributes: specialists with training in valuable fields like medicine, men who could fight, women who could trade sexual favors.

The liberation of forced laborers in Europe occurred with weak state oversight. The Western Allies established an agency called the United Nations Relief and Rehabilitation Administration (UNRRA) whose remit included the establishment and provisioning of camps for liberated foreign workers in the three Western zones of Germany. The purpose of the aid was not primarily altruistic but aimed to prevent disasters—military, political, epidemiological—that might develop from uncontrolled grouping of refugees.[19] The limited nature of these goals and the limited resources Allied governments spent to support them meant that the displaced were often self-organized. Although Soviet authorities nominally had oversight of Soviet-claimed displaced persons throughout Europe, their influence was tenuous. The historian Andrew Janco has shown how the chaos in occupied Europe allowed people to adapt identities that made them eligible for refuge.[20] A significant factor in this story was conflicting definitions of "Soviet." Western officials excluded people from areas the USSR annexed after 1939, while Soviet officials claimed them as subjects. The Allies facilitated the return of more than two million people to Soviet zones of control, but, to the dismay of Stalinist authorities, hundreds of thousands of people became nonreturners in UNRRA camps.

An implicit assumption among observers of this history has been that only nonreturners exercised agency over their fates and that most Soviet-claimed people would have avoided repatriation if they could have. This depiction of Soviet displaced persons fits the broader pattern of state actors and media outlets' presenting refugees as passive victims.[21] In some cases, Soviet displaced persons did have little agency. The Western Allies transferred under guard tens or possibly hundreds of thousands of former pro-German auxiliaries that they had captured as enemy combatants. Violent protests among would-be repatriates ensued, and some committed suicide in the face of repatriation. These ugly instances cemented Western perceptions that Soviet repatriation was largely coerced.[22] Such conflicts were not representative of all cases. Repatriation was made compulsory by an agreement between states, yet repatriates were willing or even eager to return. Large numbers of Soviet displaced persons—possibly a majority—longed to come back to their homes, to their families, and even to the Stalinist system they knew after years of forced labor under German rule. As displaced persons, returnees worked to expedite repatriation in the first months after liberation. The leadership of their camps, made up of pro-Soviet committees of displaced persons, enacted spontaneous re-Sovietization in the hopes of reclaiming their place in postwar society.

In the Soviet zones of occupation, too, state control remained tenuous through the end of 1945. Some four million people entered Soviet control from the defeat of Germany to the end of the summer of 1945.[23] This migration was just part of the massive movement of people at the war's end in Europe.[24] Meanwhile, the demands of finishing the war with Germany and occupying East-Central Europe exhausted Soviet resources. In their proclamations, Soviet leaders promised a safe and rapid return to the USSR, but many officials were often ill-disposed toward people who had worked for the enemy.

Such attitudes toward migrants were not unique to Soviet bureaucrats, but they mirrored dynamics in contemporaneous forced migrations and deportations. Two parallels are worth noting: Twelve million ethnic Germans—the legacy of settlement in the region for hundreds of years—were forcibly deported from Eastern and Central Europe to Germany at the end of World War II. The Allies, including the USSR, assisted in the expulsions, believing that a future German state might use the diaspora as a pretense for invasion as Hitler had in Czechoslovakia and Poland. The malignant indifference toward these migrants and outright hostility of local peoples and governments facilitated mass violence against them.[25] Another analogous case is Jewish migrants who survived concentration camps or evacuation in the Soviet hinterland. As they returned to prewar homes in Eastern Europe, official apathy and local antisemitism led to anti-Jewish violence. Those who fled this harsh welcome to the Western zones of Germany became "infiltratees," often treated as an undesirable drain on resources by occupation authorities.[26]

In the case of Soviet repatriation in 1945, too, chaos was a key factor in enabling abuses. The crucible of return was not the will of a vengeful Stalinist Leviathan but the absence of state control that allowed or even encouraged the violent exploitation of a vulnerable group. Red Army soldiers perpetrated widespread rape against Soviet women as revenge for alleged sexual treason with non-Soviet men. Local bosses demanded that repatriates owed them hard labor as payment for their disloyalty. For many returnees, the lack of Soviet state capacity meant being placed at the mercy of more powerful individuals and groups within society.

Soviet central authorities were frustrated with their inability to manage migration at the end of the war. In the push and pull between the "regimes and repertoires" of movement, to use the phrase of the historians Lewis Siegelbaum and Leslie Page Moch, the state regimes of ordering migration had weakened against wartime social repertoires.[27] Efforts to regulate repatriation fit into the broader attempt of Stalinist authorities to restore authority after the chaos that war had let loose. A second key argument of *Return to the Motherland* is that the Stalinist restoration was not just a return to the past but combined practices from the Soviet prewar experience with those found in other postwar states.

The officials who oversaw return under Stalin worked in the Soviet Repatriation Administration. The administration's tasks combined state security, diplomacy, and humanitarian aid. Its head, General Filipp Golikov, embodied these roles. The general, like many of the officers in the Repatriation Administration, was an experienced intelligence official. Earlier Golikov had commanded Soviet military intelligence and had then gone to the United States as the USSR's military envoy. As repatriation chief, he commanded a relatively modest staff who brought together more powerful organizations. Repatriation Administration leaders negotiated with Allied and occupied governments on the terms and logistics of return. With the Red Army, the administration monitored tens of thousands of personnel in the camp and transit systems that were supposed to bring the returnees back to the USSR. Once repatriates were in country, the administration oversaw aid and propaganda efforts through offices embedded in the Soviet state apparatus. Finally, the administration worked with the secret police to surveil returnees as potential spies and wartime collaborators. Although the Repatriation Administration operated throughout the world, this book focuses largely on Germany and areas it occupied during World War II, the places where most Soviet displaced persons lived.

In the postwar USSR, officials viewed the displaced as potential laborers. There were continuities in how Stalinist leaders channeled uprooted people like Gulag prisoners, deportees to "special settlements," and wartime evacuees to the hinterland, and their use of repatriates as a labor force.[28] The war hit the Soviet Union harder than arguably any other European state. The country lost roughly twenty-seven million people (some 15 percent of the population), and its economy was ravaged. Soviet officials saw repatriates as a vital influx of labor who, thanks to their wartime dislocation, were free to resettle per the state's requirements.

Soviet policies toward returnees as laborers present revealing parallels with wartime and postwar states. Pavel Polian has emphasized the similarities between Nazi Germany's deportation of Eastern Workers and Soviet mobilization of repatriates for postwar reconstruction.[29] This comparison has merits, but its suggestion of the totalitarian link between Nazi Germany and Stalin's USSR elides the ways that war and postwar reconstruction provoked many states to use the displaced as laborers. In Europe and beyond, authorities saw the displaced as settlers whom they could channel into schemes to rebuild the postwar world.[30] Soviet and postwar Western officials hoped to exploit displaced persons as laborers, and some were openly hostile toward them as refugees, but there was nothing like the near-universal antipathy Nazi officials had toward the supposedly racially inferior Eastern Workers.[31] Instead, Soviet officials' attitudes toward the returnees were complex, and discussions between repatriation officials and their partners in other parts of the bureaucracy reveal significant tensions between the goals of labor mobilization, reintegration, and punishment of perceived treason.

The drive to avenge perceived wartime betrayals also fused Stalinist practices with anxieties that burdened much of Europe. German occupation had been possible because of extensive cooperation from local populations. After the war, governments and peoples had to weigh the desire to prosecute wartime actions alongside the need to stabilize and rebuild.[32] Soviet efforts to punish collaboration were more pervasive and harsher than in any other country. Because they had lived for years under the enemy, Soviet returnees faced special scrutiny. A significant minority of repatriates were arrested—approximately 8 percent by my estimate—and in no other country were so many returning POWs prosecuted, some 15 percent or more.[33] It is not the goal of this book to assess whether these people were guilty of betraying the Soviet Union but to examine how the tendentious political-legal understanding of "collaborator" was produced through arrest. This is not to say that this understanding was invented from nothing. Many cases were hardly arbitrary and, in that sense, were in marked contrast to the investigations of the Great Terror of the 1930s.[34] In the earlier arrest campaign, police made huge numbers of prophylactic arrests among people whom they saw as potential threats and justified repression through forced confessions to false crimes.[35] In contrast, the core facts in collaboration cases were typically agreed on by accused and investigators. The interrogation room became a place where the accused and investigators negotiated whether these wartime actions constituted distasteful cooperation motivated by survival or criminal betrayal of the motherland.

Cases against repatriates fixated on the war years but were also inseparable from the postwar juncture. As historians like Nick Baron have recognized, the encounter with security forces during filtration and in other investigations reintroduced returnees to the Stalinist political system.[36] Although most returnees did not face arrest, they learned that their wartime experience had made them into quasi traitors. Officially they were Soviet citizens, but, as Golfo Alexopoulos argues, not all citizens were equal.[37] Soviet people's status depended on their political biography—a layered understanding that included factors such as whether they or their parents had been workers or so-called class enemies before the October Revolution.[38] The years under German control and repatriation became an ambiguous biographical element at best and more often a dangerous one. Repatriates who tried to claim a heroic wartime biography found themselves the objects of suspicion. This was especially true of those who spent time in the Western zones of occupation. As the Soviet Union and its former allies turned into Cold War enemies, police began to see repatriates as potential Western spies. Accusations of working for Anglo-American intelligence, based exclusively on falsification, were part of authorities' attempt in Stalin's last years to rein in wartime liberties and expectations for reform.[39] In postwar Western countries, the perceived danger of the USSR convinced officials to avoid discussions of collaboration and war crimes to generate social unity or to recruit anti-communist forces.[40] In the Soviet Union, too, the Cold War created silences about wartime experiences, motivating repression and discrimination that suppressed discussions of forced labor and displacement.

As the destruction of World War II and the onset of the Cold War impacted domestic politics, they also transformed Soviet conceptions about the USSR's place in the world. A third theme of *Return to the Motherland* is that repatriation efforts reflected the emergence of the Soviet Union as a nationalist state in the postwar period. This was not Russian ethnonationalism, although non-Russian displaced persons often perceived (correctly) that ethnic Russians and Russian speakers played the leading role among Soviet representatives. Instead, the country's leaders evinced patriotic confidence, even conceit, as representatives of a great power that had won the war at the head of a union of national homelands.

This development marked a shift from the first two decades of Soviet rule, when leaders of the revolutionary state viewed the world largely through the class-based ideology of Marxism-Leninism. In this earlier period, they cast workers and poor peasants as class allies and moneyed elites as enemies within their country and abroad. In the 1920s, the new Soviet regime had been content to see their former opponents from the Russian Civil War, White émigrés, leave for exile abroad rather than undermine the country from within.[41] As Michael David-Fox has shown, Stalinist leaders in the 1930s exhibited a "superiority complex." Stalin declared that the USSR had built socialism, making it the most advanced state in the world according to the Marxist framework of state formation and superior to the West.[42]

This fundamental Marxist conception never disappeared, but Soviet leaders increasingly saw nationality as an important category for assessing the loyalty of the population. Soviet leaders had attempted from the formation of the revolutionary state to shape and channel national cultures toward the construction of socialism.[43] From the late 1930s, Stalin issued orders to repress suspect nationalities—those who had titular homelands outside the USSR or, during the war, whose members were accused of disproportionately collaborating with the enemy. Meanwhile, Soviet officials embarked on campaigns to mobilize nationalism for war. Particularly notable was the rehabilitation of Russian nationalism, since it was a reversal of policies born of Vladimir Lenin's fear of "Great Russia chauvinism."[44] This turn saw attacks on so-called bourgeois nationalism, viewed as antithetical to pro-Soviet nationalism and a potential source of rebellion against the USSR. Stalinist nationality politics narrowed acceptable forms of national expression and the number of nations that the regime recognized. Yet this dynamic also bolstered the influence of national cultures with a titular homeland in the country and sought to increase their association with the

Soviet state. The shared victory in World War II was essential to the construction of these national identities.[45] In the aftermath of the war, Soviet officials presented their country as at once a supranational workers' state and an ethnoterritorial home for dozens of nations.

The fight for nonreturners—displaced persons who remained under Western Allied control into the late 1940s—demonstrated how Soviet authorities combined ethnonationalist claims with the outlook of a rising world power. They demanded that the Western Allies assist in the return of all Soviet people, against their will if necessary and regardless of would-be returnees' qualities and loyalties. In addition to the Western Allies' refusal to repatriate people from Soviet-annexed borderland regions, from 1946 the Western Allies extended refuge to people who rejected their prewar citizenship based on humanitarian principles and anticommunism.[46]

After mass repatriation ended in 1945, Soviet efforts to attract nonreturners to the USSR drew just tens of thousands of people. The quixotic effort to recruit people who obviously did not desire repatriation has puzzled historians.[47] Soviet officials remained fixated on repatriation for multiple reasons. For one, the nonreturners seemed to be a threat to security—a potential exile army abroad—and repatriation missions gathered intelligence about them. At the same time, Western refusal to comply with repatriation implied contempt of the USSR's sovereignty. What kind of great power was the USSR if it could not enforce claims over its subjects? In the contemporaneous Korean War, the inability of both the North and the South Korean states to gain authority over POWs in US camps showed that a state's ability to claim its subjects reflected its legitimacy or lack thereof, as the historian Monica Kim argues.[48] The fight over repatriation was at once about the people themselves and about the Western Allies' failure to respect the sovereignty of an equal power.

Soviet nationalist principles were an important element in these diplomatic concerns. Repatriation officers claimed that Baltic, Belarusian, Russian, and Ukrainian displaced persons, most of whom were from territories annexed after 1939, belonged in the USSR because they had titular homelands there. Western arguments about humanitarianism were merely excuses to obstruct reunion with the motherland. By the same logic, Soviet authorities were indifferent to displaced persons without homelands in the USSR, although some of these displaced persons had lived in the same areas as Soviet-claimed nonreturners. Soviet ideas about national belonging fit both Eric Lohr's characterization of the Russian-Soviet polity as a "filtering state" eager to attract and retain particular groups and the ethnoterritorial claim over subjects that the historian Tara Zahra has seen in contemporary European states.[49]

It is impossible to separate repatriation from the state-sponsored ethnic homogenization of Soviet republics, especially in Ukraine. This book explores Moscow's policy toward refugees and the actions of the displaced, but it also considers the specific case of Ukraine. Since the Maidan Revolution in 2014, researchers in Ukraine have been able to access voluminous secret police reports that are mostly unavailable in other post-Soviet republics. These reports are so numerous because Germany's long occupation and extensive efforts to extract labor from the region meant that deportees from Ukraine (mostly Ukrainian and Russian speakers) were the largest group among civilian forced laborers. Eastern Workers in Germany were colloquially known as "Russians," but national identification and awareness in the region varied significantly. Those from the east had lived under Soviet rule since the Russian Civil War and identified more strongly with the USSR than those in the annexed western territories who had only lived in the USSR since 1939 or later. The annexed regions were the main site of a ferocious fight between Soviet forces and a Ukrainian nationalist insurgency that persisted into the 1950s. In part to undercut the insurgency, authorities used deportation and resettlement to create a republic whose inhabitants would more often be identifiable as ethnic Ukrainian and Russian—a task simplified by Nazi German genocide against the region's Jewish inhabitants and nationalists' ethnic cleansing of other groups.[50]

Ukraine played an important role in repatriation after Stalin, too. By the early 1950s, most nonreturners had moved from camps in Europe to permanent emigration. The Repatriation Administration shuttered in 1953, but efforts to return Soviet-claimed people continued under the auspices of the secret police. The Committee for Return to the Motherland, a front organization formed by the Committee for State Security (Komitet Gosudarstvennoi Bezopasnosti, KGB, the secret police) in 1955, nominally targeted the Soviet wartime diaspora. Yet "repatriation" in the postwar world could entail an expansive definition of ethnoterritorial belonging, encompassing people who had resided in their nominal ethnic homeland decades earlier, if ever.[51] In Ukraine, KGB officials hoped to show that national belonging and socialist progress made the USSR an attractive home for migrants from the entire world. The migrants were not passive players in this story, though, and they used their position between the powers in the Cold War for their own aims.

The book proceeds roughly chronologically from forced labor to resettlement in the USSR. The first five chapters focus on the social history of forced laborers and the displaced during World War II and in its immediate aftermath. Chapters 1 and 2 explore labor conditions and social life in the barracks transnationalism of Nazi Germany. Chapter 3 examines the choices that informed collaboration and resistance. Chapters 4 and 5 follow the lives of displaced persons from liberation to return to the USSR.

The book's last five chapters emphasize Soviet efforts to restore order after the tumult of war. Chapter 6 looks at groups of repatriates that Soviet officials drafted into labor to consider the interaction between economic demands, gender, and punishment. The tension in secret police campaigns between investigations of real collaboration and falsified charges of spying for Cold War enemies is the subject of chapter 7. Chapter 8 explores cases in which returnees attempted to claim a heroic wartime biography and faced skepticism and sometimes repression. Continuing efforts to recruit nonreturners in the Cold War are the topic of the final two chapters. Chapter 9 follows Soviet repatriation officers to the Western zones of Germany, where their attempts to recruit returnees failed, but their efforts to provoke conflict with the USSR's former allies contributed to the hardening Cold War divide. The last chapter details the post-Stalin Return to the Motherland campaign.

Return to the Motherland recovers the history of displacement that Stalinist leaders hoped to expunge. Millions of Soviet repatriates suffered for the benefit of two dictatorships as forced laborers in Nazi Germany and then as marginal citizens in the USSR. Their stories, and the story of their erasure, are an essential part of the Soviet, German, and Allied experiences of World War II and its aftermath.

WORKERS FROM THE EAST

Deportation and Conditions of Labor among Eastern Workers

The German invasion of the Soviet Union pushed people into motion. At first the movement largely flowed eastward. Soviet civilians sought safety in evacuation as enemy forces rushed ahead in attack. Red Army soldiers retreated when they were not captured. From the fall of 1941, the tide started to shift. Reversing previous policies, Nazi officials urged the mobilization of millions of people from the occupied territories to Germany to satisfy the war economy's labor hunger. Soviet estimates suggest that the Axis powers displaced at least seven million Soviet-born people.[1] They would become a pillar of the German economy during World War II.

Many became Eastern Workers (Ostarbeiter), civilian laborers deported from the occupied territories. Although the Germans did not systematically starve Eastern Workers as they did Soviet prisoners of war, conditions for the civilian forced laborers were difficult. German forces deported most against their wishes, separating them for years from their families. Notions of Slavic inferiority encouraged Germans to abuse Eastern Workers physically and psychologically. The totemic "OST" (EAST) badge that German regulations mandated they stitch onto their clothes symbolized their status as racial inferiors.

This chapter and the next use ego sources to reconstruct the lives of Eastern Workers. In Germany, forced laborers had few opportunities to record their stories, and after their return to the USSR, Soviet memory politics also prevented former Eastern Workers from speaking openly about their experiences. Apart from a limited number of diaries from the time and German police sources, the main window into this history is interviews. These interviews, mostly taken around 2005, suffer from gaps in memory, homogenization of narratives, taboos surrounding difficult topics, and juxtaposition of contemporary life with the past. Nonetheless, reading the accounts together provides a broad picture of life in Germany among Eastern Workers.

There was no single experience of being an Eastern Worker. Age, sex, physical appearance, and, perhaps most of all, the often-arbitrary choices Germans made in allocating workers to employers determined the conditions they experienced. Workers in the bleakest factory camps were confined to barracks complexes. Eastern Workers assigned to families as farmhands or domestic servants tended to have more comfortable living situations. These relatively fortunate workers, however, also understood that they were outsiders in the Reich.

Deportation from the East

The deportation of millions of Soviet-born people to Germany was a desperate measure. Before 1941, leading Nazis had conceded that they needed foreign laborers from conquered territories like France, the Netherlands, and Poland.[2] Slavic people from the USSR were different. Hitler asserted that they were dangerous—too inferior in the Nazi racial hierarchy and too infected by communism to consider employing in large numbers in Germany. And he believed that employing them would not be necessary because he projected that Soviet rule would collapse after the initial attack against the USSR. Just as in the invasions of Poland and France, Hitler expected that Germany's task in Eastern Europe would rapidly transform from conquest to rule over a colony settled primarily by ethnic Germans and exploited for resources. Although German officials developed various proposals to implement Hitler's strategy, their assumption was that most local people would starve to death or migrate east.[3]

The initial phase of the invasion seemed to validate Hitler's plans. Operation Barbarossa, the attack on the USSR that began on June 22, 1941, devastated the Red Army's frontline units. Stalin, desperate not to give Hitler a pretense to invade, had shown a persistent unwillingness to believe an attack was possible and failed to direct Soviet armies to respond until it was too late. As the disaster unfolded, Stalin continued to insist that the war should take place on foreign soil and ordered ill-conceived counterattacks rather than attempting strategic retreats.[4] Within a week, the Germans occupied Minsk, and they would approach Moscow in the fall.

The Wehrmacht had won impressive victories but had not accomplished its goal. Operation Barbarossa was designed to eliminate organized military opposition in the USSR within weeks of the invasion. By this measure, the invasion failed by mid-August as it became clear that the war would not end in weeks or even months.[5] With increasing numbers of men deployed in the Wehrmacht and huge numbers of workbenches vacated, German views on employing people from the occupied east in the Reich changed quickly.[6] Hitler in October ordered that "Russian" workers be "extensively exploited for the needs of the war economy."[7] German authorities mobilized POWs as forced laborers and approved the use of civilians from the occupied territories as so-called Eastern Workers. These orders would lead to the deportation of millions to the Reich.

To organize this huge undertaking, Hitler appointed Fritz Sauckel in March 1942 as plenipotentiary for labor deployment. An early member of the Nazi Party, Sauckel was the party leader of the province of Thuringia and was a defense commissar during the early parts of World War II. It was his role as the chief organizer of forced labor deportations that would earn him a death sentence at the Nuremberg trials.[8] His main targets for deportation were working-age people as young as fifteen. Occupation officials deported even younger people by accident or design. At first Sauckel hoped that propaganda about the good life in Germany would convince people in occupied territories to volunteer. Occupation officials plastered posters and leaflets in local languages that described the excellent labor conditions in Germany (figure 1.1). The advertised conditions for work were attractive—room and board, plus pay and compensation to families. In some cases, people did receive such compensation.[9]

These promises drew volunteers in the initial phases of mobilization. On trial in 1946, Sauckel estimated that two hundred thousand people from across Europe volunteered to work in Germany.[10] From the area around Kyiv, some four thousand people volunteered in June 1942.[11] There were understandable reasons for going willingly. The most important factor was the desperate conditions in the occupied territories. According to one estimate, German policies of starvation meant that Kyiv residents in the fall of 1941 had smaller bread rations than people living under the notoriously harsh conditions of besieged Leningrad.[12] In addition to economic factors, some imagined that going to Germany would be an adventure. One young Ukrainian man, called to the Soviet secret police for questioning as a witness against an alleged collaborator, gave an unusually candid accounting of his decision to go to Germany: "I had little life experience . . . and was curious to see something new, to see the world."[13] Contrary to expectations, factory managers reported that forced deportees worked better than volunteers. The conditions of forced labor disappointed those who had expected the good life in Germany. Deportees had fewer illusions to meet.[14]

Volunteers decreased rapidly as the first ones to go reported to people at home on the realities of labor. Eastern Workers in the Reich wrote to people who had remained in the occupied territories. German censors monitored the letters, but

FIGURE 1.1. "In Germany things are great for me! As you see my friend, Tamara Gumych, and I, Tosia Kvinska from Rokytne, live very well in Germany." Reproduction from USHMM RG-31.117, propaganda posters and flyers produced by the German authorities on the occupied territory of the former USSR. Original held in the research library of the Central State Archive of Ukraine

having lived under the censorship regime of the Soviet Union, many deportees knew how to encode information. Exaggerations were a means of evading censors. Writing "I am well" meant everything was fine. A letter that said "I am very, very well" meant the reverse.[15] Using local knowledge, an Eastern Worker could write that they dressed like fashion models but conveyed the truth by comparing their condition to that of paupers from their home village, whose names relatives would recognize but Germans would not.[16] Letter writers could avoid the postal service altogether and send messages with soldiers returning to the Eastern Front from leave in the Reich.[17]

As initial attempts to solicit volunteers failed and occupation officials turned to forced mobilization, elements of cooperation continued amid coercion. German occupation administrators passed quotas to local officials who found people to deport. Deportee Polina E. was a student in Kharkiv before the war and continued to live in the city during the occupation. She received a notice to come to the local labor bureau (*Arbeitsamt*) and realized that it meant probable mobilization to Germany. Her mother was ill, and her relatives in the countryside had too many children to support her. As Polina E. would later admit, she was interested in seeing Germany despite her misgivings. She appeared at the labor office and was promptly detained for deportation.[18] Deportees also appeared for mobilization because of the threat of violence against their families. When Oleksandr I., a young collective farmer, went to his village head to protest his mobilization, he was told that refusal would result in his parents' execution.[19] Some deportees resisted mobilization by simulating illness or going into hiding. But complying with deportation orders made life easier in the Reich. Given notice, deportees could pack—usually just necessities like clothes, shoes, utensils, and food for the journey, although some managed to bring nonessentials like bathing suits.[20]

German racial policies conspired to bring even more forced laborers from the occupied territories to the Reich. German Jews had faced increasing discrimination since Hitler had come to power in 1933. As the Germans began the mass murder of European Jews in Eastern Europe, German Jews who had not fled the country remained in the country as workers. The arrival of Eastern Workers in late 1941 and into 1942 enabled the deportation of German Jewish workers. In September 1942, Sauckel argued to Hitler that Jewish workers would no longer be necessary in the Reich because he could mobilize enough foreign forced laborers to replace them. Many German Jews soon faced deportation to extermination camps.[21]

Events on the Eastern Front also increased the deportations. In 1943, the Red Army defeated Axis forces at the Battles of Stalingrad and Kursk, putting Germany on the retreat for the rest of the war. Fearing the Red Army's further advances westward, Sauckel authorized even more desperate mobilization measures in the occupied territories. "Not one worker, not a man or a woman should be left for the enemy to become a soldier or a worker," he wrote in September 1943.[22]

Once a person was in German control, the journey to the Reich could take several days to a week. Authorities undertook a medical examination and delousing along the way. When the convoy reached its destination, guards typically would take the deportees to a square near the labor office for assignment. Anatolii A. remembered that a German farmer approached him and demanded, "Open your mouth!" After the farmer examined Anatolii A.'s teeth and was satisfied that he was healthy, he agreed with the labor office to take the teenager as a worker.[23] Several former laborers recalled that smallholding farmers took the more robust-looking candidates, leaving the smaller, less healthy-looking workers for factories.[24] According to German statistics from 1944, the Reich used about a third of Soviet civilian laborers in agriculture while more than half worked in industry. Among foreign workers, Soviet-born people were overrepresented in metal production and underrepresented in agriculture.[25]

Before they arrived at their destinations, the journey had largely determined the conditions Eastern Workers would face. Those who acceded to deportation found themselves better prepared for the ordeal that awaited. As they soon learned, selection for factory work or labor in a household would create substantially different experiences of forced labor.

Work in the City

Every forced laborer endured deprivations, but factory workers faced particularly miserable circumstances. The dynamics of forced labor in the Reich economy encouraged meager provisions for Eastern Workers, especially in industrial workplaces. Germany's tax system meant that hiring Eastern Workers as specialists was costly, but employing them as low-skill laborers was cheap. The lowest grade of workers made 0.1 reichsmark per day after the employer deducted money for room and board.[26] Unskilled women workers were particularly valuable. German inspectors found that female Eastern Workers, in contrast to other foreign workers, were just as efficient as their German counterparts.[27] As a recent history of food distribution in the wartime USSR asserts, women workers ate well compared with men because they were eligible for the same rations, but their bodies generally required less food.[28]

The nominal provisions for Eastern Workers, meager as they were, belied worse realities. A calculation based on the standard ration for Eastern Workers suggests that they received some 1,730 calories per day—just a little less than German workers received.[29] But the flat rate workers paid for room and board did not depend on the amount the enterprise spent on provisions, allowing employers to skimp on food and housing to save money. The food allotted to many workers also was less than the official rations because privileged Eastern Workers (e.g., the cafeteria staff) exploited their positions to gain better provisions. The senior doctor at the Essen Krupp factory testified to Allied authorities after the war that Eastern Workers had received no more than a thousand calories a day in rations. This amounted to five or six potatoes or rutabagas. The prepared food was often a tasteless soup that workers called *balanda*—a Russian word that translates roughly to "gruel" and has strong associations with prison. Living quarters also failed to meet regulations. The Essen factory packed workers into barracks with beds spaced 1 foot apart rather than the prescribed 1.5 feet.[30]

Protests over conditions, especially food, were common among Eastern Workers. In the summer of 1942, after several weeks at an armaments factory in Waltershausen (Thuringia), Kursk deportee Aleksandra Mikhaleva and her campmates had made their peace with their monotonous diet but still expected to receive a reasonable helping. On a workday when they received an unusually small lunch, they refused to return to work until camp authorities gave them another portion. Remarkably, police accommodated the protest by promising a bigger dinner. The lack of serious reprisals undoubtedly reflected the enormity of the labor hunger in the country rather than sympathy with the strikers.[31]

The size of camps and conditions in them varied considerably. The largest consisted of multiple barracks on a territory and hundreds of total workers in the complex. Each room had bunk beds with straw mattresses, usually for ten to twenty inhabitants but sometimes housing more. Other "camps" were a single building or unconventional living spaces with a limited number of workers. In one case, the owner of a restaurant rented out the banquet hall as a barracks for thirty people. The location had the advantage of being close to the factory where the residents worked, and the owner managed to isolate the barracks from the still-operational restaurant.[32] A typical barrack room had a sink for basic hygienic needs, and each person had a locker or small cabinet. Most workers had Sunday as a free day for chores, private employment, foraging, or recreation. As a rule, smaller barracks complexes allowed more freedoms for residents, although most barracks were locked at night. Former workers at larger enterprises remembered having worse conditions than those at smaller workplaces.[33]

The regional economy could impact living situations as well. Ivan S., a Kharkiv province native, worked as a coal miner in southeast Germany near the Protectorate of Bohemia and Moravia (today's Czech Republic). He recalled that because of his job he could shower every day after work, unlike his counterparts at factories, who had to make do with the sink in their barracks between monthly trips to the bathhouse.[34]

Labor conditions also varied. Most former workers recalled a twelve-hour workday lasting from early morning to the evening. According to regulations, they were supposed to be under the supervision of a German and kept apart from foreign workers from outside Eastern Europe. A typical master was an older German man or one whose health would not allow him to serve in the army. In factory settings, managers might embed individual Eastern Workers in a German work team. Often their work involved low-skill tasks like cleaning. As the need for labor grew and Eastern Workers demonstrated their fluency in German and their worth as laborers, some took more specialized positions.[35] Intensive Allied bombing disrupted production, especially in 1944–45, and meant that laborers had no work at all in some cases. Transit hubs and fuel manufacturing centers in northwest Germany, where the Western Allies would soon send armies, were hit especially hard.[36] As factories shut down toward the end of the war, German authorities transferred workers to dig fortifications or sift through the rubble after bombing raids.[37]

Guards and workplace supervisors had to find a balance between repression and understanding as they attempted to maintain order and motivate workers. They needed to punish the unruly, but arrest was not always the best option because it could mean losing labor to long-term incarceration.[38] To discipline workers without involving the Gestapo, guards at work camps employed beatings and detention in isolation cells. Vadim N., a young worker in a camp at Bochum (Westphalia), remembered an incident when police caught a campmate who had run away. Rather than relinquish the worker to a concentration camp, the commandant retrieved the young man and had Vadim N., a fluent German speaker, translate his upbraiding. Then Vadim N. watched as the commandant beat his charge and sent him back to the camp to work.[39] The resort to beating also reflected racial stereotypes about Slavic laziness. When General Andrei Vlasov, the leader of the pro-German Russian Liberation Army, met Nazi leader Hermann Göring, the latter characterized the representative attitude of German work supervisors: "A typical Russian accepted the use of the whip. . . . It would not be possible to expect any results from their labor without it."[40]

Violence was gendered, with male Eastern Workers receiving the worst beatings. Valeria F. recalled an incident in which the supervisor at her factory suspected a young man of breaking equipment and hit his head with a truncheon so hard that the worker went to the hospital for two weeks. The camp's women had it marginally easier; the master more often beat them with his fists and hit only their backs, not their faces.[41] Virtually all the factory workers witnessed or experienced violence. Soviet officials interviewed hundreds of thousands of returning forced laborers about conditions in Germany. A handful of the returnees praised their employers, but most told the interviewer that the Germans had "cursed and beaten" them.[42] Former forced laborers who said that treatment had been relatively good nonetheless cited instances in which the guards locked them in isolation cells for minor acts of disobedience. This form of punishment could be particularly brutal at facilities in smaller towns. Aleksandra Mikhaleva, at a camp of some five hundred people at the small town of Waltershausen, reported to Soviet interviewers in 1945 that camp guards had locked workers away for hours or days for underfulfilling work norms and buying potatoes from local Germans. Because the town was small, the place of confinement was relatively primitive—"a musty basement."[43]

Just as punishment varied among camps, so did privileges. Among the most important was the ability to leave on days off. Authorities in some camps waited several weeks or months to allow leave until they thought the workers would not try to escape or riot. At the Otto L. Schmidt firm, a small furniture factory in Berlin converted to produce ammunition boxes, camp officials took workers on guided tours around the city after two weeks in the camp. Two or three months later, they were allowed to leave the camp on Sundays in groups of ten. If any of the ten did not return to the camp, the others would face collective punishment of two weeks without the right to leave.[44] Other camps restricted leave, but security was lax enough that the laborers could go outside at their own risk. Taisa T.'s campmates in Seeback (Thuringia) would wait until dark to forage illicitly for berries that they had noted on their march to the mine factory. When the guards caught some of the women returning, they held them at gunpoint and beat them.[45] While the ability to leave had obvious benefits for Eastern Workers, it arguably appealed to the enterprises just as much. Laborers who found work on farms or sold handcrafts could supplement their official rations, relieving the burden of the camps.[46]

To distinguish Eastern Workers from other people in the Reich, Nazi officials introduced the OST badge. Although the badge was nominally a security measure, in truth it marked Eastern Workers less as threats than as supposed racial inferiors who did not belong in places like buses and cinemas. Nazi leaders also hoped that the badge would prevent so-called racial mixing (*Rassenschande*), sexual relationships between Germans and non-Germans that Nazi leaders feared would pollute Aryan blood. Some former laborers later dismissed the practical relevance of the badge. One interviewee said, "If you needed to go somewhere, you turned the collar over . . . and that's all. If someone stopped you, you just uncovered the OST badge."[47] Employers at small farms or in households usually did not insist on their workers' wearing the badge at home, leading to a sense of false security. Police could stop those who were careless about wearing the badge and fine employers for negligence.[48] Others recalled that the badge was meaningless because it was obvious that the workers were not German, badge

or no. Mikhail B., a worker at a factory on the outskirts of Frankfurt, risked trying to take the bus to the city with friends on a free day in 1944. The young men
had removed their OST badges, but the conductor would not let them on. "She
knew from our clothes," he said. "She knew from the way we talked."[49]

Regulations called for OST badge wearers to have segregated medical treatment. According to German statistics, 14,522 Eastern Workers died in 1943—a
rate approaching 1 percent—and an economic historian has given a cumulative
death toll of approximately 6 percent. Although this rate was significantly higher
than among German civilians, it was much lower than the mortality rate among
Soviet POWs.[50] German authorities had no interest in pampering Eastern Workers but, not wanting to lose valuable labor or allow the spread of infectious diseases, provided medical care. Rather than use German doctors for the workers,
authorities usually recruited medics from Slavic foreign workers or POWs.[51]
Some medics were more qualified than others. One former worker recalled that
the head of her factory's medical room was a Polish veterinarian.[52]

Laborers who contracted infectious diseases or sustained injuries could receive treatment in a medical ward. A period of illness meant reduced rations but
also a respite from work. At Valeria F.'s camp, laborers cut themselves and applied poisonous buttercup leaves. The painful sore provided an excuse to go to
the clinic for treatment.[53] In another instance, workers at the Daimler-Benz automobile factory in Berlin drank methanol both to get drunk and because taking the exact right dose would make them sick enough to receive leave without
causing permanent damage.[54]

Conditions in most areas of life for Eastern Workers improved over time, especially after Germany's military situation deteriorated in 1943. German leaders' desire to generate as much productive labor as possible spurred these changes;
as Sauckel said, the motivation was not "mawkish humanitarianism."[55] SS leader
Heinrich Himmler backed improvement in work conditions, too, and in
April 1943 decried that many camps were "like jails" in a cynical attempt to improve morale. Himmler's and Sauckel's instructions for the treatment of Eastern Workers in the same month approved their right to leave the camps on free
days.[56] Many former Eastern Workers confirmed that such improvements occurred, although some never received the right to leave camp on their own.[57]
German inspectors visiting Eastern Worker camps in 1943 produced scathing
assessments. These evaluations may have indicated the failure to improve conditions or that there was no real desire to do so.[58] It seems possible, however, that
the negative assessments reflected an attempt to spur improvements.

As Allied armies grew closer, intense bombing raids increased the danger for
forced laborers. Bombings had been regular in 1942 and 1943, but the destruction
became apocalyptic in 1944. Amid this bombing campaign, German authorities

WORKERS FROM THE EAST

denied Eastern Workers a place in public bunkers, leaving them vulnerable if they could not get to a factory shelter.[59] During night bombings, camp guards had to unlock the barracks to bring the workers to a bunker. In some cases, nighttime raids were too sudden, or the guards were too pitiless to open the barracks. A firebombing destroyed the barracks of the Werner Werks in Berlin. The workers, released from the locked barracks by the explosion, rushed to the street in their nightclothes. They covered themselves with blankets, jackets, or whatever else they could find as flaming pieces of the roof fell. Several were hospitalized. Berlin police recorded the incident in detail because a bank official accused the survivors of having stolen a suit from his house during the raid.[60]

Proximity to factories and German callousness made Eastern Workers the disproportionate victims of bombings. Valentin Senger, a young Jewish man whose family was hiding in plain sight in Frankfurt (Main) as gentile Germans, worked with a group of Eastern Worker women killed in an attack in September 1944. As a transportation hub, Frankfurt was one of the main targets of Allied bombings meant to disrupt the German economy.[61] The city's Germans had a well-built bunker, while the foreign laborers at Senger's factory had a flimsy shelter that "the smallest bomb would have penetrated." One night an Allied bomb hit the shelter, killing seventy-eight Eastern Worker women and a handful of Germans who had gone to the shelter as a last resort.[62] Allied bombers devastated the shipbuilding city of Kiel in 1944. Of the 4,457 Eastern Workers and 307 Soviet POWs in the town, 97 (2 percent) were killed that year in bombing raids. These workers, who made up just 28 percent of the 17,322 foreign workers in the city, made up almost 60 percent of bombing fatalities among foreign workers (163).[63] Bombings also destroyed living spaces in the camps, and managers inevitably forced Eastern Workers into even more cramped and inadequate housing when it was necessary to find housing for Germans or foreign workers from Western Europe.[64]

The danger of air raids brought opportunities, too. Foreign laborers benefited from salvaged goods in their aftermath.[65] One forced laborer remembered how resourceful acquaintances burglarized houses during bombings. They glued newspapers to windows with sticky jam during raids so that they could break and remove the glass with less noise.[66] Police reports from Berlin are full of complaints about German property stolen during air raids, as in the case of the bombing of the Werner Werks barracks.[67] These investigations had a basis in the desperation of Eastern Workers who might resort to theft during opportune moments. The primary focus of the investigations on Eastern Workers, however, also reveals German stereotypes about criminality among Slavic workers.

The fear of foreign criminality apparent in these cases reflects a paradox of Germany's forced labor program. The war economy demanded labor, even recruited from the supposedly inferior peoples of the east. Yet Eastern Workers' presence in Germany fostered anxieties that they would damage the Reich more than they would aid it. From the first arrival of Eastern Workers, the leader of the Sicherheitsdienst (SD, a German security agency), Reinhard Heydrich, ordered that they be used in "Russian enterprises"—workplaces that would employ Eastern European laborers in isolation from other foreigners and Germans, excluding supervisors.[68] It was impossible to keep Eastern Workers completely isolated, though. The danger that they would conspire against Germany or simply fail to work hard motivated the police to monitor and repress supposedly dangerous Eastern Workers.

The case of Pavel (Paul) O. reveals several threats that German authorities saw in Eastern Workers. The fifty-two-year-old Taganrog native claimed to be a physician, so German officials made him into a medic for various enterprises in Krefeld and Düsseldorf. When camp authorities inspected his work in late 1942, they found that he was engaging in "peculiar behavior." Pavel O. disparaged Bolsheviks and Jews so vociferously that camp inspectors thought he was playing a role to ingratiate himself to them. An administrator at Düsseldorf's Rheinmetall found another reason for alarm. Pavel O. had exaggerated his qualifications, conflating his training as a field medic (in Russian, *fel'dsher*) with being a physician. Authorities also suspected that he was a homosexual, a dangerous fact given the Nazis' brutal persecution of gay men and, to a lesser degree, women.[69] Asked directly whether he was a homosexual, Pavel O. said he had a "strong dislike for women" and was said to demonstrate "unnatural familiarity" with younger men in the camps. He told interrogators that he felt attraction to younger men but had been impotent for five years and had not attempted any homosexual relationship.

Pavel O.'s main crime was not sexual but the organization of a protest about conditions in the camps. As a medic, he visited various sites in the area and compared the situations at each. When he visited a camp where the food was comparatively poor, he alerted the kitchen staff. According to an official at the Krefeld camp of IG Farben, a chemical manufacturer and one of the largest companies in Germany, Pavel O. was gathering signatures to petition Nazi leaders in Berlin for better conditions. Around the same time, an SD report noted that pro-German propaganda articles about the "model order" of camps that appeared in Slavic-language newspapers were creating unrealistic expectations among workers.[70]

The most revealing aspect of Pavel O.'s case is that his plans did not necessarily seek to undermine German authority. He hoped to work with authorities in the Reich to improve conditions. Unlike wildcat protests over food, Pavel O. planned to appeal to German leaders as allies against local administrators. The possibility of systemic protest was perhaps more menacing than sporadic work stoppages and earned Pavel O. an indefinite term of house arrest in the IG Farben camp. Eventually authorities transferred him to the Dachau concentration camp.[71]

In the investigation of Pavel O. and in other cases, police deployed repression to control disruptive laborers. Organized struggle against the Nazi regime by Eastern Workers was not widespread, but, as in all cases of subjugated people, small acts of uncoordinated resistance were common.[72] Workers would labor slowly, create delays by breaking instruments, or simulate illness to avoid going to the factory. As a punishment for the "work-shy" and as a means of motivating others, SD leaders in mid-December 1942 embarked on a monthlong secret campaign of arrests against shirkers from Eastern Europe. Orders called for local police departments to survey factory officials about poor workers or escapees. After summary proceedings, the police were to send these undesirables to concentration camps.[73]

Conditions at factory camps drove many Eastern Workers to attempt escape. In a June 1944 meeting between Hitler and Albert Speer, the organizer of the German war economy, Speer complained that police were depriving him of a significant number of laborers by sending escaped foreign workers (not only Eastern Workers) to concentration camps at a rate of thirty to forty thousand per month. To Speer's displeasure, the police were sending workers to punishment camps (*Arbeitserziehungslager*) when they could have gone to his enterprises.[74] Despite the prospect of incarceration in a punishment camp, unhappy workers attempted escape with the hope that they could survive until liberation outside a labor camp. Allied pressure on both fronts increased these hopes, and bombings created ruins where escaped Eastern Workers could live.

In many cases, runaways did not dream of escaping forced labor but of finding better conditions. Ivan G. and several campmates fled a Hannover-area camp just days after arrival in mid-1943. Realizing they were far from the Eastern Front, they wanted to find a farm where they believed food and housing would be better. Two weeks later police captured them and had them sentenced to punishment camp.[75] Their attempted escape represented the broader desperation of Eastern Workers assigned to factories. Confined to camp barracks and given meager rations, it is no wonder that they fantasized about a better life in the countryside.

Agricultural and Home Labor

Factory workers' rural fantasies were based in the reality that Eastern Workers in farmwork usually had more food. This was true even at large farms, where workers lived in factory-style barracks. Nikolai G. lived in a camp with almost two hundred other laborers, but the resourceful workers could forage for food in the countryside and cobbled together enough dishes, cups, and small tools from a nearby garbage dump that they could create a kitchen in their barracks. Food was not plentiful but also not at starvation levels.[76]

At family farms, an Eastern Worker might labor alongside the family from dawn until dusk in hard manual labor. Former workers remembered being responsible for an array of tasks, beginning with milking cows and tending to other cattle, and ending with field work. Farmwork was demanding, and, in contrast to the situation at factories, at small farms only Sunday afternoons were free. Milk cows have no weekends.

The intimacy of the family farm could make life nightmarish. The relative anonymity of the factory environment also had advantages. Individuals at a large enterprise might be able to take furtive breaks or escape the barracks for an evening. At a family farm there was nowhere to hide. Farmworkers who did not get along with their employers lived in the same house as their tormentors. The son of Evdokia P.'s employers harassed her constantly. Once he watched as she milked cows and, dissatisfied with her work, sprayed milk straight from the udder into her face.[77] Akulina Maksimenko came to work on the Molow family farm at age fourteen. She told Soviet officials after liberation that when she was unable to cope with the eight milk cows and several dozen other animals on the farm, the owner beat her.[78]

In other cases, the family virtually adopted Eastern Workers. Halyna K. worked at the Guggenbichler family farm in Mühlbach (Lower Franconia), where her mistress taught her to knit and sew, and gave her a sewing machine at the war's end. Sharing the family's blue eyes, and ruddy cheeks and hair, Halyna K. was sometimes mistaken for her boss's daughter (figure 1.2).[79] Even when employers were not as welcoming as the Guggenbichlers, conditions on farms were better than in the city on average, if only because the food was more plentiful. Maria Kh. claimed in a post-Soviet interview that her employers provided five meals a day.[80] These fond recollections were perhaps a trick of memory. Former farmworkers would return to a Soviet Union that experienced famine in 1946–47. The memory of the turbulent and destitute 1990s was also fresh when they gave interviews in the first decade of the 2000s. But contemporary evidence reinforces the notion of relative abundance in the countryside during the war. German authorities sometimes assigned Soviet POWs to work at farms as a de facto convalescence to recover from malnutrition before transfer to factories or mines.[81]

Like Eastern Workers at family farms, domestic servants placed in households generally had good conditions. In September 1942, Heinrich Himmler authorized the employment of Soviet women aged fifteen to thirty-five in German households. The directive demanded that the women have a "Germanic appear-

FIGURE 1.2. Halyna K. with the children of her employers, the Guggenbichler family, interview ZA481, 09.09.2005, Interview-Archiv "Zwangsarbeit 1939–1945," https://archiv.zwangsarbeit-archiv.de/de/interviews/za481, Image 05.

ance," as determined by recruiting commissions that would inspect the women on their way to the Reich. Loyal Nazi families, those of party or military officials, were eligible to hire the women.[82] Authorities often selected the women based on physical appearance. Polina E. had worked for a month in a factory when the director and his twelve-year-old son inspected the workers in search of a maid. According to Polina E.'s later recollection, the boy thought she was pretty and made his father take her home.[83] In occupied Belarus, the commander of a subunit of the German killing squads (*Einsatzgruppen*) who enacted the mass murder of Jews and other groups in the region sent his parents an eleven-year-old "Aryan looking" Belarusian girl.[84] It is possible that many cases were similar to the informal hiring in these examples, and that Himmler's order formalized the questionable practice of employing Eastern European women as servants. Just a month after Himmler's order, German authorities registered 8,131 Eastern Worker women as domestic servants, roughly 11 percent of all foreign women working in that capacity.[85]

Domestic workers became close to their employers. Zinaida B. was a native of eastern Ukraine who worked for the family of a Luftwaffe colonel in Berlin. Although the hours were long, she respected her mistress, Elisabeth, an ethnic German émigré from an aristocratic Riga family. Their philosophical discussions went beyond household affairs. When Elisabeth learned that Zinaida B. did not believe in God, she wondered, "Well, why live then?" Zinaida B. seemed to make life more interesting for Elisabeth. Although Elisabeth had five daughters, Zinaida B. was nearly thirty years old. She was a mature interlocutor who also provided a connection to Elisabeth's early years in the Russian Empire.[86]

Halyna Ia., a blue-eyed and light-haired sixteen-year-old from Kyiv province, became the domestic servant for the family of Wendula Wagener. Her husband was Otto Wagener, a general and Nazi official who had been a confidant of Hitler's in the early 1930s until other Nazi officials pushed him to the side.[87] Wendula Wagener had inherited a castle near Streckenwalde from her industrialist father and lived there with her own two children and six child refugees. Interviewed in 2005, Halyna Ia. was seemingly not aware of Otto Wagener's status in the Nazi hierarchy. She could not help but to become more like her host family. Wendula Wagener refused to call her Halyna and instead called her by the German version of her name, "Helena." They would sometimes go to the nearest town to buy German-style shoes and get fashionable haircuts. Halyna Ia.'s initial workload was limited to cooking and cleaning. After the family's French governess left, Halyna Ia. was charged with bringing up the children as well, reading them German stories at night. Although Halyna Ia. grew closer to the Wageners, there was always a barrier between them. Otto Wagener was absent most of the time but during one visit joked, "We'll make a Volksdeutsche out of you." She recalled responding that she could only be Russian. (For Germans, all Eastern Workers were "Russians," although Halyna Ia. gave her oral history interview in Ukrainian and identified as Ukrainian.)[88]

Working in a household or on a family farm did not make an Eastern Worker part of the family. When Polina E.'s employers fled the bombing raids in Berlin, they returned her to the labor pool and had her reassigned to a different workplace until the end of the war.[89] The Germans deported Kyiv natives Valentina S. and her sister to work on a family farm a village near Halle (Saxony). Because her family was from the city, she and her sister had experienced little farmwork and adjusted with difficulty. When the German family discovered that seventeen-year-old Valentina S. was not capable of the difficult labor, they sent her back to the labor office, separating the sisters. Later the family would denounce her for visiting her sister too often, leading to Valentina S.'s arrest.[90] Although conditions could be comfortable in households and Eastern Workers could become close to families, they remained racial inferiors who could be discarded.

The lives of Eastern Workers in the Reich were highly differentiated. Of the millions sent to work, only a handful of people volunteered, and fewer still would have agreed to go if they had known what awaited them. Workers at factories felt hunger constantly and experienced arbitrary violence. They resided in overcrowded camps, where illness and bombing raids threatened. Small workplaces like family farms or households usually provided better conditions. Living with a family meant some private space and more food, although it also meant working closely with one's employers.

In some senses, the conditions of Eastern Workers were not so different from those of their counterparts in the wartime USSR.[91] Evacuation and mobilization of workers in the Soviet Union increased the burden on already crowded housing stock; people lived in underground hovels (*zemlianki*) or crowded barracks. Soviet rations were also inadequate. A quantitative analysis of official rations in the wartime USSR found that only administrators in the defense industry had nominal rations that provided enough calories to meet their biological requirements. Other workers received rations that were lower, sometimes by a large margin, than their daily needs.[92] Like their German counterparts, Soviet leaders mobilized people as young as fourteen years old to work in factories and on collective farms.[93] And as in the Reich, those who tried to escape mobilization faced punishment. Tens of thousands of teenagers faced prosecution for supposedly deserting their workplace.[94]

The difference between Stalinism and Nazism for civilian workers was in the racialized cruelty of Germany. The occupiers brought Eastern Workers to the

Reich because the necessities of war outweighed their hatred of Slavic people. Or perhaps because of their racist beliefs the Germans saw them as good slaves. There were Germans who treated their forced laborers kindly, but they were still masters with extensive authority over their charges. As in other colonial empires, Germans tolerated or even encouraged beatings of subalterns from colonized regions. The comparison with Soviet treatment of workers caused one German administrator to note that Stalinist officials sent people to execution or exile for minor crimes, but they "take pains that in public and especially at work there is no manhandling."[95] German limitations on Eastern Workers' mobility were much stricter than Stalinist restrictions on laborers; workers in the USSR could not change their jobs without official permission but could travel freely within cities during nonworking hours. Above all, it is necessary to remember that Germany marked the peoples of the east for eventual destruction.

Against their initial plans, German leaders mobilized people from all territories that their armies occupied. Forced labor disrupted lives but also created new bonds. In an atmosphere of coerced contact with the outside world, Eastern Workers found replacements for family in the camp community.

FORCED LABOR EMPIRE
Community, Transnational Contact, and Sex

The deprivation Eastern Workers experienced in the Reich was communal as well as material. Deportation took many forced laborers from their native lands for the first time. Most Eastern Workers were in their teens or early twenties and found themselves beyond the supervision of elders and authorities they had known since childhood.[1] The absence of these communities reinforced regional ties and created new affiliations. As in the case of concentration camps and ghettos, camp life sowed divisions among the workers as well. Deprivation pitted groups against one another in the struggle for food and privileges. Although conditions were not as dangerous as in Jewish ghettos, the difficult circumstances of forced labor created similar dynamics that encouraged workers to find advantageous positions and allies among friends and lovers.[2]

Among the defining features of Eastern Workers' experience were their encounters with non-Soviet foreign workers from the German wartime empire. Nazi racial thinking identified foreign laborers like the Dutch or French as belonging to superior, near-German races. Slavic workers from Central and southern Europe belonged to supposed inferior races. Eastern Workers held the lowest spot in this hierarchy, and notions of their racial inferiority enabled Germans and other foreign workers to take advantage of them. Although all foreign workers shared the sorrow of distance from their occupied homelands, Eastern Workers rarely found group solidarity with their counterparts.

Sex was an important part of interactions between East European laborers and others. In other cases of extreme deprivation, like the wartime ghettos for Jews or the Soviet Gulag, sexuality meant both danger and opportunity.[3] The overwhelming power imbalance between German authorities and Eastern Workers enabled sexual violence, but sexual relationships were also outlets for resistance and a way to spend leisure time. Sex was a commodity, and female Eastern Workers could trade intimacy for resources. In some cases, barter meant prostitution, but almost all relationships had pragmatic elements.[4] The relative privilege that non-Soviet foreign workers enjoyed made them into attractive suitors for Eastern Workers. Some of these mixed relationships were based in romantic affection, and a number ended in marriage. These cases, nonetheless, would have been unlikely without the discrepancy in the rights of Eastern Workers and their supposed racial superiors.

The lives of Eastern Workers in Nazi Germany were full of risks, scarcity, and division. Hitler's forced labor empire brought Soviet people into contact with non-Soviets, but the experience was often negative. Nonetheless, social life continued as the barracks created hierarchies, groupings, and connections.

Forced Labor Communities

The German invasion of the USSR meant the destruction of social ties. Before the war, Soviet mass culture centered on official organizations run through the party and the Komsomol. The Germans persecuted these groups under the occupation, driving the most dedicated members underground and severing the connections that official culture had fostered between others. The occupiers forbid primary school education after grade four for non-Germans and outlawed forms of self-governance above the district level. The deportation of millions of individuals from Eastern Europe represented the German view on the value of local social life: the people in the area were laborers to be exploited without regard for their communities.

Their disdain for Eastern European peoples meant that the Germans made few deliberate efforts to shape society among Eastern Workers. Insofar as German leaders hoped to mobilize the deportees, they believed that Eastern Workers should subscribe to identities along ethnonational lines (e.g., as Ukrainians) that, under German leadership, would be opposed to Bolshevism. Yet Nazi officials were suspicious that nationalism could become a vehicle for mobilization against Germany and monitored "cultural services" for Eastern Workers closely.[5] Instructions from the SD in 1944 permitted Eastern Workers to attend religious services but simultaneously forbade émigré clergy from participating. Presumably, the police worried that resistance might coalesce around church officials.[6] Nazi leaders hoped to mobilize Eastern European people for the war effort but feared what would happen if they gave them autonomy.

Individual Eastern Workers were won over by the efforts of Germany and émigrés aligned with the Nazi regime. Teenager Vitalii Belikov from Kharkiv arrived as a factory worker in Berlin in 1942. He knew his émigré uncle was living in German-dominated Europe, so he paid to publish a classified advertisement in the pro-German newspaper *New Word* (*Novoe Slovo*). Soon Ioann Shakhovskii, the head of St. Vladimir Orthodox Church in Berlin and the future bishop of the Orthodox Church in the United States, connected Belikov with his uncle, a priest in Novi Sad (in wartime Hungary, now in Serbia). Packages from his uncle plus help from Shakhovskii and other émigrés made life easier for Belikov than for the average Eastern Worker. Perhaps because of his unique position—and because of repression he would face in the 1950s after his return to the USSR—he described life in Germany as better than in the USSR, even as a forced laborer. The religiosity that Belikov developed from contact with Orthodox priests in Berlin would persist throughout his life.[7] Belikov's family connections among émigré religious figures were atypical, but Belikov was like many other Eastern Workers in his use of kinship and regional affiliations to find a community in the Reich.

The circumstances of deportation helped preserve local networks from the occupied territories. Conscription orders might target dozens of people from the same area, whom Germans then sent together to the Reich. The typical deportee left behind most of their loved ones but was not entirely alone. They arrived in Germany with at least one or two neighbors or relatives. Aleksandra Mikhaleva was deported from Kursk in 1942 with her cousin Galina. When they arrived in Waltershausen (Thuringia), camp authorities kept them in the same room, where they would live together with a group of young women from Kursk until liberation in April 1945.[8] German authorities took entire families to work in the Reich, especially as the Wehrmacht retreated from the occupied territories in 1943–44. Families shared living spaces with other people, but camp administrations kept them together.[9] The proportion of workers brought to Germany as families was undoubtedly small. There is no reason to think it differed significantly from the proportion of French forced laborers living as couples, whom a historian has calculated as less than 6 percent at the Berlin Siemens factory.[10]

Deprived of their families, deportees stuck with the friends and relatives who remained with them. Anna P. was deported to Austria at just thirteen years of age alongside her older sister. When a smallholding farmer took only her sister, Anna P. pleaded that he take them both. The farmer took pity on her and kept them together for several days. Another family from the area hired Anna P., and she remained close enough to visit on Sundays.[11] The desire of Eastern Workers to remain with familiar people was a survival mechanism that ensured a forced laborer would have at least one person they could trust in an uncertain environment. Allowing neighbors and relatives to work together was probably not a conscious policy of German authorities but the path of least resistance. In some cases, though, individual Germans seem to have kept deportees together because of a combination of kindness and the calculation that they would work better under those circumstances.

Eastern Workers also stayed together to mitigate the psychological impact of separation from their communities. Deportation to Germany was the first time many were away from their families, and homesickness was common. Vadim N. and a handful of young people taken from Taganrog to Bochum would gather to share their longing for their seaside town. Over the course of their meetings, they composed a song that Vadim N. could still recall sixty years after liberation. "For us it was a kind of anthem," he said. The common experience of yearning for home and family cemented friendships among the teenagers and young adults.[12]

Miserly provisions in the camp reinforced boundaries between groups. Aleksandra Mikhaleva noted that when the kitchen staff handed out bread at the cafeteria, some of the women would enter the line again and receive an illicit second helping. Regional affiliation structured social life among the camp's 510 residents, and Mikhaleva's group, all women from Kursk, were infamous (or envied) for their ability to solicit extra food. "They say about us, about the Kursk women, that we always get two helpings," Mikhaleva wrote.[13] The appearance of relative advantage not only created hostility between groups but perhaps channeled animosity away from the camp administration.

One of the most pronounced differences was between people born within the USSR's pre-1939 borders and those from territories the Soviet state annexed in 1939–40. During the short period between the annexations and the German invasion, Soviet authorities had attempted to acculturate the westerners to their new lives. Less than two years of Soviet rule, however, could not erase significant differences in language and culture between the east and the west.[14] Anna M., a woman from the eastern provinces of Belarus, recalled that she was considered "Russian" by her western Belarusian coworkers at a farm in Germany.[15] In one instance at a camp in East Prussia, forced laborers from the western annexed territories protested bitterly that the Germans categorized them as Eastern Workers rather than Polish, a status that would have guaranteed better wages and working conditions. They launched a wildcat strike in January 1943 that ended after they spent two days without food or heat in the winter cold. They were beaten, but not arrested, and sent back to work.[16]

The importance of regional groups is clear from the cases of Eastern Workers who lost these connections. Police sent Ivan K. to a punishment camp after his failed escape attempt from a Munich-area camp in the spring of 1943. There he hoped to insinuate himself into a group but failed to find anyone from his native Cherkasy region. Instead, the eighteen-year-old fell in with a group of prisoners from neighboring Kyiv province who "adopted" him. Tellingly, regional affiliation—defined as necessary in ever-widening rings—was the connection he sought by default.[17]

Ivan K.'s story is also revealing for his use of the term "adopt." Eastern Workers were most often teenagers or young adults. According to German regulations, deportees could be as young as fifteen, but desperate occupation officials sent some children who were even younger. For many or perhaps most of them, deportation to Germany meant separation from older relatives for the first time. Some 60 percent or more began work in Germany when they were under twenty-three years old. Of those, half were eighteen or younger.[18] How many arrived without older relatives is unclear. Anecdotal evidence from interviews, German documents, and Soviet statistics suggests that young people sent without parents were in the majority.

Young Eastern Workers agonized over the separation from their relatives. Farmworker Maria K. brought her friends to tears when she sang "Hello Mother, Your Daughter Sends a Letter" at Sunday gatherings of foreign workers. This song, like many sung by Eastern Workers, was a standard in the USSR but took on new meaning as workers found themselves without parents in unfamiliar surroundings.[19]

As in "Hello Mother," workers did write letters home in their free time. Petr P. remembered that people in his village received letters from Germany from departed neighbors but that few letters gave information about the true situation there.[20] Fearing punishment for themselves or their families if censors detected damaging information or anti-German views, letter writers coded information or kept their messages nondescript. Most wanted to let their families know that they were alive and that they missed them; they also asked recipients to pass along greetings to others from themselves and their campmates.[21] A few asked for care packages—and amazingly one reported receiving a package from her family in Ukraine despite the hardships of the occupation.[22]

Correspondence stopped as the Red Army retook territory from the Germans. The westward movement of the front in 1943–44 cut off Eastern Workers from their families in formerly occupied territories. Letters had provided some assurances that their relatives lived and were waiting for them. The severance of ties was another factor that unmoored young Eastern Workers. For those from the easternmost territories occupied by Germany, the loss of contact with their families could last two years.

Eastern Workers adapted to their German lives, restricted though they were. On Sundays it was common for workers in towns to go on long strolls. Their salaries were small, and there was little they could buy without ration cards. Still, many managed to go to photography studios and purchase unrestricted food-stuffs like cabbage or lemonade. Others found ways to sneak into cinemas—a pleasure technically forbidden to Eastern Workers.[23] Those with marketable skills could make supplemental income by fixing goods, as amateur mechanic Vadim N. did by repairing watches.[24] Even more widespread was the practice of taking day jobs on local farms or in households in exchange for food.

Workers who could leave their camps were often amazed by German towns. As a child in the Soviet Union, Aleksandra A. had heard of the Dresden Gallery at school, so when she found herself in Rumburg (today Rumburk, Czech Republic), a hundred kilometers from Dresden, she went to the city to see the gallery. She only found out on arrival that the gallery had been closed during the war.[25] Mikhail B. was a young teenager from a Belarusian village taken to the Frankfurt (Main) area. He later recalled the impression that Frankfurt made on him. He had never been to a city, even in the USSR. The world of shops, bicycles, and public transit was new and wondrous. "I had never seen big cities, big houses. It all amazed me," he said.[26] For many the urban experience was just as novel as life in a foreign land.

Factory workers adapted to life in Germany but always understood themselves as distinct from Germans. Participation in German holidays is a good example of this distancing. Holidays can give meaning to the passage of time, marking the calendar with symbolically significant dates. The Soviet government after 1917 upended the traditional calendar by abolishing Orthodox Christian festivals and replacing them with revolutionary holidays like International Women's Day (March 8) and the anniversary of the October Revolution (November 7 on the Gregorian calendar).[27] For obvious reasons, German camp administrations did not honor Soviet holidays, and few Eastern Workers seem to have celebrated them on their own. Germany had holidays associated with the Nazi Party, such as Hitler's birthday, but no former Eastern Workers recalled taking part in them. Undoubtedly, many did not want to celebrate Hitler's birthday and fewer still would have acknowledged such a celebration in post-Soviet interviews. It seems equally likely that camp administrators did not want to sully German national holidays by allowing foreign workers to participate. Eastern Workers took part in the New Year's holiday, as well as religious holidays like Christmas and Easter. It is difficult to register the role of religious life in the camps. The only Eastern Workers who remembered going to church services in the oral history interviews I reviewed worked at family farms and went to German churches.[28] In general the situation with holidays reflected a symbolic vacuum among Soviet-born people. Religious holidays initiated Eastern Workers into the rhythms of German life but did not give a sense of broader belonging as revolutionary holidays in the USSR had done.

Holidays were not meaningless, though. Celebrations were vital to forced laborers for rest, to mark time, and to create small-group connections. On holidays workers typically received a day off and bonus food. In some cases, factory administrations provided a venue for a party. For the New Year's holiday, the administration at Aleksandra Mikhaleva's camp opened the large cafeteria to several hundred camp residents. The German translator consecrated the gathering with a speech of praise for Hitler before turning over the celebration to the workers. It fell upon them to organize the festivities, which included songs and dancing.[29]

Celebratory food and drink were necessary to mark the holiday. Lucky buyers might convince Germans or non-Soviet foreign workers to sell rationed food or coupons for inflated prices.[30] Alcohol was attainable but just as difficult to find as food. Desperate for holiday drinks, some workers turned to methyl alcohol. Valentina Kalashnik was a twenty-year-old schoolteacher before she was taken to be a cleaner at a chemical laboratory in Grevenbroich, near Cologne. At work she came across a bottle of methyl alcohol marked with a skull and a warning in German. Kalashnik told male Eastern Worker friends what she found, and they persuaded her to steal some for their Christmas Eve 1943 party. She brought an empty bottle to work, syphoned off three hundred milliliters of the methanol, and hid it in her cubby in the camp. At 8:00 P.M. on Christmas Eve, Kalashnik came to the men's barracks with three female bunkmates. The three men at the party produced two bottles of nonalcoholic beer and mixed the methanol into them. The revelers all made toasts and took drinks, but two of the men imbibed especially large portions of the concoction. At 10:30 P.M. the camp turned off its lights and the women went home, leaving the men in a festive mood. On December 26, the women learned that one of the men had died and another had been hospitalized. For her part in the incident, the Gestapo sent Kalashnik to the concentration camp Ravensbrück.[31]

Kalashnik and her friends were not alone in drinking methanol and perhaps understood the risks. One former POW argued in his memoirs that a campmate's accidental overdose was a product of Eastern European alcoholism.[32] There is a more charitable explanation, though, which was that alcohol was an integral part of any festivity. The inseparability of alcohol and celebration had even convinced Soviet authorities, after years of fighting against alcohol in the early postrevolutionary period, to incorporate "cultured" drinking into worker holidays in the mid-1930s.[33] For forced laborers in Germany, alcohol was a way to create a festive atmosphere and cement ties.

Socialization in the urban forced labor barracks differed from village life. An individual assigned to a family farm might be a long distance from other Eastern Workers. There were foreign workers from various lands in Germany, however, and connections with Polish workers were particularly important to Eastern

Workers in rural settings. Sociability often meant Sunday group gatherings where one of the young men would bring a harmonica or guitar and the workers would dance to the music. After a week of hard work with a German family, the dances gave Eastern Workers a chance to be with people besides their employers. With more space and less surveillance, unofficial rural gatherings could be larger than those in the towns. Even in the village, however, revelry could draw unwanted attention from Germans. One worker recalled how just days after the Soviet victory at Stalingrad, a German heard the loud gathering of singing Poles and Ukrainians in a barn. He entered the building and berated them, "Why are you singing and dancing when [German] soldiers are dying?" The man submitted the names of the meeting's participants to the police, who fined their employers.[34]

Such denunciations hint at the danger and distrust Eastern Workers faced. In forced labor camps, the lack of private spaces made it difficult to keep anything secret and precluded meetings that exceeded a handful of people. The barracks provided no shelter from prying eyes. In his autobiographical novel, Vitalii Semin's teenage narrator opined that the substance of a secret among bunkmates would not be "uncovered at first, but the people involved in it were obvious."[35] The presence of informants heightened strains. One of Aleksandra Mikhaleva's friends, Valentina, confessed to her that factory police had recruited her to inform on their room. Until then Mikhaleva had not bothered hiding her diaries from her bunkmates but began to worry that camp authorities would discover them. Camp guards could search barracks without notice. If they found Mikhaleva's diaries, would they send her to jail for anti-German activity?[36]

German recruiting of informers was one way that the camp leadership created divisions and hierarchies among Eastern Workers. Camp administrations also employed Eastern Workers and former POWs in specialist positions as doctors, translators, supervisors, and other personnel. Across Europe, the Germans authorized, and often forced, locals to help govern the area. In this regard, dynamics at Eastern Worker camps paralleled those at Nazi German concentration camps attached to factories (but not death camps) and the Soviet Gulag. Production was the main priority in these places, and officials placed inmates in positions of relative privilege to minimize the free labor needed to operate.[37]

Specialists became intermediaries between Eastern Workers and the camp administration. In Semin's novel, a Soviet-born doctor named Sofia Andreevna treated the prisoners for typhus during an outbreak. Her acts of kindness in prolonging workers' hospital stay were life-preserving and seemed to contravene the wishes of camp leaders. At the same time, dealing with an unruly patient, she threatened, "If you don't go back to your place, I'll release you tomorrow." The prisoners knew that doctors had better food and fewer roommates than they had. Some even wondered if Sofia Andreevna was extending hospital stays not for ailing patients but for herself. After all, she would have to work at a factory if there were no patients.[38] As in the Gulag, medical personnel in Eastern Worker camps occupied an awkward position between German authorities and the workers. They had the authority to grant sick leave and often used it to help camp residents. Yet their status came from the Germans, and they rightfully feared losing their position—or worse—if they took too many liberties.[39]

Interpreters navigated similar dilemmas. Official translators were often recruited among Volksdeutsche from the Soviet Union, speakers of Slavic languages like Poles or Czechs, or émigrés from the former Russian Empire. For day-to-day translation, authorities found unofficial interpreters among workers who spoke German well. POW Anatolii Derevenets, an unofficial interpreter in his camp, recalled translating a conversation that turned hostile between the German kitchen head and a Soviet prisoner named Mishka. The German mentioned a newspaper article that reported a Wehrmacht victory in a battle on the previous day. After Derevenets translated, Mishka shouted in Russian, "Well you ask him about how the Russians kicked their asses in such-and-such a place." Derevenets feared that he, not to mention Mishka, could face punishment for such an outburst and mistranslated to save them both from trouble.[40]

Other intermediaries between German authorities and Eastern Workers included barracks and room supervisors. Rather than embed a German overseer in each barracks room, the camp commandant designated one of the residents as his representative. The residents called this person the *starosta*, or elder. The limited evidence that exists suggests that the selection of the elder was typically made by the agreement of the camp boss and the residents. The elders were usually among the adult bunkmates and knew at least some German. Anna Sh., for example, was nineteen or twenty when she became a room elder at her camp in Meschede (Westphalia). Because she knew German, she could raise complaints with the camp administration.[41] The position did not replace factory work for Anna Sh., but for others it did. At Petr P.'s barracks, a converted restaurant banquet hall, the elder's full-time job was organizing the workers.[42]

Medical work and translation required skills. Room elders, too, typically had maturity, language knowledge, and social capital. In contrast, a job in the kitchen provided access to food and seemingly required little. Postwar Soviet investigators frequently accused arrestees of earning these positions by informing on campmates to German authorities.[43] Whether these accusations were genuine or the product of envy is unclear. It is apparent that the formation of kitchen cliques sparked resentment at the time. In her diary, Aleksandra Mikhaleva wrote that the kitchen workers had gained "great strength and power" through deference to the Germans. In one instance, a male acquaintance berated the kitchen staff for giving him a small serving of soup. The staff informed on him for being a malcontent, and camp guards beat him.[44]

Social groupings among Eastern Workers emerged along lines both new and familiar. Deprivation, surveillance, and camp hierarchies prohibited large-group cohesion in the camps. Demographic realities also impacted camp life. Many Eastern Workers were young people separated from their families for the first time. In this unknown situation, Eastern Workers found community in regional ties and kinship. Although there were important divisions between Eastern Workers, a more significant boundary was between them and other nationalities in the Reich.

Barracks Transnationalism

Nazi racial ideology defined the treatment of foreign workers. Westarbeiter (e.g., Belgians, Dutch, French, Norwegians) were supposed to be racially more like Germans and could work as specialists and receive comparably good wages. Even as prisoners of war, French workers received packages from the Red Cross. Italian workers had also enjoyed a privileged position while the Italian government supported Germany. In the summer of 1943, the Italian government overthrew Benito Mussolini and gave its support to the Allies, prompting Germany to organize a competing puppet government. Italian soldiers thought to support the anti-German Italian state became prisoners whose treatment was not enviable. Deported Slavic workers, such as Poles, were treated worse than the Western Workers. Still, their relative freedom of movement and higher official rations put them in a privileged position compared with Eastern Workers.[45]

One group that Eastern Workers rarely encountered were Jewish victims of the Nazi German regime. Many Eastern Workers were aware that German authorities were targeting Jews. Before their deportations to Germany, some Eastern Workers had seen Jews being arrested or murdered.[46] At train stops deportees heading westward caught glimpses of beleaguered Jewish workers from the ghettos of the General Government.[47] Most Eastern Workers, though, were sent to places far from the death camps.

People from Jewish backgrounds taken as Eastern Workers knew that these roots were dangerous. Antonina S.'s mother was Jewish, but her father was Russian and gave her his last name. Her passport listed her as Russian, and that was her nationality for German authorities, too. Somehow a campmate learned or decided that she was half Jewish and denounced her for it. The camp commandant called her to his office and questioned her via an interpreter, an émigré. Antonina S.

could understand German because she had lived in Odesa and knew Yiddish. Feigning incomprehension, she heard the translator assert that no Russian would have married a Jewish woman in the Russian Empire. The commandant accepted this explanation and dropped the matter. If he had determined that Antonina S. was part Jewish, she undoubtedly would have gone to a worse fate: penal labor, death at a concentration camp, or perhaps execution in Germany.[48]

Historians under Nikita Khrushchev depicted antifascist solidarity between foreign workers.[49] Some echoes of this solidarity are found in interviews with former workers, who undermined their bosses with veiled insults. Oleksandr I. remembered that Soviet forced laborers called their German boss "fatty" (*puzatyi*). When French workers heard the description, they were curious; they asked, "What is *puzatyi*?" and then adopted the insult too.[50] Differing tastes between cultures also brought opportunities for cooperation. Soviet laborers working at the Junkers factory at Magdeburg were hungry—but not hungry enough to eat frogs that they could catch near the camp. Instead, they traded the frogs for bread to Italian POWs.[51]

Conflict was seemingly as common as solidarity in interactions between groups of foreign workers. After he returned to the USSR, secret police questioned Evgenii Kiselev, an arrestee who had been a prisoner at Buchenwald, about rumors that he instigated a revolt in the camp. He admitted that the revolt was a simple brawl between national groups, stating, "I started a fight, hitting a Frenchman in the face because he pushed a Russian prisoner."[52] Aleksandra Mikhaleva's work camp saw violent conflicts between Soviets and Poles. On a Sunday in August 1943, the Soviet men at her camp had an extended drinking session. When the inebriated men saw a group of Polish workers, they picked a fight and attacked them with knives. After camp guards broke up the scuffle, the men vowed to continue the fight the following week. By the next weekend, cooler and perhaps now sober heads had prevailed and called off a second round of the brawl.[53]

Non-Soviet workers had better provisions and more freedom of movement, factors that made them important contacts for trading. Deals with Eastern Workers and POWs were lucrative and, though illegal, were not so risky to rule them out entirely.[54] Because Eastern Workers had little alternative to the black market, other foreign workers could charge exorbitant prices. A German police report concluded that foreign workers "all try to take each other for a ride . . . and it is almost always the Eastern Worker who ends up being the worst cheated."[55]

Eastern Workers' connections with Germans in towns were often more formal than their relationships with other foreign laborers. The Germans they encountered most often were camp administrators, police, and work supervisors. Even German coworkers usually had a supervisory role. Germans and Eastern Workers had different interpretations of their interactions. Many former Eastern

Workers remembered individual Germans as kind people who brought them food out of pity or perhaps even as an attempt to resist the Nazi regime.[56] Rather than seeing these acts as altruistic, a leading German historian argues that for the German worker, sharing food was motivated by production; a hungry forced laborer was not an industrious worker.[57] Kindness and pragmatism were not mutually exclusive. Valentin Senger's family were Jews from Odesa hiding as Germans in Frankfurt (Main), and his father became a factory supervisor for Eastern Workers because he knew Russian. He gained their confidence with small kindnesses—bringing them medicine or food. He also invited them in small numbers for visits to his family's home. Senger was not alone in inviting Eastern Workers to visit. Many forced laborers who had the right to leave the camp premises received similar invitations.[58] In Senger's case, supervisors at the factory made no complaints because the Eastern Workers were productive under his supervision.[59]

For Germans living near a camp, the presence of Eastern Workers could be a boon. On weekends Germans in need of yard work or home repair would arrive at the camp to solicit labor. Liudmila G. recalled that the head of the camp would come on free days and act as a labor recruiter. Pay was usually not in cash but in a more valuable currency—food. A farmer who hired Liudmila G. allowed her to eat berries from his garden as she worked. Others made soup or provided bread. The wage was at the discretion of the employer.[60] The glut of labor and lack of food available without ration cards meant that compensation could be as little as a bowl of soup for a day of work. It did not matter. Nina M. recalled that when there was work "you would fly forward as fast as you could . . . just so you would get something to eat."[61]

As a rule, the more social distance between Eastern Workers and Germans, the worse the relationship. A typical occurrence was German teenagers' chasing Eastern Workers in towns, throwing rocks at people they saw as racial inferiors.[62] Relationships that were not anonymous tended to be more friendly. In some cases, German employers could become almost surrogate parents. Oleksandr I. worked in a preparation shift at a coal mine with a pleasant older German named Otto. One day Otto came to the mine and informed him that his son-in-law had been killed at the front and that he had no desire to work that day. Otto and Oleksandr I.'s relationship had been friendly before, but the loss of his son-in-law seemed to bring out Otto's paternal feelings. He invited the Ukrainian teenager home for Christmas, where he showed him pictures of his dead son-in-law.[63]

At workplaces or in towns, regulations meant to segregate Eastern Workers from other foreign workers and Germans could hardly isolate Soviet people from non-Soviet Europeans. Contact did not mean solidarity. Easterners' dismal position made them vulnerable to systemic exploitation by Germans and other foreign workers. Nowhere was this exploitation more visible than in sexual relationships.

Sexual Life

An unintended result of forced labor was that it brought millions of young, unmarried women and men together in the Reich. Security measures and the lack of privacy hindered sexual activity, but the difficult conditions of the camp motivated it. Sexual relationships were pleasures that could be had under the circumstances of forced labor camps. Moreover, barracks relationships usually had elements of sexual barter, where female Eastern Workers traded sexual attention (but not always intercourse) for food, resources, or privileges.

In some cases, people from the east would have relationships with one another. Male Eastern Workers were somewhat scarcer than women, about ten men for eleven women.[64] Yet sex segregation by barracks meant that a group of Eastern Worker women might be at a factory with no Soviet-born men nearby, or vice versa. In some cases, the men claimed they were in demand. Aleksandra Mikhaleva, the Kursk diarist, had a Russian friend Grisha (Grigorii), who bragged, "There are ten girls for every guy. You go out with one, another is winking at you, and a third is waiting in line."[65]

Perhaps Grisha was especially popular with women, but Eastern Workers were generally bad matches. Camp relationships often had a material component, and Eastern Workers on average earned less and had fewer privileges than members of other groups. Male Eastern Workers faced the same expectations for courtship as other foreign workers. Mikhail Sinitsyn, an Eastern Worker and aspiring poet in a factory in Bamberg (Bavaria), wrote a poem called "Meet Up and Break Up":

> Galia cheated on me secretly,
> Her love wasn't fated to be mine,
> Galia didn't love me really,
> Only my bread, bacon, and wine.[66]

At Mikhaleva's camp, women encouraged their bunkmates to find "profitable courtiers" who would bring them gifts of food and clothes. These were generally Polish or Czech laborers at farms in the surrounding area. Mikhaleva's Polish boyfriend Jozef brought her chocolates and shoes. He also taught her to ride a bike. "The guy is really in love with me," she wrote.[67] Antonina V. was working at BMW's shipping department in Munich when she attracted the attention of a Dutch coworker who introduced her to his Dutch friends. She entered a relationship with one of the Dutchmen who worked at a local bakery. He provided her with food from work and access to entertainment that many other Eastern Workers did not have: swimming pools, photo shops, and cafés.[68] Such privileges were key drivers of transnational contact.

These relationships were notable for female Eastern Workers not only because they were with exotic men but because they were among the first experiences many had with romance and sex. The experience of work in Germany coincided with the coming of age of these teenagers and young adults. Aleksandra Mikhaleva's diaries contained detailed accounts of meetings with non-Soviet men. After the doting but oafish Jozef came a similarly named Czech, Josef, whose seeming disinterest and allure to other women in the camp attracted Mikhaleva. After a day of walking with Czech Josef (the guard let her out even though it was not a free day), she commented on her blossoming as a woman in the camp, "He lifted me in his arms like a child and pressed his lips to mine in a long, passionate kiss. How did that happen?" In Kursk she had a boyfriend who had hardly dared to hold hands. "Now a kiss means nothing."[69]

Mikhaleva rarely reflected on the pragmatic aspects of her relationships. The ubiquity of gift giving for sexual attention made these practices the norm. She sometimes wrote of her boyfriends as Polish or Czech but not exactly as members of a nationality. Poles and Czechs were factions among foreign workers, the same way she was a member of the Kursk faction. The non-Soviet men were defined by their prewar homelands, perceived differences in national character, language, and, perhaps most important, the relative privilege that German categorization bestowed. Most often, Mikhaleva wrote about her boyfriends as individuals—whether they would be good husbands and if she was prepared to be their wife.[70] Moreover, Mikhaleva's liaisons with non-Soviet men did not displace her relationship with her Kursk roommates as her primary group identity. In important ways, these romantic relationships solidified her barracks connections by creating alliances between the Kursk women and groups of male Polish or Czech workers.

Language played an important role in mixed relationships, with German as the lingua franca. When Iurii Kh. saw Maria T. on the streets of Königsberg, he thought she was a Slavic foreign worker. He did not want to seem presumptuous, though, so he used the neutral German first before Polish and then Russian when he approached her. German not only guaranteed he would be understood but also allowed Iurii Kh. to avoid assumptions about her nationality and, consequently, about her status in the Reich.[71]

Relationships based on physical attraction and even barter were difficult to sustain without a shared language. Antonina S., the young woman who hid that her mother was Jewish, was recruited for specialized work at a chemical factory because of her ten-year high school education and her good German. There she began a relationship with a Frenchman called "Zhano." They could not communicate well because he did not know German, but he would draw pictures of flowers for her and would slip them into her pocket at work. Soon Zhano fell ill and went to the hospital. Although Zhano's sickness was not serious, he would suffer a new malady—a broken heart. Antonina S. was visiting the patient when his friend Claude arrived. He charmed Antonina S. instantly, and just days later she broke up with Zhano and began a relationship with his friend. Whatever spark occurred between her and Claude, it surely helped that he was a translator and could converse with Antonina S. in German.[72]

Polish was the other important language for relationships. Having grown up in a part of prewar Poland annexed in 1939 to Soviet Belarus, Olga D. had learned Polish in school. She claimed that her ability to communicate with Poles drew many male suitors for Sunday strolls through local orchards.[73] Polish workers were more numerous in villages than Westarbeiter, who were fewer in general and were more often employed in specialist positions.[74] For this reason, Eastern Workers on farms often had extensive contact with Poles. The fluid identities of those from the western borderlands also made it easier for them to blend in with their Polish milieu.[75]

Most of these relationships had some elements of gift giving and barter, but the memoirs and diaries of former Eastern Workers, both men and women, rarely mention sex. The absence of sex reflects the limitations of these sources rather than the realities of camp life. Interview subjects who were in camps and ghettos rarely describe their own sexual relationships, which seem disgraceful, and only slightly more frequently speak about others' liaisons.[76] It is possible that uncurious workers did not know the details of others' sex lives if they confined themselves to the cramped, sex-segregated, securitized barracks. Tetiana B. recalled how young men visited her twenty-three bunkmates before curfew. These meetings were platonic, she claimed, but added suggestively, "Maybe somewhere they . . ."[77]

Sex happened, of course, despite living restrictions. Eighteen-year-old Galina G. met a French man named Emil at her factory in 1943. Although she was confined to the factory and her barracks complex, a workplace romance bloomed. The relationship continued despite their inability to meet outside of the factory. Emil gave Galina G. extra supplies, and they spoke in German "about love" and his life in France while she learned French. In 1944 her camp removed restrictions on visits to barracks by outsiders, meaning that Emil could visit. Galina G.'s bunkmates did not mind the visits—almost all of them also had boyfriends. She told an interviewer in 2005 that she and Emil married under German law in 1944. It is possible they married legally, but it is also possible that she used marriage as shorthand for a long-term sexual relationship. In either case, the camp leadership prohibited their living together. Nonetheless, by the end of the war, Galina G. had become pregnant by Emil. Undoubtedly, the elderly Galina G. felt comfortable talking about her pregnancy because it came in the context of marriage. The details of her sexual life with Emil were not something she discussed, however.[78]

Sexual relationships like Galina G. and Emil's could not be secret, and not only because of pregnancies. In the case of French workers in Germany, tight living quarters forced sex into public spaces, creating the impression that French women were especially promiscuous.[79] Similar notions of Eastern Workers' wanton behavior must have circulated. Aleksandra Mikhaleva knew about all the relationships of her campmates, and they knew about her "heated love affair" with Polish Jozef. Her cousin Galina had a clandestine relationship with a married German coworker twice her age. As Mikhaleva explained, "She meets with him during her breaks and leaves work for meetings, when we have the night shift. All the workers have already noticed. Somehow no one is very surprised, although they talk about it and laugh about it and say the most disgusting things possible." The lack of surprise was probably because Galina was just one of several women from the barracks seeing older German men. Mikhaleva had her own prospective German suitor, a coworker who visited the barracks occasionally. And though she wrote euphemistically that the women in her barracks had not "lost their honor," Mikhaleva also reported that several friends from Kursk working in a neighboring town were pregnant. At least one had arranged an abortion.[80]

Eastern Workers were also involved in purely transactional sex that might be better classified as prostitution. The German state organized brothels within the Reich and in concentration camps but seemingly avoided using female Eastern Workers because of their supposed racial inferiority.[81] Prostitution among Eastern Worker women was unofficial. At large complexes, a camp official or enterprising foreign worker might organize an unregistered local brothel. In 1943 an inspector from the German Foreign Ministry sent to Eastern Worker camps was scandalized to find that camp commanders and other bosses were encouraging women to do sex work to supplement their incomes.[82] Because of its unofficial character, assessing the scope and character of prostitution is impossible. The taboo nature of prostitution also means that oral history accounts are virtually silent on the issue. In more than one hundred accounts and interviews of former forced laborers that I reviewed, none mention prostitution, and few mention sexual barter as such. Only a handful of the women mention rape, and only in the context of unsuccessful attempts (by Germans and other nationalities).[83] A study using Holocaust survivor interviews notes that the later the testimony was given, the more likely it was to discuss rape. Arguably, previous decades of testimony and the more sexually open environment of the period after the 1990s made Holocaust survivors open to talking about these issues.[84] In contrast, Eastern Workers only began to speak about their experiences late in life—in the 1990s or early in the twenty-first century. It may not have occurred to them to discuss sexual matters, and, moreover, a lasting shame in the USSR surrounded Eastern Workers' supposed sexual treason.

Classified postwar reports by Soviet officials are products of this stigma. Their authors would find signs of wartime prostitution, but the politicized accounts should not be read at face value. A Soviet youth league official who visited a camp for liberated forced laborers in Germany wrote with alarm about some of the women in the camp, "These morally depraved people not only sold out their motherland, but also their own body." Supposedly, the women had born "little Fritzes" and now were starving the babies to death in Soviet displaced persons camps to escape condemnation. Even if these stories were apocryphal, the disgrace of sexual contact with Germans helps to explain why women did not want to talk about these relationships later in life. As proof of widespread prostitution, the Komsomol official cited derogatory poems that had gained currency in the camps.[85]

Were such rumors evidence of widespread prostitution and barter? Perhaps. What is certain is that Soviet men felt that women had betrayed the country through sex with foreigners and that they had little sympathy for Eastern Workers' motivations for transactional sex. Sexual barter, including prostitution, gave women a chance to supplement their meager rations. At the same time, the power differential between camp administrators and Eastern Workers exposed the women to coercive and dangerous relationships. In the occupied east, German soldiers raped local women as a way of showing dominance over a supposedly inferior people. Within the Reich, sexual violence against Eastern Workers was less overt, but the attitudes of Germans and West European workers toward these women were similar.[86] The possibility of rape by Germans was on the minds of Eastern Workers. Maria G. remembered her fear of her boss when she came to a family farm to work at age fifteen. Her first nights she lay awake, thinking, "God, don't let him come in here, don't let him . . ." She was relieved to discover in the next weeks that the farmer was only interested in her labor.[87]

It is possible to imagine, as in the case of the mass rapes the Red Army would commit in Germany, that women provided sex to individuals to protect themselves from rape by multiple men.[88] Muza I. recalled that the "deputy" of the group of Polish workers whose dances she visited claimed her for his girlfriend, although she refused his advances. Before he left the village to visit his home, the deputy threatened, "Don't go around with anyone. . . . I am the one who keeps you safe, only me." These parting words hinted at the relationship between sex and protection for vulnerable Eastern Workers.[89]

Nazi leaders treated sex between Germans and Eastern Workers as a violation of their prohibitions on racial mixing.[90] The fear of racial contamination also pushed the Wehrmacht in the occupied east to establish brothels and conscript local women as sex slaves. Army leaders believed that controlled sex with Slavic women would prevent the more extensive racial mixing that might occur in unrestrained relationships with local women.[91] Reich authorities tolerated but did not approve of German men's relationships with foreign women, especially from Eastern Europe. Yet they did not punish the men harshly in general. For one, sex between German men and Soviet-born women was impossible to stop, above all in the occupied east where German men were many and women few. Authorities also viewed German men's sex with foreign women as an unfortunate consequence of the Aryan race's supposed virility.[92]

Pregnancy that resulted from female Eastern Workers' sexual relationships is a painful chapter. German regulations until the beginning of 1943 allowed female Eastern Workers to go to their homelands if they became ill or pregnant, and reports by camp administrators to central authorities suggested that women were using pregnancy to escape the forced labor regime. Undoubtedly calculated pregnancies occurred, although it also seems possible that camp authorities exaggerated the magnitude of such incidents. Such reports motivated a harsher position on pregnancy. From 1943 onward, German officials demanded that Eastern Worker women remain in Germany and give their children to a nursery.[93]

Conditions for mothers and children were criminal. A Russian-language poster distributed in the occupied territories extolled German care for mothers and implied that Eastern Worker children would receive the same care (figure 2.1). Although regulations stipulated that "racially valuable" children (those with German fathers) were supposed to be fostered as German, the situation at nurseries for other children of Eastern Workers was abominable. An SS official reported that at one nursery newborns were being kept on starvation rations until they inevitably died. The SS man had no desire to save the children but instead proposed a supposedly humane solution: execute them immediately to save the food and suffering. Meanwhile, German authorities legalized and urged abortions for Eastern Worker and Polish women, even as German women faced prison for terminating their pregnancies.[94] Valentin Senger related a case in which one of his father's Eastern Worker charges became pregnant. Senger's father made the mistake of reporting the pregnancy to his supervisor, who informed the Gestapo. After interrogating the woman about the baby's father, the Gestapo sent her to a hospital to have an abortion. Women under the elder Senger's watch continued to get pregnant, but he had learned his lesson and arranged for future abortions privately.[95] A database of the nurseries estimated that the combination of abortions and death by negligence numbered more than a hundred thousand.[96]

Nazi leaders penalized relationships between German women and foreign men much more harshly than those between German men and foreign women. Although an ethnic German woman who had sex with a foreigner had broken the same law as a German man, authorities treated these incidents as much worse

FIGURE 2.1. "We saw Germany. 1. Care for mother and child. Fighting and working together with Germany, you create a happy future for yourself." Poster reproduced from USHMM RG-31.117.

violations: German men made sexual conquests, however mistaken they were in their target; German women—the bearers of Aryan children—had desecrated their purity. For this crime, German women faced public humiliation and potential concentration camp sentences more often than German men. The magnitude of the punishment for both the woman and the man involved also depended on Nazi German categorization of the foreign man's race. French or Dutch men received comparatively light sentences because German authorities saw them as racially close. In contrast, Soviet and Polish men caught having sex with German women were often executed. The Reich Security Main Office, the umbrella policing agency in Germany, in 1944 authorized an average of two to three executions per day of Soviet men charged with having sexual relationships with German women.[97]

The several hundred annual executions did not encompass all the sexual relationships between Eastern European men and German women. Still, the number of men from the occupied east in relationships with German women was almost certainly lower than the number of female Eastern Workers in relationships with German men. It was not just the threat of punishment that stopped men from the east from entering relationships with German women. A major factor that prevented these relationships was physical barriers. Male Eastern

Workers and Soviet POWs faced more restrictions on their mobility and greater scrutiny of their behavior than did female Eastern Workers.[98]

Male forced laborers in German-occupied Europe were perpetrators of sexual violence as well as victims of German punishment. Maria G., the farmworker who had overcome her fear of potential sexual violence by her German employer, was attacked by a Soviet POW coworker. The farm where they worked was large enough to support three foreign laborers, including a POW the farmer would occasionally hire from the local camp. This was Petro, a man in his twenties from Poltava province who was tall and handsome, according to Maria G. Over months of working together, he made persistent advances, and when they were alone in a field, he attacked her. Her boss and another worker heard her screams and stopped Petro before he could rape her. Police arrested Petro, and Maria G. never found out what happened to him.[99]

Presumably, the sentence for Petro was much harsher than it would have been for a German. An example of the discrepancies in punishment involves soldiers from the Turkestan Legion, a pro-German formation recruited among Soviet POWs. Formed along ethnonational lines, the units enjoyed relatively free movement within their area of operation and, rather than fighting on the front, often served as police in occupied territories. The Germans sent units from the Turkestan Legion to the Netherlands, among other places. In the fall of 1943, a group of five soldiers from the legion entered the house of a Dutch family on the pretext of searching for British spies. Upon entering, they raped the family's teenage daughter. Unlike most plausible incidents of rape that the Dutch raised to the attention of authorities, the occupiers took up this case and executed the rapists. The lack of punishment for German rapists does not excuse rape by Soviet-born legionnaires. It suggests, however, that German authorities believed the charges against the Central Asian auxiliaries because of their status as racial inferiors. Moreover, because they were racial inferiors, they were more deserving of punishment.[100]

Like sexual violence, the prevalence of same-sex relationships is difficult to assess. As in other settings of sex-segregated confinement, it is easy to imagine forced laborers engaging in homosexual acts with their neighbors. The same power dynamic between Eastern Workers and Germans that enabled heterosexual exploitation surely created the possibility of homosexual contact between these groups. It is remarkable that former Eastern Workers' interviews and diaries do not mention same-sex relationships of any kind. This absence must be partially explained by the stigmatization of homosexuality in the former Soviet Union into the twenty-first century.[101]

Despite the stereotypes and taboos surrounding Eastern Workers' sexual relationships in Germany, a picture of their sexual lives emerges from available sources. Young Eastern Workers sought intimate relationships amid deprivations. In many cases, it is difficult to distinguish the line between affection and pragmatism. Even in relationships with elements of romance, German racial hierarchies introduced dynamics that made non-Soviet people in Germany into "profitable courtiers" and, especially in the case of Germans, allowed them to pressure Eastern Workers into sexual relationships.

The Germans treated Eastern Workers as a coherent group of racial inferiors but also promoted divisions between them. The meager rations Germans allotted to forced laborers created animosity not only toward the camp administration but also toward campmates. Regional groups jockeyed for more provisions, and camp "specialists" gained privileges. Paradoxically, these tribulations created solidarity and vibrant social life at the barracks level. After returning to Kursk in 1945, Aleksandra Mikhaleva wrote in her diary, "I miss my friends, our room."[102] Tellingly, she wrote about her friends from the Kursk barracks, for these ties did not extend far beyond its walls. German policies of division and the economics of the labor camp worked against cohesion among Eastern Workers as a whole.

The same logic of deprivation shaped Eastern Workers' contacts with other foreign workers. The relative privilege allotted to groups the Germans viewed as racial superiors allowed them to profit from Eastern Workers. Sexual interactions between female Eastern Workers and others, even in the context of romantic relationships, usually had elements of barter. The exchange of intimacy for food or privileges helped female Eastern Workers survive. Yet it also exposed the disparity between the conditions of life for people from the occupied east and other national groups in the Reich, constraining the common cause foreign workers might have otherwise found against the Germans.

Deliberate German policies, social factors, and economic realities atomized Eastern Worker society. Workers' hostility to the Germans and the Germans' fear of group action ruled out mass subscription to a German-friendly sense of collective belonging. Although forced laborers disdained their overseers, social divisions and camp surveillance precluded identities that transcended the barracks.

COLLABORATION AND RESISTANCE

Wartime Agency and Its Limits in Wustrau
and Leipzig

Life in the Third Reich for Eastern Workers and Soviet prisoners of war necessitated both compromises and struggle with German rule. Most forced laborers fell into bitter cooperation, but a significant minority more actively engaged in collaboration or resistance. Soon after the invasion of the USSR, German leaders began to recruit POWs as auxiliaries, into military formations, and as minor functionaries. Most joined antipartisan units or became guards, while a minority took on more significant roles as pro-German administrators. Meanwhile, other Eastern Workers and POWs formed small, secret groups that they hoped would contribute to Germany's defeat.

Any attempt to quantify collaboration or resistance encounters problems of definition and tendentious sources. By one estimate, approximately 250,000 Soviet soldiers voluntarily surrendered to the Germans. Some of these defectors were among the estimated 1 to 1.6 million who served in antipartisan brigades, police, and other capacities during the war.[1] Many enlisted in these groups to escape starvation or because of German coercion, factors that complicate designating such people as collaborators. Resistance is even more difficult to recognize clearly. Although one Soviet-Russian historian extrapolated from German police documents a baseline number of resisters in the tens of thousands, such a calculation is fraught; ubiquitous German suspicion probably inflated these figures, while the necessity for secrecy in resistance activity and consequent lack of organizational archives depressed them.[2] There is another issue that should complicate any assessment of the scale of collaboration and resistance: people who collaborated were sometimes the same people who resisted.

Analogous dilemmas have faced historians of German society under Nazism. Scholars have long struggled with how to assess support for Hitler and what to consider opposition. A well-established part of this literature moved away from the search for violent resistance to Nazism and instead concentrated on everyday opposition (*resistenz*, or immunity); because the Nazi regime hoped for total control over society and punished perceived resistance mercilessly, behavior that contradicted official dictates (e.g., fraternizing with foreign workers) could be seen as resistance.[3] This argument contains the important insight that the structural constraints of living in Nazi Germany must inform any evaluation of collaboration or resistance. Similarly, a strain of scholarship on the history of Eastern Europeans working under German authorities has argued for a more sympathetic view of collaboration than previously. One German historian has asserted that even death camp guards, many of them former Soviet POWs, trained at the infamous Trawniki camp in today's Poland were both perpetrators and victims in the Nazi system of mass murder; the guards faced violence and potential execution by the Germans while they participated in the murder of prisoners.[4]

The question of complicity in Hitler's regime is critical, but it is as much moral as it is historical. For scholars writing about collaboration, the goal often is to criticize (or support) the harshness of Stalinist justice and postwar public opinion on both sides of the Iron Curtain.[5] Yet the dividing line between cooperation and collaboration is subjective. Any definition will simplify what was a mixture of ambiguous motivations, contradictory behavior, and coercion. It is tempting to adopt the narrow definition of a French historian who characterizes collaboration as assistance to Germany motivated by political sympathy.[6] There were Soviet-born people who perhaps fit this characterization. General Andrei Vlasov and a group of captured Soviet officers created the pro-German Russian Liberation Army (Russkaia osvoboditel'naia armiia, ROA), whose goal was to overthrow Stalin in favor of a Russian state with German help. Yet Vlasov also faced pressure from his German allies and existed on the edge of the same spectrum of coercion and compromise as Eastern Workers. Similar questions arise about resistance. A handful of POWs and Eastern Workers resisted German rule without compromises, but they were a minority among the many others who undertook small acts of resistance even as they worked under the Germans. Did these people resist because they hated Nazi German rule or because they feared accusations of treason should they someday return to the Soviet Union? Recognizing this problem, this chapter attempts to move beyond discussions that define individuals as criminals or victims, opportunists or heroes. Instead, it focuses on action to explain wartime behavior.

The rejection of such a moral definition is not a failure to recognize that some acts were more important than others. The significance of collaboration or resistance lay at the juncture of intent, impact, and agency. It mattered how someone interacted with the Germans, why they did it, and how much choice they had in the matter. Eastern Worker and POW activity on the black market, workplace theft, harvesting from private gardens, unplanned work stoppages, and sporadic violence were probably more detrimental to the German war effort than all organized resistance within Germany's borders. Yet these actions are poor examples of resistance because they were spontaneous or were conducted primarily for the purposes of survival rather than to undermine the Nazi regime. The impact of collaboration or resistance is also an important factor. Vlasov's cooperation with the Nazi regime was more consequential than that of rank-and-file ROA soldiers, and service in the ROA meant more than labor at a factory as an Eastern Worker. Perhaps the most important factor—and the one that binds collaboration and resistance most strongly—is agency. Assistance given to Germany under the imagined and real threat of coercion meant less than help given freely. The German regime gave Eastern Europeans in the Reich little freedom of action, yet some enjoyed more opportunities than others. Who among Soviet POWs and Eastern Workers had a modicum of choice? How did they use their relative autonomy?

This chapter is most interested in the question of agency and examines it through the Wustrau propagandist training camp and resistance groups in Leipzig. The Wustrau men were drawn from educated prisoners and experienced privileged conditions compared with most POWs, Eastern Workers, or even auxiliaries in pro-German formations. Because of the propagandists' relative elite status, Wustrau provides a window onto the factors that enabled collaboration and, unexpectedly, resistance.

From Captivity to Collaboration

Northwest of Berlin near the village of Wustrau, the German Ministry of the East established a ten-square-kilometer complex on a wooded lake. The ministry, headed by Nazi leader Alfred Rosenberg, was the civilian bureaucracy charged with governing the occupied eastern territories. From 1942 until the end of 1944, the complex would hold several thousand former Soviet POWs grouped by ethnonational categorization into barracks of Armenian, Azeri, Belarusian, Georgian, Russian, Ukrainian, Uzbek, and various North Caucasian peoples.[7] Almost all the residents had education and accomplishments. Among them were doctors, teachers, and engineers, and many had been in the Communist Party before their capture. There were other training facilities where German forces prepared former Soviet POWs to join pro-German brigades or to become concentration camp guards. The Wehrmacht had a propagandist camp at Dabendorf, on the opposite side of Berlin, that operated as an officer training school for Vlasov's ROA.[8] Unlike these facilities, the Wustrau camp's purpose was training former Soviet elites as propagandists for Nazi German rule in Eastern Europe.

Almost all these men had been through the ordeal of capture and detention in German POW camps. Many were taken in the first months of the war, the most dire period for the USSR. Before June 1941, Soviet propaganda had emphasized the strength of the Red Army and insisted that any war would be fought beyond Soviet borders. It was a double shock when millions of soldiers were captured in mass encirclements as German forces made their way to the outskirts of Moscow. More than half of the nearly 5.8 million Soviet prisoners taken throughout the war were captured by the end of 1941.[9]

The desperate first months of the war created opposing impulses among soldiers. The large majority of Soviet POWs came to German captivity against their will. A combination of patriotism, fear of reprisals, group loyalty, and protectiveness of loved ones made Soviet soldiers fight.[10] There was also a growing awareness of the fate that awaited prisoners. Soviet newspapers described horrific conditions in German POW camps. Articles reprinted German orders that banned the Wehrmacht from feeding prisoners who did not work and letters by German soldiers that discussed summary executions of prisoners.[11] Despite this information, and perhaps because of a skepticism of Soviet propaganda, a significant minority surrendered voluntarily—perhaps as much as 5 percent of Soviet POWs. Some claimed to be motivated by their hatred of the Soviet system, but most experienced a combination of defeatism and political ambivalence. To many it seemed that the stunning early defeats made the Soviet collapse inevitable.[12]

As prisoners of the Germans, both those who surrendered and those who were captured found themselves facing lethal forms of deprivation, as well as outright murder. Historians disagree over the scale of death in POW camps, but a minimum of 2.6 million and as many as 3.3 million died of 5.8 million Soviet soldiers captured during the war.[13] These deaths were not just a product of criminal negligence but of orders by Hitler and German military leaders. With the infamous "Commissar Order" issued on the eve of the invasion, the German high command authorized the execution of captured Soviet political activists, leaving the exact target of the order open. The ambiguity of the directive meant that its implementation was far from categorical, and a significant number of military and civilian party members survived through cooperation with their captors. Nonetheless, the "Commissar Order" provided flexible grounds for executions among various groups—political commissars (party officials embedded at every level of the army) and "Asiatics."[14] Soviet soldiers apparently knew that these were key targets, and those who fit the categories attempted to hide themselves. A former

POW later remembered his moment of capture. As a German truck approached him and a small group of unarmed soldiers, a young officer threw away his pistol and announced, "Don't call me lieutenant. I'm just Misha."[15]

There were patterns to the targeting of Soviet POWs, but killing was not confined to select categories. Soviet POWs overall were a group that Germany slated for destruction. Tellingly, the murder of Soviet POWs was an important link in the development of the death camps. The notorious complex Auschwitz-II (Birkenau) was initially formed to hold Soviet POW laborers, and it was POWs who largely built the camp. There, in August 1941, SS officers conducted the first experiments with industrial killing by murdering several hundred Soviet POWs in a gas chamber.[16]

Most POW deaths in 1941 resulted from intentional starvation. Wehrmacht regulations on the eve of the invasion set daily rations for prisoners at 1,300 starchy calories—the equivalent of seven or eight potatoes. This amount of food could not sustain a person at rest for long, and because the Germans expected prisoners to fulfill heavy manual labor, it was a death sentence for many. Moreover, the Wehrmacht was not prepared to fulfill even these paltry obligations. A German officer reported after the capture of Minsk in June 1941 that the camp outside the city had a hundred thousand POWs who had not received food for a week.[17] In 1944, Soviet investigators in liberated Minsk uncovered the corpses of eighty thousand POWs in mass graves near the camp. Of the 9,425 deaths that they found recorded in German documents, 80 percent were due to starvation.[18] Starvation and execution were linked, as well. Military doctor Mikhail Breisler, a Jew who avoided summary execution by adopting the Tatar surname Alimov, remembered an instance in which a guard, a former POW himself, beat to death a prisoner who was too weak from hunger to march from work to the camp.[19]

Starvation, hard labor, and the massing of thousands in camps made POWs susceptible to disease. In February 1942, typhus alone killed some fifteen thousand Soviet POWs daily.[20] Luck often determined survival. Prisoner Vasilii Timokhin was captured soon after the invasion and sent to a camp in Poland. His rations there were a half pound of bread and a bowl of *balanda* (thin soup) made primarily of unwashed rutabaga. After several days of this diet, he developed diarrhea. He was fortunate to find a doctor, a POW medic. Because the camp had no medicine for prisoners, the doctor could only advise a restricted diet of dried bread for several days. Timokhin's diarrhea stopped, and he did not contract any other illnesses while his body was weakened from the self-imposed ration reduction.[21]

The best way to survive POW camps was to leave them. Flight from the camps was feasible but risky. German documents registered almost thirty-six thousand escapes by Soviet POWs from the start of the war to the end of August 1942.[22]

Common scenarios included hiding during a workday with assistance from civilians; escaping during transfer to and from work; or slipping away after the Germans haphazardly massed POWs in improvised sites like stadiums.[23] Prisoners from the area had an advantage, as local knowledge and contacts facilitated escapes and hindered subsequent recapture.

Early in the war, the Germans released some POWs based on racial categorization. These were ethnic Germans, Baltic nationals, Ukrainians, and Belarusians—or at least people who claimed to belong to these categories. Taking a promise that the former prisoners would not rejoin pro-Soviet forces, the Germans believed these men would peaceably go to their homes in occupied territory, labor in the local economy, and in some cases become local police. Some were recruited as internal police for the POW camps.[24] Villages that the war had emptied of working-age laborers often welcomed released prisoners, vouching for nonlocals so they could claim them as workers.[25]

Germany abandoned the policy of release in the fall of 1941, as officials increasingly hoped to mobilize POWs for work in the Third Reich. Germany's turn to labor exploitation meant the abandonment of intentional starvation, and captivity became less deadly from the spring of 1942 onward. A Soviet POW's chance of survival was less than 50 percent in 1941, whereas the mortality rate for the rest of the war was closer to 25 percent. The latter death rate was still outrageous by international standards, but it reflected an improvement in conditions.[26] Prisoners of war who arrived in work camps in the Third Reich had already survived the deadliest moments.

Conditions in work camps in Germany were nonetheless hardly comfortable and were worse than those the average Eastern Worker experienced. German officials found that Soviet POWs were valuable because they could be used in the least hospitable areas of German-occupied Europe. More than a hundred thousand Soviet prisoners worked on construction sites in Norway, often above the Arctic Circle, where roughly one in six died.[27] Although POWs usually had Sundays free, they could rely on little more than their rations because they were always kept under guard and could not go out to work like Eastern Workers. They could not forage for food and had limited opportunities for trade.[28] Using whatever they could find—nails, small pieces of metal, wood—enterprising prisoners fashioned products to sell through the camp fence. Children's toys were especially popular because German industry's shift to wartime production had de-emphasized consumer goods.[29] Some Eastern Workers, like Georgii T., made themselves into intermediaries, selling the products that POWs made.[30]

The dire conditions in the occupied east and in labor camps farther west were the most common motivations for Soviet POWs who joined pro-German formations. In the lead-up to the war, Hitler had ruled out using local people on the Eastern Front in any military capacity, and German leaders would avoid using auxiliary units in frontline combat roles until the end of the war. Yet within weeks of the invasion of the USSR, German forces were hiring so-called Hiwis (*Hilfswilliger*, or volunteers) for noncombat roles like translators; by one estimate, their number was more than a half million in 1942.[31] In occupied areas, Germans recruited locals as police officers and as guards at POW camps. By employing more than two hundred thousand local security personnel in the east in 1942, Germany could use fewer German men in occupation forces and send more to the front.[32]

Recruiting in the first months of the war had been informal or local. By the end of 1941, Germany began to organize formal enlistment of Soviet POWs and local people into Eastern Battalions (Osttruppen) organized along ethnic lines. Beyond the practical role these units played in freeing German soldiers for frontline service, they also had a political purpose. Nazi German leaders believed that non-Russian national units would appeal to people who desired liberation from their Soviet-Russian masters. Orientalist prejudices made Nazi leaders especially eager to recruit Turkic and Caucasian peoples, whom they considered easier to manipulate than Slavs.[33] Despite the misgivings about Slavic national movements, the Waffen-SS, the military force of the SS, also formed Russian and Ukrainian units.[34] Such units generated ambivalence on both sides. Ukrainian nationalist leaders, at first optimistic about the prospects of an independent Ukraine in the German sphere of influence, split into pro-German and anti-German factions over the course of the war.[35] German leaders saw the potential creation of an anti-Soviet Russian national movement as filled with both opportunity and peril. Would such a movement be pro-German? Would it jeopardize German credibility as a liberator among non-Russian nationalities? By late 1944, Germany's situation in the war had become so perilous that Hitler risked the formation of a Russian organization under former Red Army general Andrei Vlasov in the Committee of the Nationalities of Russia (Komitet Osvobozhdeniia Narodov Rossii, KONR).[36]

Units of all nationalities served mostly as security forces. A huge number—four hundred thousand at their numerical peak in 1943—fought in a quasi–civil war against pro-Soviet partisans in the occupied east.[37] Sizable defections to the partisans made German officials question the wisdom of using Osttruppen in this capacity, but there were many other areas where they could serve throughout German-occupied Europe. Taken from guard duty in the east, some became security at work sites and barracks for Eastern Workers or became free workers themselves.[38] A comparatively small but notorious group of guards was the Trawniki men. Recruited mostly from former Soviet POWs, these men were trained at a camp near Lublin, Poland, and sent to be guards in concentration and death camps.[39]

In contrast to German recruiting of POWs as guards and antipartisan forces, the Ministry of the East sought former POWs for roles as propagandists and organizers in the occupied east. The ministry was established after the invasion of the USSR to provide a civilian bureaucracy for the Reichskommissariats (civilian governments of occupied zones in the east). Although the territories of Ukraine, Belarus, and the Baltic republics were nominally under German civilian rule, real governance was fragmented between overlapping power bases: civilian authorities, the Nazi bureaucracy, the police, and the army. Ministry head Alfred Rosenberg's goal for the occupied east, often preempted by the needs of rival authorities, was to create an ethnic German colony with limited numbers of native workers as servants. Rosenberg was a devoted Nazi but, unlike many of his counterparts, thought that German prosperity in the territories would depend on leveraging émigrés and locals as colonial servitors.[40] The purpose of the Wustrau camp was to convert educated Soviet POWs into such pro-German functionaries. The logic of recruiting propagandists followed the perceived needs of the prospective colonial regime and hopes to leverage nationalism through elites: among all defectors, a little more than half seem to have been Russian, but only a sixth of Wustrau propagandists were Russian. Ukrainians, whose value as propagandists seemed more immediate in the occupied east, were approximately a third of Wustrau trainees, a proportion some 10 to 15 percent higher than defectors overall. Defectors from the North and South Caucasus were also more prevalent in Wustrau than in the general population of defectors. It is possible that the postwar perception in Russia that Soviet POWs from non-Russian backgrounds were the most eager volunteers emerged from their disproportionate representation among more prominent groups like the Wustrau men.[41]

Almost all prisoners enlisted to help the Germans out of desperation. A characteristic case of a Wustrau trainee was Petr Astakhov, an eighteen-year-old ethnic Russian from Baku, Azerbaijan. He had barely finished school when he was drafted into the army in the spring of 1942. After basic training, Astakhov's unit went to fight in the massive Soviet offensive at Kharkiv, where Stalin hoped to regain the initiative and throw the Germans out of Ukraine. Instead, the Germans encircled the Soviet forces, capturing Astakhov and two hundred forty thousand other Red Army soldiers in May 1942. The first days at the POW camp at Pervomaisk (Mykolaiv province) taught Astakhov a harsh lesson. When he settled into the barracks, he removed his boots and fell asleep on a plank padded with his army coat. The boots were gone in the morning. The starving teenager soon sold his army coat. Better to have bread (two whole loaves) than guard the coat all summer. He would think about the cold in several months—if he survived.

In the following weeks, rumors spread around Astakhov's camp that a commission would soon arrive to recruit "specialists." The commission was one of several from the Eastern Ministry that were seeking POWs with education or professional experience.[42] Astakhov was a candidate at the margins of acceptability. He was not a real specialist but had a ten-year education, making him relatively well educated among Soviet POWs. He also could draw accurate sketches, and perhaps one of the German guards had recommended Astakhov to the commission after he drew portraits for them in exchange for food. Still, Astakhov would later wonder about the impression that he, a barefoot teenager in soiled clothes, must have made on the commission. "I tried to create the portrait of a useful person," he recalled of his ten-minute interview. Several days later, a guard called out his name and commanded, "Specialists in formation." Out of naivete or willful ignorance, Astakhov did not yet recognize that he had signed up for service to the Reich.[43]

Like Astakhov, poor living conditions made Ekaterina Timoshenko, an Eastern Worker, overlook the bargain she was entering with the Germans. Timoshenko was a nearly fifty-year-old engineer at a medical research institute in Kyiv who remained in the city after the German invasion. In April 1942, the occupiers mobilized her for work in a military factory in Güsen, twenty miles northeast of Magdeburg. Most campmates were half her age. Moreover, a German medical commission concluded that her poor health made her fit for light work only. Her masters at the factory disregarded this assessment, giving her the same workload as her younger campmates. After three months of toil, the enterprise transferred her to the easier job of cleaning the workers' camp. Her luck seemed to improve further in May 1943 when the camp head offered her the chance to go back to Ukraine. During her 1946 trial for collaboration at a Soviet military tribunal, she would claim that the camp leader tricked her; she did not know that he wanted to recruit her as a propagandist. Although Timoshenko's excuse was credible, it is equally plausible that she had understood the camp head and later wanted to soften the tribunal's judgment of her. In either case, her exhaustion made her susceptible to any proposal that would bring her home. She was trained at an Eastern Ministry camp (not Wustrau) and sent to do propaganda work at a Kyiv factory.[44]

The line between volunteering and coerced recruitment in these cases is difficult to discern. Karl Streibel, one of the heads of the Trawniki camp, testified later that most POWs had offered their service willingly but that German camp officials had nominated others.[45] In most Soviet arrest files that I reviewed, arrestees admitted they had understood that they were offering their loyalty to Germany. In the case of Vlasov and leaders in his movement, ambition and genuine ideological conflicts with Stalinism made them ready volunteers. Some of the

Wustrau men also had ambitions, if only to return to their chosen careers. Aleksei Dunchevskii, a schoolteacher from Kyiv province, told Soviet investigators that he knew he was being recruited to collaborate but assumed that the Germans would send him to work in a school.[46] Dunchevskii probably did not think he was being recruited as a propagandist, and it is hard to imagine that the Trawniki men envisioned what would be asked of them in the death camps. Future propagandists and camp guards largely seem to have understood that they were volunteering for service that would earn them improved conditions and did not know (or did not care) what that service would entail.[47]

Life in Wustrau

For the Wustrau men, the transition from prisoner to propagandist began at a holding camp. One of the main camps was at Kielce, Poland. At this future site of a notorious postwar pogrom against Jewish survivors of the Holocaust, the Eastern Ministry established a camp for volunteers to recuperate.[48] Conditions for POWs at Kielce were markedly better than in normal POW camps. Daily rations were a half kilo of bread, a liter of soup, jam, fish preserves, sweet coffee, and six cigarettes. Prisoners could buy wine, cigarettes, and beer if they had money. Best of all, the camp freed them from hard labor. Residents only had to do light cleaning and, at another holding camp, occasional work for a local farmer.[49]

Holding camp residents held a liminal status between prisoner and ally. They remained under the watch of guards and translators, themselves former Soviet POWs. According to an émigré recruiter, camp authorities tested the loyalty of the volunteers by getting them drunk so they would "lose control and babble about whatever was on their mind."[50] But the holding camps marked a point of transition, with some camps organizing pro-German and anti-Jewish lectures during the late stages of recruits' stay.[51] Even at camps without political classes, German propaganda was unavoidable. One Kielce prisoner recalled that the barracks walls were covered with antisemitic propaganda that connected prominent Soviet figures to Jews (figure 3.1).[52] After several weeks or months at a verification camp, the Germans converted the men from Soviet prisoners into stateless Eastern Ministry trainees and sent them to Wustrau.

The head of Wustrau was a German, SS Obersturmführer Frenzel, but day-to-day camp operations were handled by émigrés and eager camp graduates.[53] Aleksei Dunchevskii was one of the first trainees to arrive at Wustrau (figures 3.2A and 3.2B). He noted that "Germans' attitudes towards [them] changed dramatically" upon their arrival. He settled in a barracks assigned to ethnic Ukrainians, one of the fourteen to sixteen at the camp where as many as six hundred people

FIGURE 3.1. "The Stalin Constitution." Stalin sitting on works by Marx, Engels, and Lenin and writing in Hebrew script. Reproduced from USHMM RG-31.117.

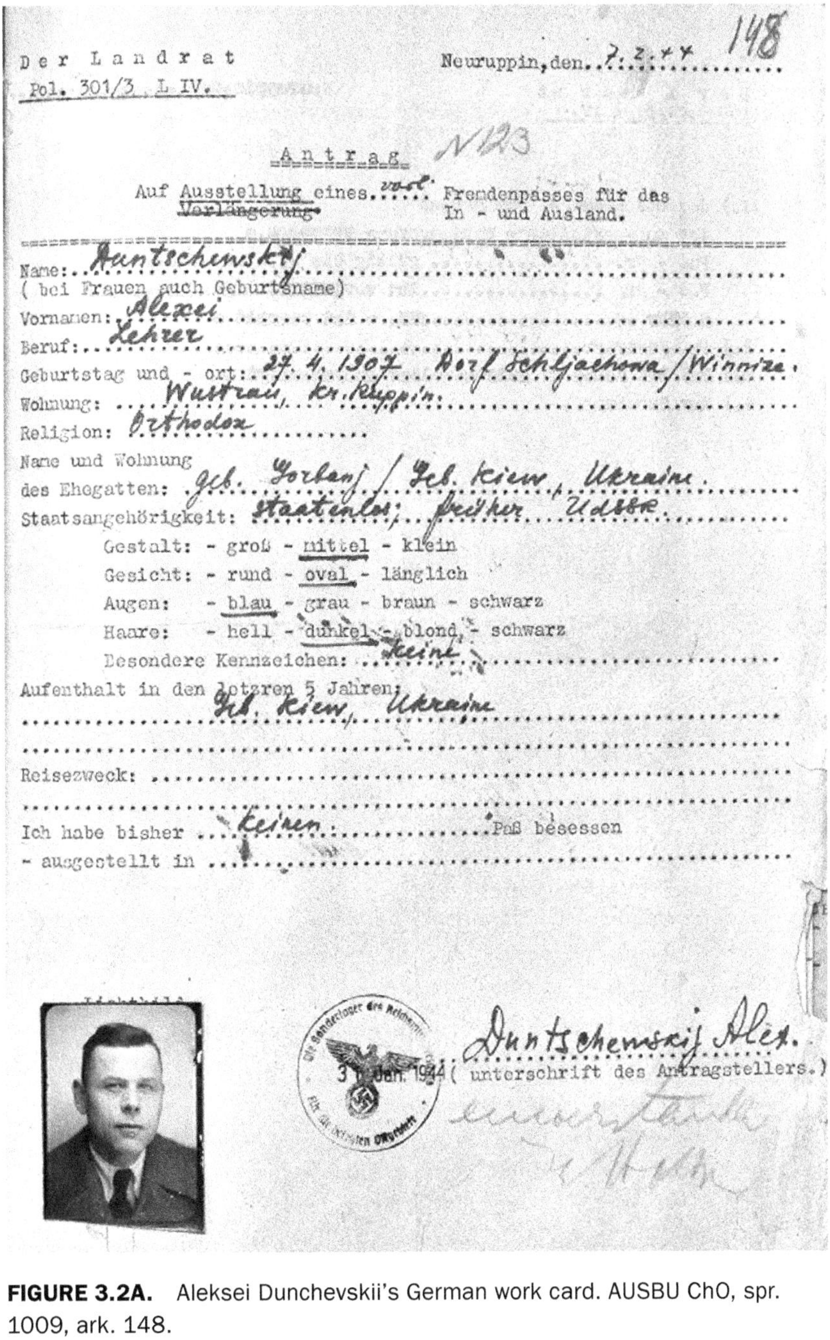

Der Landrat   Neuruppin, den.. *7.2.++* *148*
Pol. 301/3 . L IV.

A n t r a g   *N123*

Auf Ausstellung eines.. *und* .. Fremdenpasses für das
~~Verlängerung~~   In - und Ausland.

Name:.. *Duntschewskij* ..
(bei Frauen auch Geburtsname)

Vornamen:. *Alexei* ..

Beruf:.. *Lehrer* ..

Geburtstag und - ort:. *27.4.1907 Dorf Schljachowa /Winnize.*

Wohnung: .. *Wustrau, kr.Kuppin.*

Religion: *Orthodox* ..

Name und Wohnung
des Ehegatten:. *geb. Gorlanj / geb. Kiew, Ukraine.*

Staatsangehörigkeit: *Staatenlos; früher UdSSR* ..

      Gestalt: - groß - <u>mittel</u> - klein

      Gesicht: - rund - <u>oval</u> - länglich

      Augen: - <u>blau</u> - grau - braun - schwarz

      Haare: - hell - <u>dunkel</u> - blond - schwarz

      Besondere Kennzeichen:. *keine.* ..

Aufenthalt in den letzten 5 Jahren:
.. *geb. Kiew, Ukraine* ..

Reisezweck: ..

Ich habe bisher .. *keinen* .. Paß besessen
- ausgestellt in ..

                 Duntschewskij Alex.
            (unterschrift des Antragstellers.)

FIGURE 3.2A. Aleksei Dunchevskii's German work card. AUSBU ChO, spr. 1009, ark. 148.

FIGURE 3.2B.   Enlarged photo from Aleksei Dunchevskii's work card.

in total resided at a time. Like housing, training groups were determined by nationality. Ukrainians were the largest group, with some two hundred trainees at any time.[54] The Russian barracks, housing approximately one hundred people, offered bunk beds with straw mattresses and pillows—comfortable lodgings compared with POW camps.[55] Trainees traded their prisoner uniforms for suits and ties and received the same rations as Germans. For several hours a day, they listened to lectures that they were supposed to use as propaganda material in the east. Each émigré community sent representatives to lecture at Wustrau for a rumored 600 marks per month; former trainees who were hired as lecturers earned 120.[56]

The curriculum combined ethnic nationalism with the Nazi-German world-view. A Ukrainian trainee, Ilia Sherstiuk, remembered reading *History of Ukraine-Rus'* by the Ukrainian historian and politician Mykhailo Hrushevsky. The Georgian contingent learned about the economy of Georgia. The German part of the curriculum included language training, lectures glorifying Germany and the Nazi Party, and classes on the danger of "Jewish violence against the peoples of the world."[57]

The political ideology taught at Wustrau opposed Soviet Marxism-Leninism, yet its political culture had striking similarities to that of the USSR. The camp had a club with an extensive library that a former trainee claimed had been seized from a Soviet government collection in Minsk.[58] The most active figures, those who later became lecturers, sometimes joined émigré political parties that generated propaganda materials for classes.[59] What training Wustrau gave for personal behavior is unclear, but Vlasov army instructions echoed Stalinist social conservatism. Propagandists in Vlasov's KONR received a pamphlet in 1945 called "The Battle with Elements of Degeneracy in Everyday Life." It urged officers to forbid drinking, "gifts" to superiors, and promiscuity among soldiers. The pamphlet placed the blame for sexual harassment of women on "the Soviet 'drink of water' theory"—the idea popular among early Bolshevik radicals that sex was no less a biological need than water. By the mid-1930s, however, Stalinist officials had embraced the nuclear family as the bedrock of socialist society. The paper's traditionalist denunciation of "hooligans and pimps" could have been taken from the Red Army newspaper *Krasnaia Zvezda*.[60]

In the Georgian "ethnographic choir," the most famous product of the camp, Wustrau co-opted a Soviet musical ensemble for the Nazi regime. The choir was led by Davit (David) Kavsadze, whose father, Sandro Kavsadze, was a boyhood friend of Stalin's from the Tiflis Seminary. After the Russian Revolution, the elder Kavsadze founded the Soviet Georgian Choir of Song and Dance, which was an outgrowth of Soviet nationalities policy that promoted ethnonational difference within a framework of loyalty to Soviet rule. Regime-sponsored groups like Kavsadze's codified a repertoire of national dances and songs that Georgian performers had developed from the nineteenth century.[61] According to family legend, Stalin came to see Kavsadze's choir in 1937 and after the concert offered to grant the choirmaster any favor. The elder Kavsadze asked for, and received, the pipe that Stalin was smoking that instant.[62] Even in Wustrau, Davit Kavsadze regaled singers with the story of Stalin's pipe and apparently continued to toast the Soviet leader's health.[63]

After his father's death in 1939, Davit Kavsadze assumed responsibility for the choir and in the spring of 1942 took it to the Crimean city of Kerch to perform for Red Army units. German armies soon overtook the peninsula, and Kavsadze became a POW. When Georgian émigrés learned that a member of the famous Kavsadze family had been captured, they recruited him with the promise that he could practice music. Georgians at Wustrau had formed a choir before Kavsadze arrived at the camp in March 1943, but its leader was not a music professional. "Having heard a few pieces," Kavsadze later told a Soviet tribunal, "I noticed many flaws and decided to help them." Kavsadze's musicianship and the sponsorship of the Georgian emigration made the choir a sensation. In addition to money, Georgian émigrés donated *chokha*, the traditional Georgian cloak. Kavsadze became a celebrity among the émigrés. Far from his wife and children in Tbilisi, he began dating Mariam Kereselidze, the daughter of Leo Kereselidze, the émigré commander of the pro-German Georgian Legion.[64]

Kavsadze took the choir to performances across German-occupied Europe, made a record in 1944, and appeared in a German newsreel the same year.[65] The choir's repertoire included several songs about the émigré party Tetri Giorgi but was not so different from that of the Soviet ensemble Kavsadze had led before his capture. Dressed in traditional Georgian garb, the group could have been in Tbilisi as easily as Berlin (figure 3.3). In one song, the group repurposed an inspirational Soviet piece by replacing Stalin's name with Hitler's.[66] Soviet nationalities policy is often described as "national in form, socialist in content." Kavsadze's choir—and in a sense the entire Wustrau enterprise—was "national in form, fascist in content."

Beyond the Georgian singers, who had rehearsals and concerts, few of the Wustrau men had obligations outside their training. An exception was several dozen Georgians, who were sent away to the Slovenian border for agricultural

FIGURE 3.3. Undated photograph of Wustrau's Georgian choir. Davit Kavsadze appears to be the man in the back row, farthest to the left. USHMM RG-38.001, d. 46206, folder 2, l. 37.

work, apparently on the estates of Georgian émigrés.[67] Others did occasional work for farmers near the camp. Most of the Wustrau men enjoyed significant amounts of free time outside of their classes. The men received room and board, several hundred marks as start-up money, and one mark a day for various expenses.[68] They could spend that money on leave from the camp with a day pass.[69] Obersturmführer Frenzel and the émigré workers took trainees in small groups on trips around Germany. Petr Astakhov was one of many who went on the tour. First the group went to eastern Germany, then to the Tyrolean mountains in Austria. Finally, they went to Bavaria—the birthplace of Nazism. Astakhov was shocked by the comforts of the trip, noting, "The train, passengers, conversations about the sites, the feeling of freedom—it was all real."[70]

The treatment of the Wustrau men was exceptional among Soviet POWs who entered German service. At the other end of the spectrum were the Trawniki men, whose contribution to Germany's system of mass murder was far more direct than the Wustrau men's, and who faced worse conditions than the propagandists. Disciplinary infractions could lead to whippings, weeks of detention, or even execution. These conditions and the hideous task of murder they were assigned motivated a large proportion of the Trawniki men, perhaps one-third, to flee to partisan groups despite the high cost of capture.[71] These escapes highlight the instrumental motives of collaboration among Soviet POWs. Undoubtedly, the average volunteers' experience was more like that of the trainees from Trawniki than those from Wustrau. Most volunteers escaped the worst deprivations of POW camps but continued to suffer surveillance and exploitation at the hands of Germans.

The Wustrau men would remember their time at the camp with fondness. Why would they not? Before the war, they had labored in the pressure cooker of the Stalinist mobilization economy. Then they had fought a losing war in the Red Army before they saw the horrors of the POW camps. Compared with these experiences, the months of training were a welcome relief. They had classes instead of work. Food was more than adequate in comparison to the previous months and years. In significant ways, the training the men experienced was like ideological preparation in the USSR, with the important substitutions of German racialized antisemitism and anticommunism. As their instruction ended, however, the Wustrau propagandists considered what would come next.

Collaboration and Resistance

The first men to arrive at Wustrau graduated as propagandists in early 1943. Two early enrollees, Aleksei Dunchevskii and Ilia Sherstiuk, joined a group of fifteen other newly minted propagandists bound for Ukraine. Accompanied by Obersturmführer Frenzel and an émigré handler, they arrived in the town of Lutsk (Volhynia) in March 1943. Dunchevskii and Sherstiuk became roving lecturers, presenting to Ukrainian villages the talking points they had learned at Wustrau. Dunchevskii, assigned to rural Shepetivka district, later estimated that he gave between 120 and 200 talks in his nine months of work. At a typical lecture, the village head would gather residents in the square, and someone from the local Ukrainian administration introduced Dunchevskii to the audience. He then gave a talk on one of several themes: Soviet atrocities against Ukrainians, optimistic assessments of Germany's war situation, or the dangers of "Jewish coercion." After he finished, the villagers typically had few questions.[72] Sherstiuk, less active than Dunchevskii, gave 30 talks for the civilian occupation administration before the Wehrmacht poached him. In his new role, he drove along the front shouting exhortations into a loudspeaker for Soviet soldiers to desert.[73]

Both men lived well compared with their Ukrainian neighbors. In the summer of 1943, Dunchevskii went for a ten-day vacation in the village of Zaiachkivka, where he had taught at a school before the war. His arrival must have surprised his former neighbors. They had seen him last on the eve of the war, when the Red Army had mobilized him into a surveying unit. Now he appeared in the village looking well nourished and dapper in a blue woolen suit. The local German commandant gave him deficit goods—bread, cigarettes, and firewood. The contrast between his relative comfort and the desperation of his neighbors must have been striking. He deflected questions about his job when he met former colleagues from the school. When they persisted in asking, he told them that he worked for a newspaper. From his appearance alone, his former neighbors understood that he held a position with status.[74]

Dunchevskii and Sherstiuk were among the few Wustrau graduates who would conduct propaganda work. The Germans never had a chance to send the remainder to their occupied homelands. The Wehrmacht held parts of western Russia for significant periods, but these territories were never under the Eastern Ministry's civilian administration. Much of the Caucasus never came under German occupation at all. Apparently the only Wustrau propagandists who went to the east were Ukrainian, and by the fall of 1943, the Red Army was already pushing into Ukraine. The danger was growing not only from the Red Army but also from a faction of the Organization of Ukrainian Nationalists, which by 1943 had splintered into factions that fought against both German and Soviet forces. In the face of these threats, Dunchevskii, Sherstiuk, and the other propagandists in Ukraine returned to Wustrau.

Even as Germany lost its occupied eastern territories, Wustrau continued to train propagandists for the nominal goal of administering the occupied east.

German leaders never lost hope that someday Nazi Germany would need propagandists for the eastern colonies. As the Germans waited for the war to turn back in their favor, the Eastern Ministry sent the Wustrau men to work within the Reich.

Wustrau hired its best graduates as teachers and organizers. The Eastern Ministry awarded Dunchevskii a bronze medal and made him a *Schulleiter* (head teacher) in the camp. He also went as a recruiter for the camp to Berlin-area factories. He enlisted few volunteers among Eastern Workers but found love with a woman named Nadezhda Gavronskaia, whom he had first met during a lecture at a village in Ukraine. Dunchevskii had a family in the Soviet Union, but he claimed Gavronskaia as his wife and took her to Wustrau. The Wustrau-based magazine *Ukraina* hired her as a typist. When bombing attacks intensified at the camp, Dunchevskii received a position in a Berlin factory as the Eastern Ministry's representative for monitoring conditions among Eastern Workers.[75]

Émigrés worked in the national departments within the Eastern Ministry and could arrange jobs for their favorites from the camp. Aleksandr Kashia had been the leader of the Wustrau Georgian barracks from May 1943 until Obersturmführer Frenzel dismissed him in May 1944. The reasons for his dismissal are muddy. Kashia told Soviet interrogators that Frenzel fired him because of his "anti-fascist conversations." His former campmates—whom Kashia had listed as supporting witnesses in 1959 for a post-Gulag rehabilitation attempt— denounced him as being on friendly terms with Frenzel. They said that he was dismissed for misappropriation of camp goods. Camp specialists like Kashia often skimmed supplies for themselves, and possibly his theft reached unacceptable proportions. In any event, he landed lightly in the Eastern Ministry's Georgian section, making recruitment trips to POW camps and escorting Berlin's Georgian émigrés westward, presumably to avoid the imminent Soviet occupation.[76]

The Georgian emigration also supported Davit Kavsadze's choir at Wustrau until the middle of 1944. Georgii Magalashvili, an émigré working in the Eastern Ministry, took care of the choir's finances and supported Kavsadze personally. In July 1944, Magalashvili told Kavsadze that the émigré community would soon run out of money. He proposed that the choir remain together but as an SS unit. Kavsadze called a meeting of the choir, at which he stated, "Where you go, so do I." He and forty choir members opted to work for the SS from September 1944, perhaps believing that their value was higher as a singing ensemble than as solo propagandists. At first little changed, and the choir went to sing in France. In March 1945, the SS transferred them to fight partisans in northern Italy.[77]

The less established men at Wustrau hired themselves out as free workers. Andrei Kovkhaev, a Russian trainee, found a Berlin construction firm that needed workers in late 1943. With camp leaders' permission, Kovkhaev began to find work for Wustrau's Russians. Young trainee Petr Astakhov signed up to repair bomb-damaged buildings. As a stateless person in Germany, he received the same pay and rations as Germans and lived in an apartment. On weekends he visited Berlin's attractions, searched for extra ration cards at the black market on Alexanderplatz, or visited friends at Wustrau. A few of the Wustrau men had become invested in the anti-Soviet cause. For most, however, work in Germany was a way to escape reprisals and maintain the relative comfort they achieved.[78]

As the war continued, the Wustrau men increasingly worried that they were on the losing side. The Red Army won a major victory at Stalingrad in January 1943 and placed the Wehrmacht on the defensive for the rest of the war after the Battle of Kursk that summer. The propagandists knew about Germany's losses. Indeed, their repertoire included speeches about how the defeats were not as bad as they looked. But as the Red Army surged westward, some had second thoughts about their time in the camp. Astakhov brooded, "Am I guilty for what happened and should I bear responsibility . . . ? If I wasn't a traitor and didn't commit any crimes, then I can't be guilty."[79]

Some of the men later claimed that they had been secret resistance members in Wustrau. Many propagandists who returned to the USSR received Gulag sentences but were released in the 1950s under Khrushchev. Those who sought political rehabilitation told review boards that they had formed a pro-Soviet faction at Wustrau. One said that several members of the Georgian choir were expelled from the camp because they refused to go on tour when Kavsadze arrived.[80] These assertions were self-serving, but some of the singers did leave the camp to become free workers, lending plausibility to this story.

Escape from German control was a matter of opportunity as much as intention. Antipartisan units on the Eastern Front (re)defected to the Soviet side by the thousands.[81] A group of Wustrau Georgians sent to agricultural work near Slovenia used the trip to escape in May 1943. Eight of the men, including Kashia's predecessor as barracks head, planned to establish contact with Yugoslav partisans and flee. When their connection gave them just a revolver and a grenade for weapons, all but the conspiracy's leader and the barracks head refused to go. The other six men did not want to journey unarmed across an unfamiliar terrain for several days to join unknown partisans. The pair who escaped walked for two days before they found and joined the partisans. The other men were transferred back to Wustrau.[82]

Such defections caused German authorities to shift policies. The Wehrmacht pulled antipartisan units from the Eastern Front to use in other parts of Europe like France and Italy. And Wustrau residents no longer went to border areas except as propagandists. Notably, however, the Germans seem to have avoided collective punishment for guards and other volunteers when their comrades escaped. A Georgian Legion member who had served as a guard at the Kielce camp remembered that after an escape, the Germans arrested a handful of his fellow legionnaires. The rest had temporary restrictions on their passes to go to town.[83]

As Allied armies surrounded Germany and bombed Berlin regularly at the end of 1944, the Eastern Ministry dismantled Wustrau. Few of its residents had illusions that the Germans could win the war. Those who had worked as propagandists like Aleksei Dunchevskii probably knew that they had little hope of redeeming themselves in the eyes of Soviet authorities. They attempted to conceal their biographies or went into hiding. Those who had graduated from Wustrau but never worked as propagandists still hoped to clear their names. Astakhov escaped Germany for Switzerland across Lake Constance with a small group of Wustrau men at the beginning of 1945.[84] Others who had collaborated with the Germans would become key members of resistance groups as free workers.

The Limits of Resistance

Reconstructing the history of Soviet resistance in Nazi Germany is like drawing a portrait from a series of funhouse mirrors. Large-scale, coordinated resistance organized within Germany was impossible due to constant surveillance of Eastern Workers and members of pro-German formations. Soviet intelligence services had spies in Germany, including in concentration camps, but they were few.[85] Instead, most resistance groups were small operations involving a handful of people in Eastern Worker and POW camps. Contacts existed between groups within regions but were apparently not centralized. Fearful of arrest, participants left almost no documents about their activities from the time—no meeting protocols, membership lists, or declarations of principles. Only a handful of anti-German leaflets survived. German police investigated thousands of Soviet-born people as resisters. One reading of the police files would suggest that there were perhaps hundreds of thousands of Soviet militants waiting for their chance to revolt.[86] These documents have serious limitations, though. Nazi leaders were paranoid about conspiracies against the state and eager to find plots in uncoordinated acts of resistance. Postwar accounts by resistance group members present similar problems. Hoping to earn a heroes' welcome, they told Soviet authorities that they conducted anti-German work because of their love for the USSR. Meanwhile, Soviet police reports cast doubt on resistance members' accounts, even suggesting that they were agents of the Gestapo.

I present here the case of one group in Leipzig based on members' postwar accounts. It is possible that they exaggerated or even invented parts of their

reports, yet their narratives are plausible and fit with other postwar stories of resistance.[87] Their testimony, given under secret police questioning to investigators
across the USSR, appears to be uncoordinated. They also claimed to have undertaken resistance activity that would have been feasible given the constraints
of life as a forced laborer. Their main accomplishment was spreading anti-
German propaganda rather than less credible acts of violence. The final element
that fits well with the broader picture of resistance is the inclusion of an important but problematic figure—Aleksandr Dzadzamia, a former member of the
Wustrau Georgian choir.

After his release from the Georgian choir in mid-1943, the Eastern Ministry
sent Dzadzamia to work as a free physician in Leipzig's Eastern Worker camps.
Dzadzamia had been a medic and a Communist Party candidate member in the
Soviet Union. His former Wustrau campmates asserted in rehabilitation testimonies that he had been in a secret faction of Soviet loyalists at Wustrau. One
recalled how early in their stay at the camp, Dzadzamia tested him before pull-
ing him aside to reveal that they shared a hatred of the Germans. Dzadzamia
was also among the singers who left the choir in 1943 after Davit Kavsadze took
over the ensemble.[88]

Dzadzamia became a doctor at a large camp attached to the Rudolph Sack
company, which employed over a thousand foreign workers, including hundreds
of Eastern Workers, to produce armaments. According to Dzadzamia, his entry
into a formal resistance group began when a strange Russian visitor came to his
clinic in August 1943, warning that the clinic's Polish translator was an informer.
When the Russian came back in March 1944, he professed his love for Germany
and asked the doctor what he thought about life in the Reich. Dzadzamia gave
an evasive answer. Some days later, the Russian appeared again and told the doctor that the previous visit was a provocation on behalf of the camp's pro-Soviet
resistance. The group wanted him to join, and the Georgian agreed. Soon Dzadzamia became one of its key members. In April 1944, his status as a free doctor and perhaps his prewar candidate membership in the Communist Party
earned him a place on the group's organizing committee.[89]

The group's leader was Prokofii Lesnichenko, a thirty-year-old Eastern Worker
with a complicated history (figure 3.4). He had been an activist in the civil defense organization Osoaviakhim in Pavlohrad (Dnipropetrovsk province,
Ukraine) before the war and served a one-year forced labor sentence in 1937 for
the minor crime of damaging property at his workplace. His arrest apparently
did not discredit him significantly, as he returned to his position after his term.
When Germany attacked the USSR, he joined the Red Army as deputy commander of a medical battalion. The Germans captured him in fighting near
Poltava on October 30, 1941. In later interrogations with Soviet secret police, he

FIGURE 3.4.   Prokofii Lesnichenko with members of RROK in Leipzig in the spring of 1945. HDASBU, f. 1, spr. 695, ark. 24.

said that he escaped an improvised POW camp at a garage in Kyiv. He made his way to relatives in the Pavlohrad area, some three hundred miles away, staying there until Germans arrested and deported him as a POW to work in Germany. For a month in Pegau, near Leipzig, he worked on a farm for a local landowner. Lesnichenko got into a heated argument with the farm's owner, and before police could arrive, he fled to the east on foot and then by train. When police at Katowice detained him, he claimed to be Pavel Shevchenko, an Eastern Worker from Kyiv who had fallen behind his convoy. The police sent him to Dresden for investigation. Finding no compromising information about a Pavel Shevchenko, the criminal police released him to work at the Ohlhorst factory in Leipzig.[90]

In the camp, Lesnichenko sought allies among his nineteen roommates. They included four young men whom Lesnichenko deemed reliable because they had been in the Komsomol (Soviet youth league) before deportation. It seems that Lesnichenko misled his young colleagues' into trusting him by hinting that the Communist Party had sent him to Germany to organize resistance work. In 1942 they formed what he later called a party-Komsomol underground group. Although one of the Komsomol members would boast to a Soviet secret informant in 1949 that the group killed a camp security guard, by all other accounts their only work was to spread pro-Soviet propaganda among Eastern Workers.[91]

The group composed and distributed leaflets based on information members gleaned from radio and rumors. None of Lesnichenko's leaflets survived, but their content was probably like the Russian-language flyers distributed by another Leipzig resistance organization, one of which read: "Comrade POW! The time is coming when you, like your comrades who are fighting on the front, will have to take an active part in the fight for the liberation of the Motherland from aggressors and occupiers."[92] Resistance cells produced leaflets with the materials that were available. Some managed to find German typewriters, but Lesnichenko's group was probably more representative. Its members copied several dozen at a time by hand.[93]

The group seems to have been part of a loose collective of resistance cells in Leipzig. According to one account, the city had 150 or more resistance members in various camps toward the end of 1942, when the Gestapo arrested roughly 50 people as supposed resisters.[94] Another wave of arrests in May 1944 further thinned resistance members' ranks by 48. Even after these arrests, the Gestapo estimated that several hundred workers from Poland and the Soviet Union were in opposition groups in the city.[95] Communications between these groups were informal. Lesnichenko made new contacts on strolls during his free Sunday afternoons. One of these contacts was Vera Shcherbak, a medical worker and the wife of a Red Army soldier and party member, who was mobilized to work at a different camp in Leipzig. She met Lesnichenko by chance at a café in 1942 when she overheard him relaying rumors about the war to friends. After learning that her husband was in the Red Army, Lesnichenko initiated her into the group the following week. She then recruited several members at her camp.[96]

Some resistance groups found sympathetic Germans. Leipzig communists worked with Eastern Worker Nikolai Rumiantsev to create an organization called the International Antifascist Committee in the fall of 1943. According to postwar accounts, the committee covered some seventy camps in the city, a figure that probably represented a tenuous network of small, autonomous resistance groups. Rumiantsev's attempt to expand and coordinate operations seems to have drawn the attention of authorities. In May 1944, the Gestapo arrested Rumiantsev and later executed him.[97] Perhaps referring to this network, Lesnichenko told Soviet investigators about connections he had to German communists who gave his group copy paper.[98]

Resistance groups relied on the same regional ties that brought together Eastern Workers more broadly. Lesnichenko was one of many people from Pavlohrad in Leipzig.[99] One Pavlohrad deportee, Efrosinia Usenko, said that she saw Lesnichenko on the street in Leipzig in 1943 and recognized him from her prewar civil defense work in the Komsomol. After she introduced herself, he invited her to a pub and persuaded her to join his group. Usenko recruited her friend

Natalia Berkun, another deportee from Pavlohrad. They had arrived together in 1942 and, after they were transferred to different camps in the city, became regular Sunday strolling partners. They lost track of Lesnichenko (or perhaps feared joining the group) but reconnected with him in early 1945. Now instead of strolling as a pair, they met up with a group of roughly fifteen people. At the first meeting Usenko and Berkun attended, Aleksandr Kuprii led them to a secluded grove where group members set out food and wine. Lesnichenko distributed leaflets to each person for them to take to their camps. Berkun described the picnic as a disguise for the political content of the meeting, but the social element of the gathering was also real. She and Kuprii began to date and would marry after liberation.[100]

The trust that formed through social bonds was an important factor that enabled resistance work, but so was opportunity. At first glance, a free worker like Dzadzamia seems like an unlikely candidate for membership. His status in the camp must have signaled his connections with German officials and raised the possibility that he would inform on the group. Like Lesnichenko, though, he was a former party candidate member. He undoubtedly understood that if (or when) the Germans lost the war, his cooperation with them would be damning in Soviet eyes. Dzadzamia was an attractive target for the group to recruit because of the privileges he enjoyed. Beyond working unguarded and having greater access to the city, he was allowed to rent a floor of a German's apartment.[101] Having a private living space meant that he could make and distribute leaflets with fewer problems than Lesnichenko. Dzadzamia's value was also perhaps tied to his access to goods that Eastern Workers could not obtain.

Dzadzamia's participation was not an anomaly. It was common for resistance groups to organize through medical workers and clinics. The Munich-based Brotherly Union of Prisoners of War (Bratskii Soiuz Voennoplennykh, BSV) is arguably the best-known resistance group made up primarily of Soviet POWs that operated in the Reich. In September 1944, the Gestapo arrested and executed seventy-nine men at Dachau concentration camp as alleged members.[102] The main evidence for the existence of this group comes from German documents that probably exaggerated its sophistication and size. Nonetheless, there are telling similarities that suggest patterns with other resistance cells. Like Lesnichenko's group, the BSV used medical stays to organize. BSV leader Roman Petrushel, an auxiliary in a German antiaircraft regiment, arranged for visits to a hospital where he could pass instructions to other "sick" group members and send information via hospital staff.[103]

The conversion of volunteers like Dzadzamia into resistance group members was also common. Musa Dzhalil (Cälil) was a Tatar poet and a young Soviet official who joined the Red Army as a political commissar after the German invasion.

In June 1942, the Germans captured him, and he soon joined the Tatarstan Legion (Idel-Ural), a pro-German formation. It is difficult to verify the mythologizing accounts about Dzhalil that emerged in the post-Stalin period. These narratives portrayed him as a national hero who joined the legion for the sole purpose of organizing resistance. It seems clear that Dzhalil did undertake resistance activity at some point, and the Germans arrested him in 1943. The following year, after he wrote a collection of poems later smuggled out of Berlin's Moabit Prison and published in the USSR, the Germans executed him.[104]

Like Dzhalil, Dzadzamia, and Petrushel, many BSV members held positions in German military units and work camps. These positions gave them better rations and freedom of movement. BSV organizer Iosif Feldman was a former Jewish Red Army medic who adopted the Slavic-sounding name Georgii Fesenko to survive German captivity. He took work as a translator at a forced labor camp. Karl Ozolin, Feldman's comrade-in-resistance, was the camp's clerk. Both were arrested in May 1943 and later executed.[105] Cases like these made German officials wary of former Soviet POWs and Eastern Workers in positions of relative privilege. In a circular about resistance activity, German police identified domestic servants as potential resisters since they could become trusted workers in the homes of influential families.[106]

German officials simplified the supposed motives of resisters as Soviet radicalism. When Munich police arrested Feldman/Fesenko, they turned him into a figure that confirmed all their fears and prejudices. Feldman/Fesenko was supposedly a ranking officer from the People's Commissariat of Internal Affairs (Narodnyi Komissariat Vnutrennikh Del, NKVD) from Dnipropetrovsk sent to Germany as a saboteur. The Gestapo's assertion that he was a Jew from the Communist Party elite fit perfectly with Nazi expectations. Efim Brodskii, a future historian who uncovered these Gestapo documents while he was chief Soviet propaganda officer in occupied Berlin, later interviewed people who knew Feldman/Fesenko. In contrast to German police reports, interviewees said that Feldman/Fesenko was an ordinary POW, distinguished by an excellent command of German that he gained from a childhood in an area of Ukraine where many ethnic Germans had lived. Feldman/Fesenko was no NKVD officer, and it is doubtful that he collaborated only to further his resistance efforts.[107] In all likelihood, Feldman/Fesenko volunteered to improve his chances of survival and later put his relative freedom to use in resistance.

It is easy to imagine that Feldman/Fesenko, Dzadzamia, and other resisters wanted to prove their loyalty to the USSR. Soviet POWs thought they would face scrutiny or repression after the war, and those who collaborated might see active resistance as their only safe path home. The incentives to resist only increased as the war shifted in favor of the Soviet Union. In Leipzig, as in other areas of

German-dominated Europe, opposition activities intensified following the Soviet victories at Stalingrad and Kursk in 1943.[108] Nonetheless, it is probable that resistance was not only pragmatic but reflected a preference for Soviet rule. Dzadzamia and Lesnichenko had been upwardly mobile young functionaries in the USSR who had occupied a place in society they could never hope to achieve in Germany. Even among the relatively privileged Wustrau propagandists, only those who believed the Eastern Ministry's promises of national liberation could unreservedly accept their position as elites from a supposedly inferior race. And for Jewish POWs in hiding like Feldman/Fesenko, only Germany's defeat would guarantee escape from eventual murder. In this sense, the pragmatic and ideological aspects of resistance fed one another.

Lesnichenko's group presents a complex picture of resistance among Eastern European people in Nazi Germany. Like other resistance groups, their story is one that includes compromise with German authorities. Dzadzamia's record was the most problematic in this sense, but Lesnichenko and the others contributed to the German war effort too. They risked arrest by distributing leaflets but continued to work in German factories, albeit against their will, until the war's end. As liberation approached in 1945, they hoped that Soviet officials would acknowledge their work as a contribution to Germany's defeat.

Davit Kavsadze's Georgian choir, by 1945 a Waffen-SS unit, joined the thousands of former Soviet POWs in pro-German formations who defected to the Allies at the end of the war. In the middle of April, the choirmaster's lover, Mariam Kereselidze, urged him to flee and avoid repatriation to the USSR. Kavsadze had another plan. On the night of April 26–27, two days before German forces surrendered in Italy and four days before Hitler committed suicide, the choir went over to the Italian partisans. Kavsadze told his singers that he intended to meet with Stalin after returning to the USSR and explain how circumstances had forced them to cooperate with the Germans. He must have doubted this idea, though. A few days after the war ended, he secured more than a hundred Italian certificates of partisan service for his choir and other Georgians in the SS unit.[109]

Had Kavsadze and his singers earned the certificates? Clearly no. Although they participated in a skirmish between Italian partisans and pro-German Cossacks, their partisan experience was surrender in the guise of defection. Kavsadze may have hoped to make the same claim as a member of Vlasov's army, who escaped to a neutral country and argued in his memoirs that resistance had only been possible because he had joined the ROA.[110] The justification was self-serving but had an important element of truth: collaboration often put people in a better position to resist. Soviet POWs who volunteered for service to Germany mostly did so because they wondered if they could survive the desperate conditions of the POW camps. Collaboration had freed them from backbreaking labor, starvation, and harsh restrictions on mobility. Except for the few people totally committed to the Soviet or German cause, the choice to oppose or support German rule was a calculation: Was service in a pro-German formation worth the reward? What were the opportunities for resistance, and what were the costs? Would anti-German activities earn resisters absolution in Soviet eyes? As the certainty of the Allied victory grew from 1943, Soviet people in Germany—perhaps most of all those who had joined pro-German formations—chose increasingly to rebel.

Opportunity was an important factor in collaboration and resistance. The strains that the war placed upon states gave Soviet-born people in Germany a modicum of agency. Wustrau trainee Astakhov said of his recruitment that he was a boy POW trying to look "useful." This bitter comment reflects a reality of the war: both sides needed capable people and recruited them readily. Men were the main targets because states viewed them as potential soldiers and security personnel, although limited numbers of women were also recruited as propagandists and camp administrators. The Wehrmacht infamously massacred captured POWS who were Communist Party members, but German authorities also recruited Soviet elites like Kavsadze to lend credibility to anti-Stalinist groups. Former party and Komsomol members were at once leading figures in resistance groups and prevalent among the Wustrau men. As ambitious and educated people, they had joined prewar Soviet organizations because it was a path to success or because local party bosses had recruited them as outstanding students, workers, and soldiers. The Germans needed the same useful people as volunteers.

After Germany's defeat, a history of resistance would become an asset in DP camps. Former Eastern Workers and POWs presented wartime suffering and opposition as proof of their loyalty to the anti-German cause. In the vacuum of power in Allied-occupied Germany, resisters would trade on this sense of integrity to become the leaders among Soviet displaced persons.

LIBERATED IN A FOREIGN LAND

Wild Re-Sovietization and the Choice to Return
in Allied-Occupied Europe, 1945

Millions of Soviet-born people emerged from German control in the spring of 1945. Some had already fled their camps when they encountered Allied soldiers. Others awoke to find that the guards at their camps had disappeared. Still others—a problematic and sizable minority—the Allies captured while serving in pro-German formations. Allied forces urged displaced persons from all non-enemy countries to go to assembly centers in advance of planned repatriation. Many war refugees were eager to return to their homelands, while others hoped to forge a new life in postwar Europe. For both those who wished to return and those desperate to avoid repatriation, the chaos in the Western Allies' zones of occupation enabled DPs to transform themselves to suit their purpose.

In the beginning of 1945, the USSR and the Western Allies agreed to return all Allied DPs and liberated POWs to their countries of origin, regardless of individual wishes. For the Soviet leadership, the recognition of their claim over Soviet people abroad was a crucial part of the country's emergence as a great power on an equal footing with the Western Allies. In the ruins of Nazi-dominated Europe, however, the policy of compulsory repatriation belied the chaos that the Allies faced in practice. State actors prefer (and coerce) populations to fit cleanly into national categories, but the destruction of the war meant that the identity of refugees was often illegible. Eastern European understandings of national belonging had been fluid before the war and became even muddier after years of living under German rule.[1] The situation was complicated further by disagreements over who was subject to repatriation. The Western Allies refused to recognize the Soviet claim over people from western regions of the USSR that had been annexed after

September 1939. The result was that DPs could adapt their biographies or forge new ones to fit categories that would allow them to avoid repatriation.[2] Soviet-claimed DPs asked themselves: Should I risk the possibility of repression in the USSR? Could I make a new life abroad? Both courses involved risks and trade-offs. No matter their decision, the choice itself suggests that many DPs believed they had agency over their postliberation fate.

This chapter focuses on the short but critical period in the spring and summer of 1945 when over two million people would enter Soviet control from France and the Western-controlled areas of Germany and Austria.[3] For many the question was not whether to return but how to return. USSR-bound DPs, like their counterparts from across Europe, were largely self-governed under the Western Allies' control. Although DP camps for Soviet-claimed people were nominally under joint Soviet-Allied supervision, DPs were beyond the direct control of Moscow. Local leaders created unauthorized pro-Soviet political organizations and used violence to reinstate Stalinist political and social norms. I call this process "wild re-Sovietization," part of the broader dynamic of self-organization and violence that occurred in Europe on the heels of liberation.[4] By participating in these efforts, Soviet DPs hoped they could return to the USSR as citizens in good standing.

The End of German Control

Liberation began in advance of Germany's defeat as the Third Reich descended into chaos. With Allied armies approaching from east and west, camp administrations ordered workers and prisoners to embark on forced marches to the center of the country. Evgenii Kiselev was one such prisoner, an inmate at a subcamp of Buchenwald, the notorious complex based in Thuringia at Weimar with more than a hundred subcamps and hundreds of thousands of prisoners. Kiselev was a thirty-something factory specialist from the port city of Mykolaiv (Ukraine) with a thorny past. German authorities in Mykolaiv had arrested him for black market activities in September 1942, and in the local prison they made him a kitchen worker. During interrogations with Soviet police after his return to Mykolaiv, he claimed to have been a resistance member in the city; his former cellmates accused him of earning his kitchen job by informing on them. Whatever services he had offered his captors did not spare him deportation to Buchenwald. Kiselev remained within the camp system for some eighteen months except for a brief period in the fall of 1944 when he escaped to Leipzig. At Buchenwald he became a *stubendienst*, one of the prisoners the Germans trusted with distributing food to fellow inmates.

When guards at Buchenwald's Halberstadt subcamp ordered the men to gather their things, Kiselev may have feared the worst. Rumors were spreading that the Germans were murdering captives rather than see them fall into Allied hands. And in truth, there were instances when German authorities executed forced laborers because of the supposed threat they posed to the local population.[5] In an infamous episode in March 1945, SS General Hans Kammler, the head of the V-2 rocket bombing program, ordered the execution of 208 Polish- and Soviet-born forced laborers who he claimed were stealing chickens from local farmers near Warstein (Westphalia). In a trial in 1958, one of the executioners implausibly claimed that he believed the 208 victims—including a one-year-old child—had been caught marauding. The real reason behind the executions seems to have been a combination of late-war nihilism and the German conception of Eastern Europeans as racial inferiors.[6]

Unlike the atrocities at Warstein, Kiselev's guards at Halberstadt had no immediate plans for executing the detainees. Their orders were to march the prisoners away from Allied armies to the interior of the country. Kiselev's position as food distributer worked to his advantage. In the chaos of the evacuation, he and his friends took two kilograms of sugar and three kilograms of rye flour. He was also fortunate that the convoy's escort was "Russian," a former Soviet POW recruited to work as a camp guard. Kiselev persuaded the guard to let him and six campmates go to a stream to bathe, and they used this trip as a pretext to escape to nearby woods. There they encountered two friendly Eastern Workers from a neighboring village who guided them to an abandoned barn.

After several days, local police found the hiding spot and some of the men. This moment was perilous. German authorities in some regions issued orders to execute foreign laborers accused of theft.[7] Fortune turned the escapees' way again. The local police jailed some of the escapees but did not execute them. They soon broke out and returned to their friends at the barn. The men lived on their reserves for the next week until American forces came. Emboldened by liberation, they stole an Opel 6 limousine—their "tank." Kiselev directed the men to Leipzig to find other Soviet people who could help them get home to the USSR (figure 4.1).[8]

Self-liberations like Kiselev's were frequent in the last days of the war. In 1944, General Dwight Eisenhower, the Allied supreme commander, had advised forced laborers over the radio to abandon their jobs and work the land. "The safest place to hide now is the countryside," Allied radio broadcasted. "The farmers need you. Many will conceal you and give you food."[9] Anatolii A, a nineteen-year-old from Krasnodar region in Russia's Caucasus, had worked as a forced laborer near the Rhine in western Germany. He fled his camp in March 1945 with his friend and girlfriend (also from Krasnodar region) and sought refuge at a house that they

FIGURE 4.1. "Bringing our 'tank' to the camp Rudsak, Anatolii, Boris, and I. May 1945." Evgenii Kiselev and the men from Buchenwald pose with their car in Leipzig. AUSBU MO, f. 5, spr. 8042, t. 2, unnumbered folder with photographs.

came upon. As chance had it, the occupant was a German peasant who paid them to dig a hole in which to hide belongings—bottles of wine and clothing—while Anatolii A.'s girlfriend watched the farmer's baby daughter.[10]

The most common story of liberation on the Western Front was that foreign workers discovered their guards had fled in the night. Although their captivity was over, the fight to find food continued. On a Sunday in late March 1945, American bombers destroyed the work camp in Bamberg (Bavaria) where Mikhail Sinitsyn, a twenty-one-year-old aspiring poet, had been a laborer. The guards had fled, so he and his campmates went to the forest two miles from the city center. At night they crept to the train station for supplies, and Sinitsyn uncovered a small revolver while looking through boxes. Many others had weapons, too. A dangerous period set in after the Wehrmacht was defeated but before US forces occupied the city. Former forced laborers like Sinitsyn had armed clashes with German guards at Bamberg's warehouses. Only when American forces arrived and began distributing supplies did the fighting stop.[11]

Soviet people greeted Allied troops with joy. In an instant, OST badges and concentration camp uniforms became symbols of pride rather than shame (figure 4.2). It would have been easy enough to unstitch the emblems, but they were proof of suffering under the Germans. Maria G. had not worn her badge as a worker at a

FIGURE 4.2. "A memento of the girls from the Pittler camp, Zhenia Nekrasova and Valia Koshechka. May 1945, Leipzig." Note the OST badges. AUSBU MO, f. 5, spr. 8042, t. 2, unnumbered folder with photographs.

family farm but ran to the house for it when she first spotted US troops on the horizon. She did not want to be mistaken for a German.[12]

Western occupation authorities were wary of displaced persons, whom they saw as potential looters. Theft was a fact of life among displaced Soviet people, but it occurred in a broader atmosphere of disorder. One historian working with local records from Bremen found a rate of serious crimes (e.g., armed robbery or murder) among displaced persons for May 1 to November 15, 1945, as roughly 2 percent. This rate was higher than in peacetime but matched the contemporaneous rate among Germans almost exactly.[13] Such statistics, limited as they are, suggest that crime was a general problem in the spring of 1945, not one that involved the displaced alone. Yet the Western Allies viewed DPs and not Germans as the key source of criminality. Although the Allies did not resort to violence to control former forced laborers as the Germans had during the war, their attitudes toward DPs echoed German anxieties.[14] Marvin Klemmé, an American official working as a United Nations Relief and Rehabilitation Administration (UNRRA) camp administrator, criticized DPs in Soviet camps for preying on the local population. He asserted that they had agreed "more or less voluntarily to come to Germany" and now believed that "they had won the war and therefore could see no reason why they couldn't take what they wanted."[15]

Klemmé was incorrect in his assumptions about the DPs' sense of entitlement but was right to associate violence with the search for food or loot. Violent encounters typically involved confrontations over theft or revenge against former workplace masters and camp commanders. Indiscriminate violence against Germans was rare.

Soviet-claimed people in Europe became a worry to Western Allied leaders for another reason. In France and Italy, the Allies encountered huge numbers of former Red Army soldiers serving in pro-German formations. Some surrendered without a fight or even killed their officers during nighttime defections.[16] In other instances, these formations were essential to the continuing fighting power of the Wehrmacht.[17] During a heated moment in negotiations with Soviet repatriation officials, the British representative, Admiral Ernest Archer, said, "You know that your people who are in England now were caught in German uniform and forty-five thousand of them were fighting against us during the invasion of Normandy."[18]

The Allied encounter with Soviet-claimed people in Europe spurred a debate over repatriation in Anglo-American governing circles. Despite the antagonism that US and British soldiers felt toward the auxiliaries as enemy combatants, some Allied leaders worried that repatriating people to the USSR, especially captives from pro-German formations, would mean their imprisonment or execution. The international legal status of Soviet-claimed displaced persons was cloudy. The Geneva Convention of 1929 stipulated that all warring powers should repatriate prisoners of war after the peace.[19] But were Soviet defectors still Soviet, or had their status changed through their service to the Reich? Balanced against the concern and confusion over repatriation to the USSR was the Western Allies' anxiety about their own POWs. The Red Army was liberating hundreds of thousands of Allied nationals in German camps on the Eastern Front. Anglo-American politicians worried that Stalin would use liberated Allied POWs as hostages. Still another factor probably played a role. The Western Allies were not eager to care for a population of refugees indefinitely in occupied Europe. Anglo-American officials organized UNRRA, the organization that would run the DP camps until 1947, primarily because they feared that an uncontrolled refugee crisis would hinder Allied strategic goals.[20] UNRRA favored repatriation as the best outcome to displacement because it seemed to be the most expedient means of ensuring postwar stability.[21]

Ultimately leaders in both the United States and the United Kingdom agreed to repatriate all Soviet subjects. British foreign secretary Anthony Eden and Stalin came to a handshake agreement on mutual repatriation of Allied citizens at a state dinner in Moscow in October 1944. At the Yalta Conference, where Churchill, Roosevelt, and Stalin negotiated the broader postwar settlement in

February 1945, the Allies signed formal agreements about repatriation.[22] Although the principal agreement had been reached, tensions continued over implementation. Soviet officials bristled over the Western Allies' exclusion of people from the USSR's post-1939 borders from mandatory repatriation, although they avoided pressing this issue during the initial stages of repatriation from the winter of 1944 to the summer of 1945.[23] For their part, the Western Allies continued to worry that Soviet authorities would detain POWs. Exchanges of people took on the trappings of a hostage negotiation. Days after Yalta, Eden warned Soviet officials to ensure "the same number of our people" would be exchanged for the number of Soviet returnees arriving at the port of Odesa.[24] Allied fears were not without basis. When Soviet officials would later reflect on this period, they regretted that the USSR had not exploited its leverage to trade Western POWs for nonreturners.[25]

Despite these future misgivings, the agreement at Yalta was a watershed moment for the Soviet state. The conference confirmed that the USSR was entitled to a major role in the governance of postwar Europe and Asia. Yalta was significant because, besides the redrawing of world maps and the creation of the United Nations, repatriation was a signal of the USSR's postwar status. Important as it was to gain millions of potential workers and soldiers as repatriates, Soviet diplomats understood that repatriation also represented the USSR's ability to project its power in the world. Reciprocal recognition of authority over subjects and respectful treatment of these people was a de facto recognition of the country's equal standing. Moreover, Soviet claims linked populations and regions; Ukrainians belonged in the Soviet Union because their national territory, Ukraine, was part of the USSR. It may seem surprising that officials complained bitterly that Soviet POWs, many of whom had been captured serving in pro-German formations and would meet a harsh reception in the USSR, were disrespected as "Russian swine" by British military police.[26] Yet the treatment of even the most compromised Soviet POWs represented the deference owed to the Soviet state.

According to the Yalta agreement, all Soviet displaced persons were supposed to assemble at the nearest camp after encountering Allied forces. Like other DPs, Soviet people were to be housed according to nationality to facilitate aid and repatriation.[27] And like most other DP camps (e.g., for Polish or Jewish DPs), a local leadership was responsible for security and day-to-day governance. Unlike the other camps, which were administered by UNRRA, Soviet DP facilities fell under the joint responsibility of an Allied commandant from the Supreme Headquarters of the Allied Expeditionary Force (SHAEF) and a liaison from the Red Army. According to American military documents, the Soviet representative was supposed to survey camp residents and "select the best qualified senior officer of the camp as Camp Leader."[28]

General Vasilii Dragun, a veteran of military intelligence, was responsible for Soviet repatriation efforts in Germany and France at the war's end. Before his appointment, there was little Soviet supervision over the assembling points. After his appointment, too, the scale of displacement made it difficult for Dragun's officers to exercise control over the camps. At the height of repatriation immediately after the German surrender, Soviet representatives in Western Germany and France numbered roughly 160. For each of these officers, there were some fifteen thousand returnees and several thousand more nonreturners whom the USSR claimed as citizens.[29] In Leipzig there were five big camps with hundreds or thousands of residents, but many smaller camps with several dozen or fewer.[30] Moreover, as many as a third of all DPs lived outside the camp system in their own apartments or with Germans. Such "free-living" DPs gave up Allied assistance but, according to the UNRRA administrator Marvin Klemmé, enjoyed "comparative luxury" in their living situations and could survive through the black market.[31] With so many camps and with DPs living on their own, Soviet representatives could hardly cope without the help of local DP leaders who had established themselves under the Western Allies.

There was apparently no system of appointments for local administrators at Soviet camps. Dragun and his underlings seem to have issued credentials to DP leaders with little verification of their identities other than a handwritten biography. The roving officials from the USSR probably did not choose the DP administrators in many cases but empowered those already in place. Some camps seem not to have seen a Soviet representative until the eve of repatriation. A Soviet officer visiting camps in the Western zones of Germany in May and June 1945 found that he was the first official they had encountered since liberation.[32]

The figure of a typical camp leader emerges from the messy archive of credentials that Dragun's office issued. The administrators were usually men in their late twenties or thirties, often POW officers or former party members. Many claimed to have been in resistance units, and this background was probably their chief qualification. Some admitted to serving in pro-German formations before they joined the resistance. Konstantin Chegeleshvili was the head of Assembly Center 88 at Lisle-sur-Tarn near Toulouse in the south of France. A Georgian lieutenant who was captured in May 1942, he had volunteered for the Georgian Legion but ran away to the French partisans in November 1943. His partisan brigade apparently appointed him commandant of the assembly center after liberation, and Dragun's office assented to his selection later.[33] Sometimes camp residents held elections. Viktor Sh. remembered that his camp chose its own commandant "based on the rumor that he had been a commissar in the army."[34]

After the defeat of Germany, the Western Allies did not prioritize the establishment of control within DP camps, Soviet or otherwise. Although Western

Allied officers handling DP affairs were more numerous than Soviet repatriation officers in Western Europe, they were also few compared with their displaced charges. As the war with Germany ended, their main goal was for DPs to obstruct occupation regimes as little as possible.[35] Allied forces delivered supplies to assembling points but made few efforts to supervise life within the camps.

The relative independence of the DP camps was a product of the chaos and violence of the last months of the war and the early months of liberation. German authorities lost control over forced laborers and prisoners, and the Allies did not have the desire or capacity to organize DP life beyond basic enforcement of order via local governance. The consequence was that local administrators and DPs gained significant autonomy in Allied-occupied Europe.

Wild Re-Sovietization

After escaping Buchenwald, Evgenii Kiselev and his crew would become DP administrators in Leipzig. The city was in territory occupied by the Western Allies and incorporated into the Soviet zone by Allied agreement later in 1945. The Buchenwald men arrived on Leipzig's outskirts before Allied forces had secured the city. American soldiers sent them to the large Stahmeln camp—a soccer field converted into a barracks for forced laborers at Pittler arms manufacturing. The camp's head, a former Soviet POW named Vasilii Aliferenko, offered them beds and would soon enlist them as fixers. The Buchenwald men kept order in the camp, helped to organize provisions, and undertook ad hoc missions to find family members of camp residents. For some they became protective patriarchs. A young campmate, Liubov Potykalova, wrote a respectful letter to Kiselev a year after return, stating, "Evgenii Vasilevich, I told my parents so much about how you treated me well, almost like a father, although you are too young to be my father."[36]

Kiselev had come to Leipzig not by chance but to find wartime contacts. After temporarily escaping from Buchenwald in 1944, he had hidden in the city for two weeks and befriended a man at the Mangold camp named Pavel Shevchenko. Days after arriving at Stahmeln, Kiselev learned that Shevchenko was a former POW from Pavlohrad whose real name was Prokofii Lesnichenko. He had led a small resistance group during the war and now had become the de facto coordinator of Soviet DP camps in Leipzig.

When they met after liberation, Lesnichenko introduced Kiselev's group to Captain Kulikov, the Red Army representative under General Dragun in charge of repatriation in the city. "You are all politically literate people," Kiselev reported Kulikov's having told the Buchenwald men, "you've gone through the political school of the world." What the captain meant was that they had moral credibility as former concentration camp prisoners. They were also adult men, unlike most of the adolescent and young adult DPs. Perhaps most important, they had a car. Kulikov asked Kiselev's team to help him find wartime collaborators and keep order among Soviet people. He also asked them to monitor DPs who tried to avoid repatriation. In broad terms, Kulikov was asking Kiselev to help re-Sovietize the displaced persons of Leipzig.[37]

Kulikov's admonition to locate collaborators matched the thirst for payback among some former captives. Most revenge was personal. Liberated in Walter-shausen by US forces in April 1945, Kursk native Aleksandra Mikhaleva wrote in her diary that a DP named "Uncle Sasha" got drunk and "beat his former master with pleasure."[38] Others noted that Germans who had treated foreign workers well might receive a reference vouching for their good conduct to show Allied forces.[39]

In many camps, local administrators undertook vigilante justice that went beyond the wishes of Soviet officials. Air force general Aleksandr Vikhorev, rumored to be an intelligence official in disguise, was one of the first Soviet officers to tour the DP camps of France in early 1945. He reported to the Repatriation Administration about vigilante trials where DPs had executed campmates accused of collaboration. Rather than take the side of the accusers, Vikhorev asserted that the camp residents were no less guilty of collaboration than those they hanged. The trials were an attempt to shirk responsibility among people who were "rotten to their bones."[40] From the perspective of Stalinist investigators, the executions may have seemed like a pretense for traitors to silence potential witnesses. Soviet leaders also undoubtedly disapproved of vigilantism because it misappropriated the prerogative of the state to judge traitors.[41]

Kiselev and his men participated in impromptu trials in their role as troubleshooters at Stahmeln. Urged on by the residents, Kiselev's team located a man identified as a POW turned camp guard during the war. Administrators at Stahmeln then organized a trial of the guard. "After the trial, the camp residents voted for his execution," Boris Surov-Kurov-Kin, one of Kiselev's men, later told Soviet police interrogators. "The court appointed a group of people who shot that *polizei* not far from the camp."[42] The group was also involved in the execution of a German whom their neighbors in a Polish camp identified as a Nazi factory owner who had tormented them during the war.

The violent acts seem to have made Kiselev's men uncomfortable. Like other executioners in Nazi Germany and the Soviet Union, they drank during executions, perhaps to ease their psychological burden.[43] In the case of the factory owner, the executioner was so drunk that he said he might have missed his victim. Later he failed to find the body when he went back to bury it. Perhaps the German had survived, or perhaps the intoxicated executioner forgot the site of the killing.

None of the other men knew whether the German was dead because they had not gone to witness the execution, a possible sign of their distaste for the task.[44]

The men did not relish these murders, so why had they agreed to them? Kiselev could have turned the accused over to Allied authorities. Earlier the group had found a bomb crater with the corpses of fifty prisoners from Leipzig jail, forced laborers and POWs executed by the Gestapo in the last days of the war. On their own initiative, the men found a Gestapo officer whom witnesses identified as the perpetrator and took him to American authorities. The Buchenwald group had not known the Gestapo officer, but they had not known the camp guard or the factory owner either. They had no personal conflict with the people they executed. For them and other Soviet DPs, vigilante justice was a proxy for active participation in the war. As POWs and Eastern Workers, they had not come to Germany as victors, but at least they could inflict violence against the enemies of the Soviet Union after the war.

Symbolic violence also marked the reassertion of Soviet men's authority over women. Historians of France have shown how defeat by Nazi Germany and liberation by the Western Allies created a sense of lost masculinity among French men. Reacting to their feelings of emasculation, they rounded up women suspected of collaboration or sex with the Germans and enacted ritual punishments against them. The iconic act of revenge was shearing the women's heads.[45] Soviet men in Germany experienced many of the same feelings of shame as their French counterparts. Although the Red Army had triumphed, Germany's early victories had enabled the deportation of millions of Soviet people away from the motherland. Many Soviet men assumed that the women could not or did not resist German sexual advances. Or they believed that non-Soviet foreign workers had bought Soviet women with ration cards. Many female Eastern Workers had engaged in sexual barter, but Soviet officials were unwilling to accept that the deprivations of forced labor had compelled these transactions.

Feelings of emasculation led DP leaders to target Soviet women in relationships with non-Soviet men. Soviet people had entered relationships with non-Soviets even under restrictive German camp regimes, and liberation only increased opportunities for contact. Threats against mixed relationships were sometimes tinged with racism, especially toward Black Allied soldiers. Liberated forced laborer Anatolii A. recalled that women knew they were under surveillance. He remembered camp leaders saying, "If someone goes with a Black guy or one of the other new masters [American soldiers], watch out."[46]

Aleksandra Mikhaleva endured Soviet men's aggression against Soviet-Italian couples in Waltershausen. Like the Buchenwald men at Stahmeln, a group of former POWs came to Waltershausen from a nearby concentration camp and formed a band that organized the DPs. Furious that many Soviet women were dating Italian DPs, the former POWs threatened the couples with beatings. In the final weeks before liberation, Mikhaleva had begun to see an Italian named Ugo and continued to go out with him despite the hard stares of the Soviet men. At the end of May, the attacks came. On May 22, a gang of Soviet men confronted one of the "Italian" women and shaved her head. The women stopped meeting the Italians in the open and went to the Italian barracks instead. A week after the first incident, the Soviet gang armed themselves with knives, invaded an Italian barracks, and dragged out the Soviet women. Some gave up their boyfriends after this attack. Ugo and Mikhaleva continued to date but took precautions. They met only during the day and often at the home of a German acquaintance, where the gang would not find them.[47]

The behavior of the Soviet men shocked Mikhaleva. Her cousin Galina Mikhaleva did not share her feelings, and married a former Soviet POW in early May. He proposed to her almost immediately after liberation. Judging by the excitement over the wedding, Galina's must have been one of the first in the camp. Some fifty people attended the ceremony, the women all outfitted in white wedding dresses, probably taken from German stores. After the festivities, Aleksandra wrote a pensive entry in her diary: "I don't think that I'll ever get married. I'm not used to Russian men anymore. I'm afraid of them."[48] Ugo seemed to her a sophisticated Italian man. He wrote songs for her and, like her Czech and Polish wartime boyfriends, did not pressure her for sex. The Soviet men's attempts at physical domination of the women astonished her.

More Soviet women were like Galina Mikhaleva than Aleksandra, it seems. Liberation brought together thousands of Soviet people and enabled cohabitation between sexual partners. The situation was much the same as in the forced labor camps; people in positions of authority or with access to resources were the most attractive partners. As prominent figures in the Stahmeln camp, Kiselev and his men paired off with women within days of their arrival. Anecdotal evidence suggests that many camp residents continued to live with their wartime bunkmates in barracks, while couples commanded a modicum of private space by living together. The Buchenwald men and others described these camp relationships as marriages and their partners as wives. During the four months between their liberation and arrival at their homes in the USSR, the men led "more or less normal family lives," according to Klavdia Astashina, Kiselev's camp wife.[49]

Like other camp residents, Kiselev's group and their partners seem to have defined marriage as monogamous sexual cohabitation. They used the term in earnest, in contrast to wartime "field wives," a derogatory term that masked the transient and often coercive relationships between Red Army officers and female personnel.[50] Some of the older men, including Kiselev, had families in the USSR and may have assumed that their camp marriages would last no longer than the

FIGURE 4.3. "A memento to my dear comrade Evgenii from comrade Boris and his wife, Olga. Leipzig, May 1945." Note Boris Surov-Kurov-Kin wearing his camp uniform. AUSBU MO, f. 5, spr. 8042, t. 2, unnumbered folder with photographs.

stay in the DP camps. But it is understandable that the euphoria of liberation after years of captivity made it easy to fall in love. The DPs were alive and free, while a spouse who had lived under occupation or had fought in the Red Army might be dead or remarried.

There are no statistics about returnees who married in Germany, although anecdotal evidence suggests that these relationships often survived repatriation. The coordinator of Leipzig's Soviet camps, Prokofii Lesnichenko, married Evgenia Osipovich, a gynecologist, after liberation. According to her postwar account, she had lived with her husband in Minsk before the war. They remained in Belarus under the German occupation, and her husband went to the partisans weeks after Osipovich gave birth to a son in August 1941. After she fled Belarus with the child for fear that she would be arrested for connections to the partisans, the Germans deported her to work in Leipzig as a midwife for Eastern Workers. What happened to her husband and baby is unclear from her account. Osipovich possibly did not know if they were alive when she married Lesnichenko, or perhaps silence in her account implied that both had died. In either case, she moved to Pavlohrad with Lesnichenko in August 1945.[51] It is possible to see the desire for traditional marriage as a return to the conservative Stalinist ideal of monogamous relationships.[52] Yet camp relationships are probably better seen in the context of the DP experience in Europe more broadly, where refugees sought marriage as a return to normal life after years of disruption.[53]

Lesnichenko's resistance group produced several marriages in Leipzig, and it persisted in Allied-occupied Germany in other ways as well. A reputation for wartime resistance earned Lesnichenko the position of camp leader in Leipzig. In this role, his main duty was to organize supplies for the camps and keep order among the residents. Lesnichenko took another task upon himself as well—creating a documentary record of his resistance group.

The Leipzig group was hardly alone in producing material about resistance activity. Rakhmil Shmushkevich was a Jewish POW who had been a party member and ranking propaganda worker in Ukraine before the war. He claimed later to have founded a resistance group in German captivity while hiding under a false Ukrainian identity. When he became the leader of a DP camp under American forces, he directed his campmates to write memoirs of their resistance activities.[54] By producing these autobiographies, the DPs were replicating Soviet practices. The Soviet government had sponsored major projects of autobiographical commemoration to document the building of a socialist state: diaries about the building of the Moscow Metro, memoirs about industrialization, recollections of the October Revolution. Individual Soviet people had used diaries to situate their lives in the great events of Marxist-Leninist historical progress.[55] In the DP camps, future returnees anticipated the necessity of incorporating a pro-Soviet war narrative into their biographies. Affiliation with a resistance group was an important way they attempted to write themselves into the broader Soviet effort.

Postliberation resistance committees included people who had been in resistance groups and those with vague or nonexistent claims to opposition. In late May 1945, Lesnichenko formed an organization called the Russian Workers Liberation Committee (Russkii Rabochii Osvoboditel'nyi Komitet, RROK) as a way of uniting the various Soviet groups in Leipzig. The designation of the group as "Russian" probably mirrored German and Allied parlance or a slippage between Soviet identity and the Russian language, since Lesnichenko and many other members were not from Russia. At the first RROK meeting, Lesnichenko gave a speech lauding the resistance activity in the city. Some attendees were members of his wartime group, including the Georgian camp doctor and Wustrau propaganda camp trainee Aleksandr Dzadzamia. For the most part, however, the eighty to ninety attendees had only met after liberation.[56] They included Kiselev and his men, who had questionable records as oppositionists. They had escaped from Buchenwald but had not been part of Lesnichenko's group. Kiselev had encountered Lesnichenko during the war but also had been a *stubendienst* and possible informer. Nonetheless, the Buchenwald men had shown their loyalty to the USSR as camp administrators and became members, too.

Another RROK member included for his value after liberation was a young German named Willy Gehlbach.[57] He had served in the Wehrmacht as a medic but received a discharge for "nerves" in 1943. After his return to Leipzig, the German made contacts with several men from the forced labor camps and went into business with them on the black market.[58] His continued trade with former foreign workers after liberation brought him into contact with Lesnichenko. Besides offering the DP camps food and supplies, Gehlbach had a stash of German Communist Party cards he obtained from a communist friend and access to a printing press.[59]

Lesnichenko passed the limited number of German Communist Party cards to Dzadzamia and other members of the wartime group. When Gehlbach created RROK stationery and a stamp, the number of card-holding members proliferated. Lesnichenko gave cards to the DP leaders he knew. People close to Lesnichenko vouched for friends as resisters and secured cards for them as well. Dzadzamia had Lesnichenko issue a card to Iokim Kapanadze, who, like him, had been a Georgian choir member at Wustrau and a free physician in Leipzig. Vasilii Aliferenko, the Stahmeln camp head, received a card for himself and obtained one for his camp wife, Pavlohrad native Efrosinia Usenko, who had participated in Lesnichenko's wartime resistance group in the final weeks before liberation. Kiselev and his men believed that Usenko received the card primarily because of her relationship with Aliferenko and arranged cards for their camp wives as a "matter of respect." Gehlbach passed the cards liberally to DPs he knew.[60] No fewer than a hundred people received RROK cards. There were several dozen similar groups in Allied-occupied Europe, although RROK seems to have been among the most sophisticated.[61]

Besides the cards, RROK distributed posters of Stalin and Lenin, generated pro-Soviet bulletins, and put on antifascist theater shows. For his part, Gehlbach used RROK as a commercial enterprise, making Red Army star pins to sell for two marks each.[62] The German was catering to the hopes and fears of Soviet DPs, who wished to show themselves as loyal Soviet citizens. The American UNRRA official Marvin Klemmé recalled that Soviet-bound people decorated their camp with red banners and paintings of Stalin and Lenin. As the camp residents departed eastward, he observed, "One would have thought . . . that all of these folk were on a glorious holiday or picnic of some sort. They were laughing and singing and yelling."[63] Klemmé did not understand that beneath the celebratory atmosphere lurked a feeling of dread. Would the DPs be received in the USSR as citizens in good standing or as traitors?

RROK and the paraphernalia surrounding it were pledges of allegiance to the Soviet Union. Organizations like RROK were not resistance groups in the literal sense. They reflected little actual resistance activity in the war. At the same time, they were not simple ploys to falsify resistance. Instead, they were attempts at re-Sovietization. The war had forced Soviets into varying levels of complicity with the USSR's enemies. Armed resistance had been all but nonexistent, and anti-German propaganda groups had been few. A sympathetic interpretation of RROK is that the claim to resistance was a spiritual position that affirmed members' loyalty to the USSR despite their problematic biographies. With Stalin posters, Soviet-themed pins, and RROK cards, DPs showed that they had been loyal to the USSR in their hearts.

Postwar resistance organizations were one attempt at re-Sovietization without Soviet control. In these efforts, DP camp organizers in some instances unknowingly went against the wishes of leaders in Moscow. Despite their miscalculations, wild re-Sovietization demonstrated that many DPs, and perhaps the majority, wanted to return to the USSR. Former Soviet activists who became DP leaders most of all hoped to rehabilitate themselves and restore their rightful place in the USSR. The chaos of the camps not only allowed DPs to express their vision of Soviet loyalism but also gave those who wished to avoid repatriation the chance to remake themselves.

The Choice to Return

Nadezhda Severilova was eighteen when British forces liberated her on a farm near Salzwedel, in north-central Germany. Her childhood in Kyiv had not been happy. She had lived at an orphanage until 1942, when the Germans deported her for work at age fourteen to a family farm. During the final months of the war, she shared farm duties with a group of Italian POWs. Severilova, gray-eyed with midlength blond hair, caught the eye of one of the Italians, Brosildo Antilucci (Brozil'do Antilichi in Russian documents). Through their conversations she learned Italian at a remarkable pace. Antilucci suggested that she join him in Italy at the war's close, a marriage proposal according to Severilova. She liked Antilucci but did not want to marry him and decided to return to the USSR. He left his address and departed for Italy.

Soon Severilova began to regret her decision. She decided to find Antilucci in Italy, but getting there was not so simple. She first claimed to be the Italian sister of a fellow DP, an Eastern Worker from a neighboring farm who was going to Italy with her new Italian husband and their unborn child. British authorities in charge of determining nationality did not believe Severilova and ascertained that she was from Eastern Europe. According to her testimony to Soviet secret police, a British officer and a Polish translator recruited her as a spy, and the latter enrolled her in a Polish espionage school in Munich. In all likelihood, the translator sent her to a nursing program for Polish DPs to help her avoid repatriation to the USSR.

When Severilova flunked out of the school for poor attendance, the translator helped her concoct another plan. She went to the Italian consul in Munich pretending to be a Naples-born war orphan. In the story, her grandfather had taken her from Italy to Spain and then to Germany. The consul credited her story enough to send her to the Italian transit camp at Mittenwald (Bavaria, bordering Austria), where authorities were supposed to contact Naples police and confirm her identity. Not wishing to wait for the police to respond, Severilova slipped onto the next convoy going south. Sympathetic Italian POWs hid her when Allied authorities came to check identification papers on the train to Naples. The day after arriving, a Naples police official hired her as a domestic servant. For the next year, she lived in Naples under the name Nella Antilucci until, having failed to find Brosildo Antilucci, she decided to return to the USSR.[64] Severilova was extraordinary in the number and combination of identities she adopted on her journey. At the same time, she exemplified the decisions DPs faced and the tactics they used as they navigated the prospect of return.

The main factors that enabled Severilova's journey were the fluidity of national identities among Eastern European peoples and disagreements over who was subject to compulsory repatriation. Allied officials refused to recognize the legitimacy of Soviet annexations in 1939–40 and asserted that people from these territories were exempt from compulsory repatriation as non-Soviets. Displaced persons camps with nonreturners were mainly filled with people from these regions, a fact that Soviet officials acknowledged even as they insisted that these DPs were subject to repatriation.[65] At the same time, national identities were blurry among Eastern Europeans. It was rare that someone from Kyiv might claim to be from Naples, but Severilova's transformation from a Ukrainian DP into a Polish nurse trainee was less difficult. A secret police informant in Ukraine reported one returnee as saying, "All it took was to tell an American officer that you were from Poland or Latvia, Estonia or Romania, and they would offer to let you stay."[66]

This statement was a rueful exaggeration, but it was not so far off. Evidence about people's identities was often lost, sometimes intentionally. While many repatriates saved their Soviet or German documents and dutifully submitted them to police upon return to the USSR, in other cases authorities had few documents to prove who someone was. With time and effort, the Western Allies or Soviet authorities could verify someone's identity, or at least establish that an identity was false. But there were seven million displaced persons in occupied

Germany alone in May 1945. The process of identifying all would have taken years. In many cases, like that of Severilova, authorities were left to assess DPs based on their self-presentation.

The paucity of identity documents enabled DPs to enlist the help of nonstate organizations to avoid repatriation. Anti-Soviet national committees and émigré organizations were eager to aid Soviet nonreturners. The committee at a Polish DP camp in Heidenau (Lower Saxony) registered potential Soviet repatriates as Polish and provided false biographies. The camp even coached the newly registered Poles on their nominal home regions so they could give plausible answers if Allied authorities questioned them.[67] Émigrés at the Parsh camp in Austria had saved stationery and stamps from the Russian All-Military Union, an organization of anti-Bolshevik veterans of the Russian Civil War. Falsified documents backdated to the 1920s turned postwar nonreturners into post–civil war émigrés.[68]

Allied authorities sometimes accepted the crudest fake documents. In January 1946, Major I. M. Zverev of the Soviet repatriation mission in Würzburg in the American zone of occupation recognized two men impersonating Red Army officers. They were liberated POWs he had previously encountered in the American zone and had sent to the Soviet zone of Germany. In the chaos of return in mid-1945, they had returned to the American zone. After a gunfight that left one of the impersonators wounded, Zverev detained both and found a self-made pass in stilted English: "Iwan Shoukow lieutenant in the service of a Military-school, in the town Libau, worked as a commander in camps of russian prisoners and workers between Wuerzburg till Aschafenburg and Frankfurt. He has the permission to go to the russian general at Frankfurt to ask for an information." The pass had apparently raised no alarms among American authorities for the months that the two men had driven around the zone, enjoying their status as Soviet officers.[69]

Individual Allied officials sometimes went against orders and aided the unwilling to escape Soviet claims. A British interpreter working with Soviet officers told a young nonreturner woman in English, "You just cry and say you don't want to go. They won't take you." She believed she was speaking in confidence to the woman, not knowing that the Soviet officers understood English.[70] One DP, Ivan K., remembered a friendship with an American soldier who said his Russian émigré family owned a factory. Supposedly the son offered to hire Ivan K., although it is unclear if the invitation was genuine or an expression of fondness for someone who had already decided to return to the USSR.[71]

In 1945, Western Allied commanders condemned such incidents, reluctant to give the appearance of violating the Yalta agreement. An American order in April 1945 read: "Serious misunderstandings have occurred in the past through loose talk. For example, some casual remark by a junior officer asking a Russian if he would like to go to America has been interpreted as propaganda and proselytizing."[72] In July 1945, Eisenhower ordered the arrest of two Russian émigrés after Soviet officials complained that they were conducting anti-Soviet propaganda.[73]

It was possible to create new legal identities without using false documents or adapting one's national belonging. An important phenomenon in this regard, one at the center of Severilova's story, was mixed marriages. Thousands of other Soviet-claimed people, overwhelmingly women, married non-Soviets. Leaders in Moscow disliked such mixed marriages and in 1947 banned them in the USSR. A state decree nonetheless allowed Soviet people living abroad in mixed marriages to avoid repatriation.[74] Despite the efforts of Soviet DP leaders to prevent mixed relationships like those Aleksandra Mikhaleva endured, it was impossible to stop them. The French internal ministry in 1946 registered about three thousand marriages between Soviet women and French men. A thousand or more Soviet women registered marriages to Dutch and Belgian men with Soviet authorities.[75] In 1948, Soviet officials counted almost eight thousand Soviet-claimed people who had married citizens from socialist bloc countries and remained in their spouse's homeland.[76] Those figures only included people who had registered their marriage. Who knew how many refused to report marriages to non-Soviets because they feared repatriation? An early estimate by Soviet administrators placed the number of Soviet-French marriages alone at twenty thousand.[77]

Many of the women married for love. Antonina S., a half-Jewish woman from Stalingrad who managed to hide her Jewish heritage while working at a chemical plant in Germany, married her French boyfriend, Claude. They moved to France after the war, had a child, and settled into a comfortable life in the Paris suburbs. Although the Soviet government had authorized Soviet people in mixed marriages to live abroad, in 1946 repatriation authorities found Antonina S. and forced her to repatriate with her son. Perhaps Antonina S. and Claude had not registered their marriage, or perhaps the officials did not care. Similar abductions were the cause of scandals in the French press and sometimes resulted in the release of the women to their spouses.[78] In the case of Antonina S., it would be some twenty years after repatriation before she could contact Claude again.[79]

A rare case of a Soviet man's potential marriage to a non-Soviet woman involved Lev Netto, brother of the famous soccer player Igor. An ethnic Estonian from Moscow, the twenty-year-old former POW had taken work at a German farm after he escaped his camp in the last days of the war. His boss was a German woman whose husband had died in the Wehrmacht. The woman had a sixteen-year-old daughter, and she watched as the two young people grew closer over several months. On the eve of Netto's departure for the Soviet zone of Germany, the mother made a proposal: Netto could stay at the farm, marry her daughter, and eventually become the owner. Tempted though he was, Netto decided to return to his family in Moscow.[80]

Some women sought a non-Soviet husband to avoid repatriation. Soviet officers visiting DP camps in the Netherlands in 1946 found that most of the women they hoped to repatriate had Dutch husbands or had recently divorced but wanted to marry again.[81] A woman in Luxembourg, where the government agreed to repatriate almost all Soviet-claimed people, became desperate when local police came to take her to a Soviet transit camp. She made a hasty agreement with the escorting officer to act as her husband—or perhaps to actually marry. When Luxembourg officials learned of the scheme, they fired the officer and turned the woman over to Soviet control.[82]

As this case from Luxembourg shows, not all attempts to avoid repatriation were guaranteed success. In interviews taken in the first years of the twenty-first century, however, dozens of people who returned to the USSR suggested it would have been simple to stay in Europe. Russian-born Valentina G. gave a representative account: "An American officer came and said . . . 'We invite you to Canada [sic] for recruiting. We'll give you a house with furniture, plates, and linens on a thirty-year mortgage.'" According to Valentina G., many people from the camp accepted this offer, afraid that return to the USSR would mean exile to Siberia.[83] In these stories, emigration was an open door to the American dream. And in these stories, the interviewee rejected it in favor of the USSR because of a combination of foolishness and patriotism. Some aspects in these narratives were surely overstated, misremembered, or misinterpreted. The offer Valentina G. heard might have come from representatives of an émigré association rather than Allied officials. Or it might have been idle chatter—a soldier eager to compare capitalism with the Soviet welfare state. It is also important to place such assertions about the ease of emigration into the context of the first decade of the 2000s, when the interviews occurred. Valentina G. implied that she had been loyal by returning to the motherland rather than leaving for what seemed in retrospect to be an easy life abroad. Moreover, she and other repatriates had faced poor treatment as a reward for their loyalty after they returned.

Despite these exaggerations, the prospect of nonreturn was real but came with risks and problems. When Nadezhda Severilova arrived from Naples at a Soviet transit camp in Austria, she faced deep suspicion about her attempt to avoid repatriation. Her verification in the camp took nearly a year, and in 1951 the secret police in Kyiv would arrest her as a supposed British spy.[84] Vladimir Protsenko, a Kharkiv teacher deported to Germany during the war, sought to escape Soviet control for the British zone of Germany in May 1945. A British unit detained him and sent him again to the Soviet zone. A year later, after he had returned to his hometown and resumed teaching, Soviet police arrested him as an alleged British spy and Gestapo agent. It is possible Protsenko would have faced arrest even if he had not attempted to escape repatriation. At a minimum, his aborted flight to the British zone drew the attention of Soviet police and increased the severity of their accusations.[85]

Beyond the threat of Soviet reprisals, emigration carried the danger of a ruined life in an alien land. Valentina Chuliak was just sixteen when she met Julien Giles (Zhile), an older Frenchman who worked at her factory in Germany. In a petition to the Repatriation Administration in the summer of 1946, she wrote that Giles had helped her survive forced labor and married her after the war. They then went to his village in France, where she was isolated from the outside world. He beat her, kept her locked away at home, and demanded she speak only French.[86] Although Chuliak's situation was particularly difficult, Soviet women in the spring of 1945 must have worried about the possibility that the relationships that had helped them endure forced labor could transform into another kind of captivity.

Alternatively, Soviet women might find themselves abandoned. Antonina V. in a post-Soviet interview recalled the story of a coworker who had married a French man from her camp. She went with him to Paris after the war, but his parents rejected her, and she went to the USSR. Antonina V. must have learned of the story only after repatriation, but it reinforced her sense that she made the correct decision to reject the marriage proposal of a Dutch suitor.[87] A friend of Severilova's, Antonina Shubovich, had a similar story. After marrying an Italian POW and having his child in Sicily, Shubovich returned to the USSR alone with the baby.[88]

The main reason that people chose repatriation to the USSR was to see their families. Aleksandra Mikhaleva wrote in the May 9 entry of her diary, "Can it be that I will see my beloved relatives soon? Are they still alive?" Although she thought about marriage to her Italian boyfriend, Ugo, moving to Italy was inconceivable. The only future she could imagine with him was if he would come to Kursk.[89] For Nadezhda Severilova, in contrast, a childhood spent in an orphanage made the possibility of starting a new life more attractive.

Even those who believed they were likely targets of repression felt the pull of family. Ivan Tvardovskii, the brother of famed poet and *Novyi Mir* editor Aleksandr, was captured fighting against Finland and spent most of the war in a POW camp there. In 1944, he escaped to Sweden, where he evaded repatriation and took a job in a woodcarving workshop. In the early 1930s, Soviet authorities had exiled him and his family—minus Aleksandr—as supposed kulaks (rich peasants). He assumed this status made it likely that the police would see him as a traitor if he returned. Despite his plausible fear and comfortable Swedish life, Tvardovskii could not remain abroad while his wife and son were in the USSR. As he recalled: "I became convinced that prosperity could not overcome grief and yearning for one's homeland and family." He returned to the USSR in January 1947. He soon found himself serving a ten-year sentence in a Soviet labor camp.[90]

Jews who survived German concentration camps also sought reunification with their families inside and outside the USSR. Potential Jewish returnees faced a special set of circumstances. Soviet conceptions of ethnic belonging meant that officials were mostly indifferent to the repatriation of Jews, sometimes even those born within pre-1939 Soviet borders, and did not press the issue with the same insistence as they demanded the return of Ukrainians or Baltic peoples. Jews did not constitute the titular nation of any major territory of the USSR and thus were an awkward fit for the Soviet framework that equated nationality with homeland. In one case, an American official complained to Soviet repatriation authorities in August 1945 that a Red Army officer gave a group of fifty-four Jewish survivors from the Terezin ghetto a pass demanding that the US Army "assist in every way" in their journey to Palestine. Far from making a claim on the Jewish migrants as potential repatriates, Soviet officials seemed to be eager to rid themselves of the burden of caring for refugees.[91]

International relations also played a role in the liberal Soviet policy toward Jews. A telling incident was the apparently successful emigration in early 1947 of a group of several thousand Jews from the newly annexed Carpathian province of Ukraine. Aleksandr M. Aleksandrov, the head of the Ministry of Foreign Affairs department in charge of Poland and Czechoslovakia, advised officials in charge of repatriation that the Jews should be allowed to leave or risk "unwanted attention in world opinion."[92] The Polish-Soviet population exchange of 1944–46 gave Soviet Jews from the pre-1939 borders an opportunity to leave as well. One former Soviet soldier wrote to the American Jewish Joint Distribution Committee, a prominent aid organization, "Came home from the army, found no one alive in Kiev, and as I had the chance to go to Poland—had an uncle there—I went, but no uncle; all Jews trekking to Palestine, so I decided to go along."[93]

A limited number made the opposite journey. Iosif A. had grown up in Hrodno, in Western Belarus, and survived Auschwitz. After liberation he joined a group of survivors from his hometown, most of whom planned to go to Palestine from the Czech lands where they found themselves. Iosif A. had siblings who had been alive when he left Hrodno, however, and he hoped to find them there if he returned. He parted with the Palestine-bound group and presented himself to the Red Army for repatriation. When he returned to Hrodno, he learned that the Germans had killed his entire family.[94]

Each Soviet DP had a different set of calculations about return: Was family waiting? Or was a (potential) spouse abroad? Would life be better outside the USSR—where many lacked languages and skills to forge a good life? Or was it safer to go to the USSR—where returnees might be branded as traitors? Some found assistance from émigrés and Allied officials. Others could plausibly claim to be from the western borderlands or belong to another group not subject to repatriation. No matter how fraught with problems, Soviet DPs had a genuine opportunity to remain abroad. Most chose to return to the USSR.

Evgenii Kiselev left Leipzig in July 1945 at the head of a group of RROK members, including his men from Buchenwald. For nearly four years he had lived under German occupation and captivity. He had made compromises with German authorities that he feared would weigh on him when he returned to the USSR. In the absence of central authorities, Soviet DP camp leaders like Kiselev reinstituted aspects of Soviet life—often through violence—in the hopes of showing their loyalty to Stalin's regime. Kiselev's time in Leipzig promised to erase his wartime failings and turn him into a leading Soviet citizen again.

The chaotic period from the end of the war into the early occupation granted DPs a modicum of agency. The postwar situation enabled wild re-Sovietization but also allowed DPs to find ways to avoid return to the USSR. Most nonreturners were people from the USSR's recently annexed western borderlands, whom Soviet authorities claimed as subjects but the Western Allies did not recognize as such. A significant minority of nonreturners were people like Nadezhda Severilova, a woman from Kyiv who Western Allied and Soviet authorities agreed should return to the USSR. To remain in Europe, she and others used the flexible identities of the postwar period, the destruction of documentation, and the sympathies of local authorities.

Most Soviet-born DPs decided to return to the USSR. For some it was an easy choice. Enthusiastic returnees rejected a life abroad because they missed their families and their homeland. The decision was difficult for those who saw repatriation as more palatable than an uncertain future as a refugee or dependent of a non-Soviet spouse. Still others hoped for the best, even as they feared exile to Siberia or a Gulag sentence. As they came back under Soviet control, returnees found that they had as much to fear from hostile neighbors as from the wrath of Stalin.

AMBIGUOUS HOMECOMING

Social Tensions in Repatriation to the USSR

On July 7, 1945, Raisa Lashkul committed suicide. Local authorities in Smila district (Kyiv province) chalked up the incident to boy trouble: she liked him; he wanted to see other girls; she killed herself in despair. Lashkul was also a repatriate who had returned home from forced labor in Germany earlier that year. When officials from the Repatriation Administration investigated the matter, they found a shocking case of abuse. Lashkul had replaced her relative, also possibly a repatriate, for two weeks at a peat enterprise. When the relative returned and Lashkul left the job, a representative from the village council and his friend accused her of deserting the workplace. Growing angry with Lashkul, the council head threw wastewater at her and demanded that she appear before the village council. When she refused, he pulled out a revolver and shot in the air. Terrified, Lakshul went to the village council, which released her almost immediately. Neighbors said that Lashkul was not the same after, that she suffered from sleepless nights. She reportedly said, "They tormented us there, we came back, and they torment us here."[1]

Lashkul was among the wave of displaced persons who returned to Soviet control from the end of 1944 to the beginning of 1946. Soviet leaders were ambivalent at best about the returnees. Were they victims of fascism or traitors to the motherland? Should they receive assistance or face discrimination? Within officialdom there were disagreements about how to treat the returnees. Repatriation officials in Moscow were the most sympathetic and wanted to organize an efficient and vigilant process to bring Soviet people eastward. The bureaucracy charged with overseeing return was the state Repatriation Administration, headed by General Filipp Golikov. Under its supervision, the Red Army operated hundreds of transit camps across Eastern Europe that were supposed to provide food and housing for returnees on their journey. Along the way, police leaders planned to put each returnee through filtration (*filtratsiia*)—political verification that was supposed to catch collaborators. But central authorities often played a secondary role in the period of so-called mass repatriation. The pressure of millions of returnees made plans unworkable. Meanwhile, the strain of occupying Germany and the emphasis on the reconstruction of the Soviet economy took priority over the comfort and safety of returnees. As in Allied-occupied Europe, such factors led to social autonomy and self-organization. Under Soviet control, however, social agency meant that repatriates became targets for exploitation.

Contrary to popular conceptions of Soviet repatriation in the English-speaking world, there were no orders to send all repatriates to the Gulag. A significant number would go to the army or labor battalions, but the majority went to their home regions in the USSR. The inadequacy of organization and supplies made them dependent on the goodwill of lower-level Red Army personnel to find housing and supplies. The imbalance of power and the popular assertion of repatriates' wartime guilt led to violence and sexual coercion against the returnees.[2] After returnees arrived in the USSR, neighbors discriminated against them as they attempted to resume their lives. Elements of this cold reception were distinctive to Stalin's USSR. The fear of association with potential traitors that had been a key element of repression in the 1930s increased the marginalization of returnees. But repatriation also generated problems that are typical of virtually all incidents of mass displacement. Rather than exclusively a creation of Stalin's system, the often-harrowing experience of return to Soviet control was a by-product of war.

Unplanned Return

As Western Allied armies uncovered millions of Soviet-claimed people in Western Europe, advances on the Eastern Front brought the Red Army into contact with even greater numbers of displaced Soviet subjects. They were "the equivalent of an entire army," according to one commander, and needed assistance.[3] By order of the State Defense Committee, the USSR's wartime extraordinary government, the task of registering and feeding the refugees fell to the Red Army's overwhelmed Department of the Rear. Soon the department's head, General Andrei Khrulev, complained to Deputy Premier Viacheslav Molotov that the number of returnees had "grown extraordinarily" and proposed creating a separate army department for repatriation. Khrulev's estimation of the problem was laughable; he planned to hire a mere sixteen full-time workers to oversee migration.[4] In October 1944, Molotov reacted to the magnitude of displacement by establishing a state Repatriation Administration with a planned 1,710 officers and workers in repatriation departments on the front and 416 in the central administration.[5]

The new administration was charged with effecting repatriation quickly but also in a way that would prevent infiltration by spies and traitors. These conflicting priorities brought repatriation officials into conflict with police leaders. Deputy head of the Repatriation Administration, General Konstantin Golubev, recognized in January 1945 that returnees would be too many for security forces to verify as planned. He proposed that civilians, who were less likely to have collaborated, be sent "directly to their homes for local verification." Vasilii Chernyshev, deputy head of the NKVD, the bureaucracy in charge of criminal police and prisons, rejected this solution as a threat to the state.[6] As security forces failed or refused to process the refugees, a patchwork of verification emerged: on some fronts, returnees faced inspections outside the USSR; on others, the Red Army forwarded repatriates to NKVD filtration camps at the border.[7] Golubev took his conflict with security officials to Stalin in June 1945, when he wrote to denounce "senior military officials" for overvaluing security and underestimating the "political importance of the quick delivery of repatriates to the motherland."[8] In the summer of 1945, a compromise emerged: all returnees would undergo verification in their home districts.[9] This requirement did not necessarily replace filtration abroad. In many cases it was an additional verification that compensated for superficial or nonexistent filtration outside Soviet borders.

From 1944 until July 1945, roughly 1.5 million displaced people returned to Soviet control. Over the next four months, some 3 million additional repatriates would arrive.[10] The picture that emerges from the border between the zones of Germany is so chaotic that it seems likely that Soviet authorities could hardly count all the returnees. In the feverish period in the summer of 1945, Colonel A. A. Razumov, the repatriation officer for Soviet-occupied Germany, claimed that the Western Allies sent hundreds of thousands of people without lists.[11] At the Soviet border, NKVD officials lodged similar complaints about how the Red Army organized repatriation; convoys of thousands of people were arriving without registration lists, let alone documents about their political verification.[12]

Once the returnees were under Red Army control, repatriation officers divided them into civilians and POWs for processing at transfer points (*sborno-peresylochnye punkty*) spread across Soviet-occupied Europe. The army operated 157 such points, which as planned could house 1.3 million people.[13] However, the number of repatriates quickly exceeded this capacity, especially at points close to the zonal borders. Camp 272 near Meissen (Saxony) was equipped for 15,000 people but by June 16 contained over 21,000. With so many people, the camp rapidly exhausted its food stores. Colonel Razumov ordered repatriates to less burdened camps and simultaneously "forced" the transfer of 100,000 former POWs into reserve units eastward.[14]

At the transfer points, civilians returning to the USSR were supposed to join echelons for transit home by train or truck. Almost immediately, plans to use motor transport proved unrealistic. In June, GKO revised its orders for using transit and introduced a "combined" system that included marches. Of the 713,500 returnees supposed to arrive in the USSR in July, 88,500 of the repatriates—those who were healthy and unmarried—were expected to march up to thirty-five kilometers daily while their baggage traveled by truck. In the end, however, only 13,000 went by foot. Some avoided the march by asserting that they were family members of older or pregnant repatriates. But disorder in occupied Germany also meant that those capable of marching were often those capable of organizing transport independently. Meanwhile, those who needed help—the elderly, the ill, and those with small children—could wait for weeks or months while repatriation officials arranged transport.[15]

A typical case of return is that of Aleksandra Mikhaleva, a Kursk deportee. She and four other women from her hometown went from their barracks at Waltershausen to Soviet-occupied Chemnitz (Saxony) on June 9, where they slept outside with hundreds of other Soviet people. Five people died of exposure during the night.[16] The group managed to get on a slow-moving train with liberated Soviet POWs going seventy kilometers north to Riesa, where the Red Army had organized a transit camp. After spending a night at the Riesa train station, they learned that the camp was another twenty kilometers away and that they would have to walk, dragging their suitcases with them. By the time a passing truck offered a ride, they had traveled just five kilometers in two hours and abandoned much of their baggage to lighten their load. They rested for several days at the Riesa camp before its commandant placed the five women in an echelon of a hundred returnees going eastward by train. The convoy took a week to travel three hundred kilometers to Oels (today Oleśnica, Poland). At Oels an army captain, hoping to earn Mikhaleva's favor, secured a room in an apartment for the women. Mikhaleva refused his advances, and the captain left them alone in relative comfort until they could pass through filtration and be assigned transport. They stayed at Oels for two months before they received papers to go home.[17]

When returnees crossed into the USSR, they encountered NKVD border camps, called verification-filtration points (*proverochno-fil'tratsionnye punkty*). For those who had already passed verification, the facilities were supposed to provide food and shelter during a short wait for transit home. Returnees who lost their filtration records, never received them, or seemed untrustworthy might be detained for verification. Just as in the army's transit camps, the NKVD border points were ill-equipped to handle thousands of people arriving at irregular intervals. In May a group of 107 returnees arrived at the border point at Khyriv (Lviv province) with their papers in order. The commandant checked their documents and sent them away to stay at the train station while they waited indefinitely for transport. The returnees, including fifty-six children, lived outside for as long as five days, having received just two days' rations.[18] When repatriates received tickets, the itineraries sometimes took them just part of the way home. Nikolai Karpov, a twelve-year-old returning from Germany with his grandmother to Smolensk province, received tickets from the border to Viciebsk (Belarus)—some 250 kilometers from their home. They sneaked on trains the rest of the way, narrowly avoiding trouble when the conductor discovered they had no tickets.[19]

In their home districts, repatriates were supposed to receive official assistance with reintegration. In the Baltic republics, Belarus, western Russia, and Ukraine, each province formed one or more reception-distribution points (*priemno-raspredelitel'nye punkty*) to organize transport, jobs, housing, and financial assistance. Republics received millions of rubles to provide the neediest repatriates with subsidies of up to 300 rubles, the equivalent of a month's salary or more. Not all returnees knew they were eligible for aid, though. Lithuanian repatriation workers noted that returnees would settle into their homes only to petition for aid weeks later after learning that others had received cash and "American presents" of clothing and shoes. Obliviousness and disorganization led repatriates in Belarus to claim just 20 percent of the available 24 million rubles.[20]

Perhaps the main reason that few repatriates took state aid was that many did not return via officially mandated channels. They avoided filtration outside the USSR either because they feared repression or because they had tired of waiting weeks or months to return. By August 1945, the Repatriation Administration in Belarus had counted as many as 100,000 returnees. Only 40,000 had arrived in "an organized manner," via filtration camps and the administration's reception-distribution points.[21] In January 1946, a secret police report from Ukraine found that 379,228 of 652,958 repatriates had not undergone filtration in their home districts.[22]

Filtration officers could hardly process the huge numbers of people arriving daily in camps. In the Central Army Group (Austria, Czechoslovakia, and Hungary), roving NKVD commissions serviced repatriate camps. Over the summer and fall of 1945, its officers spent a combined 22,178 days investigating 237,804 returnees. Rough math would suggest that each officer saw between ten and eleven people per day, but this figure does not include rest days. And filtration officers were not conducting investigations every minute of their workdays. Under the generous assumption that they worked filtration cases six days a week for nine hours a day, each repatriate would have taken forty-five minutes on average, including interviews and paperwork. Officers could hardly have conducted a serious investigation in that time.[23]

The filtration investigation—really a short interview—was a formality in most cases. Investigators typically asked how returnees had been deported or captured, where they had been abroad, and whether they had faced arrest during the war. Some waited months for an officer to interview them for a few minutes.[24] A minority of cases became serious investigations because documentary evidence was available, informers made accusations, or the returnee had been captured in an enemy military unit. Filtration officers in most instances had returnees' own testimony as the only evidence of their conduct. Many former members of pro-German formations invented new names and identities for themselves.[25] The verification process could be so superficial, however, that even returnees with damning wartime records did not need to adopt false names. Under American occupation, Ilia Sherstiuk, a Ukrainian propagandist trained at the Wustrau camp, first lived in a barracks with a group of men who had served in pro-German units and hoped to avoid repatriation. After a few weeks there, he moved to another barracks, where the residents wanted to return and apparently had cleaner wartime records. From there he went to the Soviet zone under his own name with no apparent problems.[26] Some returnees volunteered confessions that they had been pro-German auxiliaries and put themselves at the mercy of filtration officers, who sometimes recruited them to spy on other returnees.[27]

Investigators conducted weeks- or months-long verifications of people who fit into target groups. Obvious cases for investigation were the thousands of people that the Western Allies had captured in pro-German units and transferred to Soviet control at the end of the war; almost all these people faced some form of repression. People from national groups like ethnic Germans or Crimean Tatars, whom the Germans had been especially eager to enlist, came under investigation more often than ethnic Russians. Men came under investigation more frequently than women because Germany and its allies had more often recruited them during the war. Investigators also scrutinized people with unusual paths back to the USSR. Nadezhda Severilova, the young woman from Kyiv who lived for a year in Naples as Nella Antilucci, was kept for a year in a transit camp in Austria after she decided to return to the USSR. She worked at the camp's library while police continued to interrogate her about her travels in Europe.[28]

Fearing repression in the USSR, some who had served in pro-German units resisted repatriation fiercely. At the notorious Dachau concentration camp, converted into a holding camp for POWs, the US Army prepared to give Soviet authorities 475 people accused of serving in various pro-German formations in January 1946. After the prisoners delayed their transfer through protest, US commanders acceded to Soviet demands to use force. As American soldiers set off tear gas and beat those who resisted, 14 committed suicide and 17 sustained injuries that sent them to the hospital.[29]

Of the 4.2 million people who returned from displacement from outside the USSR's borders by the spring of 1946, police arrested 6.5 percent (272,867) during filtration. Most came from the ranks of POWs, among whom the arrest rate was 14.7 percent. Among civilian repatriates, roughly 1.8 percent faced arrest (see table I.2). Overall, it is safe to conclude that most arrested returnees (but not all) were former members of various German-commanded formations, groups that state orders specifically targeted. Most were exiled to special settlements in distant areas of the Soviet Union for six-year terms. Official repression took forms beyond arrest. After the war ended, NKVD border points sent former prisoners of war and military-age, male forced laborers to labor battalions across the USSR. They amounted to 14.5 percent of returnees from abroad. As workers in coal and heavy industry, they awaited political verification indefinitely—typically several months or more—before the enterprise converted most into ordinary laborers. This was effectively forced resettlement, although few were charged with any crime.[30]

The remaining 58 percent of returnees "went home." These returnees were more often women, since men were disproportionately sent to the army or to labor battalions. In Ukraine two-thirds of the returnees through April 1946 were female.[31] The category of homebound returnees masked state repression, as the NKVD sent members of national groups such as ethnic Germans, Ingrian Finns, and Crimean Tatars away from their homes to exile or to work in industrial settlements. The number of deportees was perhaps as many as 5 percent of all returnees.[32] Most repatriates nonetheless went to their home regions. This fact does not excuse the repression Soviet authorities applied to many undeservedly. However, it suggests that Soviet policy prioritized verification, reintegration, and economic recovery over repression.

Stalinist leaders did not order all returnees to the Gulag but also did not treat them kindly. The disarray of the war and its aftermath, and the lack of resources it entailed, meant that Stalin's regime was unable or unwilling to ensure repatriation occurred in an organized manner. An element of official hostility was built into this chaos. Regime leaders tended to favor scrutiny over speed. And they could have allotted more resources to feed and transport returnees but chose not to prioritize people who, in the minds of many officials, had served the enemy. The limitations of state capacity meant that necessities—transit, food, organization—were lacking for a population whose requirements did not rank high among leaders' concerns. This factor helped people who wished to avoid verification. For most, however, it meant that soldiers outside Soviet borders and local bosses within the USSR gained considerable authority over their lives.

Displaced under Soviet Rule

Liberated Soviet forced laborers bore many of the typical characteristics of refugees. They often lacked documents to prove their identities and previous activities. Most had little in the way of belongings, savings, or helpful contacts in Europe. They depended on aid from Soviet occupation forces, placing them at the mercy of local military administrations that doled out assistance. They carried the additional burden of having worked for the enemy, albeit against their will, and compromised biographies sharpened their vulnerability as refugees in Europe.

As the Red Army occupied land beyond Soviet borders, it targeted ethnic Germans for plunder.[33] Repatriates sometimes took part in these thefts. At Frankfurt (Oder), Soviet army police detained 1,082 repatriates for various crimes, primarily theft, during the first three weeks of August 1945. Near Krakow, groups of repatriates took advantage of the marginalization of ethnic Germans, people who would soon be expelled from Poland. Returnees even joined forces with soldiers to conduct armed robbery in the German countryside.[34]

Displacement and questionable wartime records made returnees into victims more often than perpetrators. Although police verification was often superficial, its arbitrariness also allowed NKVD and army counterintelligence (SMERSH, an abbreviation of Smert' Shpionam that means "Death to Spies") officers to exploit the power they had over returnees. Repatriation administrators inspecting transfer points in Germany found that security officers routinely stole watches and gold "under the guise of a security deposit."[35] Some returnees did not need prompting to offer bribes. One repatriate woman, the widow of an executed "enemy of the people," traded a gold necklace—her husband's wedding gift, carefully hidden throughout her time in Germany—for a verification report that would eventually allow her to return to Leningrad.[36]

Most camps for repatriates were next to army settlements. Soldiers regularly invaded these lodgings, asserting that returnees deserved punishment for their wartime biography—even if the state was unwilling to mete it out during filtration. Self-righteous soldiers conducted violent robberies of returnees, their inhibitions often loosened by alcohol. On the night of November 7, 1945, near Bunzlau (today Boleslawiec, Poland), the deputy commander, chief of staff, and other officers from an artillery regiment broke into the repatriate camp after a night of drinking. Two of the repatriates supposedly insulted the officers, and the deputy commander responded, "They're Vlasovites, beat them!" One returnee managed to hide while the officers caught and beat the other. When duty officers arrived to check on the commotion, they stopped the fight but also stole a bike and a radio from the repatriates' dormitory. The two superior officers received five-day sentences while their accomplices apparently went unpunished.[37] In such incidents, soldiers took advantage of the physical vulnerability of the displaced and exercised popular conceptions of postwar retribution as excuses to abuse returnees.

Repatriate women were doubly vulnerable as the targets of sexual violence. Soldiers in World War II raped women for a number of reasons: as a show of dominance, as revenge against enemies and traitors, or because the opportunity was available.[38] When Soviet soldiers raped repatriate women, they were often driven by a sense of soldierly privilege. The explanation an arrested officer gave for his attempted rape of a woman on the First Ukrainian Front was typical: "I came from the front and need a girl."[39] Soviet authorities and soldiers assumed that many women who had lived abroad or under occupation had extensive sexual encounters with Germans. A political officer in the Repatriation Administration in Germany wrote that after the experience of living abroad "many girls drink wine, smoke, act rudely." He laid the blame for outbreaks of venereal disease on the repatriate women, rather than on the Soviet and non-Soviet men who had sex with them, frequently under coercive circumstances.[40]

Soldiers proclaimed that women's supposed wartime treason demanded punishment—often through sexual coercion. Polina E. became involved in a forced relationship with a SMERSH officer. Because she was fluent in German, the officer summoned her from a transit camp to interview for the job of translator. During the meeting he peppered her with loaded questions, "Who are you—a fascist or not?" Perhaps the most important question came at the end. The officer proposed that they "cohabitate." Polina E. in a post-Soviet interview overlooked the coercion at the core of the relationship. She claimed to have consented because it meant that she would be able to return to the USSR with a husband. Within a year she became pregnant and had to return to the Soviet Union. Polina E., like other women who had relationships with soldiers in Germany, learned upon arrival in the USSR that the officer already had a family.[41]

The disorder in Soviet-occupied territories makes any attempt to establish even an approximate number of rapes of repatriates virtually impossible. Soviet soldiers seem to have committed fewer rapes of repatriate women than of German women, which scholars have estimated variously between one hundred thousand and two million.[42] However, assaults against Soviet women existed in the same continuum of sexualized retribution. In Flatow (today Złotów, Poland) on the night of May 9, 1945, three drunken soldiers from the NKVD military police found a house where Soviet citizens due for repatriation were staying. Under the guise of an official assignment, the leader of the group had the two soldiers lead the male repatriates outside, leaving him alone with the one woman in the house. After she refused his advances, he raped her. The officer received a three-year sentence for sexually assaulting his fellow Soviet. This sentence was in line with what soldiers could expect to receive if they were convicted of raping German women. A soldier from the same unit received a two-year sentence for raping a seventeen-year-old German, and another received a four-year sentence for raping a fifteen-year-old German.[43]

Soviet officials lamented that sexual coercion occurred between soldiers and repatriates but described most incidents as "cohabitation" (*sozhitel'stvo*). This euphemism included genuine relationships alongside sexual assault but hid the coercive dynamic in most cases. A surprise inspection at a camp in Germany in August 1945 found that almost all Red Army officers in the area were sleeping with repatriate women. Just as life in the forced labor camps had encouraged women to engage in sexual barter, access to goods and privileges drew the repatriate women to Red Army personnel.[44] In a regiment in the Second Air Army in Poland, thirty-eight unemployed repatriate women lived with officers. An officer from a different unit in the army lived with a woman whom he registered as a military cook, although she did not work.[45] In the anonymous memoir *A Woman in Berlin*, the German author described how after multiple rapes by Red Army soldiers she offered herself to a single officer to gain protection from worse abuses.[46] It seems probable that repatriate women entered similar relationships with Red Army men to avoid assault by others.

In addition to providing living quarters and goods, a woman's decision to have sex with an officer could determine whether she would go home or be accused of treason. In July 1945, the commandant at an NKVD border camp sent a young woman to the local military doctor for inspection for venereal disease. When she received a clean bill of health, the commandant hired her as his personal cook. Two days later, she returned to the doctor and asked his help to escape the commandant: "I don't want to use my body to pleasure the guests of the lieutenant colonel." Days later, and surely not by coincidence, the NKVD arrested her as a spy.[47]

Repatriates had few options to repulse the violence visited upon them. In at least one case, though, repatriate women took matters into their own hands. At a transfer point in Germany in July 1945, a group of vigilantes headed by a woman organized an improvised trial of officers for sexual violence, executing those it found guilty.[48] Surely there were other occasions when repatriates answered violence with violence, just as there were many more episodes when abuses against returnees went unrecorded. As Colonel Razumov, the officer in charge of repatriation in Germany, asserted, during the massive influx of people in the summer of 1945 such incidents had received little attention.[49]

The Eastern Front was a violent place, and the coercion repatriates faced in Soviet occupied zones was in part a product of this environment.[50] The backdrop of violence cannot entirely explain the way that Red Army soldiers targeted repatriates, though. Many soldiers viewed them as traitors who were deserving targets for retribution. Just as important—they were easy targets as refugees in need of assistance in their travels. Safety only came as the occupation regime in Germany stabilized and as returnees came home in the second half of 1945.

Cold Homecomings

Repatriates arrived in a devastated Soviet Union. Eastern Workers had been deported from areas that experienced years of occupation and fighting. People in these regions saw the destruction of their homes, famine, and violent treatment by the occupiers—and sometimes again by the Red Army. In Ukraine, which had supplied the largest number of Eastern Workers, a virtual civil war raged between anti-Soviet nationalists and Soviet forces for years after 1945.[51] Despite the backdrop of conflict, overt violence against returnees abated as they returned to their prewar homes. The power imbalance between returnees and other locals was not as pronounced as between displaced persons and Red Army soldiers. Nonetheless, scarcity and the widespread notion that repatriates had betrayed the motherland fostered conflicts between those who had remained and those who had left.

One reason that locals distrusted repatriates was the popular rumor that returnees had become rich in Germany. The occupiers had promised that Eastern Workers would enjoy excellent conditions in the Reich. Realities had disappointed those who believed these assurances. Remittances sent to family in the occupied territories were rare, and wages for the laborers were minimal to nonexistent.[52] Nonetheless, it seems that Soviet people imagined their compatriots enriching themselves in the capitalist world. Soldiers returning from Germany took boxes and boxes of goods—why would civilian returnees not do so also?[53] By law repatriates could transport unlimited belongings, even cattle, into the USSR without being subject to customs. Perhaps a lucky few arrived with piles of suitcases packed with valuables. The majority had accumulated little. Ukrainian repatriates arriving by train by the spring of 1946 were reported to have taken an average of twenty-three kilograms of luggage with them—the equivalent of a full checked bag on a flight today.[54] The notion of repatriate wealth was so persistent, however, that even parents were incredulous when their children came back from Germany empty-handed. When Zinaida B. arrived at home, her father's first words were, "Let's go, where are your things? We'll take your things." She had to break the disappointing news that she did not come back with "riches from Germany" but instead with one half-broken suitcase.[55] Perhaps believing the rumor themselves, repatriation officials held "long conversations" with resentful local authorities about customs laws that allowed returnees to take "all that they were able to take."[56]

Returnees' supposed wealth convinced local leaders that there was no need to assist them. A repatriation official in Belarus noted that people who had lived through the occupation complained that returnees had suffered less than those who had remained. One person was quoted as saying, "We weren't taken to Germany but instead stayed home. We have nothing because the Germans took or destroyed everything."[57] Funds allotted to returnees seemed to disappear into local budgets. In the Ukrainian town of Smila, a returnee who found her home occupied by strangers was refused help from the town council, although it had received 300,000 rubles from the Ukrainian government to use as aid.[58] Local leaders from a district in Kyiv province argued that instead of needing aid, "More likely is that we will have to force them to work."[59]

Many local authorities shared the opinion that repatriates owed labor to their communities. In a village in Kyiv province, the local NKVD head directed the village council to put repatriates to work at night stacking grain so that the other residents could rest. In the city of Poltava, municipal leaders who received orders to mobilize a thousand people to conduct unpaid timber felling sent repatriates alone to do the arduous work.[60] A Ukrainian repatriate from Lysniaky, Volyn province, wrote that "comrades from the NKVD" advised her to find work at the local butter factory. The head of her village's council disagreed: she and other repatriates must work for him a minimum of fifty days in manual labor—loading grain or mining peat—and only then could they work anywhere else.[61]

Finding living space was difficult, too. Some cities saw virtually every building destroyed or damaged. In addition to this problem, occupation facilitated appropriation that introduced the messy problem of establishing what belonged to whom.[62] Repatriates were not the only people looking for housing as they returned to their homes. The millions of people who returned from evacuation in the Soviet hinterland faced resistance when they tried to reclaim living space or find new housing.[63] The deficit was so challenging that even demobilized soldiers had trouble finding housing, spurring state programs to provide apartments to veterans and their families.[64] Repatriates' troubles with finding shelter were compounded by their arriving later than most evacuees and the stigma they bore for having been in the Reich. When repatriates to Pleshchenitsy (Minsk province) claimed their prewar property, townspeople accused them of belonging to families with pro-German police and demanded they forfeit the houses.[65] Anna Shirokaia, who returned to her house in Staline (today's Donetsk), came home one day to find that the city's procurator had sent a woman, the head of a local government store, to live with her. When Shirokaia protested, her new roommate's brother beat her, and the municipal court dismissed her lawsuit because she had been in Germany.[66]

Many returnees had no home waiting for them. Almost a quarter of returnees to Russia received housing by begging authorities to assign them even a corner of a room in someone else's home.[67] Eight hundred returnees to Staline province who were assigned to work in heavy industry enterprises lived for months in a 720-square-meter basement. Even after a state inspector declared the basement unfit for living, 286 people continued to reside there. A visiting repatriation official from Moscow asked the chair of a factory workshop party committee, "Why do you treat people that way?" He responded, "They're just repatriates." Perhaps conditions in Staline were especially bad because city workers in charge of repatriation disparaged the returnees. One was quoted as saying, "A repatriate is not a person. A noose is waiting for all of them."[68]

Central directives barred repatriates from living within a hundred kilometers of the restricted cities of Kyiv, Leningrad, and Moscow. Although some managed to receive special permission for residency, or lived in these cities without authorization, the rule created opportunities for employers to prey upon returnees. When returnees to Kyiv were turned away from the city, representatives from enterprises in the area were on hand at the provincial reception point at Myronivka. In June 1945, an official from the local peat plant recruited new returnees by telling them that their daily walk to work would be ten kilometers shorter than it really was and that their daily norm of bricks was five hundred fewer.[69] Officials in the Repatriation Administration in Moscow theorized that they only learned about abuses at Myronyvka and the surrounding area because many of the repatriates were former students from Kyiv, and thus more willing to assert their rights as Soviet citizens.[70]

The desire of students to resume their education was another source of tension. Twenty-year-old Liudmila Goncharenko from Smila applied to finish her ten-year grade school education, but the town head demanded she work "on the rocks" at the local mine. "I'm your boss here, and you don't have the right to study."[71] When Nadezhda Podenko from Kyiv province quit her job at a peat mine to go back to school, a boss from the mine appeared at her door, swearing, "You're going to be put behind bars you German lackey, I'll get you a whole year. Oh, you German reptile, you prostitute, you German slut." Podenko appealed the case to the local procurator, but he took no action.[72] Repatriates younger than sixteen numbered 39,294 in Ukraine, and many returning young adults had never finished their education because of the war. As of April 1946, however, just 24,183 returnees were enrolled in educational institutions.[73]

Neighbors commonly accused returnees of having become "Germans." It is possible the assertion reflected real differences between returnees and their neighbors. Hundreds of thousands had been in close contact with Germans as farm laborers or servants in households. Nadezhda Severilova had not only learned German but became fluent enough in Italian that the Italian consul in Munich believed she might be from Naples.[74] Like Severilova, most returnees were under twenty-two and had spent crucial years of socialization in Germany.[75] A party official from Kharkiv province singled out the young as the most problematic among returnees: "It is very hard to make them say what they think. They speak in ready clichés." Young returnees had lost their ability to employ the discourse of Stalin's regime. Although they used the slogans political officers fed them, they did so without fluency, leading the official to assert that they were masking their "true face."[76]

Signs of foreignness among repatriates in the countryside caused sharp divisions. After the Myronivka reception point assigned thirty young repatriates to work at the Vodianka collective farm, the locals accused them of forming a faction and "boasting of their attire brought from Germany and their knowledge of the German language." Villagers at another collective farm in Kyiv province accused returning youth of speaking German and claiming that they had forgotten their native language. For a Sunday stroll at the local bazaar, a repatriate woman in the town of Kagarlyk put on the dress, hat, and veil she brought from Germany. Her appearance drew the attention of collective farmers who spat curses as they followed her. The party report on the incident claimed that an NKVD officer had to escort her from the market "to avoid excesses."[77] The accusation of "Germanness" not only portrayed repatriates as un-Soviet but implied that they had collaborated with the enemy.

The role of the police in these incidents was complex. Some lower-level officers took part in the exploitation, but others protected returnees from the whims of local bosses. When fifteen-year-old Bronislava A. returned to the Minsk area after forced labor, an NKVD officer who signed her paperwork to go to school advised her, "Never tell anyone who you are and what you are. Tell them you lived under occupation with your parents."[78] Postal censors suppressed letters returnees sent about their desperate straits. Yet police monitored the letters not only to repress unflattering information but also to act upon issues that repatriates raised. The conclusion of a police report about repatriates from July 1946 was that they were facing serious problems with housing and food. In one letter, a woman from the city of Makiivka (Staline province) wrote that she had returned to find that none of her relatives or acquaintances lived there anymore (or were alive—the language is unclear). She had ten years of schooling, a substantial education in the USSR, yet she was jobless. "To think that someone like me . . . would be a beggar in the Soviet Union," she wrote.[79] Police leaders pressured party officials to take these matters seriously and improve conditions.

Police and party officials fluctuated between sympathy and suspicion. On August 4, 1945, the Organizational Bureau of the Communist Party's Central Committee, responsible for cadre management, issued a resolution condemning the "unfounded suspicion" of party workers toward returnees: "It is necessary to remember that [they] have regained all rights belonging to a Soviet citizen."[80] Even for concerned Soviet officials, though, the danger remained that enemies were masking themselves as victimized returnees. As the head of the Repatriation Administration in Lithuania noted, enemies "could arrive in the guise of a repatriate."[81]

Official suspicion contributed to wariness toward returnees. Soviet people's experiences under Stalin had taught them that keeping the wrong friends could earn them a Gulag sentence. During the Great Terror of 1937–38, police officers had turned real social networks into fabricated conspiracies against Stalin's regime.[82] Thinking along these lines, a party leader in Slutsk district (Babruysk province, Belarus) wondered about repatriates, "What happens if we help them and suddenly it turns out that they were [pro-German] police?"[83] A core factor in both official and unofficial relationships with repatriates was uncertainty about who was a victim and who was an enemy.

Suspicion about repatriates in part resulted from the disconnect between the simple portrayal of the war in the Soviet media and the complex realities that had existed in Germany. In the press, returnees were called "victims of fascist captivity," a term that indicted the German occupiers and their allies. But buried in this stock phrase was a question: How had the enemy been able to enslave so many Soviet people? Film and artistic portrayals of repatriates, few as they were, usually depicted passive women and children liberated by the men of the Red Army (figure 5.1). In the film *The Fall of Berlin* (1949), the main character, worker Aleksei Ivanov, is with his love, Natasha, when the Germans attack his town on June 22, 1941. Gravely wounded, Aleksei falls into a coma and only three months later learns that the Germans have taken Natasha as a forced laborer. Although he was unable to protect her, he rights this wrong by fighting all the way to Berlin and freeing her. The film's narrative about repatriates was convenient: Soviet women had become forced laborers only because of German treachery and extraordinary circumstances.

A more complex treatment is found in *Girl 217* (*Chelovek* [Person] *No. 217*, 1944), directed by famed filmmaker Mikhail Romm. The hero, a young Slavic woman named Tania, becomes an Eastern Worker sent to be a domestic servant for a German family who treats her like a slave. After the murder of a fellow Eastern Worker by the family's eldest son and his friend, both German soldiers on leave, Tania musters the courage to kill the two soldiers and flee during a Red Army bombing. This unusual portrayal of active resistance is problematic in its

FIGURE 5.1.   Liberation of Eastern Workers. Drawing by Veniamin Briskin, ca. 1945. Courtesy Allan Gamborg of Soviet Digital Art.

own way, because real resistance was usually less dramatic and occurred amid compromises with German authorities. Moreover, the film shows Tania's ultimate escape as dependent on the intervention of Soviet forces and evades the question of how she became a forced laborer.

The truth of the war was more complicated and, from the official Soviet perspective, shameful than such representations. The Red Army could not stop the German offensives of 1941–42, and Soviet people who had lived under occupation could not prevent the occupiers from kidnapping millions of people.

The politics of wartime guilt contributed to the conflicts between returnees and their neighbors. Repatriate Antonina M. returned from forced labor with a child. She told neighbors, just as she told post-Soviet interviewers, that the father was a Soviet POW. Accused by a neighbor woman, the wife of a former POW, of having a child with a German, Antonina M. lashed out, "If your husband hadn't surrendered, I wouldn't have been taken."[84] People who had lived under occupation, too, faced accusations of collaboration and had to defend their wartime behavior.[85] At the peat processing plant at Myronivka, a dispatcher, Bormatov, responded to repatriates' grievances about their conditions by shouting, "Who are you to complain to us about bad food, you Fascist dogs? You should be happy we give you bread and soup." Complaints by repatriates led to an investigation that found the dispatcher had worked as a courier for the German occupation and saw him removed from work.[86] Bormatov's anger perhaps masked fear about his own precarious position in Soviet society. He may not have been a partisan, but at least he had stayed in his home rather than working in a factory in Germany. By marginalizing repatriates, he reinforced his own status in the postoccupation USSR as a good Soviet citizen.

The excessive reaction of Bormatov reflected a common attitude among people who had lived under occupation: the experience of a forced laborer or prisoner of war could have been no worse than the horror of the German occupation. As material hardships continued in the postwar USSR, many chose to believe that repatriates had gotten rich working on modern German farms for kind landowners or from sexual liaisons with German men. For these reasons, they seemed not to deserve assistance or goodwill from local authorities. Repatriation officials and secret police officers shared responsibility for the ubiquitous suspicion that followed returnees, but they also attempted to moderate abuse from below. Far from being the main source of returnees' misery, representatives of Moscow were often those that repatriates hoped would save them from the whims of local authorities.

Silenced Biographies

After the chaos of return in 1944–46, repatriates settled into Soviet lives. Nominally, they returned to their places as full Soviet citizens. In practice their status as quasi traitors among officials and fellow Soviets limited their opportunities. Discrimination encouraged repatriates to remain silent about their experiences during the war and in its aftermath in the years that followed—a fact that complicates the job of historians. As post-Soviet oral histories show, repatriation did not guarantee formal repression but meant pervasive discrimination at home.

When they applied for work or to school, all Soviet citizens had to complete a long form that established not only basic facts like their date of birth but also politically charged biographical elements like their family's status before the Russian Revolution or whether they had relatives living abroad. Another question appeared on applications after 1945: Where did you live during the Great Patriotic War? Employers knew that "Germany" was a potentially dangerous answer. For this reason, Mikhail B. went from factory to factory looking for work when he returned to the Russian town of Penza in 1945 after living as a POW at the Buchenwald concentration camp. His troubles were noteworthy because, having finished a technical school before the war, he should have had no trouble finding a job. It was a chance encounter with an old acquaintance that helped him find a job. The friend was a school director who invited him to work as a teacher.

Mikhail B. said, "I'll ruin your [political] biography." The friend replied, "There are no official directives not to hire you."[87] His friend was correct. Repatriates who had not faced official repression could technically work anywhere. It was fear and enmity that stopped employers from hiring them.

Mikhail B.'s case illustrates the problems returnees faced but also the power of personal contacts. The most successful repatriates were those who could rely on friends and family—people who were certain of a person's character and past.[88] Returnee Raisa B. was a young teacher when the Germans took her from a village in Belarus. Although the district NKVD denied her an internal passport, she went to Karelia with her cousin and her cousin's husband, an officer in the NKVD border guard, who helped her find work as a teacher there. She taught for several months until she was removed from the position after an officer in Petrozavodsk, Karelia's capital, learned that she was working without a passport. Her cousin's husband smoothed over the situation and found her a new job teaching in another school in Russia's north. Remarkably, Raisa B. was removed from several more positions—and each time her relative used his contacts to ensure she endured no serious trouble. Eventually, she gained and kept a position in the Murmansk area.[89]

Ambition mattered as much as personal contacts. Repatriates who sought higher-ranking positions had more difficulty finding work and faced more scrutiny after they were hired. Olga G. was an upwardly mobile young woman whose prewar job in radio had led her to become a radio operator in the Red Army during the war. During her first mission, she was captured and spent two years as a prisoner at the Ravensbrück concentration camp. After liberation she managed to come to Moscow, and a former boss hired her in the radio administration when he learned she had been unable to find work. Her biography soon raised questions within the administration, and she was fired with no explanation. Olga G. decided to appeal to a higher authority in Mikhail Suslov, the Communist Party Central Committee secretary responsible for matters involving ideology and communication. Olga G. recalled how one of Suslov's assistants, having summoned her and the radio official who had fired her, shouted, "How dare you fire a person based on four lines of their biographical form? Who gave you the right?" Despite this display of indignation, Suslov's clerk did not return Olga G. to her previous job but found her a position in a different bureaucracy, believing that the incident would sour her relationship with supervisors in the radio administration.[90] Specialists who had difficulties like Olga G.'s were common. In Estonia, repatriation leaders reported that no enterprise would hire a specialist worker without a letter from the deputy head of the republic's Council of Ministers.[91]

The outcome in Olga G.'s case was relatively fortunate. After her return to Voronezh, Liudmila G. only found work through her sister's friend, the mistress of an official at the Sacco and Vanzetti factory, one of the major employers in the town. Her boss, despite his better judgment, hired her knowing that she had been in Germany. Liudmila G. recalled that he treated her well, even taking her to work with him when he left the factory for a new job. Yet he always feared there would be consequences for hiring a repatriate. When party commissions inspected the factory, her boss told her to hide, and he instructed her to omit her having been in Germany on work documents. It is apparent that the boss insisted on these measures above all to protect himself. When outside officials learned that Liudmila G. had been in Germany, her boss fired her.[92]

The fear of association with repatriates also presented an obstacle to entry into political organizations like the Communist Party and the Communist Youth League. Nikolai G., a young man from Rostov, managed to find a job at a metalware factory upon return and by 1946 had joined the Komsomol. Indeed, he became the leader of the youth group in his workshop. In 1947 the chief hiring officer unexpectedly called Nikolai G. to his office, accused him of being a spy, and fired him. It is unclear what prompted his dismissal. Possibly his selection as workshop youth organizer had drawn attention to his biography. Another oral history respondent recalled that after he became his army unit's Komsomol secretary in 1947, his supervisor denounced him as a former forced laborer, which ultimately led to his arrest.[93] Alarmed by the precarity of his situation, Nikolai G. went to his local Komsomol organization to resign from the youth league, despite the insistence of the district youth leader that everything would pass.[94]

Uncertainty over repatriates' place in political organizations would continue well after Stalin's death in 1953. Petr A. attempted to join the Communist Party in 1956, the year that Premier Nikita Khrushchev forcefully denounced Stalin in the "Secret Speech," but the members of his prospective party cell "looked at me like a fascist" and rejected him.[95] Oleksandr I., who had been sixteen in 1942 when the Germans took him as a forced laborer, only joined his factory's party cell in 1967 after multiple invitations and assurances from his colleagues that his time in Germany would not be a problem.[96]

How many people tried to join the party or Komsomol only to be turned away is impossible to know. Party and youth organizations apparently kept no records of how many repatriates were accepted. Repatriation officials compiled reports about the number of prewar specialists (e.g., engineers or veterinarians) who found work in their areas of expertise and about the dozens of returnees who went on to become heads of collective farms and villages in the first few years after return. Such data allowed repatriation officers to assert that reintegration was complete and implicitly justified the administration's lack of interest in monitoring the fates of returnees beyond the initial period after arrival. After all, the Repatriation Administration focused primarily on the moment of migration and, increasingly from 1946, on appealing to nonreturners.[97] Yet these raw statistics about returnees who returned to work as specialists do not reflect the decline in status that many experienced after return. V. I. Storozhenko, for example, had been a propaganda lecturer for the Kyiv city party organization before his capture by the Germans in 1941. After he returned, he became a clerk in a photo shop. Soviet statistics would record both his prewar and postwar jobs as white-collar occupations, but his new position had none of the influence or connections of his old.[98] The omission of data about party membership in repatriation statistics suggests what is apparent from oral history testimony—that the war was a stain on repatriates' biographies that impeded promotion. Some political organizers viewed repatriates as traitors who had no place in political organizations or in significant positions. For others, including for some repatriates themselves, the stigma and the associated threat of denunciation and arrest were enough to preclude entry into political organizations and promotion at work.

Professional and political marginalization spilled over into private life. Zinaida B. aspired to a managerial role at the butter factory at Kharkiv and attributed her languid rise up the ranks to informal discrimination. The combination of ambition and her past also affected her relationships. She recalled, "The collective around me was mostly interested in their careers. They were men who wanted to gain promotions, not simple workers or collective farmers." Each relationship she started with a man from this circle ended when her romantic interest realized that her German past would be an obstacle to his career. Meanwhile, because she was unmarried, childless, and a repatriate, it was easier for the factory to send her on long work trips, which further exacerbated her relationship problems.[99]

For repatriate women who had lesser ambitions, marriage could help erase their German past. After returning to her native Cherkessk in Russia's North Caucasus, Antonina V. married and changed her last name. She moved to Leningrad in 1947 and changed her address, which further obscured her legal identity. Until the fall of the Soviet Union, she refused to talk about her time in Germany, even with her family, to avoid "any unpleasantries."[100]

The shadow of wartime forced labor led some to make compromises in their personal lives. Upon her return to Kursk, Aleksandra Mikhaleva at first longed for her Italian boyfriend, Ugo, but she soon moved on and began to date local men. In January 1947, she married a man named Konstantin after knowing him for two weeks. Had Mikhaleva found a Soviet man who was cultured like her wartime European boyfriends and fallen in love at first sight? In 2019, I found Mikhaleva's adult grandson through a journalist in Kursk and asked about the hurried nuptials. According to family lore, friends introduced the two because both had troubled biographies: she was a repatriate, and he was a social outcast who had suffered from fits of depression in his youth. Both were ready to marry but could not find anyone who would take them. Mikhaleva's final diary entry, from 1949, discusses her ambivalence about the relationship. Konstantin, a geological surveyor who was frequently away for work, treated her well but was inattentive. After this entry, she hid her journals and told no one about them until she gave them to her oldest grandson in the 1990s.[101]

The intersection of formal and informal discrimination convinced returnees like Mikhaleva to remain silent about the war. Antonina S., the former forced laborer who had moved to France with her husband, Claude, only to be forcibly repatriated with her newborn, refused to tell her son who his father was for years. She changed his last name to hers and told him that his father was a doctor who had died in the war. Only in the 1960s, during the relaxation under Khrushchev that would lead to increasing international contacts, would Antonina S. be able to call Claude and tell her son who his father was.[102] A similar case was that of Galina G.—a woman who was separated from her French husband, Emil, during his repatriation to France via Odesa. She managed to hide that she had been in Germany when she applied for admission to an institute and throughout her career. Her Soviet husband, whom she married in 1950, died in the 1990s not knowing that she had been a forced laborer in Germany. Her son knew only because she told him about his biological father in 1960. Yet continuing apprehensions about her wartime experience caused her to hide Emil's photograph until 2004.[103]

Returnees became second-class citizens in the USSR for the sin of having been the lowliest of workers in Hitler's forced labor empire. Popular resentment transformed into abuses when state and occupation authorities would not or could not defend returnees. In Soviet-occupied Europe, the chaos of the wartime and postwar periods made repatriate women a target for opportunistic sexual abuse, while accusations of their amorality justified sexualized violence as a form of revenge. The fact of returnees' displacement created conditions for exploitation that are nearly universal among displaced peoples, a condition that one scholar has termed "refugeedom."[104]

An element of official hostility contributed to repatriates' difficulties by giving license to their tormentors. Stalin and other Soviet leaders could have protected returnees with strong, public messages about their status as citizens in good standing. Instead, central leaders demanded that repatriates endure the verification of their wartime biographies, a process that signaled reasons to suspect the returnees. At the same time, higher authorities in the Repatriation Administration were as often defenders from local abuses as they were facilitators of scrutiny. Even the secret police occupied a role between protector and persecutor. As in other postwar states, the capacity of central authorities in the USSR was limited, and their attitudes toward the migrants were mixed.

Returnees endured limitations and scrutiny for the rest of their lives, even if they did not face formal punishment. As a rule, those with smaller ambitions and stronger social networks had fewer difficulties than those whose aspirations were higher and connections were weaker. In almost all cases, though, the stain of spending the war in Germany diminished opportunities. There was no central directive about how officials should rate repatriates as potential employees. Arguably, uncertainty about their status intensified informal discrimination. This dynamic was characteristic of Stalin's USSR, where it was safer to avoid contact with people with problematic biographies than to expose oneself to the potential accusation of protecting enemies of the state. Returnees themselves internalized these restrictions, eschewing job opportunities or applications for party membership because they anticipated, rightfully, that a higher profile could attract unwanted attention to them.

There were notable differences between repatriates' experiences in Soviet-occupied Europe and in the USSR itself. Above all, physical violence diminished considerably as returnees crossed the Soviet border and as the war receded further into the past. An important aspect of returnees' experiences did not change as they settled into their postwar lives, though. Official indifference and hostile relations within postwar society, rather than a central campaign of arrest, were chief factors that shaped their ordeal.

REPATRIATION AND THE ECONOMICS OF COERCED LABOR

Between Punishment and Pragmatism

The war with Germany ravaged the USSR. Wartime destruction led to the loss of a third of the prewar economy and the deaths of as many as twenty-seven million Soviets, approximately 14 percent of the prewar population.[1] Mobilizing surviving laborers was crucial to Stalinist leaders' plans to rebuild industry in the country. In occupied Germany, Soviet economic managers needed workers to dismantle factories for reparations. Within the USSR, repatriate labor was essential for reconstruction efforts, especially in areas that had previously been under occupation. While most repatriates and POWs wished to return to their homes, the leaders of economic ministries eyed them as a portable workforce to channel into reconstruction projects.

The conscription of returnees as laborers combined notions of punishment with the decentralization of power that occurred during the war and in the immediate postwar period. Officialdom was divided over the status of repatriates, but for many economic managers, repatriates' status as suspect people made it easy to justify mobilizing them for labor as penance. Throughout the war, liberated POWs spent months or years working in camps while they waited for police to investigate their pasts and send them back to the army or to the Gulag. At the end of the war, Stalin ordered those determined to be "Vlasovites"—a blanket term for people who had served in pro-German formations derived from General Andrei Vlasov's Russian Liberation Army—to work in so-called special exile in the most inhospitable places in the USSR. A second category of mobilized workers, liberated service-age men among Eastern Workers and POWs, Soviet leaders sent to "labor battalions" (*rabochie batal'ony*) while they underwent verification.

Of more than six hundred thousand members of the labor battalions, more than 90 percent received a clean political record, and in this sense, they were fortunate to avoid exile or the Gulag. They nonetheless were forbidden from leaving the enterprises where the government had assigned their battalion.[2] In effect, they became labor settlers in areas damaged by the war. For a third category of returnees, auxiliary workers in Soviet-occupied Eastern Europe, hostility toward them in the military also justified punishment in the form of indefinite employment abroad.

The postwar mobilization of returnees bore signs of Stalinist coercion that existed before and during the war. The planned economy, with its massive goals for industrial growth, created an insatiable hunger for labor, and managers took advantage of the displacement of various groups to press workers into state projects. In the early 1930s, regional governors hoped to develop their territories with millions of peasant workers evicted from their homes during dekulakization.[3] Starting with collectivization and continuing in the mass arrests of the 1930s, NKVD administrators managed an enormous number of Gulag laborers. Entire cities formed around forced labor camps.[4] During the war itself, supposedly unfaithful national groups like Germans and Chechens were conscripted into the Labor Army (Trudarmiia) or NKVD labor battalions in exile settlements.[5] Suspicion of groups' loyalty to Stalin's regime and accusations of political crime motivated these arrests and deportations. However, after detainees entered the system of forced labor, economic motivations often displaced political factors in determining their treatment. Officials in the Soviet economy were happy to accept detainees as seemingly cost-free labor. Repatriates differed from these previous groups in that the Soviet state was not responsible for their displacement. Yet the fact of their uprooting made it easy to send returnees to prioritized reconstruction efforts. The lack of supervision over their employment plus the assumption that repatriates were a group deserving of retribution ensured that many workers faced desperate conditions.

The three categories of returnees conscripted into labor—POWs suspected of treason, labor battalions, and workers kept in Central and Eastern Europe—also demonstrate the difference in the treatment of men and women as returnees. Soviet leaders cast men as more likely collaborators than women, and this possibility justified men's mobilization while they underwent a lengthy verification process. In contrast, women, alongside children and older men, were supposed to return home after filtration. Rather than see the mostly female workforce go to verification and a speedy return home, Red Army officers and economic managers kept them in Soviet-occupied territories, often against the wishes of leaders in Moscow.

There were many factors that determined how Soviet people returned to the USSR. Sex, timing of repatriation, and one's wartime past could make the difference between return and enlistment as a laborer far from home. In all cases where returnees were pressed into labor service, however, the stigma about their time under enemy rule provided a crucial rationalization for this treatment. At the same time, the logic of coerced labor sometimes contravened the hard-line goals of punishing collaboration and rooting out potential spies. The priorities of the Soviet state in postwar reconstruction placed the migrants in limbo between return and repression.

Double Prisoners

Prisoners of war occupied an ambivalent place for Soviet officials. According to an apocryphal story, Stalin said, "We have no prisoners of war, only traitors." The Soviet dictator perhaps never said this directly, but the sentiment manifested itself in official culture. It was common for Soviet officials to describe prisoners as "surrendering" (*sdat'sia*, literally to give oneself), suggesting that POWs were disloyal soldiers who had defected rather than fighting until incapacitation.[6] The infamous Order No. 270 of August 1941 commanded that "soldiers encircled by enemy units and divisions should fight until the last moment."[7] The order left open the question of what "the last moment" meant. Should soldiers fight to the death or until resistance was futile? This phrasing reflected the broader uncertainty over the difference between a prisoner and a defector, and ensured that liberated POWs would face scrutiny about the circumstances of their capture.

A mitigating factor in the treatment of returning POWs was that the Red Army desperately needed soldiers. At the same time, Soviet officials worried that uncontrolled reintegration of prisoners would allow spies to infiltrate the army. This suspicion was not altogether unfounded. Hundreds of thousands of Soviet POWs would serve the enemy in auxiliary formations or in other capacities. To combat this risk, all liberated POWs were supposed to undergo verification before reenlistment. Most POWs were eventually reintegrated into the army, but many spent long terms in "special camps" as members of the "special contingent," waiting to clear political verification.

The camps' nominal goal was to find spies and punish collaborators, but NKVD officials also viewed the special contingent as a source of labor. Red Army advances after the Battle of Stalingrad in January 1943 brought a particularly large surge of liberated POWs under Soviet control. In the spring of 1943, General Ivan Petrov, the head of the NKVD's Administration of Prisoners of War and Internees (Upravlenie Po Delam Voennoplennykh i Internirovannykh, UPVI), anticipated the growth of this labor force and agreed that the administration would take on extra responsibilities in coal mining and construction. But with most former prisoners returning to the army, the NKVD would soon run out of detainee workers to fulfill the contracts that UPVI had promised. In April 1943, Petrov complained to superiors that he was losing his workforce. A few months later, he ordered that all specialist workers should remain in the UPVI system even after they passed verification. Petrov was following the economic logic of the Soviet system. Workers were scarce, especially during the war years, and prison administrators like Petrov could not hire labor. They could only appeal to state leaders to provision them with more prisoners or prolong their terms. Lacking inbound prisoners, Petrov decided to fulfill his obligations by keeping the ones he had indefinitely.[8]

Some prisoners spent nearly a year in camps without being verified. Even following verification, many remained in the camps. At Camp 174 at Podolsk (Moscow province) in the spring of 1944, dozens of verified prisoners protested by refusing to work. A camp official summarized prisoners' feelings: "If you think I am guilty, take me to court, but I do not feel like I am guilty and I do not want to live and work under guard." In three months, 141 prisoners had petitioned to go to the army's storm battalions, units sent to the deadliest areas of the front, rather than remain at the camp.[9]

Unverified prisoners, and often those who had passed verification too, worked under guard, but inmates were hardly cut off from the outside world. Camp 303 in Kaliningrad (Moscow province) housed 1,400 prisoners in thirteen barracks. The site at first glance seemed to separate the inhabitants from the town. A ten-foot-high barbed-wire fence surrounded the complex, and guards kept lookout from four towers. Despite the security in place, the barrier between camp and town was porous. Over the first three months of 1944, camp police gave 119 men a clean political record. Most of the verified men remained to work at the same factory, and 45 continued to live at the camp but now enjoyed the right to come and go at will.[10] At a camp at Liubertsy, just outside of Moscow, three prisoners escaped when their workshop head, who was not an NKVD employee, allowed them to work outside a securitized area. Other factory workers invited prisoners home for drinks. A factory guard looked the other way when one prisoner received 1,500 rubles from a civilian through the gate. Relatively light punishments for "leaving work voluntarily" suggest that such incidents were frequent and difficult to control. The first violation earned a prisoner a warning, and subsequent infractions could mean five to ten days in an isolation cell.[11]

Not knowing how long they would face incarceration, many prisoners attempted escape. At Camp 283 at Stalinogorsk (Tula province), where most prisoners worked at the local coal mine, the administration introduced a pass system for visiting the city. Of approximately 20,000 prisoners, 30 to 40 prisoners went to Stalinogorsk each weekday, and as many at 240 received passes on the weekend.

The guards, often younger than the prisoners, joked with them, "Old-timer, you wouldn't run away would you?" The gentle reminder did little to stop escapes. In March 1944, a captain sent 5 prisoners to get lunch for the brigade at a store a kilometer away. Rather than return with food, they bought supplies and ran. One runaway was confined to the guardhouse but fled again after dismantling the brickwork around the window during the night. Of the 80 escapees from the camp in the first half of 1944, NKVD officers apprehended 24, almost all at the runaway's prewar place of residence.[12]

The special camps occupied a position between the army and forced labor in the Gulag. The prisoners were not free but also did not yet face a forced labor sentence. After the war with Germany ended, and with the war with Japan also ending soon in the summer of 1945, Soviet leaders faced a question: What to do with the prisoners in special camp limbo?

The economic logic of forced labor provided a solution. In July 1945, Stalin signed an amnesty for 700,000 prisoners serving short sentences—the largest amnesty ever from the Gulag—to celebrate victory over Germany. Typically amnesties and early releases allowed Gulag bosses to rid themselves of ill prisoners who were incapable of work. The scale of the July 1945 amnesty meant that many able-bodied prisoners would also be released, putting at risk some of the most sensitive and difficult projects in the USSR.[13] To replace these prisoners, Lavrentii Beria, the head of the NKVD, proposed sending special contingent prisoners and incoming Vlasovites to work in exile for six-year terms in special settlements in the Far Eastern camps (Dalstroi).[14] Stalin and Beria signed a series of similar orders transferring prisoners from the special camps to enterprises in Siberia, Central Asia, and the Far North.[15] From 1945 to the early 1950s, almost 180,000 returnee-Vlasovites would be sent to exile, most by the end of 1946.[16]

Six years of exile is a long sentence, but by Stalinist terms it was lenient. During the Great Terror a decade earlier, NKVD officers arrested and executed hundreds of thousands of people on falsified charges of conspiring with enemies of the regime. Soviet POWs whom the Western Allies captured in pro-German formations must had imagined this fate awaited them after return. Violent protests during transfer to Soviet control in Europe and the United States saw men commit suicide rather than return.[17] These incidents became the enduring image of repatriation in the West, where the emergence of the Cold War made officials and publics particularly receptive to the idea that all repatriates had faced some form of repression. The exile regime experienced by many returnees who had served in pro-German military units had security that was typically more lax than in the Gulag or the verification camps. In Karelia in September 1951, for example, an officer in the Ministry of State Security (Ministerstvo Gosudarstvennoi Bezopasnosti, MGB, the secret police) found that 140 of 3,030 exiles had hunting rifles. Local authorities had not known whether it was legal or not for exiles to own arms, and the rifles were only confiscated by order of the supervising MGB officer.[18]

Limited autonomy within their place of settlement belied the harsh conditions that exiles faced. Life in the least habitable locations of the USSR took its toll on many. Sergei Kruglov, the head of the Ministry of Internal Affairs (Ministerstvo Vnutrennikh Del, MVD, the criminal police and prison system), reported to Viacheslav Molotov in 1948 that more than a thousand exiles had become disabled from frozen limbs and chronic illnesses.[19] Moreover, the nominal six-year terms that the exiles received were deceptive. When the sentences of the earliest exiles approached their end in 1951, the MGB official in charge of special settlements, Colonel Vasilii Shiian, wrote to MGB head Viktor Abakumov that the "social danger" of the Vlasovites necessitated that they should be left in their places of exile "permanently."[20] Temporary exile turned into indefinite settlement in areas where few wished to live.

The exile of the special contingent of liberated POWs was a punishment for their alleged wartime treason. Yet the connections between industry and the secret police shaped the form, duration, and location of this punishment. Rather than sending the entire group to death, Soviet leaders wanted to exploit the men as workers and colonists on the edges of the USSR. As the end of the war minimized the need for recruitment to the army, the logic of coerced labor also turned returning military-aged men into potential economic settlers.

Labor Battalions

Until August 1945, the army accepted large numbers of returning POWs back into the ranks. At the port of Odesa in February and March 1945, some seventeen thousand former POWs arrived on Allied ships. Many seem to have served in pro-German formations. Despite their questionable records, after a preliminary investigation 85 percent went back to the Red Army, and approximately 10 percent were sent to detention or further investigation by SMERSH or the NKVD.[21]

Army service allowed people who had been in Germany to recast themselves as veterans. Vitalii Belikov, a former Eastern Worker with ties to leading Russian Orthodox clergy in Berlin, recalled how he entered the Red Army in April 1945. At his Berlin camp, the workers could already hear the battle nearby. In small groups, the workers stole away from the camp and went east until they found Soviet forces. When Belikov reached a unit, officers questioned him briefly and then had him fill out enlistment papers. The next morning, he received a private's uniform. By the time his unit was ready for active service again, the war was almost over, and the unit occupied parts of Berlin with virtually no resistance.[22]

The defeat of Japan in August 1945 obviated the need for a wartime army. On August 18, Stalin issued a secret resolution that modified previous state orders about the reintegration of POWs. The previous directive, of November 4, 1944, had charged SMERSH and the NKVD with verifying returning POWs and sending those that passed to the army or to continued labor in NKVD enterprises.[23] Outside the USSR, Red Army officers typically separated service-eligible men from women, the elderly, the disabled, and children for reenlistment in the occupation armies. The new directive commanded the Commissariat of Defense to form returning service-age men, both POWs and forced laborers, into groups at collection-transfer points (*sborno-peresyl'nye punkty*). It seems that most of these points were in the USSR. When a large enough group (around 800 men) had gathered at the camp, the army transferred them to work. Stalin's order assigned the men primarily to enterprises in coal mining, iron production, and timber felling. From August 1945 to March 1947, some 625,000 men were enlisted in 792 labor battalions.[24] In many instances, they were going to the same areas where special contingent prisoners had recently worked, sometimes to the same verification camp. Like the special contingent they replaced, labor battalion members were supposed to receive salary, lodgings, and provisions. Unlike the special contingent, the local enterprise was responsible for the men's upkeep. Meanwhile, the directive commanded security services to verify battalion members' wartime biographies within three months. Labor battalion members who passed verification would not go back to the army but remained as ordinary laborers with the enterprises where their battalion had worked.[25]

Security services did not rush to conduct verification, despite the deadline that central orders provided. In Nikopol (Dnipropetrovsk province), three battalions arrived in September 1945 and a fourth came in December. By March 1946, police had conducted verification of only one. A police official explained, "We have no people in the department and the provincial MGB administration won't send us help."[26] The delay in Nikopol was long but not a total outlier. At the end of March 1946, SMERSH, MGB, and MVD officers had verified 14,572 of 22,119 battalion members (68 percent) in Dnipropetrovsk province. This rate of filtration was not so far from the 69 percent verification rate of the 174,685 labor battalion members in Ukraine.[27] While police delayed verification, the directors of mines and construction sites were happy to keep the battalions longer.

Scholars have argued that there was no truly free labor in postwar Stalinism, but labor battalion members were among those who faced the most restrictions on mobility. In June 1940, the Soviet government introduced a labor law that criminalized changing jobs without the authorization of one's employer.[28] This law, along with labor battalions' settlement without regard to prewar residence, allowed authorities to implant a workforce in devastated territories via the battalions. The damage of the war was not spread evenly in the USSR but instead hit its western regions the hardest. For this reason, regions that had seen fighting received more than half of the men, with Ukraine taking almost a third on its own. The battalions also went to hinterland provinces like Cheliabinsk, Sverdlovsk, and Kemerovo that had benefited from the labor of evacuees during the war. Another 15 percent of laborers went to distant locations in the Far East or Far North. Overall, the distribution of the battalions suggests that they were meant to rebuild relatively hospitable areas of the USSR rather than settle harsh terrain away from the country's main population centers.[29]

Most labor battalion members had never lived where they were sent to work, and the men depended on their new employer for food and shelter. For managers, however, it was tempting to ignore the needs of these outsiders. The privations of the immediate postwar period meant that enterprises lacked the resources to provide adequate food and housing, or even to pay salaries on time. When directors had money, they prioritized the salaries of regular workers over the captive workforce. Why invest in people who might go to the Gulag after verification or find a way to leave? A secret informant spying on his comrades for the MGB quoted one battalion member who explained, "We have no money, and everything is expensive. I haven't worked for thirty-eight days. I lie barefoot on the planks [of the bed]. When it gets warm, I'll steal the planks and sell them at the market." Another battalion member was quoted via an informant as saying, "I get 700 grams of bread and a half liter of hot rations in the form of coffee or slop. Sometimes you just sit hungry, because there is no money, and you can't find any. I am not living but surviving."[30]

In addition to salary and food, workplaces denied medical care and equipment to labor battalion members. When a worker at a mine in Kemerovo province approached a staff doctor for treatment, the doctor responded, "A ton of coal is more valuable than your life."[31] The army commander in charge of a battalion working at a Cheliabinsk tube-rolling plant wrote in a complaint that his men had arrived in summer clothes and never received any other clothing. Now, in January 1946, they faced a two-mile walk from their barracks to work without winter dress. Many of the workers slept in the workshop to avoid freezing to death on the walk to the barracks.[32]

Battalion members, prompted by poor conditions and the uncertain length of their service, wrote hundreds of petitions to repatriation officials. From November 15 to December 10, 1945, alone, the Repatriation Administration received 165 individual or collective petitions from workers and even commanders. Leaders of industrial sites denied accusations of mistreatment. Islam Islam-Zade, the head of the construction site at the Mingachevir Dam in Azerbaijan, responded with a counteraccusation that the complaints against his administration were "provocations" and the authors were criminals who had robbed a neighboring village. It is unclear if this charge was valid, but it is apparent that it coincided with the worst suspicions about former POWs as traitors and criminals.[33]

The petitions and counterpetitions prompted Repatriation Administration chief General Filipp Golikov to launch an inspection of the battalions. In February 1946, he commissioned twenty-six army officers to visit some sixty-seven battalions across the USSR. Although Golikov and his inspectors confirmed the inadequate conditions described by labor battalion members, they framed poor living standards as a question of effective management rather than rights. An "incorrectly organized" brigade for Golikov was one that failed to meet its production norms. Using these criteria, Golikov wrote a report to leading politicians in which he asserted that a quarter of the inspected battalions were not up to standards.[34] Inspections continued in 1946 as a famine struck the USSR that summer. The later visits focused increasingly on living standards rather than on the battalions' norm fulfillment. Because of new criteria or because of the famine, the inspectors found a greater number of inadequate battalions. Fifty-two were "at a very low level."[35]

The inspections put pressure on economic ministers and police officials to accelerate verification and convert battalion members into free workers. In May 1946, more than 80,000 men went through verification and left the battalions. On July 12, the Soviet General Staff ordered that all battalions be disbanded in the near future. By September 1, 96 percent of members had left the battalions. With some notable exceptions, most repatriates passed through filtration after a few months. At least 51,018 (about 8 percent) of the men would face accusations that they had served in enemy forces. Most went to six-year exile, but there were 4,477 cases that security authorities judged as more severe. These men were arrested and presumably sent to the Gulag or execution.[36]

After most labor battalions passed verification in 1946, some continued to operate illegally by agreement between local army officers and enterprises. A particularly flagrant violation occurred at Dniprostroi in Zaporizhzhia (Ukraine). The construction battalion with 280 remaining members had passed filtration and on June 7, 1946, was scheduled for disbanding. The head of Dniprostroi petitioned to delay the disbanding of the battalion, and the deputy chief of staff in the military district consented. A year later, Golikov learned that the battalion still existed and alerted police head Lavrentii Beria that the men had not been freed.[37]

Formal action in the case was slow to come. In late 1948, the procurator of Zaporizhzhia province found that the battalion was still in operation as a moneymaking scheme for its commander, Lieutenant Colonel Tsibrenko. Dniprostroi paid the battalion around 300,000 rubles per month. Each man generated

1,100 rubles per month for the battalion but received around 300 rubles in salary. The profits partly went toward upkeep, but a great deal went to the officers. Tsibrenko and his deputy took home a combined 12,000 rubles while subunit commanders received 2,500. The military had written the men off as civilians, while the director of Dniprostroi thought they were the responsibility of the army. Both sides believed the men deserved their indefinite term of service "as punishment." The battalion members' apparent compliance suggests that they may also have believed it was legal. How Tsibrenko managed to set himself up as a labor contractor is unclear. The chaos of the postwar period and the extreme concentration of the economy in state enterprises could enable unauthorized private entrepreneurship on a surprisingly large scale.[38] It seems apparent that Tsibrenko controlled the information that battalion members received. He hired guards and surrounded the barracks with barbed wire. Only under pressure from Golikov and local prosecutors was the battalion disbanded in February 1949. Tsibrenko's fate is unknown.[39]

Most battalion members passed through verification more quickly, but their transfer to the Soviet labor force also included restrictions. Like all Soviet people, former battalion members had to remain at their workplaces or face arrest for unauthorized abandonment of their jobs without special permission. During the war and in its immediate aftermath, the penalty for "desertion" of a job in prioritized defense industries was a Gulag sentence of up to eight years. In 1947 the punishment lightened significantly to several months in a local jail. The change stemmed in part from the many cases in which procurators failed to prosecute reported deserters, presumably because they were wary of the harsh penalty.[40] Unlike other Soviet people subject to these labor laws, battalion members had been sent to places far from their homes. The labor battalions were spared the fate of exiled special settlers, who were often sent to faraway corners of the USSR. Yet the battalions became a kind of exile when Red Army officers assigned men to workplaces with no apparent regard to their prewar residence. A group of former POWs from Kazakhstan sent to work in the Far East in Suchan (Primorskii territory) wrote a petition to Golikov in 1947 begging for help returning to their families after absences as long as five years. A deputy minister from the Ministry of Coal Production rejected this plea, citing the 1940 labor law as justification for their settlement so far from their homes.[41] How many of the labor battalions' members became permanent laborers at their assigned workplace is unclear. Even if half managed to leave their place of settlement, those that the threat of prosecution kept in place would have numbered in the hundreds of thousands.

The men who left their assigned workplaces without permission put themselves in danger. Holocaust survivor and Hrodno native Iosif A. was assigned to a labor battalion after repatriation. He recalled telling the recruiting officer, "I wasn't a prisoner of war. I was in a concentration camp." The officer replied, "We can't let you go and keep everyone else here." Iosif A. was still operating in German categories. In the Reich, he had been a Jew slated for extermination and not a Slavic POW or Eastern Worker. Once Iosif A. returned to the USSR, he became a returnee of military-service age. He went with a battalion to work in the mines of Donbas. Later, on leave from the mine, he went to his hometown of Hrodno. The main reason he had returned to the USSR was to search for relatives, but in Hrodno he found that the Germans had killed them all. During a second visit, in 1948, he found a childhood friend who convinced him to stay and got him a job. After a short period, an officer appeared at Iosif A.'s new workplace and threatened him with a multiyear Gulag sentence. He was prosecuted but, because the government had lowered the penalty, served two months of jail and forced labor.[42]

Iosif A.'s jail sentence was an injustice, but it was also far lighter than other conceivable outcomes. Initial prosecution for labor desertion could transform into more significant accusations. A repatriate named Blonskii went to work at a labor battalion in a coal mine near Moscow. In February 1947, he used his vacation to visit his hometown of Kamianets-Podilskyi in Ukraine and decided to stay. After a year, informants told the police he was living there illegally. The charges the police ultimately pursued were not only Blonskii's real violation of labor laws, but also that of being a spy for the United States.[43] Iosif A.'s case could have easily concluded like Blonskii's, with investigators accusing him of having connections with suspicious foreigners. Moreover, despite the Soviet tendency to merge Jewish victimhood into a broader category of "peaceful Soviet civilians" killed under German occupation, officials understood that the Germans had targeted Jews for annihilation and that few had survived in the occupied territories.[44] A group of Jewish camp survivors who had returned to Mukachevo (Carpathian province in Western Ukraine) complained in a letter to Soviet authorities that local police were detaining Jewish returnees and implying that they had collaborated to survive.[45] A more aggressive investigator might have similarly wondered whether Iosif A. had made serious compromises with the occupiers to ensure his survival.

Some battalion members deserted without consequences. Adolescent Oleksandr I. had worked in the mines of Germany as an Eastern Worker. When he returned to the USSR, he was old enough for military service and was sent to a labor battalion working in mines near Leningrad. Comparing the two workplaces, he noted that the German mine was already constructed and so the tunnels had been dry. The Soviet mine was still being built, and thus the workers were often deep in water underground. Perhaps for this reason he fell ill when he took leave to visit his parents in Chernihiv (Ukraine) in March 1946. His parents took him to the hospital, where authorities found him several weeks later. The mining enterprise demanded that the local procurator in Chernihiv province prosecute Oleksandr I. for leaving the mine without authorization. Eventually the authorities acceded to Oleksandr I.'s request for a release based on his illness, and he enrolled in a technical school in Kyiv.[46]

Complicated regulations allowed some men to dispute their assignments. Specialists and men with large families were exempt from permanent settlement with the labor battalion after verification. Per a secret decree in April 1946, verified repatriates from the Caucasian and Baltic republics also could go to their home regions.[47] It seems that Soviet leaders hoped the effects of the decree would show nonreturners, many of whom were from the Baltic republics, that they would not face persecution upon return to the USSR.

In practice, labor-hungry police officials found ways around the law. On May 23, 1947, a group of Baltic repatriates arrived at a camp near Hrodno on their way to Tallinn. The camp commandant stopped the convoy and told the twenty-three service-age men, "You can forget about going back to your families." He announced that they would have to serve up to five years in the military. The surprise conscription confirmed the worst apprehensions of the remaining repatriates, who had overcome fear of exile and the Gulag to return.[48] Golikov appealed instances of seemingly arbitrary labor mobilization, but the cases often came before Beria, who decided in favor of the police. In Narva (Estonia) police formed a construction battalion with men who repatriation officials argued should have been released as Baltic nationals. But on the back of an April 1948 letter from Golikov about the case, Beria issued a simple decision in pencil: "Leave [the workers] at the construction site for an indefinite period."[49]

Why did labor battalion members become targets of forced labor and resettlement? To be certain, bosses in the police and industry felt little sympathy toward these men. Their status as potential collaborators marked them as targets for exploitation. The essential reason for their condition, though, was the Soviet economic system. Managers needed resources to fulfill plans for the restoration of the postwar economy. Funding and supplies were hard to get, but the labor battalions seemed to be a free influx of workers that entailed few responsibilities for the enterprise. Repatriation officials criticized the arbitrary abuses that the battalions experienced. Golikov and his subordinates are hard to credit as workers' champions, though. Although they criticized the harsh conditions the workers faced, their principal complaint was not about the violations of the men's rights. Instead, it was that these violations made the battalions economically inefficient. Like managers in the economy, repatriation officials accepted that the labor battalions were necessary as a safeguard against the infiltration of traitors and a way to leverage workers into postwar reconstruction.

Laborers in Soviet-Occupied Europe

An analogous conflict over the use of repatriates as laborers emerged between repatriation officials and Soviet forces abroad. After Germany's defeat, Soviet commissariats began to take reparations from Germany in the form of dismantled factories. In the summer and fall of 1945 alone, Soviet forces took roughly a quarter of the 17,024 medium to large factories that planners identified in the Soviet zone of occupation.[50]

Charged with effecting this hasty removal, leaders of economic commissariats deluged Golikov with demands to allot hundreds or thousands of repatriates for dismantling work. The invariable response from Golikov and his subordinates was that economic commissariats could only hire returnees by order of Stalin's military government. Stalin obliged in many instances. He signed orders for nine commissariats to recruit a total of 44,500 people in March and April 1945.[51] They were only a fraction of Soviet workers abroad. On October 15, 1945, there remained 452,611 returnees working in Soviet-occupied Germany in various capacities. Roughly half, 221,179 people, worked for the military, and the remainder worked for economic commissariats.[52]

Military leaders were aggressive in recruiting returnees in Germany and on army bases across Eastern Europe. During the war and after, Soviet armies provisioned themselves locally via army-managed farms.[53] Occupation officials wanted people to tend the army's cattle, to work as service personnel (e.g., cooks and cleaners), and to fill other positions. The Repatriation Administration's liaison in the Northern Army Group (Poland), Colonel Nechiporenko, reported to Golikov in November 1945 that a "flood" of officers from military units was demanding repatriates as workers.[54] Golikov persuaded military leaders in Moscow to oppose these demands in favor of returning these people to the USSR, but officers abroad continued to press for more laborers. Marshal Ivan Konev, the head of the Central Army Group (Austria, Czechoslovakia, and Hungary), asked deputy minister of defense Nikolai Bulganin not only to keep the 9,914 repatriates the army group was already employing in March 1946 but to hire an additional 5,820.[55]

The recorded totals accounted for only some of the returnees working abroad. Officially, the Northern Army Group in Poland employed just 18,088 returnees in November 1945. But an inspector found 41,567 workers, including 12,131 who had never gone through filtration. Many had started working for the army before regulations for filtration were in place.[56] Large numbers were also being kept without their consent. Facing long delays in their transit to the USSR, many took work by choice or necessity. When the head of repatriation for the military administration in Germany, General Sergei Vershinin, sent officers in February 1946 to inspect the status of repatriates working in Germany, they found that just 1,113 returnees of some 27,000 had given their written permission to remain. Many repatriate workers told the inspectors that they wished to go home but their bosses had refused.[57]

The power imbalance between the workers and authorities enabled soldiers' abuses. The 227 repatriates of a unit working under the Ministry of Construction received no soap for eight months. One of their bosses, a Lieutenant Korchagin, found them digging a garbage pit one day. "Why are you digging a pit for garbage?" he asked. "We'll need it to bury you repatriates."[58] Arbitrary violence occurred when the returnees challenged their superiors. An army officer in charge of a group of repatriate fishing workers in Poland beat one of his subordinates, breaking two ribs. When a woman working in one of the army group's herds refused to sleep with her boss, Senior Lieutenant Belov, he shot her in the stomach. It is possible she was not his only victim. Authorities found two other women's corpses hidden away in a pile of hay near the unit.[59] Some officers used their influence to rid themselves of former lovers. After a Soviet captain in Poland impregnated one woman, he sent her to the USSR so that he could be with another. He then sent the second woman away to work at a factory when he tired of her.[60] Golikov concluded from these instances in a letter to Stalin, Molotov, and Malenkov, "The treatment of these repatriates has been soulless and, in a number of cases, criminal."[61]

Practical concerns about security also made Golikov worry about the extended use of repatriates as workers abroad. He wrote to Nikolai Voznesenskii, a party leader involved in economic affairs, that repatriates could use work abroad as way to avoid verification.[62] He suggested that some were avoiding their hometowns, where neighbors knew what they had done during the war. As of November 1, 1945, the occupation army in Germany continued to employ 15,000 people it classified as Vlasovites.[63] In the Central Army Group, a repatriation inspector accused one woman working in a military canteen of having been a Gestapo informant. She was just one of 5,476 returnees who had never undergone filtration in that army group alone.[64] Incidents like this one stoked fears that large numbers of collaborators or spies would evade justice or actively work against Soviet forces.

As in the case of the labor battalions, repatriation officials worried about the efficiency of using repatriate laborers abroad. In the USSR, salary often depended on whether workers fulfilled their plan. Workers abroad earned a flat wage, and repatriation officers argued that they had no incentive to do more than the minimum required.[65] Work abroad also complicated repatriation. Multiple commissars successfully petitioned the Soviet government to retain thousands of repatriates after they returned from Germany to work in the USSR.[66] General

Golubev worried that this path home was a ploy to expedite the repatriation process. Once the repatriates arrived in the country, they would leave the enterprise. Of the 1,518 people who had crossed the border as would-be workers at the Kharkiv tractor factory, 1,436 left their jobs.[67]

These issues convinced Bulganin to institute stricter control over the recruitment of civilians to work for the army abroad. In August 1946, he ordered all army groups to sign civilian workers to formal contracts within a month or send them home. Repatriation officials reported that officers fulfilled this order through predictable coercion. A colonel in charge of a cattle herd in the Northern Army Group threatened that any workers who refused to sign consent forms would face repression upon return to the USSR.[68] A major cautioned a worker, "You won't go home if you don't sign a work contract, you will be sent to a labor battalion for six months." Other officers reportedly forged signatures on consent forms.[69]

Despite these instances of coercion, other evidence suggests that many workers remained voluntarily. In a letter excerpted by military censors, one woman wrote, "I didn't want to sign the agreement for another year [of work] until our bosses yelled at me. If I was alone, I would have signed up for five years, but I have two old people without help at home."[70] A shallow reading of this letter suggests that the author only remained because of pressure from her boss. It is worth noting, however, that she wrote that she would stay abroad for five years were it not for her family. It is even possible the woman wished to remain abroad but did not want to upset her relatives. In the Northern Army Group, 4,773 workers decided to return to the USSR. Repatriation officials noted in frustration that the army had failed to check with another 11,629. Nonetheless, the majority (18,516) signed contracts to continue working.[71]

Against the backdrop of a famine in the USSR, the prospect of return may have seemed daunting. A bad harvest followed a drought in the summer of 1946. Stalin and his subordinates did not want to cease grain exports, however, believing that the influx of capital was crucial to rebuilding Soviet industry after the war. This combination led to a severe grain shortfall. As in the famine of 1932–33, peasants in Ukraine and the grain-growing south of Russia faced starvation conditions from July 1946 until the next summer. Historians have estimated that one to two million people perished from hunger and related issues.[72]

Outside the USSR, repatriate workers and their bosses undoubtedly knew about the famine. Among 12,800 letters sent abroad from Ukraine in the first two weeks of August, police censors found 1,300 whose authors wrote "in a panicked manner" about the lack of food.[73] Some used thinly veiled references to the devastating famine of 1932–33. One letter writer informed a friend or relative in Czechoslovakia, "We live 'well,' remember how things were in 1933."[74] A

Repatriation Administration official claimed that employers abroad "scared re-patriates who wish to go to the motherland with talk about the difficult life in the Soviet Union." It is plausible that army officers informed their workers about the famine not just out of their own interest but because they wanted to help repatriates avoid a challenging return.[75]

Compared with the situation in the USSR, many repatriates working abroad enjoyed enviable conditions. Those registered as workers received the military's third ration. Their official daily ration was 650 grams of bread, 25 grams of sugar, 75 grams of meat, 120 grams of fish, 20 grams of butter, nearly a kilogram of potatoes or vegetables, 100 grams of grain, 20 grams of pasta, 10 grams of flour, 30 grams of salt, and a gram of dry tea. Civilian workers were also supposed to receive two suits or dresses per year. The pay was between 200 and 300 rubles per month, depending on the job.[76] The nominal rations seem to have been not too far from reality. Inspectors from the Ministry of Defense in 1946 noted that workers in Germany generally had their own rooms, if not entire apartments.[77]

As groups of migrant laborers, there are strong similarities between the em-ployment of Soviet repatriates and DPs living outside Soviet control. Both So-viet officials and their Western counterparts viewed the migrants as a resource, whether for the coal mines of Belgium or the Donbas, or for agricultural work in England or cattle herding for the Red Army in Poland.[78] Both groups posed the challenge of (re)integration, whether in the form of assimilation in Western Europe or reintroduction to Soviet life after years abroad. Repatriates in Soviet-occupied Europe became dependents of the Soviet army or economic ministries, virtual prisoners in some cases. As in other parts of postwar Europe, though, the demand for labor could also give repatriates a degree of physical mobility. Employment abroad meant delaying repatriation, but that was not always an un-welcome development. In a sense, repatriates could become temporary nonre-turners, waiting for circumstances in the USSR to normalize before return. Although Golikov worried about exploitation of returnees, his fundamental con-cern over repatriates working abroad was that they delayed the real work of postwar restoration that would come with their return to the USSR.

The special contingent, labor battalions, and civilian workers in Soviet-occupied zones became captive workers for different reasons. The characteristic they shared was that Soviet leaders in the economy perceived their displacement as an opportunity. Unable to rely on market-based incentives to hire workers, they lobbied central leaders and used ground-level coercion to retain labor. Economic mobilization sometimes overrode the other goals of repatriation. Stalin chose working exile over harsher penalties for most former members of pro-German formations. The need for labor in occupied Eastern Europe meant that military officials forced—and in some cases allowed—repatriates to delay filtration and return.

These people were only displaced because the Germans had captured or deported them to work in the Reich. In important senses, German deportation and Soviet postwar mobilization bore similarities. Both regimes viewed the displaced as a mobile workforce to be molded to the needs of the economy. And officials in both regimes discriminated against the migrants. In Germany, Eastern Europeans became forced laborers because of pervasive notions of racial inferiority. For their part, Soviet officials justified mobilization as a debt repatriates owed to the motherland.[79] Unlike in the German case, though, Soviet officialdom was divided in its attitudes toward the migrants. Whether, and how, returnees faced forced labor obligations differed significantly by sex, wartime biography, time of return, and haphazard implementation of state decrees. Repatriates in the USSR could also call upon an advocate in Golikov's administration, albeit one that often fought the worst forms of exploitation not on humanitarian grounds but because its officials viewed the arbitrary, inefficient use of labor as a hindrance to the country's reconstruction. Above all, Soviet economic mobilization of returnees was opportunistic more than it was principled; the desire for labor was more important than the impetus for punishment. In this sense, the Soviet case was comparable to programs in non-Soviet Europe that channeled displaced persons into employment, often in prioritized, low-status fields (e.g., nursing and mining). Through these efforts, DP administrators used displacement to address economic needs while supposedly reforming freeloading migrants.[80]

Golikov and other repatriation officials were unlike their European contemporaries in an important way. Economic officials in Western Europe wanted to use select foreign migrants to rebuild industries. Golikov's mission was to restore stability by returning Soviet people to their rightful places after the chaos of war. Return meant more than arriving in the country and going back to work, though. Repatriates had to reintegrate politically after years abroad. Their encounter with police would be particularly important in reintroducing them to Soviet rule.

A RETURN TO POLICING

Collaborators, Spies, and the Cold War
under Late Stalinism

Filtration was the moment when most arrests of repatriates occurred, but not all. For years after return, police continued to monitor repatriates as a suspect group, and thousands would face arrest as traitors and spies. In many cases, the charges turned real cooperation with Germany and its allies into the postwar crime of collaboration. Other returnees confessed to obviously fabricated charges of spying for postwar capitalist powers. Both types of investigations enacted vengeance for perceived wartime betrayals and used Stalinist policing methods to construct the postwar order.

Before the war and at its start, Stalin authorized police to arrest millions of people based on their social profile. During the Great Terror of 1937–38, secret police officers received quotas to arrest so-called socially harmful elements. These were people from diaspora nations (ethnic Germans, Poles, Latvians, Koreans, and others) or with bad political biographies (prerevolutionary elites, dekulakized peasants, recidivist criminals, and others), to whom investigators ascribed exaggerated or fabricated charges. Similar arrests of "unreliable" people occurred in the first days after the German invasion. These actions did not punish crimes that had already been committed but isolated or eliminated unwanted people to prevent future offenses that Stalin feared they would commit.[1]

Postwar investigations of collaboration were different because there was little need to fabricate anti-Soviet acts. Evidence of complicity with Germany and its allies was everywhere. The Red Army captured German documents with lists of volunteers, and there were witnesses and survivors who could testify to their actions. The investigations of collaboration were hardly fair or impartial. Soviet officials were rarely moved by the circumstances of hunger and coercion that pushed many to cooperate with the Germans.[2] They investigated people who committed minor acts of self-preservation alongside those who had actively participated in mass murder. In only a few cases were they willing to give defendants the benefit of the doubt. Investigators coerced the accused and witnesses into confessing and took the evidence to closed military tribunals for secret trials. Despite the bias of postwar investigations, the charges were not without basis.[3] Most involved real assistance to the enemy. Police actions to punish collaboration reflected the worries of Soviet leaders about regulating society after the turbulent wartime period.

The emergence of the Cold War motivated the partial return to preemptive arrests of enemies. Police monitored all returnees but focused espionage investigations on those who had lived under the Western Allies. Under pressure to find spies, investigators forced arrestees to recount fictitious meetings with American and British intelligence officers. Hundreds became the victims of false accusations, and tens of thousands of returnees came under police surveillance as potential arrestees.

Although World War II unleashed unparalleled violence, it also freed Soviet people from the strictures of Stalinism. After the war, Stalin and his subordinates launched a campaign to curtail the license Soviet people had enjoyed during the previous years. The cases against returnees were part of the restoration of Stalinist normalcy after the war and the USSR's fight against its new enemies in the Cold War.

Finding Treason

Every government in Europe that was occupied by or allied with the Germans was forced to reckon with widespread collaboration among its people. Had citizens cooperated with the occupiers to survive, or had they collaborated willingly with the enemy? This question challenged postwar societies for decades.[4] There was a technical side to these problems as well. In many cases, fleeing German forces had destroyed evidence. Potential witnesses were dead or had fled westward in advance of the Red Army. It was easy to find evidence of widespread collaboration, but finding specific people was often more difficult.

While the war continued, the thirst for revenge prompted vigilante justice against supposed traitors. When Red Army units arrived in towns, unrestrained soldiers, partisans, and civilians punished the people they believed were guilty.[5] Continuing military danger from pro-German agents also motivated arrests. Shortly after the Red Army arrived in the eastern provinces of Ukraine, the republic's head of the People's Commissariat of State Security (Narodnyi Komis-sariat Gosudarstvennoi Bezopasnosti, NKGB, secret police), Sergei Savchenko, warned his underlings about the danger of people who had gone to work in Germany and returned. Based on evidence in forty-five cases of returnees arrested by October 1943, Savchenko asserted that Germans had sent spies back to Ukraine under the pretext of illness or political opposition. He estimated that there were hundreds of pro-German propagandists who might still be in Ukraine.[6]

The desire for revenge and concerns about security cooled in the weeks and months after the liberation of territories. Summary executions usually gave way to a more understanding view of cooperation with the occupiers. Because the Red Army was desperate for soldiers, some former auxiliaries changed sides in the weeks before Soviet forces arrived or were able to join the army by hiding their collaboration. In other cases, army recruiters looked the other way or solicited auxiliaries to leave German service and join the Red Army again or "re-defect."[7] At the beginning of 1946, police in Ukraine found that at least 22,375 former pro-German police or auxiliary forces had avoided repression and were living freely in the republic. Incomplete data suggest that more than half of the former auxiliaries had gone to the Red Army after collaborating.[8] Some of the men subsequently received medals for their service fighting against Germany.[9]

After Germany's defeat, Soviet authorities took a harsher view of collaboration. They worried that superficial filtration investigations abroad were allowing collaborators to evade punishment and return to their homes. Bogdan Kobulov, the deputy head of the secret police, ordered regional counterintelligence officers in August 1945 to compile reports three times a month on the registration and investigation of repatriates. The police suspected all returnees, but the investigations focused primarily on people who had served in enemy units. In October, Kobulov and his counterpart in the regular police, Vasilii Chernyshev, issued Directive 119/118 ordering all police organizations to conduct secondary investigations of repatriates who might have been in pro-German units.[10]

Among the most damning sources about collaboration were German documents. In some cases, Soviet investigators began with a significant evidentiary base. One such instance was Trawniki, a village in eastern Poland that housed a training facility for former Soviet POWs who were convinced by hunger, coercion, or disillusionment with Soviet rule to volunteer for service to Germany. Trained to be concentration camp guards, the Trawniki men became ground-level perpetrators in the Holocaust.[11] The camp operated from the fall of 1941 to the summer of 1944, when rapid Red Army advances prevented the Germans from removing or destroying the camp archive before Soviet forces arrived. Military intelligence gained a mass of documents about Trawniki—training materials, personnel files, and a directory of some five thousand trainees.[12] The world learned about these documents during the notorious trials of John Demjanjuk. A Trawniki trainee who emigrated to United States as a nonreturner from the USSR, Demjanjuk came under investigation in the 1970s as "Ivan the Terrible," an infamously cruel guard at the Treblinka death camp. It came out that Demjanjuk had been misidentified, but materials from Soviet archives (above all his German identification card) proved that he had been a guard at the Sobibor death camp, where he assisted in the murder of tens of thousands of people. The evidence was strong enough to earn his conviction in a German trial in 2011.[13]

Documentary proof was not available in most cases, and the starting point for investigations typically came from postwar testimony. An important source was a returnee's registration file with local police. In the Soviet Union, all people were supposed to register at their place of residence. The system of internal passports and registration allowed police to monitor citizens' domestic migration.[14] As part of their local registration process, returnees underwent filtration irrespective of whether they had passed through verification at the border and/or abroad. At the local police office, repatriates had an interrogation with an officer in which they (again) explained where they had been abroad and what they had done. The police collected supplementary material, including a short biography, filtration certificates, and German records. Returnees sometimes presented documents that demonstrated they were loyal citizens, like reference letters from their Soviet employer. All these materials went into a file that remained with police for years.[15]

For returnees this process was enervating. Rumors of exile to Siberia had been ubiquitous in the DP camps abroad, and it seemed that one wrong step might make them come true. In another way, verification was the reinitiation of repatriates into Soviet political culture after years abroad. Interrogators became instructors on the proper biography returnees should present to officials.[16] In interactions with state and party institutions, in job applications, for instance, Soviet people had to provide their official biography, where they recounted their class background, their education, and their participation in Soviet campaigns.[17] The war period was another chapter in this story. In the formulaic questioning sessions with police officials, repatriates rehearsed their wartime biographies, learning the safest way to present their time in the Reich was as a period of passive victimhood.

From the perspective of security officials, each registration was the start of a potential investigation. In Ukraine a relatively small number of returnees faced arrest after they arrived at home—a little over 1 percent (about fourteen thousand) by the start of 1948.[18] Statistics after February 1948 are unavailable, but police continued to investigate returnees until January 1952, when an order from the MGB in Moscow removed most repatriates from its list of target groups.[19] Because summary statistics about repatriates from Moscow's secret police archives remain classified, comparable data on postfiltration arrests of repatriates in other republics are unavailable. The number of arrests for wartime crimes was highest during the war and its immediate aftermath, then declined in Stalin's last years.[20] Accounting for this trend, I estimate that in addition to the 6.5 percent of returnees who were detained during their filtration in Soviet occupied zones and at the border, roughly 1.5 percent of Ukrainian repatriates faced arrest.

There is reason to believe that the arrest rate in Ukraine was no lower than in other regions and was possibly higher. Soviet forces in the republic faced not only the Wehrmacht but also a war with nationalist insurgents.[21] The conflict was most violent in the western provinces, where a faction of the Organization of Ukrainian Nationalists positioned itself as the liberating army of the Ukrainian nation.[22] As a counterinsurgency force, Soviet police in the NKVD formed the Main Directorate for the Struggle against Banditry. Although most people the directorate arrested as nationalists were not repatriates (the number of people arrested as insurgents was several times the number of arrested returnees), there was some overlap between the categories. Anecdotal evidence from reports about the counterinsurgency shows that police identified some arrestees as repatriates and nationalists at once. By April 1946, police had arrested 294 repatriates as "participants in anti-Soviet groups" and 605 as "various anti-Soviet elements," categories that probably included nationalists.[23] The number of repatriates arrested as Ukrainian nationalist insurgents was perhaps lower than it might have been because relatively few people from the western provinces returned. Many did not consider themselves citizens of the Soviet Union, their home regions having been annexed after September 1939, and the Western Allies agreed, exempting them from compulsory repatriation. In Lviv province in the west, roughly 20 percent of people registered as deportees to Germany had returned (27,278 of 132,000) versus 55 percent of all Ukrainians (1.26 million of 2.30 million).[24]

These complicating factors make it difficult to extrapolate an arrest rate for the USSR from the case of Ukraine. Accepting that the Ukrainian arrest rate was probably no lower than the national rate, though, it seems safe to conclude that no more than 8 percent of repatriates were arrested in total (6.5 percent during filtration plus 1.5 percent after return).

This figure is large by international standards but lower than commentators have assumed was the case. France's national government, for example, ruled out prosecuting people for volunteering for work in Germany, even as many French people clamored for revenge.[25] In the case of the USSR, Western observers assumed that Stalin's police arrested or executed almost all returnees.[26] On the contrary, wholesale repression of repatriates did not occur, but police investigations were nonetheless a step in the direction of mass terror. The fact of returnees' registration is significant, since each file was the beginning of a case that police could resume if additional incriminating evidence materialized. Security officers marked some 6 percent of returnees as unreliable enough to put their case in the operational records (*podsobnyi uchet*, a record of people who were suspect but faced no charges). Police also ordered follow-up investigations of nearly 2 percent of returnees whose subsequent status is unknown.[27]

Some people avoided registering with the local police out of fear. Repatriation Administration officials in Minsk in early 1946 found dozens of people who had not registered and asserted that an unknown number of people had not gone through filtration after return to Belarusian villages.[28] By June 1947, Ukrainian police had uncovered 3,855 "illegals" who had been caught after failing to undergo local registration.[29] Some must have avoided registering because they feared repression. Others perhaps thought filtration abroad had been enough. How many people avoided registration and were not caught is unclear. Official reports from Ukraine show that the number of returnees was a million fewer than the number of people counted as having been taken to Germany.[30] Many of the missing people had not returned to the USSR at all. Hundreds of thousands of people from Ukraine, especially from the western provinces, remained in the Western occupied zones with Allied approval. A significant number of forced laborers and POWs from the republic died during the war. There were also prewar residents of Ukraine who had repatriated to different republics, to army service, or to the Gulag. Still, some of the missing people must have simply not registered. Their number was probably in the tens of thousands or more in Ukraine alone.

People who avoided registration were doubly suspect once they were caught. Anna Petrenko was a returnee from Kyiv province who had worked for a farmer in Germany during the war. She returned to the USSR while pregnant and said the father was a former Soviet POW. On the journey home, Petrenko went through verification a total of four times abroad and in Ukraine. After she moved with her mother to Khabarovsk territory in the Far East in 1946, she married a soldier in the military police. She told secret police interrogators that her husband and friends advised her not to register as a repatriate or else "they'll send you to jail for six years." Perhaps she feared that her son would face questions about his father. Who was to say that he was Soviet and not German? When she moved from Khabarovsk territory to the Far Eastern territory in January 1948, Petrenko had to write a short biography for a job application. In it she said that she had lived in Khabarovsk territory during the war and had married her husband in 1945. Police in the Far East requested her file from their colleagues in Ukraine and learned that she had been in Germany during the war. In interrogations in April and May 1948, she and her husband admitted that the biography was false. Despite her falsification, Petrenko was not arrested. It is possible her husband's position in the military police helped her or that her lie was not reason enough to arrest her. She continued nonetheless to be an object of interest for police until at least 1952.[31]

Registration allowed police to find informants, in addition to suspects. During filtration some returnees who had served in enemy formations confessed to treason and volunteered to exculpate their sins by spying on their fellow returnees.[32] The most important characteristic of informants was that they could insinuate themselves among persons of interest. People who had worked as interpreters or clerks for the enemy were especially attractive informers in the USSR. Soviet police assumed that they had special knowledge about the workings of labor camps because they had served as conduits of information between German administrators and the laborers.[33] Informers who could tell police about noteworthy returnees were also valuable. For example, Kyiv police in 1946 recruited an opera performer who had toured Germany during the war and returned to the USSR in September 1945.[34] Through her and other agents, police infiltrated groups of performers who had worked in pro-German propaganda organizations.[35]

Officers pressured repatriates who achieved a modicum of success after return to become informers. When Maria S. returned to Kursk province, she gained admission to a technical college and even became a leader in its Komsomol organization. Her position brought her to the attention of police, who harassed her until she agreed to become an informant. For months she avoided giving compromising information to her handler but eventually agreed to denounce a woman from her street. The woman was said to have collaborated with the Germans, and now the investigators needed a denunciation to solidify the case. "I hated her myself," Maria S. rationalized in a post-Soviet interview, "because everyone said that [she] went around with Germans and everything." Maria S. soon after graduated from the technical college and moved to Donbas, where she assumed her work for the police would end. In her new home, too, police had her file and made her an informant at her new factory.[36]

A small but significant number of returnees became informers. In Kyiv province by February 1947, police had recruited some 762 of the 135,449 returnees registered in the province. Informers in Vinnytsia province numbered a little over 300 of nearly 50,000 repatriates. Because active investigations of returnees would continue into the 1950s, it is possible that one in every hundred returnees was recruited to inform.[37] This was hardly a secret. An informant reported that Leonid Popov, a teenager who returned to Vinnytsia province, boasted that he could have emigrated to the United States. He also complained that Moscow leaders were unaware that Jews dominated life in the USSR. Finally, he warned the informer not to talk about their conversations: "Be careful because there are lots of secret MGB workers."[38]

Some informants provided false evidence. The investigation of two former ranking party members is illustrative. Mikhail Romanov and Vladimir Storozhenko had been party members for over a decade when the Germans invaded. Both became POWs and lost their party status as a result. Because they had formerly been in the party, the police suspected them of having collaborated to save themselves under the Germans. Their records were doubly questionable because they had lived in the British zone of Germany before repatriation. In 1947 the police sent an informant code-named "Sigodinov" to meet Romanov at a hotel in Kyiv under the guise of having mutual friends. "Sigodinov" reported that the suspect admitted to having been recruited by a British colonel as a spy. Unknown to the informer, the police had bugged the room and heard a completely different conversation in the recording. The police pulled "Sigodinov" from the case and recommended his arrest. Although the investigators demonstrated an aversion to using false evidence, they also saw no reason to discontinue the case against the two former party members.[39]

Investigations also began when Soviet people sought retribution for wartime actions. In August 1945, several residents of Myrhorod (Poltava province) accused a returnee named Grigorii Maliar of having razed several buildings as a member of pro-German police. On September 1, police recorded Maliar's confession that he had served in the occupation police. After he retreated with German forces, the Germans placed him in a fire brigade in Berlin. The military tribunal gave him ten years in the Gulag, a relatively light sentence compared with those of other former occupation police.[40]

The typical catalyst for arrest was evidence from previous investigations. Arrestees sometimes named dozens of people they knew from training camps and pro-German units. If police had a name and a home region, they contacted authorities in that area, alerting them to the possibility that a suspect was living there. Case files of people who had collaborated in prominent ways could contain dozens of memos from other investigations in which the suspect had been named as a collaborator.[41] When information about a suspect was imprecise, police could call for an all-union search. Central police authorities in Moscow issued an all-union search in 1946 for a thirty-something Leonid or Lev Beznos, who had lived in Mariupol (Staline province) before the war. A man accused of working as a pro-German propagandist had named Beznos as a fellow propagandist. Police from Staline province found thirteen men with a matching name. They sent photographs of the thirteen men to Beznos's accuser, who identified one as Beznos.[42]

Did the arrestee recognize Beznos or identify him under pressure from the police to name one or any of the candidates? As was the case with the informer "Sigodinov," it is possible that the arrestee hoped to benefit from the denunciation. And police were eager to punish wartime collaboration. Unlike the investigations of the Great Terror in the 1930s, however, the accusations were not fabulous tales. Cases in the 1930s often involved people's supposed intentions to commit crimes—peasants' plots to kill Stalin or factory workers' schemes to divulge national secrets to a foreign power. The police forced arrestees to sign confessions to these crimes, which, although fantastical, were impossible to disprove because they involved plans and attitudes, not real actions.[43] Accusations about collaboration had a basis in people's real experiences in the war. In many cases, the arrestees agreed to the basic facts of their wartime interactions with the enemy, even after release from the Gulag after Stalin's death. Disagreements arose over whether collaboration automatically made someone a collaborator.

The Margins of Collaboration: Three Cases

According to Soviet law, almost every Soviet person who had lived under German rule could have been guilty of treason. The Soviet law code criminalized "counterrevolutionary crimes" under the infamous Article 58. (In Ukraine the article was numbered 54.) At the beginning of the war, the charge investigators used to punish collaboration of all kinds was treason, 58-1a for civilians or 58-1b for military personnel. The circumstances of war, especially the distinction between mass violence against civilians and widespread cooperation with the occupiers, motivated Soviet leaders to define gradations of complicity. The Soviet government issued a decree on April 19, 1943, that distinguished "spies and traitors" (*izmenniki*) guilty of violence against civilians and POWs, from the "accomplices" in these atrocities. The former could receive the death sentence while the latter were to receive a fifteen-to twenty-year forced labor sentence. In a comment on that decree, issued in November 1943, the Soviet Supreme Court asserted that local tribunals were misinterpreting it and using charges of collaboration indiscriminately. The court demanded that lesser punishments apply to less serious cases of cooperation with the enemy. In the latter cases, tribunals could use Article 58-3, "encouraging an armed intervention . . . [or] assisting a foreign government in its existing war" against the USSR, that carried a sentence of three or more years of forced labor. The Supreme Court also asserted that certain factors—assistance to partisans or voluntary submission to authorities—could mitigate punishment.[44]

Although this intervention attempted to provide clarity amid overlapping prewar laws and wartime decrees, lower-level courts would continue to use a hodgepodge of charges and sentences throughout the war and into the postwar years. The inconsistent handling of cases was a result not only of misunderstood laws but also of the necessity to interpret wartime actions within this legal framework. After all, everyone who had worked in the Third Reich had assisted Germany in its war effort. The strictest reading of Article 58-3 could have justified the incarceration of millions. Where was the boundary between survival-motivated cooperation and criminal collaboration?[45]

Moderation generally won out as Soviet officials attempted to restore life in formerly occupied areas. Komsomol Central Committee secretary Olga Mishakova told a group of youth leaders from newly liberated territories in February 1944, "Not everyone can be a hero."[46] Police instructions named as the main targets of repression people who had taken active, formal roles as officials, police, guards, and soldiers under the enemy.[47]

Aleksandr Kashia was an obvious candidate for arrest. He had been the head of the Georgian barracks at Wustrau, the Eastern Ministry's training camp for propagandists. Rather than hide abroad, he decided to come back to the Soviet Union. He told investigators that he returned because he wanted to see his mother again. When the war ended, he presented himself to Red Army authorities for repatriation and, obscuring his wartime activities during filtration, received permission to return to his home in Kutaisi, Georgia. Perhaps he believed his wartime ordeal was over. But as Kashia rested at his sister's home in Tbilisi in the fall of 1945, other former Wustrau residents named him as one of the main figures in the camp. On January 4, 1946, police surrounded his sister's house. Kashia later recalled the scene in a petition for political rehabilitation—to have his arrest invalidated—in 1959 under Khrushchev: "They arrested me as if I was some bandit. There was no order from the procurator. . . . The head of counter-intelligence from Kutaisi behaved rudely. His first words were filled with the filthiest swearing."[48]

For two months, investigators questioned him about Wustrau and its residents. Based on the start and stop times in interrogation documents, it is apparent that officers were using sleep deprivation to compel his compliance. The investigators do not appear to have used physical force, however. Kashia never mentioned being beaten and presumably would have written as much in his rehabilitation petition.

Investigators had two main goals in the case. First, they wanted Kashia to admit that he had been the "assistant commandant" of the camp and a member of Tetri Giorgi, the fascist-leaning Georgian émigré political party. He would admit to being the assistant commander, although at points he called himself the "barracks elder." The interrogator's second goal was to procure a complete list of his contacts in the camp. As leader of the barracks, Kashia had known all the

Soviet and émigré Georgians who passed through Wustrau. He signed off on a list containing 143 names, at least 20 of whom were later arrested.[49]

Sentences for the Wustrau men generally corresponded to the severity of the accusations. Most of the arrestees had trained at the camp but had not worked as propagandists, and a typical sentence was ten years in the Gulag. Even choirmaster Davit Kavsadze received ten years, despite his choir's transformation into an SS guard battalion; he would die in the Gulag in 1952.[50] Arrestees who faced more serious charges could receive harsher sentences. Wustrau men Aleksei Dunchevskii and Ilia Sherstiuk, who had been among the few who graduated in time to go to Ukraine as propagandists and later worked as instructors, received twenty-five years each.[51] As for Kashia, a military tribunal sentenced him to execution, and he spent almost two months on death row before his lawyer successfully appealed for a resentencing to ten years in the Gulag. Like most of the Wustrau men sentenced to ten years, Kashia would have his sentence commuted in an amnesty that followed Stalin's death. Kashia was fortunate in this regard, because review boards often refused amnesty for men serving longer sentences, like Dunchevskii's and Sherstiuk's, opting instead for a reduction in the term.[52]

Were the accusations against Kashia real, or had interrogators forced his testimony? Undoubtedly investigators pushed him to confess in unflattering terms. Yet the evidence leaves no doubt that Kashia was the head of the barracks in Wustrau and later worked for the Eastern Ministry's Georgian section. After he was convicted, Soviet investigators uncovered a German list of Wustrau Georgians with his name included. They also found his Eastern Ministry work card from 1943. The photograph from the card captured Kashia wearing a neat suit and tie, his dark mustache a small square resembling Hitler's.[53] None of the investigation documents mention his choice to style his mustache this way, although the photograph presents a notable contrast to his Soviet documents (figures 7.1A and 7.1B). Perhaps most important, he and the other Wustrau Georgians never denied that they had been at the camp. Kashia acknowledged that he had been the barracks head at Wustrau in his rehabilitation petition.[54]

The conflict in the investigation was not over the fact of cooperation but its meaning. The title Kashia bore in Wustrau had crucial significance in this regard. In rehabilitation petitions, he described himself as the elected representative of his fellow prisoners, the barracks elder. He equated the position to the barracks head in the Gulag. It is likely that by this comparison he hoped to evoke sympathy among officials during Khrushchev's campaign of de-Stalinization. It implied that conditions at Wustrau and at a Soviet forced labor camp had been similar. Kashia suggested that he had resisted even as he collaborated: "As much as possible, I tried to make life easy for my countrymen. You won't find anyone who can say that he suffered punishment because of me."[55]

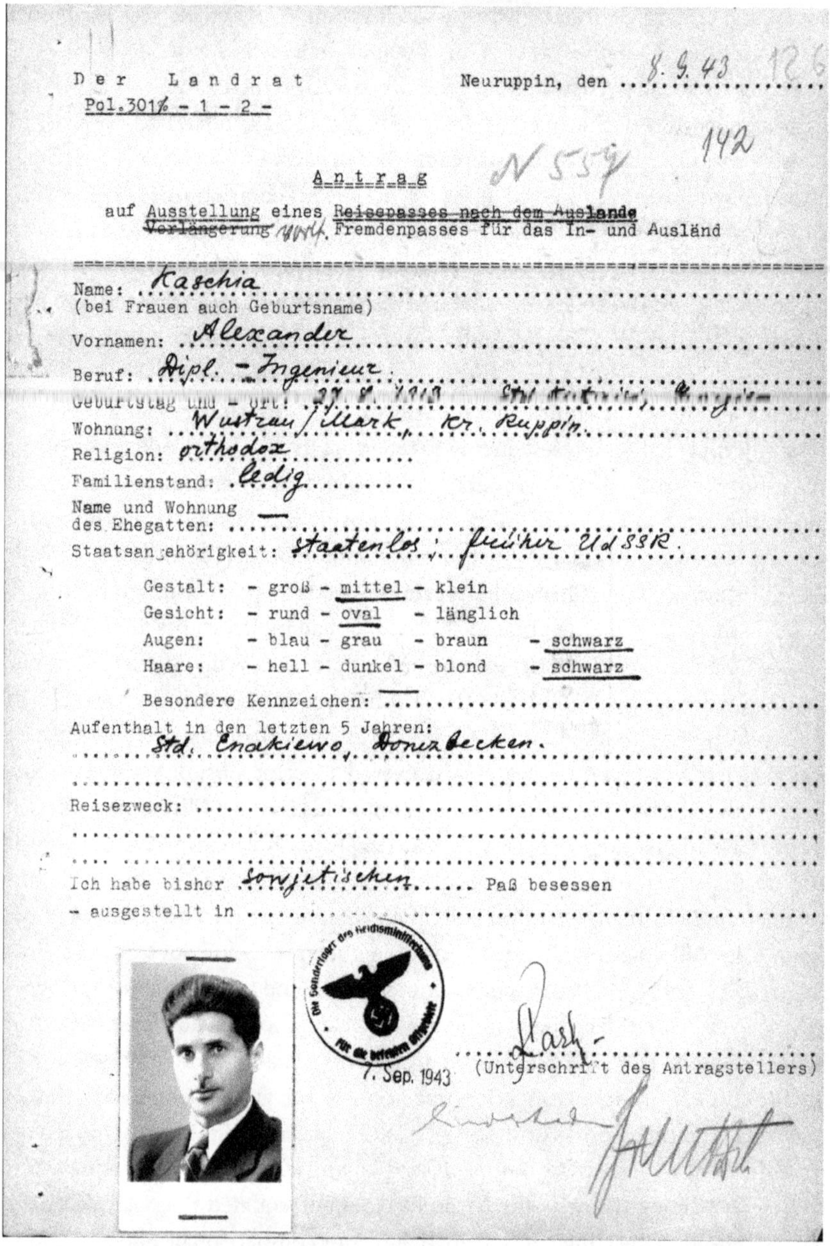

Der Landrat Neuruppin, den ...8.9.43... 12 6
Pol.301% - 1 - 2 -

A n t r a g N 557 142

auf Ausstellung eines ~~Reisepasses nach dem Auslande~~
~~Verlängerung~~ Fremdenpasses für das In- und Ausländ

===

Name: *Kaschia*
(bei Frauen auch Geburtsname)

Vornamen: *Alexander*

Beruf: *Dipl. - Ingenieur*

Geburtstag und - ort: *27. 8. 1919* ....

Wohnung: *Wustrau/Mark, Kr. Ruppin*

Religion: *orthodox*

Familienstand: *ledig*

Name und Wohnung
des Ehegatten: ___

Staatsangehörigkeit: *staatenlos; früher UdSSR.*

    Gestalt: – groß – <u>mittel</u> – klein
    Gesicht: – rund – <u>oval</u> – länglich
    Augen: – blau – grau – braun – <u>schwarz</u>
    Haare: – hell – dunkel – blond – <u>schwarz</u>

    Besondere Kennzeichen: ....

Aufenthalt in den letzten 5 Jahren:
......*Std. Enakiewo, Donezbecken.*

....

Reisezweck: ....

....

Ich habe bisher *sowjetischen* ...... Paß besessen
– ausgestellt in ....

7. Sep. 1943 ...*Nash.*... (Unterschrift des Antragstellers)

FIGURE 7.1A. Aleksandr Kashia's German work document. USHMM RG-38.001, d. 46256, folder 2, l. 142.

FIGURE 7.1B. Aleksandr Kashia's Soviet temporary identity card. USHMM
RG-38.001, d. 46256, folder 2, l. 230.

Kashia would fail to convince authorities that he had not committed treason. The evidence that he had collaborated with enthusiasm and success under the Germans was strong. He named four character witnesses for his rehabilitation case in 1959, all people who had been in the Georgian barracks at Wustrau. Like Kashia, they did not deny this fact, and some had gone to the Gulag as collaborators. All described Kashia as having been eager to cooperate with the Germans and having enjoyed the trappings of authority.[56] It is possible that they feared corroborating his story, but the same witnesses vouched for other Gulag returnees as secret resisters in Wustrau. The rehabilitation board denied Kashia's appeal in 1959, and it seems that he never had his sentence overturned.

Other arrestees admitted their guilt but hoped mitigating circumstances would warrant lenience. Fifty-year-old Ekaterina Timoshenko had been trained as a propagandist for work in Ukraine after her deportation to a camp in Güsen (near Magdeburg). After her return to the USSR, Soviet police arrested her in April 1946. It seems probable that another detainee had denounced her, as the file contains no German work card or other documents that might have motivated the arrest. For corroborating evidence, police summoned her neighbors in Kyiv and campmates at Güsen as witnesses. They confirmed that she had gone to Kyiv for a monthlong "vacation"—the time when she had worked as a propagandist in one of the town's factories. Timoshenko asserted that the Germans had drafted her into the training against her will. She had only become a propagandist because of German obfuscation and her own ill health, not because she had betrayed her fundamental loyalty to the USSR.[57]

These explanations had only a marginal influence on her case. A military tribunal sentenced her to ten years in the labor camps. She served nearly nine years before officials commuted her sentence in 1955, when she was sixty-two years old. In 1992, post-Soviet Ukrainian procurators absolved her of "treasonous activity."[58] By that point she had almost certainly died. Police convicted Timoshenko on less evidence than Kashia and for less serious offenses. She did not conduct much meaningful work as a propagandist, and perhaps did nothing at all. Like Kashia, she did not deny her deeds but contested whether they could be considered anti-Soviet collaboration under circumstances of duress.

Unlike the previous arrestees, Zinaida Zhidkovskaia-Patsukevich had done almost nothing recognizable as collaboration. At age seventeen in 1943, the Kyiv native fled for Kirovohrad instead of being deported to Germany for labor. That summer German police arrested her for listening to Soviet radio. The police stripped her nude to leer at her, beat her, and made her tell them the names of others who had listened to the radio with her. She then went to a series of concentration camps. After liberation in 1945, she returned to the USSR and married a demobilized soldier in March 1946.

Zhidkovskaia-Patsukevich's postwar life unraveled because of a small lie. During her registration interview, she told her interrogator, Major Smaglov, that the Germans had arrested her because she had listened to Soviet radio on a receiver her brother had given her. Police in Leningrad questioned her brother, and he denied having a radio during the war. The discrepancy made Kyiv officers suspicious. They arrested her in July 1946 when she repeated her claim about her brother's radio under repeat interrogation. It eventually came out that she had listened to the radio with a German soldier who was apparently dating her friend. Catching her in the lie, her other interrogator, Lieutenant Timko, made her confess that she had identified two Soviet men to the Germans as fellow radio listeners. Her confession made her a Gestapo informant in the eyes of Soviet police. She argued that the Germans had tortured her until she gave them names, and she never provided information to the Gestapo after this incident. The military tribunal at her closed trial did not recognize these circumstances as excusing her cooperation with the Gestapo and sentenced her to ten years in the Gulag.[59] In her appeal in 1956, Zhidkovskaia-Patsukevich revealed that Timko had beaten her until she agreed to confess. Violence had been particularly effective in her case because she had been pregnant. The baby was stillborn, perhaps a result of the beating.[60]

Zhidkovskaia-Patsukevich was undeniably a collaborator in one sense: until 1956 she stood convicted of treason under Ukraine's Article 54-1a. The judicial review of Kyiv's military district court overturned her conviction that year. "As a result of vicious [German] beatings and provocations," it reported, "she confirmed the names of those who had listened to the radio."[61] The author highlighted that Zhidkovskaia-Patsukevich had demonstrated remarkable loyalty to the Soviet state by avoiding deportation to Germany for labor. Yet the reviewer did not write that the accusation of collaboration against Zhidkovskaia-Patsukevich was a fabrication. Rather than deny that she had cooperated with the Gestapo, the review agreed with Zhidkovskaia-Patsukevich's argument that it was absurd to call someone a collaborator for what she had done under the circumstances.

The investigations of Kashia, Timoshenko, and Zhidkovskaia-Patsukevich varied considerably. They had not committed acts of violence, guarded concentration camps, or fought in the Vlasov army. The Georgian had collaborated in a managerial position. The older Timoshenko had trained to be a propagandist but did little or nothing in that role. Zhidkovskaia-Patsukevich had given names to German police under torture. In each of the cases, the arrestees defended themselves by distinguishing between the acts of collaboration that they acknowledged and ascription into the category of collaborator that they rejected. Regardless of the circumstances of their cooperation with the Germans, the investigators and judges argued that they were all traitors.[62]

Why were these three arrested at a time when most returnees did not face arrest or even investigation? The cases of Kashia and Timoshenko provide an easy answer. They had enlisted for training under the Germans and thus had defected formally. Zhidkovskaia-Patsukevich is more difficult to explain. Her arrest by the Gestapo signaled that the Germans had perhaps recruited her to spy on other Soviet people. Her lie about listening to her brother's radio suggested to investigators that she was hiding a bigger crime. It is possible to imagine a scenario where Zhidkovskaia-Patsukevich told the truth from the start, or told a lie that could not be verified, and escaped a sentence. The lesson of these cases is not that Stalinist investigators arrested all repatriates with the slightest blemish on their wartime record. Instead, the investigations showed that once police had identified someone as a collaborator, the desire for punishment meant a Gulag sentence was almost certain.

Falsified Spies

Accused spies never made up the largest contingent of arrestees among repatriates. Collaboration always held first place. By April 1946, police in Ukraine had arrested 6,618 repatriates, of whom more than 80 percent faced accusations of wartime collaboration. Another 14 percent were accused of belonging to anti-Soviet groups, like Ukrainian nationalist organizations. Police at the time had arrested only five people as alleged spies for the United States or United Kingdom. At the same time, the republic had opened cases involving 9,351 repatriates, of whom 469 were suspected of spying.[63]

The relatively small number of repatriates suspected of being spies in the spring of 1946 belied the shifting concerns about them as tensions mounted between the USSR and the Allies. After the war, Stalin had hoped that the capitalist states would fight one another for influence in the world. The USSR would adopt a neutral stance, profiting from the United Kingdom's and the United States' struggle with one another to become the dominant imperial power.[64] Contrary to Stalin's predictions, however, there would be no rift in the American-British alliance to exploit. In March 1946, former British prime minister Winston Churchill delivered his famous "Sinews of Peace" ("Iron Curtain") speech that criticized the USSR's increasing domination in Eastern Europe. That Churchill gave the speech at the invitation of US president Harry Truman in his home state of Missouri underlined the solidarity between the Western Allies. By the same token, the speech reflected and deepened East-West tensions.

The emergence of the Cold War motivated Soviet leaders to eliminate ties with the West in all spheres of Soviet life. This reaction was part of a broader culling of wartime freedoms that is sometimes called the *zhdanovshchina*, after Andrei Zhdanov, the party Central Committee secretary associated with cultural affairs under Stalin. As declassified documents have demonstrated, Stalin himself pushed Zhdanov to attack "servility to anything foreign" among scientists and the cultural intelligentsia.[65] In perhaps the most famous episode from this period, Zhdanov publicly condemned poet Anna Akhmatova and writer Mikhail Zoshchenko for producing works "alien to Soviet literature."[66] Soviet people who had made connections to foreigners during the war were also targets in the campaign. Stalin famously denounced "cosmopolitanism," understood as a euphemism for Jews with connections outside the USSR. Police arrested dozens of prominent Jewish officials and cultural figures at Stalin's orders. Ironically, many of the arrestees had made foreign contacts on official missions for the Jewish Anti-Fascist Committee that had generated sympathy and monetary aid for the Soviet war effort.[67]

There were reasons for Soviet leaders to be concerned about British and American espionage. Western intelligence services were recruiting displaced people who could be used as insurgents in the annexed territories of the western USSR. Members of Ukrainian nationalist organizations, whose histories of collaboration with the Germans were often extensive, became especially prominent recruits for US intelligence.[68] Some Soviet defectors to Germany defected again to the United States and became key figures in Western plans to combat the USSR from abroad and from within.[69]

Unlike national oppositionists and ranking defectors among former Soviet POWs, most returnees had little or no intelligence value and experienced no interaction with foreign intelligence services. The logic of Stalinist spy mania cast these ordinary returnees as likely foreign agents nonetheless. During the 1930s, the slightest interactions with foreigners within the USSR could lead to arrest as a supposed spy.[70] What would police do now that millions of people were returning after years of foreign contacts in territories outside of Soviet control? The DP camps were especially disquieting as dens of anti-Soviet activity where émigrés were turning Soviet people against their country. Ukrainian secret police head Sergei Savchenko believed that Anglo-American intelligence officers would have no trouble recruiting spies in this atmosphere and sending them to the USSR under the cover of repatriation.[71] After Churchill's "Iron Curtain" speech in early 1946, the proportion of repatriates under investigation as spies rose significantly. In February 1948, of 19,280 open cases of repatriates in Ukraine, 4,978 involved espionage for the United Kingdom or the United States. The proportion was 25 percent of cases in 1948 versus 5 percent of cases before 1946.[72]

Most of these spy cases started from accusations that are hard to consider espionage. There was little overlap between the significant number of returnees accused of being nationalist insurgents and those accused of espionage. Instead, police focused spy cases on repatriates who made remarks about the high quality of Western rations or about the kindness they had experienced in Western zone DP camps. Other cases began when postal censors discovered repatriates who maintained correspondence with foreign contacts. Another motivation for espionage occurred when returnees speculated that a war between the USSR and its former allies was inevitable. This rumor was especially popular in rural areas, where peasants asserted that the United Kingdom and the United States would defeat the Soviet Union and disband collective farms.[73] When investigators heard of these instances, they summoned returnees for interrogation.

Returnees were recorded as giving investigators testimony that was both farcical and generic. Many agreed to a variation of this confession:

> In ____ DP camp in the ____ zone of Germany, an unidentified intelligence officer proposed that ____ emigrate permanently. ____ insisted on going to the USSR. In exchange for safe passage to the motherland, the intelligence officer forced ____ to sign an agreement to conduct anti-Soviet work after repatriation.

The work in question was usually praising conditions in the Western occupation zones or in the West broadly. Sometimes the supposed mission was to find a job at a factory and gather information.[74] Although these people confessed to being recruited by the Western Allies, most cases did not end in arrest. Of the approximately five thousand spy cases initiated by February 1948, Ukrainian police arrested 173 people, a little more than 3 percent.[75]

One of the people arrested was Mefodii Gritsai, whose case began with an unfortunate coincidence. In 1948, secret police officers in Kyiv started an investigation based on a SMERSH (army intelligence) search request for a collaborator who had returned from Germany. The suspect was in his midtwenties and had the last name of Gritsai and possible first name of Aleksandr. Kyiv officers searched their directory of repatriates and found twenty-four-year-old Mefodii Gritsai in Pohreby, a village a short distance to the north of the Ukrainian capital. When they visited him in Pohreby, they quickly learned that he was not the Gritsai they wanted but found other reasons to detain him.[76] The occupiers had taken Mefodii Gritsai to Germany in 1943, when he was twenty years old. American forces liberated him in Dusseldorf in April 1945. He went to the Soviet zone of Germany two months later and served in the Soviet army until his demobilization in 1947. After four years abroad, Gritsai returned to his home in Pohreby and took up work at the local collective farm. It seems that when the police interviewed the workers at the farm, one mentioned that Gritsai had recently praised American rations in occupied Germany. This misstep provided the grounds for the officers to take Gritsai to Kyiv police headquarters on August 3, 1948.

During the interrogation that followed, a pair of officers coaxed the unwilling Gritsai to confess that American intelligence had recruited him. First the young man said that an American officer in Dusseldorf had summoned him for a conversation. The investigators refused to accept that this incident had been for registration alone. Gritsai offered, "Maybe the Americans summoned me to [propose] conducting counterintelligence missions." He said that Americans had attempted to persuade Soviet citizens to go to the United States. Investigators asked him how he knew about these missions. Gritsai understood where the interrogation was leading, realized he had made a mistake by suggesting the scenario, and refused to respond. The interrogation protocol says he kept silent for a tense ten minutes. After the officers repeated their question, he assented that the American officer had proposed that he do counterintelligence missions but insisted that he had not undertaken them. The final step for the interrogators was to have Gritsai admit that he had formally accepted this mission in writing. This confession was enough for officers to charge him as an American spy.[77] Later Gritsai said that the interrogators had promised to release him if he agreed to this story. When he expressed doubts, they cajoled and threatened him.[78]

Gritsai remained in custody as investigators finalized his story and extracted potential contacts who might also be arrested. One day he discussed the investigation with a cellmate. Evidently more experienced in these matters, the cellmate chastised Gritsai for yielding to the investigators so easily. Gritsai retracted his testimony on September 7. After Stalin's death, he told a review commission that his retraction prompted one of the interrogators to beat him twice and to send him to an isolation cell. A few days later, Gritsai affirmed the original testimony, but on November 24 he retracted his confession again. He told the interrogator what was undoubtedly the truth: he had praised the Americans to fellow villagers but made these comments not because he was an American agent but because it was "how things actually were."[79]

The investigators lost Gritsai as a witness against himself but brought the case to the military tribunal nonetheless on December 28, 1948. The key witness was Petr Kovalenko, a forty-year-old former party member who had been a forced laborer alongside Gritsai. Kovalenko was also arrested as a spy and confirmed the prosecution's accusations against Gritsai. When the court asked the younger man to respond, he accused his interrogators of having beaten him until he confessed. His lawyer also presented a handwritten statement from forty-nine of the collective farmers at Pohreby vouching for him. The procurator asked for more time to investigate the case, but the court denied the request, setting Gritsai free after nearly four months.[80] Although relatively few espionage cases resulted in arrest, it was perhaps rarer for an arrestee to be acquitted. Gritsai's fortitude, support from his village, status as a veteran, and luck saved him from the Gulag.

The exceptional outcome in Gritsai's case reveals what was unexceptional in the other spy investigations. The investigators' primary coercive tool was verbal. It is even possible to read the false confession as a coauthored document by Gritsai and the investigators. Although the officers compelled Gritsai to offer his story of espionage, they did so based on promises and threats, not violence. Only after he recanted did investigators use physical force. Perhaps most important, Gritsai agreed that he had been at fault for praising the Americans. He only denied that American officers had recruited him for this purpose. The investigation taught Gritsai an important lesson. Maybe he hoped that with the existential threat to the USSR gone, it would be possible to compare Soviet life to what he had experienced abroad. He now understood his mistake. During one of his final interrogations, he told the officers, "In the American camp, I really did live well compared to the German camp. That is why I said that Americans are good people. I understand that it is forbidden to do that, that I committed a crime."[81]

Most cases involving supposed spies like Gritsai ended without arrest after the coerced confession during the preliminary investigation. The effect of these cases was to warn returnees from the Western zones of Germany about the danger of praising the Cold War enemy.[82] Gritsai's case was unusual in that he was arrested and spent several months in jail. It is possible the investigators decided to arrest Gritsai because he was so reluctant to admit his fault during the initial investigation.

Gritsai was fortunate compared with the witness in his case, Petr Kovalenko. Secret police officers detained Kovalenko in Khalepia, a village not far to the south of Kyiv, on the night of August 4, 1948, in connection with Gritsai's case. Kovalenko had been a clerk in a Red Army tank division during the war. In the Battle of Kyiv in September 1941, Germans encircled and destroyed his unit west of the city. He journeyed to his home village, some sixty kilometers across the Dnepr. After he had been living for nearly two years under the occupation government, the Germans arrested him in June 1943 and sent him to work in the Reich. Kovalenko met Gritsai as a forced laborer in a camp near Dusseldorf. The two were nearly twenty years apart in age, and Kovalenko had a wife and five children. Kovalenko said that he and Gritsai had not been close but that they had a trusting relationship because they were "countrymen" from the Kyiv area. After the war, he arrived in his home village in the summer of 1945.[83]

Kovalenko was not on record as having praised the Western Allies. He was probably more adept at reading political signals than Gritsai, having been a Communist Party activist in the 1930s. He came to the attention of investigators when Gritsai told them that Kovalenko had worked as a DP camp administrator in Dusseldorf under the Allies. As an older Soviet loyalist, Kovalenko fit the mold of a DP administrator. Like his peers, he may have viewed his role as a return to activism. During filtration interviews, some returnees pointed proudly to their work with the Allies, even bragging about their work for Western "counterintelligence."[84] Because of their contacts with Allied personnel, postwar DP administrators became a suspect group in the campaign against Western spies.[85] Instructions for counterintelligence officials as late as 1952 listed as targets for surveillance "repatriates who occupied command-economic positions abroad in camps for POWs, internees, or so-called displaced persons."[86] By 1948, returnees must have understood that wartime ties with the Allies were now dangerous. In testimony from the mid-1950s, Gritsai claimed that Kovalenko had denounced him as revenge for his having exposed Kovalenko as a DP camp administrator. The young bachelor Gritsai misunderstood Kovalenko's motivations. When he appealed his arrest in 1955, Kovalenko testified that the investigator Demianenko had threatened, "If you don't give us the necessary evidence, we'll arrest your wife and children."[87]

Demianenko wanted Kovalenko to denounce Gritsai, but that was not all. Kovalenko also had to admit that he had collaborated with the Germans. It was common for police to link wartime collaboration with postwar espionage. Ukrainian secret police head Savchenko asserted in a June 1946 report to Moscow, "British and American spies often recruit agents among people who compromised themselves with the Germans."[88] A Kyiv man named Aleksandr Kovalenko (no relation) was arrested in 1947 for having served with the police under the occupation. Besides the detailed account of his time working in pro-German police, his interrogators also extracted generic testimony that he had agreed to be an American spy so that he could return home.[89] For Petr Kovalenko, it was a matter of course when interrogators made him confess to a sketchy incident where he supposedly denounced Soviet people to the German police in 1943. Fearing for his family, he did not fight the charges of collaboration or espionage. The military tribunal in Kyiv sentenced him to twenty-five years in the Gulag. In 1955, he successfully contested the verdict, insisting that the interrogators had forced him to sign a false confession. Gritsai corroborated the testimony in the appeal.[90]

As in the Great Terror, Stalinist police fabricated postwar espionage accusations against returnees based on biographical details. The main factor was repatriates' having lived under the Western Allies, but histories of collaboration could also draw a secondary charge of spying. In contrast to the 1930s, several hundred people faced arrest as spies instead of several hundred thousand. The importance of the postwar espionage cases should not be underestimated, though. The mass arrests of 1937–38 had only been possible because investigators had archived thousands of incomplete cases and compiled lists of people whose biographies made them potential suspects. When police received huge quotas for arrest, these suspects became the first victims.[91] Postwar investigations offer a parallel to the 1930s. Although the spy cases did not yield thousands of arrests or convictions, they laid the groundwork for a potential campaign of repression.

It is worth comparing the postwar espionage cases to investigations of collaboration. Petr Astakhov, the young Russian trainee from Wustrau, had signed up to serve with the Germans and made no effort to deny his actions. Arrested in December 1945, he received a "tolerable" five-year sentence. He would still be in his twenties when he left the Gulag, he reasoned. Like many other educated Gulag prisoners, he avoided hard labor and found a relatively safe white-collar job at the camp at Vorkuta, in Russia's north.[92] Police had arrested Astakhov before they had begun to focus on Western espionage. In 1948, they rediscovered his case in connection with an investigation of the Wustrau men who had escaped from Germany to Switzerland with him in early 1945. In addition to repeating accusations about Wustrau, they made false allegations in 1948 that Astakhov had become an American spy in Switzerland. He signed a new confession and received an additional ten-year sentence. In the mid-1950s, a review board would overturn the conviction for espionage. Eventually Astakhov successfully appealed for the collaboration charges to be reversed as well.[93]

Astakhov's case demonstrates the distinction between accusations of collaboration and espionage. Investigators in collaboration cases used coercive techniques and demanded harsh sentences. They showed little understanding even in cases when collaboration had perhaps been the only way to survive. Nonetheless, most collaboration cases had a basis in some concrete incident where the accused had cooperated with the enemy. The accusations against returnees as spies, in contrast, were almost all fabricated. Even though not every spy investigation resulted in arrest, the investigatory techniques show a return to the mass policing practices of the 1930s. Returnees were profiled not because of what they had done while abroad but because they had lived under the rule of the USSR's Cold War enemies. Tellingly, officials after Stalin's death reversed many convictions for espionage that came under review even as they upheld a significant number of convictions for collaboration.[94]

Despite the differences in these charges, there were also connections between them. Police saw espionage for the Western Allies as a natural continuation of service to the Germans. The link between collaboration and espionage highlighted the potential military danger of the United States and the United Kingdom. As capitalist states, the United States, the United Kingdom, and Nazi Germany all shared common features. Soviet leaders believed they were all predatory at their core. The intersection of collaboration and espionage also revealed a Stalinist assumption about the nature of treason. Wartime collaboration was not based in the desperate circumstances on the Eastern Front. Nor did police imagine that postwar espionage was a product of opportunism in a chaotic postwar situation. Neither phenomenon was contingent on their specific context. Instead, treason was a sign of character flaws that promised that subsequent betrayals would follow the first.

The cases against collaboration and espionage were one way Soviet officials shaped postwar life. The disorder of war and its aftermath had allowed or forced Soviet people to do things that the USSR's leaders saw as contrary to the country's interests. Officials did not think it was necessary to make former Eastern Workers and POWs serve a Gulag sentence for working in the German economy under coercion. In contrast, people accused of informing or of formal service in an enemy formation or administration tried to justify their actions but found the police had no sympathy. Cases against Anglo-American spies also provided a reinduction into Soviet norms. The war brought millions of people into contact with non-Soviets. Soviet people now had to relearn those connections with foreigners were nothing to brag about. Investigations against repatriates showed that they could not expect the liberties of wartime to continue, especially as a new conflict loomed.

Interactions with the police taught returnees to shape their wartime biographies to the postwar moment. Many simply avoided talking about their interactions with the Western Allies or about their time abroad altogether. A small but significant number of returnees believed they had nothing to hide but instead should be applauded as heroes. As claimants to wartime resistance returned, they found that their expectations of a patriot's welcome were sorely mistaken.

UNHEROIC RETURNS

Returnee-Resisters, Historians, and Police

Prokofii Lesnichenko, the leader of Leipzig's Russian Workers Liberation Committee (Russkii Rabochii Osvoboditel'nyi Komitet, RROK), came home in August 1945. As soon as he arrived in Pavlohrad, he sent a large packet of documents to communist officials in Kyiv.[1] The folder was evidence of his committee's work in wartime resistance and postwar administration, and the party recognized his deeds by reinstating him in its ranks. Lesnichenko's return to Soviet life seemed complete after he regained his position as head of the town's branch of Osoaviakhim, the USSR's civil defense organization. Over the next year, his life took a dramatic turn. Police hounded him, claiming RROK was a sham. In March 1947, Lesnichenko would flee Pavlohrad for fear of arrest on charges of collaboration and espionage (figure 8.1).

Lesnichenko was among many returnee-resisters who attempted to write their lives into the heroic narrative of World War II. They recognized that the war was more than just a massive military conflict. It would become a central episode in Soviet mythology, like the October Revolution of 1917 or the Great Break of 1928–29, when the country embarked on rapid industrialization and the collectivization of agriculture. In the aftermath of such momentous events, authorities commissioned historical projects to document the experiences of participants.[2] Soviet leaders replicated these commemoration practices during World War II, ordering historians and museum workers to collect evidence of people's wartime heroism. For the Soviet state, these stories provided examples of heroic behavior, mobilized popular support, and justified Soviet actions after victory. Establishing a war record was no less important for individuals. Signifi-

FIGURE 8.1. Prokofii Lesnichenko on a picnic in Pavlohrad. HDASBU, f. 1, spr. 694, ark. 186.

cant episodes like World War II took central places in the biography of each person. The narrative they gave of their life impacted every official encounter they had: in job applications, university admissions, petitions to power, and more. People who had a pro-Soviet biography could expect advantages, while those with black marks faced obstacles to advancement.[3]

Most returnee-resisters hoped their biographies would help them avoid repression, but the most ambitious expected to return to the USSR as heroes. Hundreds of returnees, or more, claimed to have been in resistance organizations as Eastern Workers or POWs. By early 1948, the secret police in Kyiv province alone had registered twenty-five resistance organizations, some with dozens of members.[4] Repatriate-resisters would find advocates among the workers of the Soviet historian Isaak Mints's commission—a state-sponsored collective of historians who recorded oral histories with participants in the war. They would also find a supporter in Lieutenant Colonel Efim Brodskii, a military historian who had worked as a propagandist in the army's political administration. Historians and resistance members alike would discover that the stories they wanted to tell did not mesh with Stalinist official expectations about the war.

The most skeptical about repatriate-resisters were secret police officials. Counterintelligence officers played a central role in deciding who was a war hero. Their investigations of people who claimed to have been Soviet loyalists dovetailed with investigations of collaboration. Police uncovered instances where partisans had become police and vice versa.[5] Among returnee-resisters, too, they found undeniable evidence that some resistance group members had also collaborated with the Germans. In other instances, police discovered that the repatriate-resisters had exaggerated or falsified claims. These faults cast doubt on all resistance organizations, which police investigators deemed "false undergrounds." The threat in this falsehood was that wartime collaborators or current Anglo-American spies would infiltrate the USSR as heroes. At the same time, the alleged deception was also in the type of heroism the groups claimed. The best resister was a martyr who committed violent acts and died on the orders of Soviet leaders. Returnee-resisters, who had opposed Germany as they could while they tried to survive, made poor postwar heroes.

Writing the Resistance

Soviet leaders presented World War II as an epochal event from its start. On the day after the German invasion, articles in *Pravda* described the conflict as a "patriotic war," evoking Russia's epic struggle in the Patriotic War against Napoleon more than a century earlier.[6] A monumental fight deserved commemoration efforts to match. After the Battle of Moscow in early 1942, the Soviet government appointed historian Isaak Mints to head a commission in the Academy of Sciences to document the war. Mints had led the project to create the multivolume *History of the Civil War in the USSR*. Now commanding a team of dozens of historians, Mints would document the Soviet-German war as it unfolded. The more than four thousand interviews with war participants that his team conducted are still a major source for historians.[7]

In addition to interviewing Red Army soldiers, commission members gathered testimony about irregular forces. The commission had a branch in each Soviet republic, and in Ukraine a major goal was to document the history of partisans and life under the occupation. Commission historians also collected stories of resistance in Germany. In many cases, returnee-resisters took the initiative to contact the commission. M. Ia. Kogan, a historian in Moscow writing about the partisan movement, received a packet of documents from Chernihiv via the commission's Ukrainian branch. The centerpiece was a collection of poems compiled by Nikolai Shevchenko, a museum worker who had been a forced laborer in Germany. Shevchenko wrote that the compilation was the work of the Central Committee for Struggle, a group he had led in Bavaria. Kogan was intrigued. He visited Shevchenko in April 1946 and afterward created a seventy-three-question survey for the group's thirty-two members. He exhorted Shevchenko in a letter that the work of commemoration was not only "imperative for you but above all for history."[8]

Unlike the historians of the Mints Commission, army propagandist and historian Efim Brodskii had unique access to sources outside the USSR. Born in 1913 to an educated Jewish family, Brodskii was a product of postrevolutionary upward mobility. His father was an agricultural specialist whose position in the Mykolaiv provincial government perhaps helped Brodskii receive a leadership position in the city's Komsomol and become a specialist in factory construction. For a period of several months, he was arrested in one of the industrial trials of the late 1920s and early 1930s, when Stalin instigated the arrest of non-Bolshevik factory specialists. Unlike many others caught up in this campaign, Brodskii was exonerated. In 1935, he enrolled in the Department of History at Moscow State University and graduated in 1940 with a specialization in modern German history. When Germany invaded the USSR, Brodskii joined the Chief Political Administration of the Red Army (Glavnoe Politicheskoe Upravlenie Raboche-krest'ianskoi Krasnoi Armii, GlavPUR), which assigned him to a department that propagandized to German soldiers and POWs. After Germany's defeat at Stalingrad, Brodskii worked with German defectors in the National Committee for a Free Germany. The organization mirrored the anti-Soviet Vlasov army in its goals and activities, although German defectors were fewer than their counterparts. The committee served primarily to spread propaganda among German soldiers but also organized a limited number of operations involving Soviet partisans. Brodskii's unusual experiences nurtured his sympathies for German prisoners and perhaps for POWs in general. Most Soviet citizens encountered German POWs as the enemy.[9] Brodskii tried to understand their plight and cooperated with some as a pro-Soviet force.[10]

After Germany's defeat, Brodskii became the Soviet occupation administration's head of propaganda for Berlin. It was a historian's dream. Brodskii had access to piles of secret German documents, including reports from Gestapo investigations of resistance among Eastern Workers and Soviet POWs.[11] The most important was a report on the arrest of a network of Soviet resisters in Bavaria called the Brotherly Union of Prisoners of War (Bratskii Soiuz Voennoplennykh, BSV). The Gestapo claimed that the group had hundreds of members and ties with German antifascists. Many of the Gestapo's accusations were paranoid fantasies of Judeo-Bolshevik espionage based on confessions extracted through torture. Despite implausible conclusions, the report gave credible evidence that pro-Soviet oppositionist groups had operated in Germany. Police found that their main accomplishments included propagandizing among foreign workers and helping POWs escape from their work camps. These would have been feasible activities for resistance groups in Germany. The participants were also plausible. Many arrestees had freed themselves from POW camps by enlisting in German formations, where they had the comparative freedom to organize resistance.[12]

As Brodskii gathered data from Germany, his writing took two paths, both involving resistance. The first was his candidate dissertation (PhD equivalent) about the July 20, 1944, military conspiracy led by Claus von Stauffenberg that attempted to assassinate Hitler. While he finished his dissertation, Brodskii also laid the groundwork for a publication about Soviet resistance in Germany. In August 1947, he received an enthusiastic request for an article from General Aleksandr N. Shcherbakov, the deputy editor of the Soviet army newspaper *Krasnaia Zvezda*. Brodskii submitted a draft and waited. After some time, Brodskii wrote to Shcherbakov but received no response. Later he learned that a secret police leader had read the manuscript and warned *Krasnaia Zvezda*'s editor, "This is all a Gestapo provocation."[13]

Concerned by Shcherbakov's silence, Brodskii dropped the project for several years while he focused on his dissertation. After his successful dissertation defense, he took a position teaching at the Syzran Infantry School in Kuibyshev province. He returned to the topic of Soviet resisters but, chastened by his experience with *Krasnaia Zvezda*, sought approval to publish from Communist Party leaders. He sent a manuscript to the Central Committee secretary Georgii Malenkov with a request to proceed with the topic. Malenkov forwarded the manuscript to the party's propaganda department and to GlavPUR. At a meeting with leaders in the propaganda apparatus, the assistant head of the party Central Committee's Department of Agitation and Propaganda, L. A. Slepov, told Brodskii that he should abandon the work. If the topic merited attention, "the corresponding organizations," a euphemism for the secret police, would take it up. Brodskii understood that the project was being shelved but could not comprehend the decision. The story of Soviet resisters, he wrote, had "immense moral value . . . [as] an indelible page of the history of the Great Patriotic War." Historians might also sympathize with Brodskii's frustration over possessing "a large amount of top-quality sources" that he was unable to use.[14]

In the spring of 1951, he tried once again to receive approval for the project. Brodskii met with Mikhail Suslov, the Communist Party Central Committee secretary and chief ideologue, who organized a commission in the Central Committee's Department of Propaganda and Agitation to review a potential publication. Brodskii sent a 162-page manuscript titled "The Patriotic Struggle of Soviet People Taken by Force to Hitlerite Slavery and Its Influence on the Internal Situation in Imperial Germany in the Final Stage of the Second World War." Propaganda officials sent the manuscript for review to representatives of interested groups in the party-state.[15]

Officers from the Repatriation Administration received a copy and wrote a scathing response. They asserted that Brodskii was writing about unknown people—possibly enemies of the Soviet state.[16] Commission members criticized

Brodskii for being too credulous of Nazi German reports and worried that he would unwittingly introduce German provocations into the Soviet press. Over the years, Brodskii himself would revise aspects of the work that were too trusting of the German documents in the initial manuscript. The "Patriotic Struggle" text repeated the Gestapo's implausible claim that Iosif Feldman, a Jewish POW who had survived under the false identity of a Ukrainian translator named Georgii Fesenko, was sent by Soviet secret police to conduct anti-German work behind enemy lines. Some years later, having tracked down information about Feldman in the USSR, Brodskii would find that he was a Soviet-Jewish medic with no ties to the secret police.[17]

A fundamental problem with Brodskii's work was that it made Soviet people in Germany into autonomous historical agents. Brodskii quoted (via the Gestapo) a Soviet resister named Roman Petrushel: "We know that we will be responsible to our [Soviet] government for preparing and carrying out a revolution in Germany." To repatriation officials, the quote implied that Soviet resisters were autonomous participants in the potential creation of postwar Germany. The Repatriation Administration's review criticized Brodskii for publishing materials that implied that "the activities of the underground organization [were] undertaken in the name of the Soviet Government."[18] Brodskii's portrayal of the resisters misappropriated the prerogatives of the party-state in initiating resistance against the Germans.

The postwar narrative of the war showed it to be a centralized effort, led by Stalin. In truth, the desperation of the war had forced Stalin to reverse the centralizing tendencies of the prewar period and allow some delegation of authority to local elites and irregular military forces like partisans. The end of the war marked a return to centralization both within the USSR and in Soviet-dominated Eastern and Central Europe.[19] Partisan resistance on the Eastern Front, where commanders had enjoyed significant autonomy, was recast after the war as party-led opposition. The problem with Brodskii's manuscript was that resisters claimed to act in the interests of the Soviet state, but their autonomy broke with the postwar assertion that the party and, ultimately, Stalin were the chief historical agents in the war.

Despite their criticisms, repatriation officials evaluated Brodskii's manuscript with more generosity than the other reviewers, who probably included secret police officials. The discussion of the manuscript at high levels in the party-state indicates the importance ascribed to the promotion of wartime heroes. It suggests that they took Brodskii's research seriously as well and now made an example of his mistakes. The commission that convened to discuss the manuscript criticized him for writing about people who were not real resisters, implying that any oppositionist in Nazi Germany could not have survived except by becoming a Gestapo informant. Any survivors were thus either provocateurs peddling false stories or German agents. Even if resisters had survived, it was not politically appropriate to make POWs into heroes. Would it be fair to equate the bravery of prisoners with that of soldiers who had not been captured? Soviet soldiers were supposed to have fought until they were dead or incapacitated. Capture was abnormal, and Brodskii's work threatened to normalize or even glorify it.[20]

Brodskii chose a terrible time to push for the work to be published. Soviet Jews from the late 1940s until Stalin's death faced increasing discrimination and sometimes arrest. Traditional antisemitism influenced the campaign, but the main reason for the persecution of Jews was the foundation of Israel. It seemed to Stalin and other officials that Soviet Jews' loyalties might be divided between the USSR and the new Jewish state. The euphemistic accusation of "cosmopolitanism"—which hinted at foreign allegiances and strong connections abroad—dogged Soviet Jews. Brodskii was potentially vulnerable to these accusations because of his work with German soldiers and officers. Who could have been a better spy than a Jewish officer with a network of hostile foreign contacts? In 1952, Brodskii lost his job at the infantry school, was discharged from the army, and found himself the director of a kindergarten in Riga.[21]

Undoubtedly his Jewish background was problematic, but Brodskii's advocacy for resisters made him a target as well. His persecutors in the military's political administration charged him with transforming compromised individuals into war heroes. Not only were their reputations tarnished as POWs, but their resistance activity had occurred outside Soviet control. Who could say what they had done in Germany without party-authorized witnesses and documentation?

Stalinist leaders set impossibly high standards for public wartime heroism. Besides resisters' having to prove that they had undertaken a feat during the war, their biographies before and during the war had to be impeccable. After Stalin's death, the superhuman criteria for resistance lessened, and Brodskii would help resisters in Germany gain recognition for their acts. Although Brodskii's Stalin-era critics were uncompromising, there were also good reasons to be skeptical about some of the returnee-resisters. The benefits that accrued to people whom Stalin's regime recognized as wartime heroes encouraged exaggeration or outright lies about the war.

Inventing Resistance

Wartime legends and exaggerations of military exploits are not unique to the Soviet Union. States use them to boost morale and provide material for propaganda. Embellishment of heroic deeds in war is also perhaps a product of the difficulty of their verification and the benefits, formal and informal, that they can yield. In the USSR, demobilized soldiers with medals—or con artists who obtained them illicitly—could demand better living conditions and other forms of special treatment.[22]

One of the people who aspired to a heroic biography was Nikolai Shevchenko, the returnee who contacted M. Ia. Kogan at the Mints Commission about his resistance group. Born in 1903, Shevchenko finished grade school and even had some higher education, which allowed him to find work at the Chernihiv Historical Museum. After the German invasion, he enlisted in the army and was captured at the end of August 1941 near Kremenchuk (Poltava province). He escaped captivity in October, but six months later while he was working in Bila Tserkva (Kyiv province), local police deported him to labor in Bavaria, where he worked on a railroad loading team until the end of the war. After liberation he ran the club and newspaper at the transit camp for repatriates at a Soviet army base in Poland. In November 1945, he returned to the USSR with Florisa Galetskaia, a Soviet woman in her midtwenties whom he had met in Germany. It seems probable that they were romantic partners. Shevchenko resumed his work at the museum and arranged for Galetskaia to receive a job, too. Together they promoted the history of Soviet insurgents—including themselves as resistance leaders.[23]

Shevchenko and Galetskaia claimed for themselves a faultless record of anti-German feats in their organization, called the Central Committee for Struggle. They gave an auspicious date for its founding, November 7, 1942—the twenty-fifth anniversary of the October Revolution—when Shevchenko and a handful of campmates met to create the group. In August 1945, its members gathered in Bolkenhain (today's Bolkow, Poland) to reflect on their wartime activities and, more important, collect materials to show to Soviet authorities after return. The group's members assigned themselves revolutionary-style nicknames. Shevchenko was "Zheleznov," a last name derived from the Russian word for iron. He did not shy away from personal glorification. The poetry collection he sent to Kogan included an ode titled "That Name Is Our Great Stalin," which he attributed to Soviet forced laborers in a work camp in Nuremberg:

> Zheleznov, our senior comrade,
> We'll go into combat at your yell,
> A fire in the hearts of millions was had,
> When we heard your warning bell.
>
> You were the first on that November day,
> Who made the antifascist flag shown,
> And now we know that along the way,
> With you nearby, we won't be alone.

Your call set the people's hearts aflame,
They read it again and again,
Because you wrote a sacred name,
That name is our Great Stalin.[24]

The Bolkenhain documents asserted that Zheleznov-Shevchenko led the Soviet resisters in Bavaria to a stunning record of achievements. The highlights included the destruction of a dynamite factory in Fürth in April 1943, a train crash near Aschaffenburg that killed three thousand people, organizing thousands of people as strikers, and illegally obtaining a metric ton of butter.[25]

If these feats sound improbable, it is because Shevchenko and Galetskaia almost certainly took credit for accidents and for the sum of sporadic, individual acts of resistance that occurred in the area. For example, Libuše Hittmanová, a Czech forced laborer, recalled later in life how she was injured in an accidental explosion at the Fürth dynamite factory in April 1943. The explosion was probably the same one as the incident the resistance group claimed.[26] Shevchenko and Galetskaia included other acts of resistance retroactively. In February 1944, the Gestapo arrested Eastern Worker Mikhail Sinitsyn in Bamberg (Bavaria) for writing anti-German poetry. After his release, Sinitsyn met Shevchenko and Galetskaia and joined their group. They counted his anti-German poetry as one of the group's achievements.[27]

The group was not entirely fabricated. Like many small groups in Germany, it had undertaken intermittent anti-German propaganda work. Group member Pavel Primak told police in an interrogation that the group's main activity had been to gather, translate, and redistribute pamphlets that American planes dropped.[28]

Shevchenko and Galetskaia apparently believed that the group's plausible activity was not enough to merit attention from officials. Distributing flyers was a real, dangerous form of resistance in Germany, but as museum workers charged with curating the history of wartime partisans, they probably understood the importance of violent resistance in partisan groups' self-presentation. After Soviet rule returned to formerly occupied territories, hundreds of groups came forward to claim partisan status. The number of claimants and the significance of the partisan movement for the history of the war motivated Communist Party officials to organize commissions to review petitions for partisan status. The decision often involved local patronage politics. How claims and claimants fit into local politics was at least as important as the facts of resistance.[29] Partisans who had come to the movement closer to the time of liberation were seemingly more successful applicants because they had better chances of survival and fewer chances to compromise themselves through collaboration. Their violent exploits also more often dovetailed with Red Army operations on the eve of liberation and were easier to document than actions that took place earlier in the occupation.[30]

Becoming a partisan was more than a matter of pride. Partisan status could support people's reputation as local leaders or earn them promotions.[31] There was also the possibility of remuneration. In Shevchenko's case, a secret police report asserted that he was interested in a 5,000-ruble award and was exploring his chances of joining the party.[32]

The two museum workers pressed their case by sending materials about the group to officials and publications in Moscow, Kyiv, and Chernihiv. These efforts promised increased scrutiny on the group and the record it claimed. When members received surveys from Moscow, the extent of their supposed wartime activity made some uncomfortable. Primak politely wrote to Shevchenko about the questionnaire that he did not remember all the details of the group's history. Shevchenko replied, "If you have forgotten some moments of our work, I'll remind you briefly." Shevchenko proceeded over several pages to detail all the group's would-be achievements, punctuated with phrases like "you yourself remember." Shevchenko sent similar prompts to other group members.[33]

Some group members chafed at Shevchenko's account. Petr Druz, who had promoted the group as much as anyone besides Shevchenko, came to envy his friend's position as leader. After submitting materials to Kogan, Druz soured on the enterprise and wrote to Primak about Shevchenko, "He is trying to get all the glory and fame for himself on everyone else's effort."[34] Group member Natalia Kolomeets was angry that Galetskaia occupied such a prominent position in the group. She wrote to Druz, "I don't care if he [Shevchenko] is the leader, but he is talking her [Galetskaia] up too." Kolomeets accused Galetskaia of taking ethnic German (Volksdeutsche) status during the war. As a domestic servant for much of her time in Germany, Galetskaia had been "clean and satiated" while other forced laborers suffered.[35]

Police discovered Shevchenko's group through his correspondence with Kogan. Soon authorities were studying all the members' letters to each other. Police had arrested Primak earlier on suspicion of distributing Ukrainian nationalist leaflets in his village in Kyiv province. They released him only after a handwriting expert from Moscow determined that he was not the author. Now in conjunction with the Shevchenko group, police summoned Primak for interrogation. He told investigators that he had drafted an answer to Kogan based on Shevchenko's letter. Anxious about endorsing Shevchenko's claims, he decided against responding to Kogan.[36] The investigation had tragic consequences for the group's poet, Mikhail Sinitsyn. After receiving several orders to appear for interrogation, Sinitsyn hung himself in his childhood room in the attic of his mother's house. Witnesses said that Sinitsyn was on the verge of divorce with his wife, whom he had met in Germany. But they also claimed that he did not seem suicidal before the police summons.[37]

Shevchenko remained free until 1949, when police arrested him on charges of anti-Soviet agitation. Witnesses, including several members of his resistance organization, claimed that he had denounced the Soviet collective farm system during the war. Although it was not the formal charge, it seems that his real offense was that he "created fictitious materials about a supposed underground organization that he led."[38] Before a tribunal, Shevchenko said that he had comforted teenage girls being deported alongside him. He said that "Germany is a cultured, wealthy country" and that the girls would work in comfort for landowners, not in factories. He also admitted that he had lived better than other forced laborers because he had worked in the camp kitchen. Shevchenko nonetheless insisted that he had organized anti-German activities such as the destruction of a dynamite factory.[39] He would serve five years in a labor camp in the Far East until an amnesty in 1955 freed him.[40]

Returnees with a more dubious claim to resistance than Shevchenko also attempted to take their place as wartime heroes. When Evgenii Kiselev was a concentration camp prisoner at Buchenwald, he had not blown up a workstation or killed his guards. A week before US forces liberated his subcamp, he managed to escape with six friends on the eve of a forced march to the German interior. The escape went against German designs, but Kiselev's main goal seems to have been self-preservation. After liberation he became a fixer at the Stahmeln Soviet DP camp in Leipzig and joined Prokofii Lesnichenko's group, RROK.

After the Western Allies transported Soviet DPs from Leipzig to the Red Army's zone of control, Kiselev took command of a group of RROK members traveling home in mid-July 1945. They included his Buchenwald friends who had helped him run the Stahmeln camp, plus their romantic partners and friends. Kiselev had obtained a letter from the head of the transit camp at Wohlau (today Wolow, Poland), testifying that he and his group had undertaken "special tasks for the General Staff of the R[ed] A[rmy] in Germany." Kiselev later said that the Wohlau camp commandant had rewritten a letter from the head of repatriation in Leipzig, Captain Kulikov. The phrasing in the letter almost certainly was Kiselev's.[41] The document worked, and compared with the ordeals many repatriates faced, Kiselev's group returned quickly. It took a week to pass through verification. They then set off eastward and, several days later, arrived in Moscow. Police and repatriation officials were shocked to learn that a group of approximately twenty returnees had entered the restricted city by using a letter about an undocumented organization called RROK as an entry pass. Authorities in Moscow ordered the group's verification and, after they passed, sent them all to their prewar residences. Kiselev arrived in the port city of Mykolaiv in southern Ukraine on August 5, 1945.[42]

Before the war, Kiselev had been prone to deceit. His good looks and easy smile belied that he was a "shady person," according to his wife, Maria Gavrichkova. She knew he was an orphan from Saratov but had heard him give his birthplace as Tashkent. She also wondered if he had pretended to have a higher education to get his job as an engineer. The war had made Kiselev restless. After his return to Mykolaiv, he avoided the apartment he shared with Gavrichkova and went to live with a friend, Viktor Sinkevich. In Kiselev's defense, Gavrichkova was not at home on the day he returned; she was serving a short jail sentence for having left her work early, a crime under the June 1940 labor law. When Gavrichkova came home, Kiselev saw her for two hours before announcing that he had to leave for Moscow. Kiselev would come to Mykolaiv for intermittent visits over the following weeks, sometimes staying with Sinkevich. Although Kiselev never said so, it seems probable that during his absences he was seeing Klavdia Astashina, his camp wife in Leipzig. After he had spent a month roaming, Gavrichkova demanded that he settle in Mykolaiv, and Kiselev agreed. He said that he was going to stay anyway, telling her the dubious story that the Mykolaiv secret police had recruited him to work as an engineer.

When he settled in Mykolaiv, Kiselev concealed his whereabouts from Astashina. In November 1945, she managed to find his address and came to Mykolaiv to inform him that she was pregnant from him. Kiselev hid Astashina from Gavrichkova until the former moved with their newborn daughter to Sinkevich's apartment in April 1946. When Gavrichkova learned about Astashina, she and Kiselev had a "scandalous argument." Things calmed down when Kiselev agreed that they would go to tell Astashina that Gavrichkova was his real wife. But at Sinkevich's another fight erupted when Gavrichkova found a document on which the last name Kiseleva appeared instead of Astashina. (Kiseleva would be the married name of Kiselev's proper wife.)[43] Gavrichkova went through the seventy-some photographs her husband had taken as keepsakes from Leipzig and blacked out Astashina's image in them (figure 8.2).

On July 12, 1946, police saved Kiselev from his love triangle by arresting him. Investigators would study his case for the next ten months. The investigation file consists of two volumes, containing some six hundred pages of interrogation protocols and witness accounts, plus photographs and letters. After the investigation, the province's military tribunal convicted him of having informed to the Gestapo about pro-Soviet resisters in the Mykolaiv jail. The file presents a tangled collection of narratives, but the approximate story of Kiselev's time in occupied Mykolaiv is the following: German police arrested Kiselev in

FIGURE 8.2. "Photographing [us] in Stahmeln camp. May 1945." Evgenii Kiselev (left) with campmates. Klavdia Astashina's face was blacked out by Kiselev's wife, Maria Gavrichkova. AUSBU MO, f. 5, spr. 8042, t. 2, unnumbered folder with photographs.

September 1942 for black market activity after a business partner denounced him. For the next year, he lived in the Mykolaiv prison and concentration camp, sharing cells with arrestees accused of participating in the local pro-Soviet underground. He held positions of relative comfort in the kitchen and as cell monitor. Witnesses noted that he could leave the cell and suggested it was no coincidence that the Germans always seemed to call people for interrogations just after he had left. A coworker in the kitchen told investigators that Kiselev had encouraged her to tell the Germans everything she knew about the resistance. Others mentioned that as cell monitor, he beat fellow prisoners for smoking and stealing. Several also made fuzzy accusations that Kiselev denounced a cellmate as a Jew.[44]

The investigation materials are problematic and conflicting. It seems possible that Kiselev's former cellmates were conspiring against him or that investigators compelled them to denounce him. The sketchy story about Kiselev's denunciation of a Jewish prisoner was possibly invented because, unlike the other accusations, Kiselev denied it fervently and pointed to significant contradictions in the accounts. For example, the incident was said to have occurred in a cell where he had never been held. Most of the testimonies, however, gave plausible and largely matching stories about Kiselev's cooperation with the Germans. Small discrepancies between the accounts suggest that they were based on memory rather than police coordination. Among the most questionable pieces of evidence in the investigation are Kiselev's confessions. In an early interrogation, Kiselev said that he signed an agreement to become a police agent for the Germans. This admission became the central evidence against him, and it seems likely that the interrogators coerced him into making the confession. Nonetheless, at the trial he acknowledged that he had become a police agent in the prison even as he denied having committed any concrete anti-Soviet acts. The tribunal sentenced him to ten years of hard labor in the Gulag camp at Karaganda, Kazakhstan.[45]

The fact or extent of Kiselev's work as an informant is debatable, but the investigation materials leave no doubt that he misrepresented himself as a resistance hero throughout the war and in its immediate aftermath. Kiselev began to create a legend about himself as a resister in Buchenwald. He claimed to his team to have worked before the war for the Soviet government in Moscow. Kiselev also told them that a Soviet intelligence officer had ordered him to conduct sabotage, and that his resistance work under the occupation had led to his arrest. He regaled Soviet DPs in Leipzig with the story of how the Germans had planned to execute him for resistance activities in the Buchenwald subcamp at Jena but let him go for unexplained reasons.[46] It seems that the DPs took the handsome and intelligent Kiselev, beret thrust back on his head, at his word.

After he returned to the USSR, Kiselev continued and intensified his efforts to create a heroic war past. It is possible that he learned from the experience with RROK. He watched as Prokofii Lesnichenko dispensed RROK cards, inducting dozens of people into the ranks of wartime oppositionists, regardless of their wartime records. One of the men who received a RROK card asked Kiselev if it was legal for them to claim membership. "Don't worry, it will all be OK," Kiselev soothed.[47] Far from suffering because they exaggerated their resistance accounts, the group's members had only seemed to benefit.

Upon his return to Mykolaiv, Kiselev began a campaign to commemorate the local resistance. The city's Soviet loyalists had formed an anti-German underground organization called the Mykolaiv Center during the first days of the occupation. The Red Army had sent codenamed officer Anatolii Palagniuk to organize resistance activities.[48] Kiselev had known Palagniuk among other resisters in the Mykolaiv prison. Although the Germans executed the most prominent resisters, others survived and remained in Mykolaiv. Kiselev began to gather the survivors and positioned himself as protector of the group's memory. He arranged meetings with Mykolaiv Center members and said that he had been in the resistance, too. He told them that after Mykolaiv, as a prisoner in Buchenwald, his resistance activities had involved French and Belgian political prisoners. After returning to the USSR, Kiselev went to the Red Army's General Staff in Moscow. He found a familiar person there—Palagniuk. Kiselev said that the Red Army officer was now working for the General Staff and had asked his wartime resistance comrade, Evgenii Kiselev, to gather the recollections of fellow resistance members.[49]

Some of the resistance members were receptive to Kiselev, although they later denied it, because he worked to gain them the status of partisans.[50] Apparently he had made similar promises to Leipzig returnees. His Buchenwald comrade, Boris Surov-Kurov-Kin, asked in a letter from Kazakhstan, "Is it possible to get a letter through you from the NKO [People's Commissariat of Defense] that I participated in the war as an officer?"[51] By interviewing resistance members, Kiselev seems to have wanted to learn enough about the Mykolaiv underground to insert himself into their stories. After meeting with a few surviving members, Kiselev visited Vsevolod Bondarenko, a leading resistance member and regional party official, at home. He extracted a promise from Bondarenko to introduce him to Mykolaiv province's party secretary. Kiselev wanted to request recognition for Mykolaiv's resistance members, including himself.[52]

Kiselev never followed up with Bondarenko and shortly after their meeting stopped trying to become a retroactive leader in the resistance. Perhaps he learned that in 1943 the Germans had executed Anatolii Palagniuk, Kiselev's supposed contact in the General Staff. Palagniuk became famous in local history; today one of Mykolaiv's central streets bears his name (hyphenated with his real name, Vladimir, Andreev). The information about Palagniuk would have alerted Kiselev to a new reality of postwar life. None of his campmates in Buchenwald and Leipzig had been able to verify his stories. Even German authorities would have struggled to untangle his biography had they bothered. In the Soviet Union, too, chaotic conditions allowed people to claim false achievements or manufacture identities outright.[53] Nonetheless, Stalin's police had the resources and will to sort out such accounts and refute Kiselev's story.

During his first interrogations, Kiselev said that he knew Palagniuk and other visible partisans. But Soviet investigators were able to find former Mykolaiv Center members as easily as Kiselev had found them and summoned them to verify his claims. They all testified that they had met Kiselev in jail during the war. According to witnesses, Palagniuk also had only known Kiselev through their mutual incarceration. An underground member who had worked with Kiselev in the prison kitchen said that one of the arrested leaders of the resistance had warned her that Kiselev might be an informer.[54] Confronted with the evidence contradicting his account, Kiselev admitted, "My previous testimony about this issue was false."[55] Maria Gavrichkova said that her husband had not conducted any conscious resistance activity. He spent the war trying to survive by selling stolen goods on the black market.[56] On trial at a military tribunal, Kiselev admitted, "Yes, I wasn't a member of the underground, and I wasn't a representative of the General Staff of the Red Army. Yes, I lied about all that."[57]

Almost a decade after Kiselev was sent to Karaganda, Khrushchev's government began to issue amnesties and offered the prospect of rehabilitation to Stalin-era arrestees. Both Kiselev and Shevchenko were released from the Gulag by amnesty and sent appeals to Moscow to clear their names. Their letters remained silent on important aspects of their cases. Kiselev wrote nothing about RROK and his claims of resistance. In a petition to Khrushchev, he backdated his arrest to the start of Mykolaiv's occupation, allowing him to avoid awkward questions about his time under German rule in the city.[58]

Shevchenko and Kiselev both concentrated on their victimization by investigators. Their claims of police coercion were plausible but could also be seen as calculating echoes of official rhetoric. In 1953, Khrushchev had maneuvered the party's collective leadership to oust secret police leader Lavrentii Beria from his posts and place him under arrest. Beria and underlings became the primary scapegoats for Stalin-era crimes. Both appellants emphasized Khrushchev's enemies as their tormentors. Shevchenko claimed that "Beria's little investigators" had invented the accusations against him.[59] Kiselev also seems to have understood that his case would be more compelling if he could fit into this narrative and described himself as the victim of Beria's "lackeys." He wrote that the investigators had beaten him until he confessed to the crimes, knocking out two teeth. State lawyers reviewed Kiselev's complaint and found his accusations were credible. In 1956, the three officers who had handled Kiselev's case were still security officials, now in more senior positions. They signed statements that they had not used force in the case. The review, however, found other arrestees who made similar accusations against the officers. Based on these findings, one of the three was fired, and another received an official reprimand.[60]

Despite the evidence of torture during interrogation, the review still found Kiselev guilty of informing on fellow prisoners to the Germans. A post-Soviet review in 1993 also found the evidence against Kiselev to be overwhelming, although the state lawyer reclassified the crime to a lesser offense.[61] Shevchenko demanded rehabilitation in 1954, 1956, and 1964. These reviews all upheld Shevchenko's conviction on counterrevolutionary propaganda. In 1990 Shevchenko's son Vladimir successfully appealed on behalf of his dead father. Soviet Ukrainian procuracy officials argued that the elder Shevchenko "had not called for the overthrow, undermining or weakening of Soviet rule" and thus had been wrongly convicted of counterrevolutionary propaganda.[62] The appeals process, like the trials, did not dwell on claims to resistance and evident misrepresentations. Still, one can imagine that the reviewers, many of them veterans, would have had little sympathy for men who misappropriated the honor that they believed belonged to others. V. Tsyganenko, a Chernihiv assistant procurator, commented on Shevchenko's case in 1964, "It is obvious that citizen Shevchenko N. N. . . . . collected materials about the struggle of forced laborers, amalgamated them and tried to place himself personally in the foreground."[63]

Why had these men engaged in such falsifications? Both understood that their wartime biography would be crucial to their advancement as postwar Soviet elites. And both sensed that in the tumult of war and its immediate aftermath, it would be possible to write their own stories. Constructing such biographies in peacetime became more difficult. Police could call witnesses and find German documents. Just as important, investigators were wary of claims to wartime resistance and jealous of the heroic memory of the war.

The Return of the Russian Workers Liberation Committee

The members of Prokofii Lesnichenko's RROK group mostly avoided the exaggerations that Nikolai Shevchenko committed. Unlike Evgenii Kiselev's attempts to insinuate himself into the Mykolaiv Center, most RROK members said they committed plausible acts of resistance such as distributing leaflets. Affiliation with RROK earned Lesnichenko a few quiet months after his return to Pavlohrad in August 1945. He brought his new wife, Evgenia Osipovich, to town. As a graduate of a Minsk medical school, she found work quickly as a gynecologist in the local hospital. Police noted Lesnichenko's arrival, but he dealt with them as openly as he had with the party officials in Kyiv whom he sent the packet of RROK documents. Pavlohrad investigators called him for questioning on September 8, 1945, and he sent authorities a report in October 1945 outlining encounters with Allied authorities who had asked loaded questions about the quality of life in the USSR. He also told Soviet police about his meetings with Allied officers regarding the theft of cattle by DPs. For the sake of transparency, he mentioned that Allied military intelligence officers had also been there.[64]

It was a bold decision for Lesnichenko to be so forthright, and especially to volunteer information about interactions with foreign intelligence officials. Other returnees believed the safest path was to remain silent after return. A RROK member and one of Kiselev's Buchenwald men, Anatolii Popov, took this approach. Investigators in Russia's Vologda province questioned him about his RROK card in late 1945. During the interrogation, they asked why he had not applied to reinstate his prewar party membership. Popov said that as a POW, he had not yet earned his place back in the party's ranks. He continued, "I consider myself guilty for being taken prisoner and not fulfilling the oath to shoot my-self instead."[65]

By the beginning of 1946, authorities across the USSR had encountered doz-ens of returnees who had presented RROK cards during filtration. All the cards were signed by Lesnichenko. Eventually police would register more than a hun-dred people associated with the RROK case. Some RROK cardholders faced charges of collaboration based on real wartime activity. Besides Kiselev, police arrested Aleksandr Dzadzamia and Iokim Kapanadze, the Georgian doctors who had come to Leipzig from the propaganda camp at Wustrau. Dzadzamia was in Lesnichenko's group during the war, but Kapanadze seems not to have been. In a judicial confrontation between the two men, Kapanadze denied having spread resistance materials. "I'm not tired of living," he had said when Dzadzamia of-fered to include him in the resistance group.[66] In his first interrogations Dzadza-mia insisted that he had participated in a resistance group with Lesnichenko, although he admitted that the postliberation RROK organization had included people not involved in the resistance group. Dzadzamia's story changed in future interrogations, in which he signed wooden confessions that RROK had only ex-isted after liberation and was not a real resistance group.[67]

Finding members spread throughout the USSR, Ukrainian police believed RROK could be a nationwide plot against Soviet rule. Hints that the group had ties to Anglo-American forces raised even greater alarm. When reports about RROK members accumulated, officers in Pavlohrad reviewed their materials in early 1946 and found that RROK cardholder Anna Maslova, the girlfriend of a DP camp leader, had said during local filtration that British forces had printed the cards. Pavlohrad police ignored the comment initially. Amid growing Cold War tensions, they returned to Maslova's testimony, which indicated that RROK not only was helping collaborators escape justice but also was allowing spies to embed themselves in the USSR. Ukrainian counterintelligence leaders began a broader investigation into Lesnichenko and the other RROK returnees. In Feb-ruary and March, Pavlohrad's counterintelligence officers interrogated members of the group in the city: Lesnichenko, Efrosinia Usenko, and the young married couple Natalia Berkun and Aleksandr Kuprii, who had met in Leipzig. The in-terrogations revealed little that the police did not already know. The accounts largely corroborated one another and confirmed the story of a small resistance group that transformed into RROK after liberation.[68]

Police remained suspicious of the group despite the corresponding accounts. Most of all, authorities refused to acknowledge the complexities of the war that drove people to collaboration and resistance. Authorities wanted people's war-time biographies to fit into clear categories—treasonous collaborators and ac-complices, heroic resisters, and passive victims. People like Dzadzamia, with a complex wartime biography of concurrent accommodation and resistance, did not fit into any of these roles exclusively. More broadly, the charges of collaboration were incompatible with the presentation of RROK as a resistance group and discredited the entire organization. When officers questioned Lesnichenko about Dzadzamia and others, he understood that the connection was dangerous. Giving these men cards had been "idiocy" and "mistakes" enabled by ignorance of their pasts.[69] Lesnichenko may not have known Dzadzamia's whole biography in Leipzig, but he must have understood the compromises that POWs made with German authorities for survival. He knew what he was doing when he gave Dzadzamia and others RROK cards. Affiliation with the group bestowed authority in occupied Leipzig and promised redemption upon repatriation despite a problematic wartime biography.

The forms of resistance Lesnichenko claimed also caused him problems. Most RROK cardholders acknowledged under questioning that they did not conduct wartime resistance activities. In contrast, Lesnichenko and those from the smaller wartime group insisted that they had produced anti-German leaflets. These acts were plausible, but did they qualify as resistance? In official culture, resistance conjured the infamous, gruesome image of Zoia Kosmodemianskaia, the young partisan woman whom Germans tortured, executed, and left hanging in public for weeks in 1941. Kosmodemianskaia provided an example to be emulated of violent, martyred defiance to the invaders. Similarly, of the three Eastern Worker heroes in Mikhail Romm's film *Girl 217* (*Chelovek no. 217*, 1944), the sole survivor, Tania, escapes her brutal life as a domestic servant by killing two German soldiers of the household; the others died for their resistance at the hands of Germans. Genuine opposition meant violence, usually resulting in the death of the resister. Tania in *Girl 217* was an outlier among repatriates, whom the Soviet media largely portrayed as passive victims—often women and children liberated by the Red Army.

Compared with these expectations, Lesnichenko's leaflet operation must have seemed like an adolescent affair to police officers. He had been a party member and Red Army officer. Why had he not killed his overseer or destroyed a factory? If he had participated in a real conspiracy, investigators expected that the Germans would have arrested him. And if he had been arrested, his survival suggested to police that he had saved himself by becoming a German informant. Only a few documents are available about the investigators handling the case, but the records hint at their anger over Lesnichenko's perceived betrayal of the USSR. A Pavlohrad counterintelligence officer involved in the case, Captain Skidin, reportedly planned to unmask Lesnichenko in an "active interrogation." During the war, Skidin had served in military counterintelligence fighting German spies. He wanted to treat Lesnichenko the same way.[70]

The goal of Skidin and the other investigators was to connect Lesnichenko with Anglo-American espionage, despite emerging evidence that contradicted this story. When police in Zaporizhzhia found a returnee with a RROK card, they asserted that misspelled Russian words on the card indicated that British officials had produced them, as Anna Maslova had said (figure 8.3).[71]

Investigators ignored or did not know that the English on the card was also riddled with errors—a sign that the printer had probably been Lesnichenko's German associate, Willy Gehlbach. Maslova also changed her statement. After she moved to Dagestan, police arrested her on charges unrelated to the case. She told investigators in Dagestan that she had no idea who produced the cards. She was a peripheral member of the group and had wanted her story to match her friends' accounts. She thought she had heard Efrosinia Usenko saying that they received the cards from Allied authorities and repeated this statement.[72] Although the investigation materials contradicted Maslova's initial filtration interrogation, police continued to cite it as evidence because it justified the accusation of espionage.

As an espionage case, RROK came to the attention of counterintelligence leaders in Moscow. Isaak Altshuler, the head of a counterintelligence department in Moscow, upbraided his underlings in Ukraine for ignoring the obvious conclusion that Lesnichenko was a spy. He began to direct the case from secret police

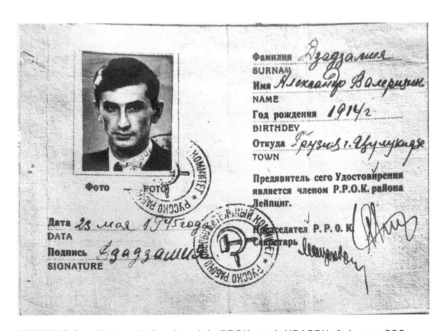

FIGURE 8.3. Aleksandr Dzadzamia's RROK card. HDASBU, f. 1, spr. 692, ark. 81.

headquarters at Lubianka.[73] Altshuler demanded that Ukrainian counterintelligence officers open investigations against all "false undergrounds" like RROK. In Ukraine alone, these investigations may have involved a thousand or more people.[74] The scope of the false underground investigations is unknown because central police archives in Russia remain classified. Based on the importance that Ukrainian counterintelligence officers assigned the cases, Altshuler probably initiated similar investigations in other republics.

Moscow's attention launched a new phase in the RROK case. The Dnipropetrovsk secret police recruited informants to spy on Lesnichenko and Osipovich. Police recruited the informant code-named "Martianov," who lived in Lesnichenko's building. He reported that Lesnichenko had lost his job for unknown reasons but continued to live suspiciously well. The physician informant "Doctor" (Vrach) went to Osipovich's work to ask about her husband.[75] Over the course of less than a year, officers in Pavlohrad summoned Lesnichenko for interrogation eight times. During the most confrontational sessions, interrogators accused him directly of being a British spy. Later Captain Skidin and his fellow investigators admitted that they had mishandled the case, keeping Lesnichenko for days at a time and producing interrogation protocols from memory long after the questioning.[76]

The clumsy investigation backfired. Two of the people the police recruited as informants seem to have told Lesnichenko that he was in danger—a fact he must have realized already from the frequent interrogations. Rather than panic, Lesnichenko told an informant that he wanted to leave town but had to "finish security verification by the MGB in Pavlohrad." Osipovich told another informant that she was planning to take Lesnichenko to Dnipropetrovsk for a medical treatment. Lesnichenko disappeared on March 8, 1947. Local police only learned about his flight a week later.[77]

The escape from Pavlohrad brought increased scrutiny of the remaining RROK members. Counterintelligence officials from Dnipropetrovsk province recruited an agent code-named "Sashko" to visit Aleksandr Kuprii, one of the original members of RROK, and establish Lesnichenko's location. "Sashko" was a repatriate who had spent the war in Leipzig. He and Kuprii had probably not met while abroad, but their mutual contacts made it feasible that "Sashko" would have a RROK card. The informant appeared at Kuprii and Natalia Berkun's home in August 1947, supposedly on a work trip that had brought him through Pavlohrad. His cover story was that he had presented a RROK card at filtration without understanding what it was. Now authorities in Dnipropetrovsk were questioning him about the organization, and he had no idea how to answer. "Sashko" explained that he came to Kuprii only because he could not find Lesnichenko. Kuprii invited "Sashko" to dinner and told him that he did not know where Lesnichenko was. He was reluctant to talk at all about RROK. He said that the organization had existed during the war, but that Lesnichenko had "ruined the whole thing" by giving cards to anyone who asked. He recommended that "Sashko" distance himself from RROK as much as possible: "Don't try to explain it to anyone because they will cross you up immediately."[78]

The ongoing investigation made Kuprii paranoid. In the summer of 1948, he and Berkun moved closer to his native village in Vinnytsia province, but the investigation followed. Kuprii was dismayed when local police summoned him for questioning. Perhaps for this reason the couple soon returned to Pavlohrad. Tensions over the investigation bled into their marriage. According to an informant who talked to Berkun's mother, Kuprii had wanted to leave her, but she threatened to denounce him. During a fight he beat her, and she left him. Kuprii now threatened to denounce her.[79] Amid this marital strife, "Sashko" visited Kuprii again. Kuprii told the informant that police interrogations had made him avoid meeting anyone who had been in Germany. He feared that police might construe even a chance encounter at the market as part of a conspiracy.[80]

What happened to the group next is unclear. The last evidence available in Ukraine's secret police archives is from mid-1949. At that point, 105 people were associated with the case as potential suspects, at least 4 cardholders had been arrested, and 22 were under active investigation.[81] It seems that few if any arrests resulted from the 22 open cases. As for Lesnichenko, authorities in the Siberian town of Barnaul found him in 1949. Although Dnipropetrovsk's secret police attempted to transfer the investigation to Ukraine, Barnaul's police apparently wanted to handle the case on their own.[82] Lesnichenko does not appear in directories of Stalin-era arrestees from Siberia, and limited access to police archives in Russia makes it impossible to verify his (non)arrest. Given the eagerness of Dnipropetrovsk authorities to extradite him, however, it is hard to imagine he was not arrested.

Lesnichenko and other RROK members miscalculated during their return to the USSR. They thought that a RROK card would ensure their restoration as full Soviet citizens. A generous interpretation of RROK is that its members had been Soviet loyalists who had done what they could to resist under the harsh conditions of German forced labor. Few could claim that they participated in concrete resistance activities during the war. Their spiritual loyalty, however, made possible the exuberant pro-Soviet activities in postliberation DP camps. Secret police investigators were not generous, though. Arrested collaborators among the group signaled that the entire organization was a fabrication, possibly a conspiracy. Insofar as Lesnichenko's resistance might have been genuine, authorities dismissed it as a weak form of opposition. Ultimately police only arrested people like Kiselev or Dzadzamia, who faced tangentially related charges of collaboration rather than accusations directly concerning RROK affiliation. Nonetheless, the encounter with the police taught RROK cardholders that their biographies would give them no claim to heroism.

Stalinist standards for resistance precluded most people who had lived abroad during the war from claiming that status. There were exceptions, such as Aleksandr Pecherskii, the Soviet-Jewish organizer of the escape of several hundred Jews from Sobibor death camp in 1943. Pecherskii's heroism in the face of certain death was indisputable, and he published an account of the uprising with the state press in his hometown of Rostov-na-Donu in 1945. He nonetheless saw his case ignored amid the anti-Jewish turn in the late 1940s.[83] Eastern Workers made poor heroes because their claims were difficult to verify. The attempts of Nikolai Shevchenko and Evgenii Kiselev to cast themselves as resisters show that suspicion of exaggerated or fabricated wartime feats was often warranted. In more plausible cases of resistance, too, the memory politics of late Stalinism worked against returnee-resisters. Resistance efforts had operated independent of the Soviet party-state and cut against the party-centric narrative of victory that emerged at the end of the war. Perhaps most important, resistance group members had complex pasts of accommodation and opposition rather than uncompromising records.

After Stalin's death, Soviet official commemoration of the war recognized a broader range of heroism. In 1956, Marshal Georgii Zhukov proposed to party leaders that POWs should have a place in the history of the war after years of disgrace. Soon party leaders began to credit resisters who had been ignored or repressed under Stalin. The Tatar poet Musa Dzhalil received the Hero of the Soviet Union award posthumously that year. Dzhalil, whose poetry written in a German prison was first published in 1955, had been a member of the pro-German Idel-Ural Legion but was executed by the Germans for organizing resistance from within. Even living resisters would become public heroes. Mikhail Deviataev, a POW pilot, led a group of captives who overtook their German captors and flew a German plane over to Soviet lines. After his return, Deviataev was arrested, apparently on unrelated charges. Only in 1957, after his amnesty, did he receive the Hero of the Soviet Union award.[84] The historian Efim Brodskii was also prepared to take up Zhukov's call to rehabilitate POWs. He published an article about Munich-based Soviet resisters in the USSR's leading history journal, *Voprosy istorii* (Issues in history), and then published several articles in the flagship thick journal of the Thaw, *Novyi Mir.* His work rejected the Stalin-era assumption that Soviet people could not have resisted as forced laborers in Germany.[85]

Brodskii was an advocate for former POWs and forced laborers, but he could not escape all aspects of Stalinist war memory. He knew that many of the resisters he depicted had also collaborated, but hardly acknowledged these circumstances and never grappled with the phenomenon. His works reflected a similar logic of official heroism as that used by Stalinist police: someone was either a collaborator or a resister, not both. Brodskii's search for uncomplicated war heroes is perhaps unsurprising and hardly unique to the Soviet Union.[86] The exceptional aspect in the Stalinist case was the central role of the secret police in vetting and, most often, rejecting claims of heroism.

Members of RROK presented themselves as having undertaken relatively modest forms of resistance. Its leader, Prokofii Lesnichenko, claimed nonviolent acts, and many participants did not point to any specific resistance during the war. They hoped that Stalinist officials would accept RROK as a pledge of fidelity to the USSR. Although they had worked in the enemies' farms and factories, they had remained true to the Soviet cause. A more understanding political regime might have accepted this form of loyalty. In France, a country whose officials and people had largely cooperated with the German occupation, postwar authorities began to rehabilitate wartime officials from 1947. By the 1950s, this rehabilitation evolved into the notion that all French people had resisted in their hearts.[87] In contrast, Stalinist police rejected a limited conception of resistance as a provocation that contradicted their view of returnees as fundamentally untrustworthy. The correct stance for repatriates was the quiet gratitude of a passive victim or the remorse of a coward liberated by the Red Army and Stalin. Returnees adapted to this expectation as such investigations continued. As the Cold War developed in 1946 and beyond, returners also shaped their biographies to fit the current political moment in the conflict between East and West.

WAYWARD CHILDREN OF THE MOTHERLAND

The Soviet Fight for Nonreturners in Western-Occupied Europe

After most Soviet-claimed people returned to the USSR, hundreds of thousands remained in Western-occupied Europe. Most were from the annexed western provinces of Ukraine and Belarus, and from the Baltic republics. Among these people and the displaced who had come from the pre-1939 borders, many feared that going to the USSR would mean repression or that their quality of life would be worse. Whatever their reason, they refused to concede to Stalinist assertions that they were Soviet subjects. The Western Allies agreed that they were not subject to forced repatriation but consented to the Soviet military's forming repatriation missions that could consult with potential returnees and organize the journey of the willing. Although they worked around the world, the repatriation officers assumed the most importance in the Western zones of Germany and Austria, which held the largest number of nonreturners. Tasked with bringing nonreturners home to the motherland, these Soviet officers found themselves on the front lines of the emerging Cold War.

The work of repatriation shifted with geopolitical winds. The relationship between Stalin and the Western Allies had been tense during the war and its immediate aftermath, but the alliance had endured these strains. As the number of returnees diminished, repatriation reflected and sharpened tensions between the USSR and its former allies. Nonreturners' vigorous and often violent protests against repatriation in displaced persons camps resonated with the increasingly anticommunist stance of Western Allied leaders.[1] The Western Allies' rejection of forced repatriation compelled Soviet officers to change tactics and persuade nonreturners that the motherland would welcome them.

For Soviet officers, repatriation became a conflict of principles. It was impossible for them to imagine that Soviet people—even those from recently annexed territories where a virtual civil war raged—would not rush to the USSR if they had an honest chance. Their arguments rested on the fusion of Marxism and the ethnonationalism that animated the Soviet nationalist state in the postwar period. Nonreturners belonged in the Soviet Union both because it included their nation's ancestral homeland and because the war had unmasked the cruelty of capitalism. Repatriation officers asserted that nonreturners refused to go to the USSR only because of the duplicitous Western Allies and their nationalist lackeys in the DP camps, who were alleged to have collaborated with the Germans. They were threatening would-be returnees, poisoning their minds with anti-Soviet propaganda, and keeping them enslaved with capitalism. The Allies' obstruction seemed to impact children most of all. As minors in the care of occupation authorities, war orphans of disputed origin became the objects of heated debate over national belonging.[2] Although evidence mounted that few nonreturners would consider migrating to the USSR, Soviet officers continued this hopeless mission, using repatriation as a forum to highlight the contrasts between the principles of the socialist bloc and the dishonesty of the capitalists.

Displaced persons were not passive objects in the Cold War struggle, however. They had choices, however imperfect, for permanent settlement outside of the Soviet Union. A minority chose to go to the USSR. These late returners faced difficult questions from Soviet officers: Why had they waited? Why return now? The real motivations were usually family or economic desperation. Most returnees did not focus on these factors when they spoke to Soviet officers, though. Late returners feared that such an explanation might cast doubt on their loyalty after living for years under German and Allied rule. They framed return as liberation from fascist collaborators and Western capitalists. The specter of moral corruption applied not only to returnees but also to repatriation officers abroad. The relationship between the officers, displaced persons, and Allied personnel both grew out of and hardened the conflict in postwar Europe.

Entering the Zone

When Soviet repatriation teams arrived in the Western zones of occupation in Germany and Austria in August 1945, occupation officials feared that repatriation would be a cover for espionage. The American Counter Intelligence Corps (CIC) received a report about "a rather wet party" attended by an American CIC informant, where repatriation official Colonel V. N. Gavrilov shouted, "What do you think I am over here for—just the repatriation of Russian DP's [sic]? No,

I have a much more important and much bigger job than that. Do you know what I am? I am a secret intelligence investigator." Gavrilov opened his shirt to reveal an eagle tattoo—the insignia of his unit in the Red Army's Main Intelligence Directorate.[3]

Despite this imprudent boast, Soviet repatriation missions were more than fronts for unrelated espionage work. Gavrilov and other repatriation officials spent hundreds of hours each month driving to DP camps to conduct meetings and collect data toward the repatriation of Soviet citizens. Intelligence was an important part of repatriation officers' work—but not in the sense of cloak-and-dagger missions to infiltrate the US occupation government or assassinate pro-Western officials. The officers' intelligence operations were most often part of efforts to persuade or force nonreturners to go to the USSR.

By the autumn of 1945, the Western zones of Germany and Austria contained approximately 1 million people from various countries who refused to go to their prewar places of residence. Many were Jews who had survived the Holocaust only to face harsh conditions in their homes in Eastern Europe. Others from Eastern Europe feared the Sovietization of their countries. Internal Soviet reports asserted that there were 450,000 Soviet nonreturners, primarily people from the western regions annexed during the war. This figure probably underestimated the number of nonreturners.[4] Soviet leaders asserted that all these people were Soviet subjects, even if they had lived in a different state before wartime annexations.

After the war, many officials in the Western zones of occupation thought that repatriation to prewar countries of residence was the preferred outcome for the displaced. The United Nations Relief and Rehabilitation Administration (UNRRA) set up camps where displaced persons could live and receive aid. These camps were organized primarily along ethnonational lines where camp residents selected their own local administration and had their own police. Some Allied officials were sympathetic to the DPs, but others viewed them as an unnecessary burden.[5] The chief of DP affairs in the British zone of Germany, General A. G. Kenchington, told a Soviet repatriation officer, "If they [displaced persons] wish to go home they are welcome. . . . If they go to their homeland, that will make my work all the simpler."[6]

As part of repatriation efforts, the Soviet government received Allied permission to establish missions in each of the occupation zones in Germany and Austria in the fall of 1945. Fifty-six Soviet officers went out on their own or in small teams.[7] They recruited dozens of Soviet displaced persons as office staff and unaccredited repatriation officers. In the first months of the missions, relations between the Soviet officers and their counterparts were cordial. The head of the mission in the American zone of Germany, General Davydov, described one interaction with the notoriously anti-Soviet General George S. Patton as a "pri-

FIGURE 9.1.   A performance in one of Leipzig's DP camps from RROK material. HDASBU, f. 1, spr. 695, ark. 15.

vate, friendly conversation."[8] In December 1945, Soviet officers in the British zone invited their counterparts to view a New Year's show staged by a troupe of returnees. The mission's political officer wrote with pride, "British officers were sure they [the troupe members] were professionals" (figure 9.1).[9]

Soviet officers' stance toward the Allies may have reflected Stalinist diplomatic calculations following World War II. Stalin believed that the United Kingdom and the United States were fated to clash over postwar spheres of influence, just as capitalist states had in previous wars. The Soviet Union would preserve good relations with one power or the other and consolidate gains.[10] This opinion apparently filtered down to repatriation officers. A CIC investigator reported that Colonel Gavrilov had suggested that "Russia really might consider forming an organization of the Big Two, United States and Soviet Russia."[11]

Soviet officers counted on Western assistance in the repatriation of the remaining displaced persons from Germany. But by the beginning of 1946, most volunteers had already gone east. The Soviet mission in the American zone of occupation received 3,669 people in the first half of 1946. This figure was smaller than the number of returnees who arrived in the Soviet zone of Germany on a typical day in the summer of 1945. Moreover, some three-quarters of the returnees in the first half of 1946 had fought in pro-German military formations and were repatriated under guard.[12] General Fedor Skrynnik, a former intelligence official for the wartime Soviet partisan administration who was now the head of the mission in the British zone, said that even the voluntary returnees were mostly "traitors to the Soviet motherland and criminal elements."[13] General Davydov concluded in early 1946 that repatriation would only be possible "by using administrative measures, that is, by force."[14]

Under these circumstances, officers tried to identify people whom the Allies would repatriate by coercion. Davydov sent his underlings to DP camps to comb through records for residents who were from pre-1939 Soviet borders or who had served with the Germans. The first operations were apparently successful. They allowed Soviet officers to compile lists of dozens of people eligible for compulsory repatriation under US occupation policies and to uncover hundreds of additional candidates.[15] Davydov was also gathering records to facilitate repatriation if the Western Allies agreed to the unconditional return of all Soviet-claimed DPs. Such a turn seemed possible to Soviet officers as late as 1946, when a repatriation officer in Austria reported his British liaison as saying, "We [British forces] are still deciding whether we will use force to repatriate Soviet citizens."[16]

The prospect of forced repatriation alarmed displaced persons. An UNRRA poll in 1946 found that 82 percent of all nonreturners in camps did not want to go to their prewar homelands.[17] Understandably, residents elected the most fervent anti-Soviet activists as leaders in the camps because they would be the strongest opponents of return. Contrary to Soviet hopes and to displaced persons' fears, Anglo-American officials do not seem to have contemplated forced return as a possibility.[18] The threat of repatriation nonetheless became a rallying cry for displaced persons.

When Soviet officers visited UNRRA camps, fear turned into violence. On March 6, 1946, Captain S. E. Lobanov and a team (translator and driver) visited the UNRRA camp at Mainz-Kastel in Wiesbaden (west of Frankfurt, US zone of Germany). Mining another camp's records, he had learned that Mainz-Kastel housed at least fifty-two people from the USSR's pre-1939 borders and a thousand Baltic nationals. Mainz-Kastel's UNRRA director offered to give Soviet officers his camp's archive too. When Lobanov arrived, though, one of the DP leaders, a Ukrainian, refused access to the documents, stating, "You aren't the NKVD and you have no need to write down any names." The camp director deferred to the DP leader, and Lobanov started to leave. When his team exited the camp, nearly a thousand displaced persons confronted them at the entrance. The team fled under a hail of rocks as the mob gave chase. US military police fired warning shots near the group chasing Lobanov's assistant, who escaped to the French zonal border with a knife wound in his back. Camp residents beat Lobanov and his driver until they were unconscious. They woke up days later in an American hospital.[19]

The violence at Mainz-Kastel coincided with growing Western apprehensions about repatriating Soviet-claimed DPs. Individual Allied officers had expressed concerns over the fate of Soviet returnees from the start, and they sometimes urged and helped nonreturners to avoid repatriation. After US General Lucian Truscott in early 1946 directed the forced transfer of a group of former POWs who had served in pro-German formations, Archbishop Nikolai of the Orthodox Church in Germany visited him to protest. Truscott said that he was following orders, but the archbishop responded, "You are not a soldier but an executioner, and the Orthodox Church condemns your actions." Moved by the archbishop or his own conscience, Truscott issued an order to cease compulsory repatriation in his command and wrote to President Truman and the US Congress to protest the use of force against displaced persons.[20]

Meanwhile, Anglo-American intelligence services increased surveillance efforts against Soviet repatriation officers. In the US zone of Germany, the CIC monitored all groups of displaced persons and repatriation missions, not only Soviet, under the code name Operation Bingo.[21] The operation began no later than February 1946, often targeting unaccredited Soviet officers, especially those carrying weapons. On April 25, CIC officers came to the Soviet mission in Frankfurt to detain several repatriates working as drivers and staff. During their interrogations, one of the CIC officers supposedly asked about Captain Lobanov's health.[22] Although the CIC released the detainees, they would face the second ordeal of detention by Soviet counterintelligence. In June, MGB deputy head Nikolai Selivanovskii advised Repatriation Administration head, General Filipp Golikov, to send the repatriates to the USSR, "considering the possibility that the arrestees were recruited by American counterintelligence." Golikov complied.[23]

Anxiety about the repatriation missions dovetailed with the growing rift between the Western Allies and the USSR. Over Soviet protests, the United Nations General Assembly approved a resolution on refugees in February 1946 that exempted refugees and the displaced from repatriation if they "expressed valid objections to returning to their countries of origin." The resolution set notable exceptions for "war criminals, quislings and traitors," who were still subject to compulsory repatriation. Yet it revealed the fundamental difference between Soviet and Western approaches. The Western delegations promoted "entitlement to resettlement elsewhere as a basic human right." The USSR's delegation, led by the notorious Andrei Vyshinskii, Stalin's chief prosecutor during the Great Terror, derided the Western policy on refugees as a concession to war criminals who had collaborated with the Germans. Referring to the Franco-British agreement with Germany in 1938 over the occupation of Czechoslovak territories, Vyshinskii argued, "This so-called tolerance [of refugees] is known to history by one name: Munich."[24]

By the spring of 1946, repatriation seemed to Western occupation officials to be both an unnecessary source of chaos and the immoral work of an enemy state. For the next several years, Soviet officials worried that Western occupation governments were on the verge of expelling the repatriation teams. Despite these fears, American forces only expelled the Soviet mission in March 1949, and the British occupation government followed suit the next year. The missions' surprising longevity was the product of a backroom deal between the former allies. The USSR had repatriated Allied POWs from the Eastern Front, but not war dead buried in Soviet-controlled territory. Although Allied officials refused to deport DPs to the USSR, they allowed the Soviet missions to advocate for repatriation while Western graves teams disinterred the dead in the Soviet zones of Germany and Austria. When, in August 1947, the US War Department proposed expelling the Soviet repatriation mission, occupation government leader General Clarence Huebner successfully pleaded for "milder action." Expulsion, he wrote, "may result in cancelling or further complicating arrangements for the US Grave Registration Teams to operate in Soviet Zone Germany."[25] Nonetheless, Anglo-American forces increased the security details that accompanied Soviet officers after the Lobanov incident. Eventually, the British occupation government denied access to any camp unless a significant number of residents requested a meeting with a Soviet representative.[26]

Between Allied restrictions and refugees' unreceptiveness, Soviet mission officers became frustrated with their impossible task. Meanwhile, Moscow demanded to know why so few Soviet citizens were returning. A sense of outrage and fear of disappointing their commanders led some officers to kidnap people they believed were Soviet subjects. Reports of abductions began as soon as the missions appeared in the Western zones. Alexander Wachowiak, a man who claimed to be Polish, told the CIC in early 1946 that Soviet officers had held him for several weeks. They threatened arrest if he did not declare that he was a Soviet subject. In March 1946, a colonel from the Third US Army found thirteen cases in which Soviet officers had detained DPs and forced them to affirm that they were Soviet.[27]

Leaders in the Repatriation Administration were enraged when they learned about such abductions. General Sergei Vershinin, who oversaw the German missions from the Berlin office of the Soviet military occupation, inspected the British zone team in March 1946. During his visit, he learned that officers had conducted numerous kidnappings. In February officers embedded with the British First Corps planned to kidnap a woman named Valia. Instead of the refugee, however, they took a different woman, a Russian translator for the British military government. The team scurried to cover its tracks. The men gave Valia alcohol and took her on a joy ride in their car. They claimed that there were no consequences, that Valia left believing the affair was an ordinary night of carousing. That group had acted with relative restraint. Soviet officers with the British Eighth Corps admitted they could not recall how many people they had abducted because there had been so many incidents. Vershinin, a veteran secret police officer, did not question the morality of these methods. He worried, however, that they would invite "provocation" and retaliation. The US occupation force in Austria had recently expelled the Soviet mission on charges of attempted kidnapping.[28] If British commanders discovered the abductions, "in the best case, they would demand the entire team leave immediately."[29]

The kidnappings occurred in part because officers did not know how else they could find returnees. Vershinin claimed that the British zone mission chief, General Skrynnik, had not adapted to the conditions he now confronted. He had supposedly acquiesced to the British definition of Soviet subjecthood that excluded people from the Western borderlands, and waited for politicians to decide rather than acting. British officers were said to mock Skrynnik as being "very accommodating." Vershinin's accusations had a self-serving element, deflecting blame from himself onto subordinates. He was correct, however, that Skrynnik and other repatriation mission officers believed that most nonreturners were unpersuadable.

With their free time, many of the officers enjoyed the temptations of life outside Soviet control. By Vershinin's count, a third of the accredited officers were conducting work directly related to repatriation. The others were engaged in black market activities or flings with German and émigré women. Captain Saakov, an Armenian former POW recruited to work for the mission as an unaccredited officer, was alleged to have obtained a Turkish passport to move freely about the zone on the business of his boss Lieutenant Colonel Shapovalov. When he stopped in Hamburg, he stayed with a German woman in an apartment that Vershinin assumed was "a safe house for meetings with British agents." The conclusions were disturbing for repatriation leaders in Moscow. Golikov forwarded the report to party and secret police leaders and recalled several of the officers, including Skrynnik.[30] The ouster marked not only a change in personnel but also a transition from cooperation to antagonism.

Persuasion and Provocation

Replacing Skrynnik was Colonel Aleksei Briukhanov, who had worked under Skrynnik during the general's tenure as wartime head of the intelligence department of the Soviet partisan movement in Belarus. In contrast to Skrynnik and Vershinin, who could be diplomatic with their Western counterparts, Briukhanov evinced an aggressive dogmatism. The colonel would not entertain the notion that most displaced persons opposed return or that they were anti-Soviet at heart. He asserted during an August 1946 meeting with his liaison, Brigadier General Carthew, "Are there Soviet citizens in the zone who want to go to the motherland? Yes, there are very many, the majority."[31] Echoing diplomat-prosecutor Andrei Vyshinskii's arguments at the UN, Briukhanov blamed local administrators in UNRRA camps who ensured that thousands of residents "lived under Fascist terror."[32]

Repatriation officers increasingly saw the Western Allies as the main culprits in the failure of repatriation. Zonal authorities set up commissions that determined camp residents' nationality in disputed cases. These commissions had frequently sided with Soviet officials through the winter of 1945. When there was no evidence that a person was exempt from repatriation to the USSR, the commission often deferred to the Soviet representative's claim. The commissions were especially amenable to repatriating people accused of collaboration with the Germans.[33] The benefit of the doubt shifted to displaced persons in 1946. It was no longer enough to demonstrate that someone had probably lived in the prewar Soviet Union. Western officials expected Soviet officers to bring written evidence like registration lists, call-up cards, or party documents to show that someone was a USSR national. Moreover, from the spring of 1946 the Western Allies in accordance with UN declarations refused to repatriate people who feared persecution in their country of origin.[34] As forced repatriation seemed less and less likely, Soviet officers concluded that they would need to persuade DPs to return to the USSR.

An important aspect of this shift was the recognition that most nonreturners were not Russian.[35] The DP camps were organized along national lines, and their leadership typically came from national committees that were fervent proponents of (re)establishing independent nation-states in their respective homelands. In this hothouse atmosphere, national consciousness among residents grew and hardened. To many DPs, the overwhelmingly Russophone composition of the Soviet officers symbolized Russian rule over their homelands.[36] This dynamic was particularly bitter because of the resurgence of Russian culture within the USSR. In the 1920s, Soviet leaders had attempted to combat Russian nationalism and foster pro-Soviet ethnic-national cultures.[37] As part of the prewar mobilization in the 1930s, Soviet authorities placed an increasing emphasis on Russian figures and the imperial Russian past.[38] Yet Soviet authorities had also bolstered the influence of titular nationalities in their republics (e.g., Ukrainians in Ukraine), strengthening the idea of national homelands in a socialist empire unified by the Russian language.[39] The representatives of Soviet rule wanted to convince non-Russians that they would return to their national homelands, rather than to an imperial holding dominated by Russians.

Baltic refugees posed a distinct challenge. The repatriation officers could hardly communicate with speakers of Baltic languages, which, unlike Ukrainian or Belarusian, was not a Slavic language like Russian. Responding to this problem, the Repatriation Administration in Moscow sent multiple officers from the Baltic republics to the Western zones of Germany in 1946.[40] According to repatriation officials, the appearance of "their countryman," the Lithuanian Captain Repshis, "made a great impression" on a Lithuanian-Estonian camp in October 1946. At a time when officers described visits to DP camps as increasingly hostile, they noted that Repshis inspired a friendlier reception.[41] Residents of the Latvian-Lithuanian camp at Watenstedt asked Repshis if they could send a fact-finding delegation to the Baltic republics before committing to return to see if returnees were being sent to exile in Siberia.[42]

Although the inclusion of Baltic officers helped, they could not resolve the tensions between people from the annexed territories and the representatives of Soviet-Russian rule. In October 1946, Repshis went with the lead officer Major Mokriakov to a Lithuanian camp in the British zone. The camp commandant, unaware that Repshis knew Lithuanian, told the gathered crowd, "I can't stand to look at these [Soviet] representatives." He asked if anyone wanted to join the Lithuanians who had remained in the USSR. People in the crowd shouted, "No, we don't want to go to Siberia." When Repshis translated for Mokriakov, he ended the visit.[43]

Such visits to the camps demoralized the officers. Displaced persons continued to be hostile, and few volunteered to repatriate. Even Briukhanov, the most ardent advocate of repatriation, came to doubt the effectiveness of camp visits. He wrote to Moscow at the end of 1946, "Literally in every camp the people are not interested in repatriation with the exception of a few individuals."[44]

The visits continued, not only for the purpose of persuasion. Increasingly, the rationale behind the trips was to expose the supposed criminality of the Allies and the camp leadership. On October 13, 1946, an incident occurred at a camp at Blomberg in North Rhine–Westphalia. The deputy head of the mission in the British zone, Colonel Kutuzov, went to the camp with an unusually large entourage in two cars. The camp was also large, with fifteen hundred ethnic Estonian and Latvian residents. The UNRRA director warned Kutuzov that the residents would be hostile toward him, but the colonel insisted on holding an open assembly. The director proved correct, and residents attended only to jeer at the Soviet officers.[45]

Frustrated, Kutuzov left with his team. A crowd of as many as eight hundred people gathered outside to taunt the officers as they drove away. Amid flying rocks and rotting produce, another object—a grenade—bounced off the lead car and exploded in the road some twenty to thirty feet from the second car. A handful of

Germans watching the spectacle received light wounds. The officers fled the scene, regrouping at a safe distance from the camp. That night Kutuzov went to British authorities to demand action: "All the people in that camp are war criminals. They must be surrendered to military authorities." A few days later, Colonel Briukhanov asked that the British isolate the camp and arrest its leaders. British authorities complied with the first demand and set up an inquiry to find the perpetrators.[46]

The inquiry convened on October 16, 1946. Although its aims were limited to investigating the bombing, Briukhanov made the inquiry into a referendum on the DP camps more broadly. When British authorities stopped Briukhanov from asking about supposed war criminals at Blomberg, he interrogated camp administrators and guards as potential accomplices in the bombing. With little difficulty, he provoked Blomberg's Estonian and Latvian leaders to profess their hatred of the USSR. Their statements were proof to Briukhanov that the DP leadership was thwarting repatriation.[47] The inquiry concluded that a camp resident had thrown the grenade, but it could not establish a specific perpetrator. Its chair reprimanded the cagey witnesses who had avoided naming anyone who had thrown objects at the Soviet cars.[48] The apparent support the British inquiry showed the Soviet side belied assertions UNRRA authorities made privately about a potential Soviet provocation. General Evelyn Fanshawe, the UNRRA director in the British zone, wrote to the occupation government that the distance of the gathered crowd from the explosion and the make of the grenade suggested that a passenger in the second Soviet car had thrown it.[49] Despite these secret misgivings, UNRRA closed the camp and relocated its residents.

Repatriation officers invited conflict, although it seems that they had no official directive to provoke the DPs. Violent exchanges between camp residents and Soviet officers were more intense and frequent when Allied security teams were absent. Despite the danger these unsupervised encounters posed, repatriation officers complained that security teams impeded their contact with camp residents.[50] Soviet pressure against hostile camp committees achieved results at the diplomatic level. In April 1947, the foreign ministers of the four wartime allies met in Moscow, and Soviet representatives secured a resolution that banned antirepatriation propaganda.[51] This policy aimed to persuade or force the Western Allies to disband national committees in the camps altogether. Presenting themselves as victims of fascist attacks, Soviet officials demanded the resignation of UNRRA directors and the jailing of camp administrators.[52]

This goal was perhaps the product of Soviet misunderstandings about the nature of the DP camps in the Western zones. Soviet officials had difficulty envisioning DP self-organization. Since the chaotic spring and summer of 1945, the occupation government in the Soviet zones of Germany and Austria had tightened control over camps that housed a much smaller number of newly arriving return-ees. To Soviet repatriation officers accustomed to centralized command struc-tures, it probably seemed that nationalist leaders in DP camps were the agents of the Western occupation governments rather than the representatives of camp resi-dents. By this logic, once Western officials removed these anti-Soviet nationalists, displaced persons would awaken from their spell and return to the motherland.

Provocative Soviet tactics backfired and convinced Allied officials to enact stricter policies to limit contact and conflict. Personal animus also played a role in the deterioration of relations between the former allies. Briukhanov's relation-ship with British liaisons became particularly toxic. In March 1947, Brigadier General Carthew proposed combining the repatriation and liaison missions in the zone. When Soviet occupation head Marshal Vasilii Sokolovskii assented, liaison head General Konovalov became Briukhanov's superior.[53] The British found Konovalov to be "co-operative, sympathetic and pleasant," in contrast to the "truculent" Briukhanov.[54] Konovalov agreed that it would be impossible to repatriate all DPs that the USSR claimed. Moreover, he supported Carthew against Briukhanov, whose untactful behavior—banging his fist on the table dur-ing negotiations and grimacing when British officers were speaking—he said was unproductive.[55] With the general's permission, Carthew barred Briukhanov from meetings entirely. The conflict drew the attention of General Vershinin, who came from Berlin for an inspection in April 1947. Apparently at Vershin-in's insistence, Briukhanov wrote a report dedicated to the question of "why the British do not like me." The accusations, he asserted, were a conspiracy against him because his dogged advocacy for repatriation cut against British interests.[56]

Before long Briukhanov gained the upper hand, and Vershinin lost his job. At an April 29 meeting with General Alec Bishop, the deputy chief of staff of zonal forces, Vershinin made a plea for cooperation. According to Bishop, Ver-shinin asked for the British to organize a visit to each camp with Soviet-claimed people as "a final chance to come into contact with displaced persons." Kon-ovalov, who was at the meeting, said Vershinin had meant "another chance" but admitted that the British translation was also plausible. Bishop wrote in an internal memo that the opportunity was "too good to be true" and began to or-ganize Operation Swan-Song.[57] On May 31, Briukhanov raised alarms in Mos-cow when he reported that Bishop was preparing the team's expulsion. Repatriation Administration deputy head General Konstantin Golubev sacked Vershinin and wrote to state security officials that he had acted "very carelessly," but he stopped short of accusing Vershinin of sabotage. Konovalov was also recalled soon after. After several months of pressing for Operation Swan-Song, British authorities yielded, and the mission continued as before.[58]

Did Vershinin really agree to the British plan? It seems plausible in the context of refugee politics in 1947. UNRRA and Allied officials had initially hoped that mass repatriation would resolve their refugee problems.[59] Soon, though, Cold War tensions encouraged Western leaders to see permanent resettlement as preferable to repatriation. President Harry Truman asserted in July 1947 that displaced persons feared persecution in their homelands, and "it is unthinkable that they should be left indefinitely in camps in Europe."[60] Some governments also saw the displaced as attractive workers in low-skill industries.[61] In addition to these economic and political motivations, both American and Soviet officials noted that many nonreturners were military-age men.[62] US intelligence hoped to leverage these men as a potential anticommunist force if the Cold War turned hot.[63] The new Western policy of resettlement worried Soviet officials, and Vershinin may have seen a last round of visits as the last, best chance at repatriation.

For Briukhanov and Moscow-based repatriation officials, though, the opportunity for a final visit to the camps was not worth the closure of the missions. Soviet officers used the missions as a stage to demonstrate the criminality of nationalist leaders among nonreturners and the duplicity of the Western Allies. Provocation had become at least as important as the nominal goal of repatriation. The most potent emblems of Western deceit were those displaced persons who seemed to have the least agency—children.

The Motherland's Orphans

World War II took the parents from millions of children. Many of these orphaned, abandoned, and lost children found themselves in Allied-sponsored institutions in the Western zones of occupation. Displaced children raised philosophical and practical issues for the Allies. Since the nineteenth century, government officials and nationalist organizers had claimed it was not only a nation's right to bring up its children but best for children's welfare to grow up within their own nation. In contrast to this view, child psychologists of the twentieth century argued that children should grow up in an environment where they receive care and experience stability. The mass death of World War II added another factor for deciding the fate of children. For the rebuilding nations of Europe, young people were a potential resource. Unlike older immigrants, it seemed possible to assimilate malleable youth with ease. Complicating the issue further, occupation authorities were unwilling to give children the same choices as adult DPs. Conflicting principles and the outsize role of occupation authorities in deciding their fate made displaced children a charged issue between the USSR and the Western Allies.[64]

Soviet officials in Germany were determined that displaced children born within the USSR's borders or whose parents were Soviet subjects should return to the motherland. This reasoning in part had an ethnonational foundation. When Soviet officials lobbied for the custody of a Ukrainian child, the claim of Soviet Ukraine over all Ukrainian people was an essential justification. At the same time, Soviet officials relied on Marxist polemics about the superiority of socialism to capitalism. Displaced children, they said, would have a better upbringing in the USSR because they could rely on a generous welfare state rather than be left with exploiters.

In territories that the Red Army occupied or where there were pro-Soviet governments, repatriation officials took children in stealthy operations. Even in cases where children were living with adoptive parents, officers asserted that the motherland's claim was more important than the bond between child and caretaker. The head of the repatriation department in occupied Austria reported to Moscow in 1948 that adoptive parents in the Soviet zone were not willing to give up children after living with them for as long as six years. In one case, the Austrian parents' resistance had forced him to call the local police to help. "All the time while we are taking the child," he wrote, "there is great displeasure, shouting, crowds gathering." The problem was not that the seizure of the children was the wrong policy but that the implementation had been misguided. Such "excesses" could lead to anti-Soviet news coverage.[65]

Hasty repatriation of children led to mistakes. A repatriation official in Moscow discovered that Soviet officers in Yugoslavia had taken several dozen children from families of postrevolutionary Russian émigrés. Separated from their relatives during the war, they had lived at an orphanage whose director consented (perhaps under pressure) to release them into Soviet custody. Andrei Vyshinskii, in his role as deputy foreign minister, agreed to reunite the children with their parents several weeks later.[66] Not all such cases ended with reunification. General Mikhail Iurkin replaced Vershinin as the repatriation department head in the Soviet occupation administration after the Operation Swan-Song debacle. When he took up the post in late summer 1947, Iurkin found that authorities in the Soviet zone had sent children to the USSR without keeping records of who had gone where. There was also a significant backlog of letters from parents in the USSR and elsewhere requesting help finding lost children. The best answer Iurkin could give in many cases was that the children were in one of the hundreds of orphanages of the USSR.[67]

In the Western zones of Germany and Austria, Soviet officials could not simply take children they believed were Soviet. Like the treatment of other persons of disputed nationality, occupation government commissions determined children's nationality. The commissions had total discretion over the fate of children under six years old, while older children had some input into the decision. In October 1946, Soviet major Chernov visited a camp at Prien am Chiemsee in the American zone in Bavaria where there were sixty-eight children between five months and sixteen years old. Chernov claimed that all but three were orphans and that all requested immediate repatriation. When a lieutenant from the US occupation force interviewed the children some days later, twenty-three of the twenty-seven over six years old rejected repatriation. Colonel Oreshkin, the lead officer in the area, asserted that the children were not capable of making the right decision. He reasoned that once the children had a proper Soviet upbringing, they would understand that they had always belonged in the USSR. American officials dismissed this argument, and the unwilling children remained in Germany. A Soviet officer escorted thirty-eight children to the east, of whom thirty were under the age of three.[68]

The efforts of mission officers in the Western zones became a celebrated cause in the Soviet press. Sergei Mikhalkov, the cultural impresario who penned the Soviet national anthem, wrote a play about the issue called *I Want to Go Home* (*Ia khochu domoi*, 1948), later made into the film *They Have a Motherland* (*U nikh est' Rodina*, 1949). In the play, Anglo-American officers and Latvian war criminals sell young Sasha Butuzov into virtual slavery. Butuzov has even forgotten Russian. At the story's climax, the boy escapes captivity with the help of Soviet officers and good-hearted displaced persons. Captain Peskaev, the repatriation official who is the story's hero, shows the boy a photograph of his mother, and Sasha instantly rediscovers his Russian and agrees to return. Mikhalkov's play reflected the widespread presentation of Anglo-American officials in the Soviet media as monsters who obstructed family reunions to feed capitalism.

Mikhalkov based the play on real events at the orphanage at Haffkrug in the British zone of Germany. The institution housed seventeen children of apparent Slavic descent who had arrived from camps in the Schleswig-Holstein area. Major Vitalii Chekmazov, the model for Peskaev, visited the orphanage on July 8, 1947, as part of a commission to determine the children's nationality. The inspiration for Sasha Butuzov was apparently Volodia (Vladimir) Prokofev, a teenager from Minsk. His father had died when he was younger, and his mother had disappeared during the war. He had spent several years in an orphanage. Although he wanted to see his mother again, it was unclear if she was alive. Meanwhile, he was content in Germany. He was taking classes to become an electrician and had German guardians who visited him at the orphanage. Volodia's age was unknown. A British report placed him at nearly eighteen while a Soviet account described him as fifteen. The commission determined that the near-adult's wishes to remain in Germany should be honored. Chekmazov protested, "It cannot be that the members of the commission believe that this child would be better with a German in Germany, eking out a paltry existence, than in his motherland, where he would receive an education and know the care of his government." Because Volodia knew nothing about his motherland, Chekmazov suggested that the Soviet mission should adopt him so that he could get a sense of his country from the officers. The commission denied this proposal.

The core dispute between the major and his counterparts was not over facts but over principles. The British presiding officer made an argument that echoed Western child psychologists' focus on material and mental well-being. He informed Chekmazov, "Our commission has the goal of uniting children with their parents and, if they have no parents, then to make a decision the commission thinks will be best for the child." Chekmazov argued that the Soviet commitment to education would ensure a better life for the children. Yet he also stressed that national homeland was an important factor. The commission referred to a girl with a Ukrainian surname as Polish, asserting that Ukrainian was not a nationality in the British understanding. Chekmazov was dumbfounded. Was a Scottish person living in Poland Polish? No, that person was a British subject and belonged in Great Britain, just as Ukrainian children were Soviet subjects and belonged in Soviet Ukraine.[69]

Unlike Sasha Butuzov in Mikhalkov's play, Volodia Prokofev did not go to the USSR. Many children from Haffkrug and elsewhere did go with Soviet officers, though. In most cases, Anglo-American commissions resolved Soviet-born children's citizenship based on the following factors: first, the parents' wishes; second, the will of older children; finally, in the absence of parents and maturity, the state of origin. As a result, a significant proportion of the children whom Soviet officers received were infants and toddlers who went to orphanages in the USSR.

Orphaned children were a small number among nonreturners overall. A repatriation official in the British zone estimated that there were roughly two hundred disputed orphans.[70] Despite their comparatively small number, orphaned children took on an outsize significance. In Soviet official culture, they represented the essential injustice of repatriation. Orphaned children were a special case because they were under the guardianship of the Western Allies and were more dependent than adults on the occupation governments. But Soviet officers asserted that these children were fundamentally like adult nonreturners. They would never belong except in their homelands and were denied this reunion through the machinations of the Allies and nationalist DPs.

Late Return from the Capitalist Underworld

A tension existed between the Soviet presentation of DPs as victims and the reality that people returning to the USSR after 1946 had avoided repatriation for months or years. From 1946 through 1951, a total of 20,386 people returned to the USSR from the Western zones of Germany and Austria.[71] This was roughly 5 percent of those whom Soviet officers counted as potential returnees. Moreover, perhaps a third or more of this number had been returned by force. By March 1947, American forces alone had sent 3,766 people to the Soviet zone of Germany under guard.[72] Repatriation officers even began to target people serving prison sentences in the Western zones of occupation, some of whom faced death sentences on murder charges.[73] Nonetheless, it seems likely that more than 10,000 people voluntarily went to the USSR from Allied-occupied Europe. How could they explain their reluctance to return at the war's end?

Information culled from censored letters demonstrates that the main attraction of return was usually family and community. One person living in the USSR wrote to a relative in the Western zones of Germany to dissuade them from returning, "I'm surprised that you write that you miss home. . . . You should know that it's impossible to write everything. But I urge you again to dismiss these stupid thoughts from your mind and quit thinking about home."[74] A frequent opposition in the letters was the longing for return versus the fear of reprisals. One woman asked her family in the USSR what might await her when she returned: "Mama, write me if there are other girls at home who were taken like I was."[75]

Based on such intelligence, General Golikov and other officials urged the heads of borderland regions to make repatriates write reassuring letters to nonreturners. State security officers apparently did not systematically monitor the collection of the letters at first. Only in late 1947 did Generals Golikov and Golubev order the verification of all letters by secret police to ensure that they were pro-repatriation and had no coded messages.[76] Mission officers delivered 1,017 letters to the Western zones of Germany in 1947 and 5,722 in 1948.[77] Police in Ukraine said that officials from the republic had forwarded approximately 4,000 letters abroad in 1949.[78] Western occupation officials generally prohibited Soviet officers from receiving and distributing letters except by the German mail service. Soviet officers were mistrustful of the German mail since many letters, a fifth of all sent in August 1948, were returned unopened. The letters that were not returned may not have reached their targets either. The solution was to distribute letters privately, either discreetly during a visit or by invitation to a Soviet repatriation office.[79]

Soviet officials believed that the best letters were written by people who had returned recently and could assuage fears about repression of late returnees. Colonel Briukhanov reported that some DP camps were sending "unofficial delegates" who planned to come to the USSR and send word about conditions in the country. He learned of this practice from Bronius Saulitis, a returnee from Lithuania who claimed to represent the nonreturners of the Bocholt camp in Westphalia. Did Saulitis really wield such authority over his former campmates? Or was his claim to represent them a bluff that he hoped would smooth his return to the USSR? Bluff or no, Saulitis probably believed the assertion would help him avoid repression, and he was partially correct. Briukhanov urged police in Lithuania not to arrest Saulitis—at least until after he had written to Bocholt.[80]

A small number of returnees tried to ensure their safety by becoming informers for the repatriation missions. In every zone, Soviet repatriation officers cultivated moles among potential returnees. After declaring their intent to return, a typical informer would remain a month or two at their camp and find more potential returnees.[81] Soviet officers believed that this service was partial payment for the debt repatriates owed the motherland for their alleged disloyalty. A CIC informant report from March 1946 suggested how recruiting occurred in practice. A repatriation official would engage a potential returnee in political discussions about the problems of displacement. The recruiter then would offer the possibility of repatriation without repression, regardless of the person's wartime record. The price of safe return was covert work for the Soviet mission. "When the victim is beginning to waver," the informant said, "the last attraction is produced in the form of a large sum of money or other advantages."[82]

When they crossed over to Soviet control, late returners often wrote testimonials that justified delayed repatriation. Explanations that involved German exploitation were relatively common for the first year following the war. These accounts asserted that German employers had blackmailed them into remaining by threatening a denunciation to the Soviet secret police.[83] Although these testimonials were plausible, they also evoked a sense of victimhood associated with Germany's use of forced laborers. Over time returnees increasingly referenced the antagonisms of the early Cold War. One returnee in 1946 claimed that at his camp in the British zone of Austria, a White émigré learned that a group of residents planned to return. In response he organized a mob of forty people to hound them out of the camp. When the returnees sought refuge with the local British commandant, he turned them away.[84]

Late returnees offered these accounts of their own accord at first, and repatriation officials soon developed a system of interviews. Briukhanov apparently first thought to record interviews methodically as evidence against British authorities in Germany. On January 31, 1947, he gathered a group of returnees for interviews at his headquarters. The repatriates were mostly those from the Baltic republics and undoubtedly understood the appropriate line. They stressed how war criminals dominated the local administrations and lived as so-called camp aristocrats, misappropriating Allied supplies to sell on the black market. When the returnees attempted to leave the camps, administrators threatened them with violence and withholding of benefits.[85] Others said that after being seen with a Soviet repatriation officer, death threats had forced them to seek refuge at the Soviet mission. Many said that anti-Soviet propaganda about the Gulag was ubiquitous, although they now recognized it was false.[86]

Occasionally those who had left Germany for work in neighboring countries decided to come back to the USSR, too. Their accounts highlighted the miserable workplace and living conditions that had awakened them to the ills of capitalism. Twenty-one-year-old Anatolii Fedorov testified after arriving from Belgium that capitalist recruiters had deceived him about the life of a miner. When he arrived at the mine, he found "protections for laborers and safety equipment are absent and you receive no medical assistance." After guards beat him for being a member of the Union of Soviet Patriots, a pro-Soviet émigré organization, he decided to return to the USSR.[87] The claims about working conditions and the anti-Soviet atmosphere in the camps were not invented. Yet the prominent references to capitalist exploitation and anti-Soviet camp leaders were also a way for late returnees to cast themselves as loyal Soviet citizens.

Materials from interviews and statements reached top Soviet leaders. On November 6, 1947, General Golikov forwarded a summary of the interviews to top police and diplomatic officials, including foreign minister Viacheslav Molotov. Based on the findings, police officials demanded that repatriation officers debrief all returnees arriving from abroad. The interviews combined the goals of state security and repatriation. Besides questions about Allied obstruction, the secret police demanded that repatriates give answers with intelligence value such as the names and addresses of vehement nonreturners.[88] The interviews demonstrated the shift from World War II to the Cold War. Police interrogators during filtration in 1945 had focused on wartime biographies, even in cases in which the returnee had lived under Allied control. Now the interviewers were supposed to focus on the situation in the DP camps.[89]

On both sides of the Iron Curtain, the Cold War rewarded displaced persons who tailored their biographies to the political environment. Nonreturners cannily adapted their views and life stories to the increasing anti-Soviet sentiment among Allied authorities. Among rank-and-file operatives, the Anglo-American intelligence community frequently looked past the problematic biographies of people who had served in pro-German outfits when recruiting anti-Soviet assets.[90] Refugees from Eastern Europe referenced the horrors of Stalinism as the reason for their flight. Many claims were justified, of course. Still, nonreturners highlighted and exaggerated elements that the Western Allies expected.[91]

Similarly, late returners to the USSR cast themselves as loyal victims of Allied manipulation rather than doubters whose love of family overcame their fear of return. Among Western and Soviet officials, DP testimony heightened fears about the enemy. On the Soviet side, the explanations of returnees reinforced the understanding that the Western Allies and their nationalist lackeys were the main obstacle to repatriation. The cycle of animus intensified Soviet anxieties about the loyalties of repatriates who had spent so much time among such a nefarious enemy.

These concerns also impacted repatriates who had worked for the missions since liberation. Because Allied authorities accredited a limited number of Soviet officers in each zone, one or two mission officers might cover entire provinces. The problem of translation between European languages plagued officers in Germany, not only in the repatriation missions but also at the International Military Tribunal at Nuremberg.[92] The repatriation missions needed other staff too: cooks, cleaners, and typists; managers and security to run transit camps; drivers and unaccredited officers for visits to displaced persons. Mission officers were reluctant to hire non-Soviets for fear that the Western Allies would plant spies. Soviet officers worked around Allied restrictions by hiring repatriates, it seems mostly from pre-1939 Soviet borders, already living in the Western zones. Despite Western protests, the missions would include more repatriate staff than accredited officers for much of their time of operation.[93]

Having been in Germany as forced laborers, mission staff were vulnerable to denunciation by their bosses. Mission officers used this threat to pressure the homesick repatriates, who had not seen their families for years, to remain on staff. One officer in the British zone of Germany suggested his colleagues were withholding letters from mission workers' families in the USSR as leverage.[94] Pressure could also persuade repatriate staff to undertake dangerous work, like infiltrating UNRRA camps as informants.[95]

Mission officers used their power over repatriate staff for personal gratification as well. Major A. Slesarev was the only repatriation officer in Denmark from August 1945 until he was removed at the end of 1946. He used his monopoly over the mission's resources to force repatriate women to have sex with him and to buy the silence of the others. In one of many incidents, the major plied a female worker with alcohol until she went to bed in a room she shared with other workers. He barged into the bedroom at 11:00 p.m., evicted the other women, and demanded sex. When she refused, he twisted her arms, prodded her, and raped her after she stopped resisting.[96]

These abuses were shocking but only drew superiors' attention after Slesarev propositioned multiple female Danish officials.[97] The Soviet ambassador in

Denmark heard of Slesarev's offenses and wrote to his boss in the mission in the British zone of Germany. A superior arrived to meet with the repatriates on the major's staff. The workers had remained silent because the major threatened to send them to the USSR. Sometimes he promised to arrange for their arrest, but at other times it seemed that return itself implied repression. Slesarev's translator defended himself against the implication that he feared return, "I will go home today, but you don't need to try and scare me."[98]

Some of the repatriate staff tried to escape their precarious situation.[99] Lieutenant Anatolii Belashov, a former POW and translator in the British zone of Germany, disappeared while waiting with two comrades for a car to be repaired near Osnabrück (Lower Saxony). The next day, March 21, 1946, Soviet officers found him dead in a British barracks in the town. During the occupation government's investigation, Captain R. H. C. Fowler testified that Belashov had come to his barracks and asked for asylum. The translator told Fowler that he believed his bosses suspected he was a spy and were "watching his movements day and night." The captain promised nothing but for the night put Belashov in an unlocked jail cell across from a British soldier jailed on a minor offense. In the morning, British soldiers found Belashov dead, hung by linens tied to the bars on the window. The British inquiry into the incident determined that Belashov had committed suicide. A Soviet military investigator who reviewed the inquiry's materials disagreed, concluding that the British had murdered Belashov because he had refused to become their spy.[100]

The Soviet account is conceivable but not likely. An important fact that the Soviet investigator omitted was that Belashov's death had come on the heels of General Vershinin's investigation into kidnapping and corruption in the mission. The visit would soon result in General Skrynnik's dismissal, and rumors surely had spread about the impending recall—or worse—of mission staff. Belashov could not have known that he was not a target of Vershinin's accusations and possibly fled because he feared that he would face repression. Once he was in British custody, Belashov may have discovered that defection would be impossible or that British intelligence wanted him to become an informant. Realizing that there could be no clean break, he killed himself. The full story remains obscure, but almost all the plausible scenarios begin with Belashov's defection.

Such escape attempts increased the officers' suspicions about their repatriate staff.[101] In March 1948, Colonel Briukhanov gave cook Polina Paraskeva the unexpected news that she would be repatriated that evening. Paraskeva was dating a liaison officer from another department and was devastated. Although Briukhanov claimed that transport logistics had necessitated her hastened departure, he probably feared she would flee if given enough time. Briukhanov nonetheless gave her the day to make last-minute purchases, assigning a driver and officer as an escort. At a shoe repair shop, Paraskeva escaped her handlers and vanished through a back door. Meanwhile, Briukhanov discovered that ten thousand marks were missing from the mission's funds. The repatriate security guard, whom witnesses had seen with Paraskeva earlier in the day, was sent to Berlin in her place. He was arrested by Soviet security forces upon his arrival, although it is not clear if his arrest was related to the incident. Paraskeva's boy-friend and a repatriate friend were recalled for fear that they would assist her.[102]

The treatment of repatriate workers created resentments and anxieties that boiled over into denunciations. Repatriates who had been involved in the seed-ier aspects of the missions' work were especially likely to accuse their former superiors. It is possible the shady dealings funded espionage, but they seem pri-marily to have been a response to the missions' lack of resources. The Soviet occupation of Germany was supposed to feed itself, which limited the supplies the army could secure.[103] It seems that for this reason, Soviet leaders in Berlin were only willing to share a minimum of resources with the repatriation mis-sions in the Western zones. The missions uncovered money that Soviet forced laborers had accumulated in German banks, nearly 15 million marks in the Brit-ish zone alone. These funds seem to have gone primarily to occupation authori-ties in Berlin, however.[104]

The missions' operations were expensive. Accredited officers received Soviet rations and could buy price-controlled Allied kits, but the missions also had to support unaccredited repatriate workers. During the winter of 1946–47, the mis-sion in the British zone received an average of half a ration kit monthly for each of the combined eighty accredited and unaccredited workers. Upkeep on the mis-sions' cars was also expensive, and German marks had little buying power. Re-pair shops demanded payment in cigarettes, coffee, or alcohol in addition to the nominal bill in marks, a practice Colonel Briukhanov described by the German term *geschäft* (business). When allegations of black-market dealings in the Brit-ish zone surfaced in Moscow, Briukhanov defended the mission: "No *geschäft*, no car repair."[105]

Accusations against Briukhanov's officers first came from a former POW known alternately (for unclear reasons) as Mikhail Kukh or G. L. Sigal. After liberation the Red Army lieutenant became an unaccredited repatriation officer and managed the transit camp in the British zone at Lübeck. In this capacity, Kukh-Sigal devised moneymaking schemes to pay for the mission—and perhaps more. As thousands of repatriates passed through the transit camp at Lübeck in the final months of 1945, mission officers offered or pressured the returnees to exchange marks for rubles at a rate of two for one. Kukh-Sigal took the marks to a Jewish DP from Poland, Isak Ryb, to exchange for rubles at a more favor-able rate. The officers exchanged for 550,000 marks in total. Although marks were not valuable on the open market, Soviet officers could use them to buy British supply kits that included items like cigarettes that they then sold or traded. Grander arrangements followed the first dealings. At the end of 1945, repatriation officers used contacts with the Max-Moor textile firm in Hamburg to make a handshake deal for more than two hundred pieces of high-quality wool fabric. The officers turned at least some of the pieces into suits for personal use and distributed other pieces to repatriates. Most officers also bought luxury items like gold watches for themselves and their relatives in the USSR.[106]

When Kukh-Sigal went to the Soviet zone of occupation in the fall of 1946, he spent some six months under verification. In April 1947, perhaps anxious about his future or under pressure from investigators, he denounced his former bosses in the mission. The officers at Lübeck confirmed Kukh-Sigal's basic story but claimed the profits had been modest, about 75,000 marks. Most of the money they spent on mission business like repatriate workers' salary, provisions, and alcohol for *geschäft*.[107] Inspectors from the Soviet military occupation in Germany investigated and reprimanded the officers. At a meeting of Moscow repatriation officials in mid-1947, General Golubev commented, "It's clear that our officers are not doing what they need to do but instead are drinking, exchanging currency, selling cars, and sleeping with German girls."[108] The officers were not recalled, probably because officials in Moscow thought it was likely that British authorities would deny entry to replacements.

To repatriation leaders, it seemed that life in the Western zones corrupted officers and repatriates alike. General Iakov Basilov, the Moscow-based repatriation official in charge of work outside of Soviet-controlled territories, said that Kukh-Sigal and others had been spoiled by years abroad. Was it any wonder that "they begin to think of themselves as suspects and invent antirepatriation stories?"[109] Basilov's assertion that repatriates had been contaminated with bourgeois values applied to the accredited officers too. From 1946 to the end of 1950, 245 Soviet officers had gone abroad as repatriation workers. Of those, at least 35 were recalled for workplace negligence or "amoral offenses." They included Major Chekmazov, the model for the child-saving repatriation officer of the film *They Have a Motherland*. He had figured in Kukh-Sigal's accusations, although it is unclear if his recall was related.[110] Until the relevant secret police records are declassified in Moscow, it will remain unknown how many mission officers went to the Gulag and on what charges.

Accusations about the corruption of officers contributed to paranoia in the mission. In the spring of 1948, Briukhanov prepared to leave his position in the British zone of Germany. His final reports depicted an atmosphere of desperate paranoia. The officers lived "in a state of tension" because anti-Soviet displaced persons rang the mission's phone day and night. After the escape of the cook Paraskeva, all repatriate staff were recalled, and the mission hired Germans instead. When he and his officers fell ill, he fired the cooks. "Now we make our lunches ourselves, or rather we live on dry rations," he moaned. "Perhaps our illness was incidental, but maybe the German women were purposefully poisoning our food, slowly trying to take us out."[111] Briukhanov did not die from poisoning or starvation. Instead, he returned to the Soviet Union and soon after was training Repatriation Administration staff to go abroad. He summarized his experiences for his audiences: "Every meeting with British military forces under today's conditions is a battle."[112]

The animosity Briukhanov and other officers expressed about Western intransigence and fascist camp administrators had some truth but also corresponded to the expectations of Soviet leaders. Late returners, repatriate workers, and mission officers all became objects of suspicion during their return to the USSR. In their interactions with officials in Moscow, they emphasized the criminality of the Western powers and the obstacles created to prevent DPs from repatriating. These statements not only demonstrated their loyalty to the Soviet Union but also solidified opinions about the battle lines of the Cold War in displaced persons camps.

Repatriation officers were products of a Soviet labor culture that emphasized fulfillment and overfulfillment of plans. Although they did not have quotas like factory workers, they felt pressure to send large convoys of returnees to the USSR. At first they counted on Allied authorities to use coercion or turned to abduction themselves. After Western leaders definitively rejected forced repatriation, Soviet officers hoped that persuasion would stimulate return. When the hundreds of thousands of DPs did not rush east but emigrated permanently, Soviet officials abroad and in Moscow were deeply disappointed.

Why the repatriation missions stayed open for so long is a puzzle, although not from the perspective of Western occupation forces. Western officials received permission to repatriate their dead from the Soviet zone in exchange for access to the living. Amid the tensions that accompanied the Berlin blockade, Anglo-American teams largely finished retrieving their dead by 1949 and ejected the Soviet missions.[113]

The mystery is why Soviet leaders insisted on retaining the missions abroad despite the apparent impossibility of persuading almost all nonreturners. The missions were a cover for espionage at times, but much of the spying was related to repatriation work itself. Part of the explanation is that Soviet leaders did not comprehend the pervasiveness of anti-Soviet attitudes among the displaced, that nonreturn was a product of sentiment from below rather than manipulation from above. In a sense, Soviet tenacity was a response to feelings of outrage at the Allies' supposedly having stolen people who belonged to the motherland.[114] If only the capitalist governments would call off their nationalist henchmen in the camp leadership, Soviet officials thought, DPs would see that the Soviet motherland that represented their national homeland was the only place they would belong.

The stated goal to return every Soviet-claimed person was not the missions' only aim. In the growing conflict between East and West, repatriation provided a platform to demonstrate the deceitfulness of the Western Allies. They had failed to uphold their end of the agreement at Yalta and reunite Soviet families. By visiting camps filled with hostile nonreturners, Soviet officers provoked clashes meant to reveal the link between pro-German collaboration during the war and anti-Soviet activity under Western rule. In the Soviet view, the Western Allies used the pretense of humanitarianism to conceal exploitation and prevent the real humanitarian outcome—reunion with the motherland.

Contrary to this view, which emphasized DPs' lack of agency, repatriates had a role to play in the drama between the USSR and the Allies. Soviet officials' belief that the camps were dens of anti-Soviet activity demanded that late returners explain why they had remained in Europe so long. Repatriation officers, too, had to account for their time outside the Soviet Union. Stories of anti-Soviet crimes in DP camps and obstructionism by occupation governments fell upon receptive ears in Moscow. Although anti-Allied narratives did not begin with returnees, they reinforced expectations about the misdeeds of the Western Allies. Moreover, they perhaps gave repatriation officials hope that they might bring the Soviet diaspora home. Although the repatriation teams withdrew from the Western zones of Germany and Austria by the early 1950s, repatriation of Soviet citizens would remain a symbol of the Cold War struggle after Stalin's death.

RETURN AFTER STALIN

The Return to the Motherland Campaign
in the 1950s

Soviet-born people dispersed from the displaced persons camps of Europe to countries throughout the world in the late 1940s and early 1950s. The project of repatriation shifted, too, moving to embassies in Argentina, Australia, and elsewhere.[1] After Iosif Stalin's death in 1953, repatriation efforts gained new force when the Soviet government under Nikita Khrushchev initiated an effort called Return to the Motherland. Under the supervision of the Committee for State Security (the KGB, the secret police), more than eight thousand people came to Soviet Ukraine alone from 1954 to the end of the decade.[2]

In its publications, Return to the Motherland portrayed migrants as members of the wartime diaspora, but most new arrivals had never lived in the USSR. The majority were so-called re-émigrés—people who years earlier had left territories that the Soviet Union would annex after September 1939. They arrived in the USSR from around the world but above all from Latin America. The largest group, accounting for approximately half of the migrants, were ethnic Ukrainians who had come to Argentina from the Ukrainian lands of interwar Poland. Although the migrants differed in their motivations and backgrounds, officials treated them in public as a single Soviet diaspora, united by its devotion to socialism.

Why did Soviet leaders want to recruit these people? They had largely lived outside of the USSR, and their return came at significant cost to the country. The campaign manifested the Soviet ethnoterritorial claim over the displaced that emerged in World War II. Like the repatriation missions in Western-occupied Europe, the Return to the Motherland campaign insisted that people whose ethnic homelands were in the USSR—especially the titular nations of Soviet republics—had an innate bond with the Soviet Union. Repatriation officers had mostly focused on the wartime displaced, while the post-Stalin campaign extended this idea to the diaspora broadly. Soviet officials asserted that groups of Ukrainians abroad deserved reunions with their families and neighbors in the motherland, and with the bigger family of Soviet Ukraine and the USSR.

The post-Stalin campaign had motivations that were both general and specific to its moment. In a broad sense, its targeting of the Soviet diaspora for return fit into efforts that Eastern European countries had made since the nineteenth century to reverse emigration.[3] The return campaign took on immediate urgency because of the recent struggle between Soviet forces and a tenacious nationalist insurgency in Western Ukraine.[4] As anti-Soviet nationalist movements went abroad, they hoped to define a form of patriotism that could survive outside the homeland. Moreover, the émigré leadership was dangerous because it worked closely with Anglo-American intelligence.[5] Against this Cold War backdrop, the return campaign attempted to undercut émigré groups by claiming that émigrés' only true home was the territory of their ancestors.

Return to the Motherland also fit into the broader turn in Soviet politics when, after twenty-five years of Stalin's rule, his successors attempted to revitalize the Soviet system. The Khrushchev period is most strongly associated with the end of mass repression, but his efforts to reform the Soviet economy were equally ambitious. Khrushchev made material comfort a centerpiece in the struggle between West and East, asserting that victory would come not only by winning the arms race but also by providing a better quality of life.[6] The return campaign promised material comfort alongside spiritual well-being. By providing prosperity to migrants who had known life under capitalism, Soviet authorities believed they would demonstrate the superiority of socialism.

Assurances about a comfortable life, feelings of estrangement abroad, and the promise of reunions with family resonated with potential migrants. When they arrived, however, they often faced disappointment with Soviet life. The way the KGB would approach this problem is an example of how the party-state offered rewards for participation in Soviet life, fighting the Cold War with material comfort as well as repression.[7]

Recruiting the Soviet Diaspora

For officials in the USSR and other states, the aftermath of World War II offered the opportunity, even the necessity, to create ethnically homogeneous states. The governments of East-Central Europe, with the help of the Allies, expelled local ethnic Germans for this reason, arguing that doing so would prevent a future German state from claiming to defend its diaspora abroad as Hitler had.[8] Migrations defined national belonging in places like Italy, where administrators ascribed citizenship to ethnic Italians "repatriated" from former colonies in Africa and Europe but not to people authorities determined were not Italian by race.[9] These campaigns highlighted the preeminence of titular nationalities in states and territories. In the USSR, such efforts came at the expense of smaller national groups, which officials marginalized and merged on paper into titular national groups.[10]

Amid repatriation, expulsion, and ascription, officials saw the possibility of bringing diaspora nationalities to their nominal homelands. After the Red Army expelled the Wehrmacht from Poland, the governments of Poland and the USSR agreed to a population exchange that sent a half million ethnic Ukrainians from Poland to Ukraine and eight hundred thousand Poles and Polish-born Jews to Poland.[11] The promise of an ethnic homeland brought some ninety thousand Armenians to Soviet Armenia in the second half of the 1940s.[12] The amalgamation of Russian and Soviet patriotism would motivate many of the hundred thousand migrants from China, mostly ethnic Russians from Manchuria, from 1954 to 1962.[13]

Propaganda appealed to diasporas' attachment to their homelands, but recruitment campaigns also used material incentives. In 1946, as an alternative to shuttering the Repatriation Administration after most of the wartime displaced had returned, General Filipp Golikov partially repurposed it as a recruiting office for diaspora groups whose titular homelands were in the USSR.[14] The implicit motivation for this extension of the repatriation program was nationalist. Just as the Soviet-claimed children living in German orphanages were connected by heritage to the USSR, so were Ukrainians or Belarusians who had left interwar Poland to live in France. In contrast to the repatriates of 1944–45, diaspora groups were under no compulsion to come to the USSR. Golikov instead offered special conditions for migrants. He wrote to deputy minister of defense Nikolai Bulganin to ask for ration kits with tobacco and extra food for the first group of re-émigrés coming from France to Ukraine in 1946. The request came at a time when a combination of drought and excessive government requisitions created a famine in the USSR that killed as many as two million people.[15] Yet Golikov deemed the provisions "especially important" because the first migrants would undoubtedly report back to the diaspora in France.[16] Despite the deprivations in the country, all new arrivals were to receive an apartment, a month's pay, and other help to start their Soviet lives.[17]

Not all petitioners received permission to come to the Soviet Union. In June 1946, a state decree offered post–civil war White émigrés citizenship but did not guarantee entry into the USSR. Feeling postvictory Soviet patriotism or perhaps leftist sympathies, thousands took citizenship. A repatriate turned defector who knew many émigrés in Paris maintained that Soviet officials refused to allow them into the USSR because they would become disillusioned with Soviet realities. They were more valuable as loyalists living abroad than as dissatisfied residents.[18] In June 1946, the government issued a secret order capping the number of White émigrés arriving from France at 2,000, just a fraction of the total émigré population. Soviet authorities were wary about allowing potential spies into the country, but White émigrés were even more wary of coming to Stalin's USSR. By the beginning of 1947, only 267 White émigrés had returned from France.[19]

Repatriation officials had better luck recruiting among other diaspora groups, but the new Soviet homeland would disappoint the re-émigrés. On December 2, 1946, the *Rossiia* arrived at the port of Odesa from France with 1,116 Ukrainians, 707 Belarussians, and 267 Russians. Most had left Polish Ukraine for Western Europe before World War II and had never lived in the USSR. They nonetheless made posters with Stalin's image and prepared patriotic speeches. After a day waiting on the ship while fog cleared, they deboarded to an empty waterfront. The ship's captain reported, "There was no delegation, no orchestra, and no flowers." Worse still, the train designated to take the group to their new homes arrived late, forcing the émigrés to remain in Odesa for five days. Golikov wrote to then Ukrainian party leader Nikita Khrushchev that information about the disappointing reception "could spread abroad for use by elements hostile to the Soviet Union."[20] Their first introduction to the USSR hinted at what the migrants would experience when they arrived in their places of settlement. The war had done significant damage to France, and the migrants might have believed that the situation in the victorious USSR would be better. This perception was mistaken; the war had left the USSR in shambles, especially the formerly occupied areas where the migrants were settling.[21]

For their part, Soviet leaders became frustrated with recruiting among the diaspora. Leaders in Ukraine's government had budgeted for several hundred thousand re-émigrés to arrive in 1947.[22] Instead, the Repatriation Administration's campaign resulted in just 16,008 re-émigrés arriving to the entire Soviet Union in 1947, most from Romania and China. The small number of returnees must have disappointed given the expense of the effort. Repatriation from France alone cost some 5 million francs—more than 1,000 francs per person—and each re-émigré then claimed more than 4,000 rubles in cash subsidies alone.[23] An irony of the campaign is that the representatives of the workers' state seem to have expected the re-émigrés would be wealthy and educated, like the White emigration that had come disproportionately from prerevolutionary elites. They were disheartened to learn that most of the re-émigrés of the 1940s were manual laborers.[24] The meager results of the recruiting campaign of 1946–47 apparently persuaded the Soviet government to abandon the project in 1948.

The end of the diaspora campaigns coincided with the closure of repatriation in Allied-occupied Europe. After wavering for several years about how they should treat DPs from Eastern Europe in postwar Germany, Western leaders opened visa programs that allowed almost a million people to emigrate to the Americas, the United Kingdom, Scandinavia, and Australia.[25] From March 1946 to the end of 1951, repatriation officers had organized by persuasion or force the repatriation of 20,386 people from Germany and Austria. The Soviet count of nonreturners, which captured only a portion of the emigration, included 313,696 people who had emigrated permanently.[26] The repatriation mission had outlived its usefulness. In 1952 its duties passed to diplomats in the Ministry of Foreign Affairs and to secret police in the Ministry of State Security.

The closure of the Repatriation Administration occurred less than a year before Stalin died in March 1953. The dictator's death opened the possibility for major reforms. The most significant change was that Stalin's successors softened the party-state's approach to repression. The new collective leadership ended the infamous "Doctors' Plot"—the arrest of prominent Jewish physicians accused of attempting to murder Soviet leaders. In April 1953, Stalin's successors published a notice about the release of the doctors. The exoneration, let alone its publication in the press, would have been unthinkable under Stalin. Indeed, it drew angry, antisemitic letters from Soviet people. But the public reversal, alongside the pardoning of many categories of Gulag prisoners, was an unmistakable signal within the USSR and to foreign observers that the new leaders had rejected the harshest aspects of Stalinist rule.[27]

One of the amnesties that followed Stalin's death was the September 1955 "Amnesty of Soviet Citizens Who Collaborated with the Occupiers," which granted releases and commutations to people convicted of nonviolent cooperation with Germany and its allies. Although the amnesty had implications for hundreds of thousands of people within the USSR, it also targeted potential returnees who feared that they would be accused of collaboration upon return. The final paragraph of the amnesty order called for easing restrictions on immigration by Soviet-born people abroad, presumably those who had collaborated.[28]

This last paragraph was conspicuous because of the recent formation of an organization called the Committee for Return to the Motherland. Its nominal leader was an obscure general, Nikolai Filippovich Mikhailov, a former POW who returned to the USSR in 1945. The committee propagandized return in its four-page newspaper, *Za vozvrashchenie na Rodinu* (For return to the Motherland), published biweekly or monthly in 1955–56 and twice monthly after 1957.

In addition to the Russian edition, the committee produced a Ukrainian version (*Za povernennia na Bat'kivshchynu*) with a circulation of five thousand.[29] Published in the committee's headquarters in Berlin, the paper reached diaspora communities via Soviet embassies and friendship societies across the world. It also broadcast Russian-language radio shows from Germany and produced books about return. These efforts garnered international attention. The *New York Times* reported from Buenos Aires in April 1956 that "the Soviet Embassy here is well on the way to establishing a record this year in getting Soviet émigrés and exiles in South America to return to their homeland."[30] The *Times* took the recruiting campaign at face value, but others did not. As many observers suspected, the committee was a front organization of the KGB.

The shadow of Soviet police in the Return to the Motherland campaign suggested to nonreturners that its main goal was espionage. They were partially correct. Counterintelligence officers were particularly interested in the return of former members of émigré organizations because they could provide intelligence and because their defection was valuable for propaganda. The campaign for return was a form of psychological warfare against anti-Soviet émigré organizations. The prospect of members' redefecting to the Soviet Union made politically active émigrés suspect one another and exacerbated existing cleavages within the community. Because of the important role these groups played in the plans of Western intelligence agencies, the disruption the campaign wrought should not be underestimated.[31]

At the same time, police were invested in repatriation not only or even primarily to recruit intelligence assets. The purpose of the campaign was to demonstrate the achievements of the Soviet Union and the joys of national reunification. These goals were on display in the production of the committee's publications. The KGB in Kyiv recruited a journalist named Nikolai Smeshnov in April 1955. The thirty-four-year-old repatriate had apparently worked as an informant for the police before and now would receive 1,200 rubles a month to work for the paper.[32] Smeshnov and others had orders to write about returnees who had been members of émigré committees but were now repentant about their anti-Soviet past. They also solicited articles from returnees working in the professions to highlight their successful transition to Soviet life. Police in Volyn province recruited a re-émigré journalist code-named "Girnyi" in the summer of 1956. He had emigrated from Poland to Argentina in 1927 and had been a member of leftist organizations, including the Argentinean Communist Party during the years 1939–47. "Girnyi" had standing instructions to report any re-émigrés who had worked with foreign intelligence, but his daily beat was to write and solicit articles for *Za vozvrashchenie na Rodinu*.[33]

As a re-émigré, "Girnyi" was unusual among the KGB's journalists. The public face of the campaign was the World War II diaspora. One of the most prominent portrayals of return was the film *Liudi i zveri* (*People and Beasts*, Sergei Gerasimov, 1962). The main character, POW Aleksei Pavlov, was played by Nikolai Eremenko, who had been a POW in real life. After the war, Aleksei moves to Argentina and then Germany, believing that his family and country would reject him. At the movie's end, Aleksei reunites with his brother's family and earns a place in Soviet society. The drama of Aleksei's story is twofold: Can he receive absolution for remaining abroad so long? And can his family overcome the fear that led to their shunning of unfortunate members of the wartime diaspora?

There was seemingly no direct connection between the film and the KGB's repatriation campaign, yet they overlapped in their concerns over family reunification. In the film, a kindly young Soviet woman connects Aleksei with his estranged family. In the real world, KGB officers weaponized family connections. *Za vozvrashchenie na Rodinu* published classified advertisements and articles where families pleaded with their lost relatives to return. The targets of such advertisements may have seen them as a threat—was the KGB informing them that their families were being held captive?[34] The hostage scenario seems especially likely in cases involving prominent émigrés and nonreturners whom KGB officers hoped to investigate as war criminals. Since the 1940s, police had been keeping catalogs of nonreturners and their relatives and now used the relatives to bait traps.[35]

Not all instances of family outreach were attempts at blackmail. In Volyn province, the KGB recruited agent "Zhukov" to persuade his daughter to return to the USSR after she wrote to him from Paris, where she had settled after the war with her French husband. "Zhukov" probably provided a classified notice in *Za vozvrashchenie na Rodinu*, and KGB officers also considered putting "Zhukov" on the committee's radio program. In this case, there was seemingly no intelligence motive. The KGB handlers sought the reunification of the family on Soviet soil, including the French husband, and no more.[36] Differentiating hostage taking from family reunification is impossible in many cases. In a sense, these incidents highlight the connection between the KGB's role in repression and in social work. The KGB used family for both goals as a tool to bind people to the bigger family of the motherland.

The wartime diaspora dominated the presentation of the repatriation campaign in public, but re-émigrés outnumbered repatriates significantly as migrants. KGB counterintelligence officers in Ukraine kept lists of new arrivals from late 1955 into 1959 that include more than eight thousand people. More than half came from South America, with some four thousand coming from Argentina alone. In the nineteenth and early twentieth centuries, huge numbers of immigrants arrived in Argentina from Europe, attracted by a welcoming government and the promise of farmland. Seventy thousand people came from Polish Ukraine in the interwar years alone, and another six thousand arrived after World War II.[37] The economic decline in Argentina in the postwar period and the accompanying political struggles between Juan Peron's government and the military perhaps unsettled Ukrainian Argentineans. The bombing of the Plaza de Mayo in Buenos Aires in June 1955 and the subsequent overthrow of Peron seem to have spurred many to return.

Although re-émigrés were more numerous, the smaller group of returnees from the wartime diaspora better represented Soviet goals for repatriation. The members of the wartime diaspora had experienced both socialism and capitalism. Their ability to compare made their return a more meaningful endorsement than that of re-émigrés, who would live in the USSR for the first time. And because many members of the wartime diaspora had lived for a significant part of their lives in the USSR, their arrival was a return to their Soviet motherland, as well as to their families and ethnic homeland.

The return campaign of the 1950s built on repatriation efforts under Stalin. When numbers of willing returnees dwindled after 1945, repatriation officials had attempted to find willing migrants by recruiting among diaspora groups. As intelligence officers took over the work of repatriation, they continued earlier efforts, using spiritual and material incentives to lure potential migrants.

The Lives of Returnees

Overtures to returnees emphasized the good life that they would have as Soviet citizens. These promises fit with the broader turn under Khrushchev to reverse the Stalinist policy of consumer shortages. Although Stalin's government had always promised a future of abundance, the state had favored heavy industry over consumer goods to produce war matériel in advance of what seemed to be an inevitable conflict.[38] After the USSR defeated Germany, the potential for clashes in the Cold War motivated Stalin to accelerate postwar reconstruction efforts, eschewing a retreat from the shortage economy that many people desired.[39] In contrast, Khrushchev made consumption a priority for the first time in decades, directing resources into mass housing and the agricultural sphere. He promised that the USSR would catch up and overtake the capitalist West not only in military capacity but also in clothing and home appliances.[40] The Repatriation Administration under Stalin had offered some benefits to re-émigrés as enticements, but not as a central part of propaganda for return. Under Khrushchev material rewards became a core element of recruiting efforts in the press.

Returnees boasted about their Soviet lives in *Za vozvrashchenie na Rodinu*. In January 1956, the paper featured one who had finished a doctoral dissertation at Moscow's Veterinary Academy and became a professor in Irkutsk. There he received a car—an undeniable marker of prosperity.[41] Another returnee enjoyed an enviable 3,000-ruble monthly salary. One Muscovite returnee assuaged potential migrants who worried that the government would prevent them from living in the capital or other major cities.[42] A returning coal miner in Staline (today's Donetsk) wrote an extended article for the newspaper on the bounty of Soviet life, complete with a spreadsheet of his income and expenditures.[43] By way of contrast, depictions of life abroad played on familiar tropes about nonreturner physicians forced to work as janitors or former engineers who drove taxis. An article in *Pravda* asserted that in West Germany there were tens of thousands who "continue to remain [abroad], deprived of rights, eking out a wretched existence in camps and settlements for displaced persons."[44]

These images fit into the broader endeavor to present the Soviet Union as a modern, prosperous state. As part of the Cold War struggle with the United States, the USSR portrayed itself as an alternative model of development for the postcolonial world and developing countries. Soviet officials put on exhibitions abroad that portrayed the USSR as a leader in technological modernity and high culture. These demonstrations were perhaps most effective in the global south, where the contrast with local equipment was impressive.[45] Novelist Iurii Slepukhin (born 1926) was a nonreturner who had been sent to forced labor in Germany after growing up in the North Caucasus region of Russia. After the war, he joined the National Alliance of Russian Solidarists (Narodno-Trudovoi Soiuz Rossiiskikh Solidaristov, NTS), an anti-Soviet émigré party, and left Europe for Argentina. In 1957, he denounced the NTS and returned to the USSR. Return offered him the chance to start a writing career with articles about devious émigrés, his former comrades in the NTS, in *Za vozvrashchenie na Rodinu*.[46] Later in life, he would write an autobiographical novel, *Iuzhnyi krest* (Southern cross). Its main character, technician Mikhail Polunin, visits the Soviet pavilion in Buenos Aires and assesses Soviet radio equipment and observes, "Not bad optical equipment, modern machine tools and measuring apparatuses. Truly, it wouldn't be an embarrassment to display in the States, let alone in Argentina."[47] Like Slepukhin, Polunin takes the next step of visiting the Soviet embassy and completing an application for return.

The promise of affluence in a technologically advanced state was not the only reason people came to the USSR. Most returnees seem to have had leftist sympathies. Statistics about how many returnees held membership in leftist political organizations are unavailable. Anecdotal evidence suggests that over half of the adult returnees had belonged to Soviet sympathizer groups like the Friends of the Soviet Union. Maria Delakova (born Oleinik) and her Belgian husband came to her hometown of Zaporizhzhia (in central Ukraine) in November 1955 after more than a decade in Germany and Belgium. Delakova claimed that they had wanted to return in 1947 but that Belgian authorities thwarted them. In the meantime, she enrolled in the Soviet embassy's sympathizer group, and her husband joined Belgium's Communist Party. The latter supposedly posted illegal pro-communist posters around their town under the cover of night. They told Soviet officials that they had returned to the USSR believing it was "a country of communists where they would be accepted with open arms."[48]

A re-émigré named Khariton Andreichuk came from Buenos Aires to his home village in Volyn province. As a member of the prewar Communist Party of Western Ukraine, he had left Poland for Argentina at age twenty-three because he feared Polish repression. It is conceivable that he also fled possible expulsion from the party during Stalin-era purges that had spilled over to non-Soviet communist organizations. The USSR had annexed Volyn province permanently in 1945, so fear of party discipline could explain why Andreichuk did not return while Stalin was alive. Instead, he spent the first postwar decade gathering information for Soviet authorities about Ukrainian nationalist organizations in Argentina.[49] The KGB was particularly eager for people like Andreichuk to return because they seemed to make the most trustworthy informants.

A sense of alienation in their adopted countries drew many returnees back to their homeland. The impossibility of assimilation is a key idea in Slepukhin's *Iuzhnyi krest*. Its hero, Polunin, complains often about the strangeness of South American culture. He is affronted by minor differences, like local drinking habits; what Soviet person could drink hard liquor without *zakuski*—snacks of pickles and kielbasa? These small discrepancies he could endure, but the fate of his potential children frightens Polunin. He reflects on the prospect of marrying his émigré girlfriend, Duniasha, and staying in Argentina permanently: "Sooner or later Duniasha will want to have a kid, at first everything will be fine but then he will go to school. Then there will be a little Argentinean in the family with his own interests, different from his parents', and an internal world far removed from theirs as well."[50]

These "little Argentineans" were a significant number among the returnees. Many re-émigrés came as entire families, bringing their teenage or adult children with them. The nearly nine hundred families from Argentina included some 3.5 family members on average. In one case, three brothers returned with their wives, children, and father—fifteen people in total—to the village of Pustomyty in Volyn province. More than a thousand had been born in South America, and of those about half were teenagers or young adults.[51] It is easy to imagine that the re-émigrés who came with foreign-born children shared the anxieties of Slepukhin/Polunin. The nationalist diaspora could deploy patriotic symbols in denunciations of the Soviet-Russian occupation of Ukraine and organize classes to support the Ukrainian language. But diaspora culture would never substitute for life in the homeland.

Dreams of raising a family in the homeland crashed against harsh realities. Children who had lived abroad for most or all their lives often spoke no Russian or Ukrainian. The younger generation who came from Latin America wrote letters home in Spanish and loitered in seaside cities like Odesa, hoping to befriend Spanish-speaking sailors in port.[52] A KGB official wrote, "Almost all of them [the young re-émigrés] speak Russian very poorly." The promise of giving their children a superior education in the Soviet Union had attracted some of the families. Those fluent in a Slavic language or who learned one quickly saw this dream realized. For those without Russian or Ukrainian, admission to higher education was impossible.[53]

Some re-émigrés felt a greater allegiance to their non-Soviet homelands than to the USSR. A young re-émigré from Argentina studying at Odesa's art institute, Alberto Pavliuk, was denounced after he told fellow students that "his Motherland is Argentina, because he was born and grew up there. His childhood friends were all there and, after all, life is good there."[54] A KGB officer in Odesa reported that the young re-émigrés "continue their foreign way of life . . . spending time drinking and listening to Brazilian or Argentinean music. They do not go to the theater and do not read books or newspapers."[55]

Some migrants were disappointed by the limits of reform in the Soviet Union. Fedor Patorzhinskii was one of a small number of returnees who had emigrated in the aftermath of the Russian Revolution. In 1920 he left Ukraine at age nineteen with Petr Wrangel's defeated Volunteer Army and settled in France. Over the next thirty years, his career as a choir director flourished. Despite his success in France, Russian Orthodox belief drew him back to the motherland. He had hoped that Stalin's wartime cooperation with the Orthodox Church and reform under Khrushchev would enable him to work in the church without consequences. He was mistaken. Although repression in the Soviet Union diminished overall, renewed revolutionary fervor after Stalin led to a revival of official atheism.[56] In a conversation taped by the KGB, Patorzhinskii confessed to a friend visiting on a mission from the Orthodox Church in France that he faced a difficult choice. He wanted to work as a church choir director but believed that doing so would mean exile from secular Soviet cultural life. Moreover, his brother

Ivan had lived his entire live in the USSR, making a career as a singer and official. Would Fedor Patorzhinskii's move to church activity force a split with his family or hurt the career of his brother? The choir director had hoped for spiritual renewal but found himself caught between his faith and his family of loyal Soviet citizens.[57]

Every person came to the USSR for a different constellation of reasons—leftist beliefs, family, religion. Whatever other factors motivated them, returnees all hoped for a comfortable life in the USSR, and bread-and-butter issues often drove migrants' dissatisfaction. Rumors about potential deprivations in the USSR had spread to the émigrés of Buenos Aires. Before leaving they had heard that bread and pork fat (salo) would be in short supply. But the shortages extended beyond what many had anticipated. One re-émigré complained in a letter to friends in Uruguay that he had to buy drinking water and boil soy to make ersatz coffee. Future returnees could "forget about meat."[58] The absence of meat was particularly troubling to South American re-émigrés. Alberto Pavliuk complained that if he found meat, it was ten times more expensive than in Argentina.[59]

Apartments and work also caused problems. Soviet officials abroad promised returnees an apartment and a start-up subsidy of roughly one to three months' salary at the time. There was often a disconnect between these promises and what local authorities could provide. A repatriate from pre-1939 borders and her Belgian husband arrived in Kyiv in November 1955 and had to squeeze into the woman's parents' apartment for six months while they waited for their own living space. Even after the city government settled the couple in a new building, they complained that the 22 square meters (approximately 240 square feet) were not enough to hold the furniture they brought from their four-room apartment in Belgium.[60] Returnees were also disappointed when their salaries were lower than anticipated. Some couples who returned from Western Europe complained that the man's salary was too low to support the family alone and that the wife "did not come to the USSR to work."[61]

Local authorities were often reluctant to help the incoming people. They had their own worries—longtime residents who were petitioning for apartments, raises, and better jobs.[62] Because repatriates were usually not plugged in to local networks, it was easy to ignore their requests. One repatriate claimed to have slept in "random locations" with his mother and four siblings after arriving in the USSR in November 1955. The reason for their misfortune was local elites, he claimed. "To resolve any issue," he reportedly said, "you have to have vodka and get local bosses drunk."[63] The migrants had expected authorities to welcome them after decades abroad, but many found that they were now outsiders.

Other returnees realized that the homeland they remembered was different from the reality they encountered. Most re-émigrés had left Western Ukraine in the 1930s, and the twenty-some intervening years had brought tumultuous change to the area. They had departed a rural, multiethnic region of Poland. In the intervening period, the territory saw the mass murder of Jews in the Holocaust and of Poles by Ukrainian nationalist groups. Soviet authorities contributed to the ethnic cleansing of the territory by removing Poles and ethnic Germans through arrests, deportations, and population transfers. Under Stalin what it meant to be Ukrainian also became more homogeneous, as cultural authorities elided regional differences in the republic. Small farms had dominated the region before, but after campaigns of collectivization and industrialization, it became a Soviet landscape of collective farms and factory cities.[64]

Many returnees chose their native village as their destination in the USSR. Some perhaps thought of it as their first stop or used it as a placeholder residence. Others may have intended to live there but were shocked by the reality of rural Soviet life. The Goliks, a married couple with teenage children, Bill and Nadia, came to Volyn province from Canada. The father had moved to Toronto in 1929 and opened a store. His wife joined him in 1938. It was the mother who pushed the family to return. She had trouble integrating into Canadian life, never learning English or gaining citizenship. Through a pro-Soviet organization that Nadia Golik called the "Russian Club," they learned about the possibility of coming to Ukraine and left for the USSR in July 1956. The father was born in Hishyn, a village not far from the town of Kovel, so the family stopped there to see relatives after arriving in the USSR. Nadia remembered later, "It was the first time I ever saw my father cry." Compared with Canada, or even her father's memories, the village seemed impoverished. The head of the collective farm in the village was welcoming, telling them, "We'll help you build a house. We'll give you a job in the collective farm, and you'll live like everybody else." The thought of staying was too much for her father. His world was not theirs; he had imagined his life in Ukraine would be like his life in Canada and hauled an outboard motor to Ukraine so he could go boating. Her father left the village for Dnipropetrovsk, a city on the Dnepr River, where he found an attractive job and could go out on the water.[65]

The Goliks were among the many migrants who converged on cities. The arrival of returnees in urban centers made the scarcity of housing even worse. Of the three hundred migrants living in Odesa province in May 1956, about 90 percent were living in Odesa proper. More than a quarter of them had not come to the USSR with plans to live in the city. There was no coordinating committee at the national or republican level that could arrange for housing, and the city government refused to give housing to migrants ahead of other Odesans. Many were left spending as much as three hundred rubles monthly on rented rooms.[66]

The difficulties that returnees experienced caused many to seek an escape from the USSR. Soviet officials had promised an improvement in returnees' lives—both moral and material. Migrants found that reforms were few and apartments were cramped. Perhaps worst of all, they had hoped to return to a welcoming homeland but often discovered that they did not belong. Soviet authorities wanted the migrants to be a symbol of socialism's superiority to capitalism. As the migrants wrote angry letters to contacts abroad and visited foreign embassies to express their grievances, they now threatened to become a symbol of its inadequacy.

Exit Negotiations

Before leaving Canada for Ukraine with her family, Nadia Golik asked officials at the Soviet embassy if she would be able to return to Canada if necessary. "No problem," they said. "Canada's your country. You were born here."[67] The embassy officials misled Golik, although they did not lie. The Canadian government would welcome her back as a citizen. Exiting the USSR would not be as easy. Soviet authorities would not let anyone leave the country without an exit permit and rejected most returnees' demands to leave in the 1950s. The ensuing struggle pitted hundreds of returnees like Nadia Golik against the KGB as they tried to leverage their connections to their non-Soviet homelands. KGB officers responded to this challenge with threats, even arrests. But attempts to leave the country also drew the police into efforts to improve conditions for the migrants.

Although some returnees from the wartime diaspora attempted to leave the USSR, re-émigrés were disproportionately those who sought an exit. Unlike repatriates, who had lived in the USSR and had a sense of what life there would entail, the re-émigrés had not lived under Soviet rule before. They were less likely to feel that they belonged in the socialist motherland, and their decades abroad distanced them from their native villages and regions. The administrative barriers for re-émigrés to leave were also fewer than those repatriates faced. Many re-émigrés held a non-Soviet passport or had family with another citizenship.

Some re-émigrés became dissatisfied almost as soon as they arrived and enlisted foreign officials to assist them. In Odesa in the summer of 1956, KGB officials found that 20 of the 150 re-émigrés from Latin America were trying to leave. The re-émigrés' dissatisfaction drew the attention of an Argentinean consular official named Pietropaolo, who visited Odesa that August. KGB officers placed listening devices in his hotel and recruited re-émigrés to spy on him. Agent "Nina" seems to have initiated a romantic encounter with Pietropaolo (standard practice for KGB surveillance of foreign diplomats) that involved trips to the theater and the beach; the KGB concealed photography equipment in her room and took pictures of her and the diplomat that were sent to Moscow. An informant reported that Pietropaolo counted some 700 re-émigrés who had asked the embassy for help leaving the USSR.[68]

Contacting the embassy meant traveling to Moscow or sending a message with someone who was going there. Nadia Golik visited the Canadian embassy in the summer of 1957. She had been there once a half year earlier and, as a Canadian citizen, hoped diplomats would help her obtain an exit permit. When she hailed a cab from her hotel, the taxi driver started for the embassy before slowing to let two KGB officers into the back seat and driving to secret police headquarters at Lubianka. For six hours KGB officers tore apart her baggage, looking for illicit messages or material. When they found a letter in Spanish— Golik promised an Argentinean re-émigré that she would send it via the Canadian embassy to avoid censors—they chastised her that carrying such letters could be punished as a counterrevolutionary crime. After they finished the interrogation, an officer escorted her to a train station and waited on the platform until she had departed.[69]

Some re-émigrés tried to leverage other identities to leave the USSR. Around the time that the Return to the Motherland campaign began, Soviet authorities initiated another population exchange with Poland. Tens of thousands of ethnic Poles went from Ukraine to Poland voluntarily or by force. The re-émigrés and their families had lived in interwar Poland, and some still had relatives in the postwar Polish state. It is possible that some re-émigrés identified as much with the Poland of their youth as with their new Soviet Ukrainian homeland. KGB officers were skeptical about these claims of Polishness and believed that re-émigrés would leave for Argentina as soon as they reached Poland. How KGB officials made this conclusion is unclear. It seems likely that they were unwilling to believe that the migrants could have unstable ethnic identities, that once migrants had declared themselves Ukrainian, this official identity overrode real ambiguities. In some cases, the same migrants' concurrent attempts to leave for Argentina suggest that claims to Polishness were pragmatic. Whatever their motivation, at least ten families in Odesa province had petitioned Polish authorities by mid-1957, and four families had received letters of support from Polish relatives.[70] Counterintelligence officers were apparently not concerned by re-émigrés' visits to the Polish consulate in Kyiv, though. It seems possible that Soviet officials felt confident that they could coordinate policy toward the migrants with socialist bloc diplomats in a way that they could not with Argentinean officials. Anecdotal evidence from reports on several cases implies that the KGB rejected the applications to leave for Poland because the re-émigrés were classified as ethnic Ukrainian and were thus ineligible.[71]

KGB treatment of re-émigrés who visited capitalist states' embassies became more sophisticated over time. Officers recruited re-émigré informants to stage problematic cases at the embassies, where KGB officers knew the diplomats would refuse to help. News of these failures would then discourage the other re-émigrés. Aleksei Arteniuk (code name "Dmitruk"), a friend of Odesa art student Alberto Pavliuk, visited the Argentinean embassy on KGB orders in March 1958. He reported disappointing and apparently genuine news to Pavliuk: the embassy officers told him that recent Argentinean elections had made it impossible to know what the country's policy toward the petitioners would be. In the meantime, the consul urged re-émigrés to stop visiting. "You killed me with that," Pavliuk responded. "What should we do now? Accept everything and begin to set up our lives here or what!"[72]

The KGB arrested the most reckless re-émigrés. Vasilii-Jose (Khose) Chuiko was born in Argentina in 1937 to Ukrainian parents from the city of Ternopil. In February 1956, he moved to Odesa with his parents and younger brother. He quickly became disillusioned with the USSR and went to the Argentinean embassy in December to discuss his exit from the country. The Odesa KGB asserted that Chuiko was a key figure fomenting discontent among re-émigrés. He also seems to have exaggerated the re-émigrés' plight, telling the consul that seven re-émigrés had killed themselves. I have uncovered no evidence of these suicides in Ukrainian KGB records, which would almost certainly track such occurrences. Chuiko's fervor made him the center of a case the Odesa KGB gave the code name "Nomads." Police recruited an acquaintance of Chuiko's named Vasilii Silich ("Chaikovskii"), who learned in late 1958 that he and another re-émigré hoped to cross the Turkish-Soviet border in Georgia illegally. Chuiko even invited Silich to go to Turkey with them. Days before the planned escape, KGB officers arrested Chuiko, who would spend a year in a Gulag camp.[73]

KGB officers believed that the arrest of one or two re-émigrés would set an example for the rest of the community. In March 1960, two counterintelligence officers assigned to manage re-émigrés in Volyn province were recommended for commendations for their successes in preventing re-émigrés from visiting embassies. In the case of Leonid Melnichuk, a young re-émigré from Argentina, they had held a "prophylactic discussion"—a interrogation meant to deter unwanted activity. They then arranged a meeting at his workplace where colleagues criticized him for wanting to leave the USSR. When those efforts failed, they arrested Melnichuk on charges of being a hooligan and saw him sentenced to two years of forced labor.[74]

Repression did not work on all re-émigrés, least of all on Vasilii-Jose Chuiko. Upon release in 1960 he set off for the Argentinean embassy. In November he flew with his friend Silich to Moscow. The trip had many ironic moments. When their plane stopped in Kyiv to refuel, he advised Silich to stay in the plane with him because KGB officers might try to detain them. At the embassy they unexpectedly encountered two other re-émigrés from Odesa, both young women. Once they were out of earshot, Chuiko confided to Silich that the women were working for the KGB and that he would warn the consul. (The women, unlike Silich, do not seem to have been informants.) Chuiko was mistaken in his hope that hypervigilance would endear him to the Argentinean diplomat. Consul Mendes was only interested in the women as sexual objects and asked if Chuiko or Silich had slept with them. After Chuiko told his bravura story of attempted illegal border crossing and prison sentence, Mendes said, "What are you, a child?" The meeting upset Chuiko, and KGB surveillance had made him paranoid. Nonetheless, the encounter did not dull his desire to leave the USSR.[75]

The most effective KGB tactic was not repression but improving conditions for returnees. Officers were preoccupied with living conditions in their reports, perhaps because they could resolve problems in this sphere. The five-member Savchuk family arrived in the town of Rivne at the end of 1955. According to the KGB report on the family, Petr Savchuk had sent multiple petitions to the town administration for an apartment, which Soviet authorities in Argentina had promised the family. However, local officials refused these petitions because Savchuk was registered in a district in the province rather than in Rivne. Facing these difficulties, the Savchuks began to petition to move to Argentina. KGB officers in Rivne did not want the Savchuks to take this step and instead recommended that the migrants get an apartment.[76] In some cases, the migrants recognized that they had leverage to make demands. A re-émigré from Argentina named Piatokha told an informer that he had only gone to the embassy "to come into the field of vision of the Soviet organs [i.e., the KGB] and get better living conditions." Even though authorities believed that Piatokha was trying to manipulate them, the plan succeeded in gaining him "normal" living conditions.[77]

The combination of reward and threat wore down many re-émigrés. Art student Alberto Pavliuk received permission to leave the USSR in 1960. Two years earlier he would have been elated. But by October 1960 he had settled into life in Odesa. Under the influence of a KGB officer, he joined a youth *druzhina*, a Komsomol-sponsored group charged with maintaining public order, and submitted his military draft card. After receiving the exit permit, he appeared unexpectedly at the Odesa KGB office to inform his handler that he intended to stay.[78] After several visits to the Canadian embassy, Nadia Golik also decided to remain in the Soviet Union and was accepted at the prestigious Kyiv Foreign Languages Institute. She met and married a Soviet-born Ukrainian classmate and began a successful career at Radio Kyiv. Golik's story was common. Migrants' educations and language abilities enabled successful careers in translation or international affairs. Golik would emigrate in the 1970s but admitted to Canadian interviewers that people like her had enjoyed privileges in the USSR.[79]

Some returnees continued to insist upon leaving the USSR. A frequent reason they cited in petitions was the inhospitable Soviet climate. Ukrainian Lidia Klimenchenko arrived with her Italian husband, Rosario Petta, and their young son in Dniprodzerzhynsk (today's Kamianske in Dnipropetrovsk province) in September 1955. KGB officers were confounded when Petta petitioned to leave shortly after the family settled. The officer monitoring the case reported that the family was poor in Italy and had all the comforts the USSR could offer: a seventeen-square-meter room with two beds, one cabinet, a table, five chairs. The town administration allotted them a brick barn housing a 140-pound pig, ten chickens, and a milk cow for their personal use. Per his request, Petta worked as a horsekeeper with a pay of 500 rubles per month. Petta and Klimenchenko had received subsidies that would have thrilled other Soviet people. Much to the frustration of their KGB handler, Petta raised challenges that had no easy resolution. He said that the Ukrainian climate was making him ill. Informants reported his wife as saying that Petta had no local friends and cried at night from homesickness.[80]

Petta was not alone in claiming that weather was driving him away from the USSR. Of course, Ukraine in the freezing winter was perhaps not as comfortable as Palermo or Buenos Aires. Yet these excuses were perhaps a stand-in for issues that repatriates could not broach. Could they tell a KGB officer that they now realized Ukraine was no longer their homeland, at least in its Soviet form? Could they say that they preferred life under capitalism? About a re-émigré who said that his children were ill because of the Ukrainian climate and that they did not know Ukrainian, a police official asserted that it was really "hatred of the Soviet system" that made the disgruntled newcomer want to leave.[81]

Unsolvable problems and years of pressure from re-émigrés made Soviet officials relent. In 1960, a Communist Party Central Committee resolution authorized a limited number of exit passes for the re-émigrés.[82] How many people attempted to leave the USSR is unclear. Police did not report consistently on the number who hoped to leave, and they probably did not discover all the people who had raised the issue. By April 1966, Ukrainian authorities registered 1,598 petitions by returnees from Argentina alone to leave the USSR; they approved 1,382. Vasilii-Jose Chuiko was among the 865 re-émigrés who decided to go by 1966. This was approximately 20 percent of the Argentineans who came to Ukraine and 10 percent of all returnees to the republic.[83] Anecdotal evidence from KGB reports suggests that re-émigrés from Argentina and Canada were more likely than other returnees to leave the USSR. Members of the wartime diaspora would have lived abroad for a little over a decade before return, much of that period in forced labor and DP camps. In contrast, re-émigrés from Argentina and Canada had spent more time away from their native lands and had established stronger connections abroad. Considering these groups' probable overrepresentation among petitioners, it seems likely that as many as 15 percent of all those who arrived in the Return to the Motherland campaign left by the 1960s.

The KGB continued to fight for the re-émigrés as they began to leave. In one instance, a family of re-émigrés from Canada living in Rostov-on-Don received their own apartment after living in a shared house for more than a year. The adults in the family were working in good jobs that promised career growth. The children were in school, and the eldest had received a place in Rostov's foreign language institute. After the family's Soviet lives had fallen into place, officials granted them permission to exit the country if they still desired. The elder son, previously the strongest advocate for leaving, naively told Canadian officials that his persistence had earned them the exit pass. Similar cases from Ukraine suggest that the KGB handler in the case had waited until conditions in the USSR would make the decision to leave difficult. To the chagrin of Canadian diplomats, who had also worked to secure the family's exit, the elder son told them he was uncertain whether the family would now leave.[84]

Some of those who left the USSR became spies. From November 1956, taxi driver Aleksei Arteniuk ("Dmitruk") had worked for the KGB under the guise of a dissatisfied re-émigré. Although he had received rewards from the KGB—new housing and help for his parents' move to Odesa—his act had so convinced Argentinean officials that in 1962 they offered the thirty-year-old a visa to return to Argentina. Arteniuk agreed to his KGB handlers' proposal to go to Argentina for several years as their agent.[85] Despite this success, KGB counterintelligence officers probably derived little comfort from recruiting a handful of spies amid the embarrassing departure of hundreds.

Soon party and police leaders would reconsider the Return to the Motherland campaign, a turn perhaps motivated by the experience with the disgruntled migrants. The public face of the operation evolved from an effort to generate migration to the USSR to one that encouraged affinity between the diaspora and the motherland. At the end of 1959, *Za vozvrashchenie na Rodinu* announced this shift as a supposed response to readers' letters to the paper.[86] In January 1960, the Committee for Return to the Motherland's newspaper and radio programs became *Golos Rodiny* (Voice of the Motherland), a title that mirrored outlets like *Voice of America*. By the end of Khrushchev's rule in 1964, the committee would become the Committee for the Development of Cultural Connections with Compatriots, later known as the Motherland Association (Obshchestvo "Rodina"). The committee continued to publish notices about families searching for loved ones abroad but less conspicuously on its platforms. Instead, it turned to Soviet achievements, foreign friendship societies, and language learning for the diaspora.

The Return to the Motherland campaign attempted to mobilize individual families in the diaspora to return to the big family of the USSR. The effort united a conception of ethnic belonging with the aim of building a socialist state that would outshine capitalism. Although the campaign nominally targeted postwar nonreturners who would have been familiar with Soviet life, most migrants were re-émigrés. Many of these migrants became disenchanted with their new homelands. KGB officers became intermediaries where it was possible, resolving problems with local authorities such as arranging for apartments and jobs. The more tenacious problem was that a large number, especially among the re-émigrés, learned that their hopes of finding a homeland were mistaken. The lands they left had been transformed, and they themselves had changed from years or decades of life abroad.

Party leaders abandoned the project of return at the end of the 1950s. It seems that the Return to the Motherland campaign proved to be more trouble than its results warranted. Unhappy migrants threatened to undermine the campaign by demanding to leave and airing their grievances to foreign officials. Under Stalin the police perhaps would have arrested a significant number of them, but Khrushchev had abandoned Stalinism's most ruthless practices. Rewards and less coercive methods could not reconcile the migrants with the motherland. By 1960, active recruiting subsided, and Soviet authorities found that granting exit permits to disaffected migrants was the most palatable solution.

The lesson of the Return to the Motherland campaign was that the Soviet diaspora mostly did not desire return. Many of its members nonetheless wanted continued contact with their homelands. The campaign for return would evolve to create these connections—to cultivate a sense of belonging to the USSR through cultural ties rather than through return migration. In this sense, the conception of the unity of the Soviet diaspora with their homelands and with the Soviet state persisted. Soviet officials had failed to bring the diasporas to the motherland, so they brought the motherland to the diasporas.

NO ONE IS FORGOTTEN, NO ONE IS FORGIVEN

For the 1960 opening of the Piskarevskoe Memorial Cemetery, the main World War II burial site in Leningrad, the poet Olga Berggolts wrote a dedication that ended with the line: "No one is forgotten, nothing is forgotten." The phrase entered the mythology of the war as a vow to remember the courage of the Soviet people. But the Soviet Union produced other, darker calls for remembrance. The author of "Of Life and Death," a pamphlet Soviet officers distributed to DP camps in 1945, used a phrase that anticipated Berggolts. After describing the execution of a Soviet man as a traitor, the booklet concludes: "Nothing is forgotten, no one is forgiven." Repatriation officials withdrew the pamphlet from the camps when they realized it was contributing to repatriates' anxiety over return.[1] The work nonetheless represented a call to retribution that coexisted with the uplifting sentiment of the Berggolts dedication. For the history of Soviet displaced people, the slogans might be reformulated as questions: Who will be forgotten? Who could be forgiven?

Stalinist leaders forgave returnees in the sense that most were not arrested upon return. To describe that as forgiveness is a cruel joke. During the war, the Germans made deportees from the occupied east into forced laborers. After liberation, returnees faced a hazardous journey to the Soviet Union. As repatriates in the USSR, police monitored them as collaborators and spies for years to come. No, the worst fears of Siberian exile or the Gulag did not come to pass. Instead, their repatriate biography meant discrimination for most of their lives.

Returnees were not forgotten, although important aspects of their lives were. The war created new experiences and new moments for social agency. Forced labor in Germany released Eastern Workers and POWs from the strictures of Stalinism, removing the foundations of Soviet identity among many. In its place, smaller identities of kinship, region, and the barracks emerged to define social life. For the first time, millions of people from the USSR encountered non-Soviets, albeit in the harsh setting of Hitler's empire, where they were at the lowest rung of the racial hierarchy. Amid the cruelty Eastern Workers and POWs faced, these interactions contravened the Stalinist xenophobia of the 1930s that had forbidden foreign contacts.

The war and its immediate aftermath offered other choices, however compromised and constrained, to Soviet people. Life between belligerent powers enabled them to collaborate or resist, decisions that often depended on pragmatic considerations rather than ideological preferences. For those liberated on the Western Front, the pivotal choice was whether to return to the USSR or attempt to remain abroad. Most chose to return, and some embraced their decision by throwing themselves into autonomous pro-Soviet organizations in DP camps. The chaos of the immediate postwar period also unleashed forms of social agency that harmed returnees. The lack of state support they received during the journey to the USSR reflected central authorities' apathy, even antipathy, toward the plight of the displaced. Yet it also shows the limits of state power—German, Soviet, and Allied—over social forces as the war ended. Moscow had neither the will nor the ability to restrain soldiers and neighbors who exploited the returnees based on the assertion that it was the just deserts of those who had worked for the enemy.

Repatriation was part of a larger effort to restore order after the war. Stalin's police sought to punish Soviet people who had shown support for Germany and its allies, although the line between regrettable cooperation and criminal collaboration was never clear. It was impossible to arrest every one of the millions of people who had cooperated in some way with the occupiers. Instead, investigators primarily targeted people who had worked formally in enemy units or bureaucracies. Cases against collaboration dovetailed with the broader effort to investigate activities that fit poorly with Stalinist orthodoxy. Police turned unauthorized resistance organizations into groups of collaborators and foreign contacts into spy rings. The investigations combined the methods of 1930s policing with the postwar situation, introducing a new enemy in the form of Anglo-American espionage. There would be no campaign of mass arrests in the mold of the Great Terror of the 1930s. The primary effect of interactions with the police was to scare alleged spies into silence and reinforce popular notions that returnees had committed treason. The transnational Soviet experience of World War II, good and bad, was forgotten in the transition back to Stalinist normalcy.

The phrase "no one is forgotten" might best apply to the Soviet wartime diaspora. The struggle to bring nonreturners to the USSR by persuasion or force became a key front in the Cold War. From the start of repatriation, Soviet leaders understood the issue as a matter of sovereignty; a measure of a state's status in the world was its ability to have other states respect its power over subjects. The repatriation of millions in 1945 also had economic implications as Soviet leaders channeled returnees into reconstruction after a destructive war. In this sense, officials in the USSR were like their European counterparts, who saw displacement as an opportunity to direct labor to wartime and postwar projects.

Efforts to bring nonreturners who remained in Allied-occupied Europe to the USSR held less economic value but immense political and ideological importance. Soviet repatriation officials wanted these people not only for pragmatic reasons involving the economy, military, geopolitics, and intelligence but also because they believed that the USSR had a special claim over people from ethnic groups that were Soviet republics' titular nationalities. Despite the apparent hostility of most nonreturners, repatriation officers asserted that it was only the Western Allies and nationalist-fascist camp administrators who kept the DPs from their joyous reunion with the motherland. This notion connected World War II and the Cold War. Soviet officials accused the Western Allies of victimizing the displaced, detaining them in camps run by the same people the Germans had enlisted during the war. The limited number of Soviet-claimed people who opted for repatriation after 1945 reinforced this belief with their tales of harassment in DP camps. These stories had an element of truth—DP camp officials were often violently anti-Soviet. The narratives also served the purposes of the returnees, framing the years that they had spent in the Western zones of occupation as captivity rather than a choice. Returnees and Soviet repatriation officers alike were eager to align themselves with Soviet narratives of the Cold War to avoid accusations of disloyalty.

The motherland did not forget its children, even as they went to distant lands. In the 1950s, repatriation efforts blurred the Soviet diasporas of various eras and experiences. In the post-Stalin Return to the Motherland campaign, the goal was no longer repatriation in the strictest sense. Most of the migrants were re-émigrés—people with roots in Soviet territories but who had never lived in the USSR. According to officials, they would always be out of place until they returned to their homeland and joined the socialist motherland. Unlike repatriates at the end of the war, diaspora re-émigrés from around the world, and mostly from Latin America, received substantial assistance from authorities who hoped they would demonstrate the advantages of socialism over capitalism. The results were often disappointing. The re-émigrés' alienation and their attempts to leave the USSR created headaches for Soviet authorities.

Unlike the re-émigrés, repatriates mostly recognized the Soviet Union as their motherland despite the tribulations they faced. Even the youngest forced laborers had spent years in Soviet schools and found relatives waiting for them. As time passed, they integrated into the USSR. Women married and hid their past under their husbands' names. Others risked omitting their wartime biography on job applications or reconciled themselves to stunted career opportunities. Over time, police surveillance diminished, yet there was also never a formal rehabilitation of repatriates. They had, after all, never been officially repressed. After years of marginalization in public memory, works by historians like Efim Brodskii carved out a place to represent Soviet people in Germany as heroes in the war. Despite the relaxation after Stalin, returnees mostly remained silent about their experiences because of the legitimate fear that they would face repression for embodying aspects of the war that cut against official narratives.

In the 1990s, a half century after the war's end, Germany sought forgiveness from former forced laborers. After years of debate, the Bundestag (Germany's parliament) in 2000 established a fund called "Remembrance, Responsibility and Future" with several billion euros to distribute as compensation. Throughout Europe some 1.66 million people received payments from the fund. The largest contingent of post-Soviet applicants, former Eastern Workers who had been at factories but not in punishment camps, received some 2,500 euros each, while those who had faced incarceration received extra.[2] Former forced laborers had to show proof of their labor in Germany. In this regard, the Stalinist system had unwittingly done them a service. The piles of documents the police had gathered during filtration and investigations now served as evidence for repatriates to claim compensation. Discussions surrounding the campaign also spurred new interest in the history of forced labor in wartime Germany. Initiatives in virtually every German province and city formed to study the local story of forced labor. At the national level, foundations from Germany and post-Soviet countries conducted the oral history interviews that I have used in this book.

Were these initiatives for reparations and remembrance sufficient? By the time they received compensation, the former Eastern Workers who were still alive were in their seventies or older. Many desperately needed the money, like so many older people after the fall of the USSR. Post-Soviet states experienced massive inflation in the 1990s, obliterating the buying power of retirees' pensions. Money and attention were welcome but could never fully compensate for the trauma of the war years and decades of discrimination. The story of Mikhailo K., a former forced laborer from Kyiv province, about his family's compensation is revealing. While discussing the compensation programs with his cousin, Mikhailo K. was surprised to learn that the cousin had taken documents for his wife. She had never mentioned that she had been a forced laborer in Germany. Later, when Mikhailo K. asked her why she kept silent, she denied having been to Germany at all. Her husband, she said, "probably misspoke." Even the fall of the Soviet Union could not assuage her fear of discrimination for having worked in Germany.[3]

Today we still live with the memory of World War II that Stalinism and the Cold War created. Officials in Vladimir Putin's Kremlin promote mythical war heroes and ignore the evidence of soldiers' morally complicated actions.[4] Repatriates remain a poor fit in this official history. At a talk about postwar trials for treason that I gave with a research team of my students at Moscow's Gulag Museum in 2019, I expected the audience to fault the work for being too uncritical of Stalinism. Our research suggested that police had been interested in investigating real wartime activities, not just in generating falsifications to fulfill arrest quotas. The reaction was the opposite, though. Most of the audience was dismayed that collaboration had not carried harsher penalties. Like Stalinist officials, they saw collaboration as a black-and-white issue and had little appreciation of the difficult compromises that the war pressed upon Soviet people.

At the same time, anti-Stalinist popular memory has integrated the Anglo-American story of the victimization of repatriates. I told an acquaintance, a Moscow composer, about this book, and he responded with a typical view among post-Soviet intelligentsia: "I thought Stalin had all the Eastern Workers shot." In Ukraine scholars working on the topic have followed the historian Pavel Polian in portraying the displaced as victims of both Nazism and Stalinism. As the historian Gelinada Grinchenko asserts, post-Soviet Ukrainian memory of forced labor and repatriation echoes Soviet concepts of victimhood, even as it cast this history as anti-Soviet.[5] By the 1990s, there were no longer restrictions on what repatriates could say about their lives. Many restrictions on relevant archives fell away in the 2010s. Nonetheless, popular representations of Soviet displaced persons continue to fit into neat categories: martyrs, traitors, and victims.

These categories, which emerged from the last years of Stalin's rule, mask the complexities of the period. Soviet displaced persons represented the tumult that war had brought—the violence of forced labor but also the social agency that armed conflict generates. Soviet officials countered this chaos by trying to reinstate Stalinist discipline in society after the war. No one was forgotten, and no one was forgiven as they attempted to bring repatriates back to the USSR. The restoration of Stalinist orthodoxy made a casualty of Soviet displaced people's complicated, transnational history of deprivation and liberation.

Notes

INTRODUCTION

1. Aleksandra Mikhaleva, *Gde vy, moi rodnye: Dnevnik ostarbaitera* (Moscow: AST, 2015).

2. Viktor Zemskov, *Vozvrashchenie sovetskikh peremeshchennykh lits v SSSR. 1944–1952 gg.* (Moscow: Institut rossiiskoi istorii, 2016), 139. The number of presumed dead civilian repatriates was more than a million, and this category probably hid nonreturners. GARF, f. 9526, op. 6, d. 235, ll. 21–22.

3. Nicholas Bethell, *The Last Secret: Forcible Repatriation to Russia, 1944–7* (London: Andre Deutsch, 1974); Mark Elliot, *Pawns of Yalta: Soviet Refugees and America's Role in Their Repatriation* (Champaign: University of Illinois Press, 1982); Julius Epstein, *Operation Keelhaul: The Story of Forced Repatriation from 1944 to the Present* (Old Greenwich, CT: Devin-Adair, 1973); Nikolai Tolstoy, *Victims of Yalta: The Secret Betrayal of the Allies: 1944–1947* (1977; New York: Pegasus, 2013).

4. "Accused of Role in Sending Cossacks to Their Death in 1945," *Irish Times*, December 16, 2000, https://www.irishtimes.com/news/accused-of-role-in-sending-cossacks-to-their-death-in-1945-1.1121487.

5. Viktor Zemskov, "K voprosu o repatriatsii sovetskikh grazhdan, 1944–51 gody," *Istoriia SSSR*, no. 4 (1990): 26–41. Zemskov, *Vozvrashchenie sovetskikh peremeshchennykh lits*, was the culmination of his research on the topic over several decades.

6. Pavel Polian, *Zhertvy dvukh diktatur: Zhizn', trud, unizheniia i smert' sovetskikh voennoplennykh i ostarbaiterov na chuzhbine i na rodine* (Moscow: ROSSPEN, 2002).

7. Nick Baron, "Remaking Soviet Society: The Filtration of Returnees from Nazi Germany, 1944–49," in *Warlands: Population Resettlement and State Reconstruction in the Soviet–East European Borderlands, 1945–50*, ed. Nick Baron and Peter Gatrell (Basingstoke: Palgrave, 2009), 89–116; Igor Govorov, "Fil'tratsiia sovetskikh repatriantov v 40-e gg. XX vv.: Tseli, metody i itogi," *Cahiers du Monde russe* 49, no. 2–3 (2008): 365–82; Vanessa Voisin, *L'URSS contre ses traîtres: L'épuration soviétique: 1941–1955* (Paris: Publications de la Sorbonne, 2015); Voisin, "Retribute or Reintegrate? The Ambiguity of Soviet Policies towards Repatriates: The Case of Kalinin Province, 1943–1950," *Jahrbücher für Geschichte Osteuropas* 55, no. 1 (2007): 34–55.

8. Christian Streit, *Keine Kameraden: Die Wehrmacht und die sowjetischen Kriegsgefangenen 1941–1945* (Bonn: Verlag J.H.W. Dietz, 1991) (in Russian translation as *"Oni nam ne tovarishchi": Vermakht i sovetskie voennoplennye v 1941–1945 gg.* [Moscow: ROSSPEN, 2009]); Ulrich Herbert, *Hitler's Foreign Workers: Enforced Foreign Labor in Germany under the Third Reich* (Cambridge: Cambridge University Press, 1997).

9. "Ziele und Arbeitsschritte des Projekts," Zwangsarbeit, 1939–1945, https://www.zwangsarbeit-archiv.de/projekt/beschreibung/index.html, accessed June 4, 2015. See also the edited volume that resulted, Christoph Thonfeld, Almut Leh, and Alexander von Plato, eds., *Hitler's Slaves: Life Stories of Forced Labourers in Nazi-Occupied Europe* (New York: Berghahn Books, 2010).

10. Kirill Aleksandrov, *Russkie soldaty Vermakhta: Geroi ili predateli* (Moscow: Eksmo, 2005); Angelika Benz, *Handlanger der SS: Die Rolle der Trawniki-Männer im Holocaust* (Berlin: Metropol, 2014); Peter Black, "Foot Soldiers of the Final Solution: The

Trawniki Training Camp and Operation Reinhard," *Holocaust and Genocide Studies* 25, no. 1 (2011): 1–99; Martin Dean, *Collaboration in the Holocaust: Crimes of the Local Police in Belorussia and Ukraine, 1941–44* (Basingstoke: Palgrave, 1998); Diana Dumitru, "The Gordian Knot of Justice: Prosecuting Jewish Holocaust Survivors in Stalinist Courts for 'Collaboration' with the Enemy," *Kritika* 22, no. 4 (2021): 729–56; Mark Edele, *Stalin's Defectors: How Red Army Soldiers Became Hitler's Collaborators, 1941–1945* (Oxford: Oxford University Press, 2017); Tanja Penter, "Local Collaborators on Trial: Soviet War Crimes Trials under Stalin (1943–1953)," *Cahiers du Monde russe* 49, no. 2/3 (2008): 341–64; Aron Shneer, *Professiia—Smert': Uchebnyi lager' SS "Travniki": Prestupleniia i vozmezdie* (Moscow: Tretii Rim, 2019).

11. See the Note on Sources at the end of this book. K. M. Grin'ko and E. V. Poltoratskaia, eds., *Repatriatsiia sovetskikh grazhdan s okkupirovannoi territorii Germanii, 1944–1952: Sbornik dokumentov v dvukh tomakh,* 2 vols. (Moscow: ROSSPEN, 2019), published a selection of documents from the archive of the Repatriation Administration at GARF. Although the Russian security service (Federal'naia Sluzhba Bezopasnosti, FSB) archive remains shut to most historians, it released a collection of documents about the wartime activities and postwar trials of prominent collaborators available in A. N. Artizov and V. S. Khristoforov, eds., *General Vlasov: Istoriia predatel'stva,* 2 vols. (Moscow: ROSSPEN, 2015), translated as *The Vlasov Case: History of a Betrayal,* 2 vols. (New York: Columbia University Press, 2020).

12. Benjamin Frommer, *National Cleansing: Retribution against Nazi Collaborators in Postwar Czechoslovakia* (Cambridge: Cambridge University Press, 2005); Jan Gross, *Fear: Anti-Semitism in Poland after Auschwitz* (Princeton, NJ: Princeton University Press, 2006); Atina Grossmann, *Jews, Germans, and Allies: Close Encounters in Occupied Germany* (Princeton, NJ: Princeton University Press, 2007); Anna Holian, *Between National Socialism and Soviet Communism: Displaced Persons in Postwar Germany* (Ann Arbor: University of Michigan Press, 2011); Mary Louise Roberts, *What Soldiers Do: Sex and the American GI in World War II France* (Chicago: University of Chicago Press, 2013); Fabrice Virgili, *Shorn Women: Gender and Punishment in Liberation France*, trans. John Flower (London: Berg Publishers, 2002); Mark Wyman, *DPs: Europe's Displaced Persons, 1945–1951* (Ithaca, NY: Cornell University Press, 1998).

13. On sexual barter, see Anna Hajkova, "Sexual Barter in Times of Genocide: Negotiating the Sexual Economy of the Theresienstadt Ghetto," *Signs: Journal of Women in Culture and Society* 38, no. 3 (2013): 503–33.

14. Streit, *"Oni nam ne tovarishchi,"* 8, provides a higher number for deaths that has come under dispute. For a discussion of these numbers, see Edele, *Stalin's Defectors*, 124; Christian Hartmann, *Wehrmacht im Ostkrieg: Front und militärisches Hinterland 1941/42* (Munich: Oldenbourg, 2009), 568.

15. See Edele, *Stalin's Defectors*, 95–119, for a discussion of motivations.

16. For more sympathetic treatments, see Benz, *Handlanger der SS*; Voisin, *L'URSS contre ses traîtres*. For a less understanding interpretation, see Shneer, *Professiia—smert'*.

17. This approach is similar to Franziska Exeler, *Ghosts of War: Nazi Occupation and Its Aftermath in Soviet Belarus* (Ithaca, NY: Cornell University Press, 2022).

18. Stathis Kalyvas, *The Logic of Violence in Civil War* (Cambridge: Cambridge University Press, 2006).

19. UNRRA also interacted with Eastern Europe through delivery of aid to formerly occupied regions, including to Belarus and Ukraine. For an overview of the creation of UNRRA, see Jessica Reinisch, "Internationalism in Relief: The Birth (and Death) of UNRRA," *Past & Present*, no. 210, supp. 6 (2011): 258–89.

20. Andrew Janco, "Soviet 'Displaced Persons' in Europe, 1941–1951" (PhD diss., University of Chicago, 2012).

21. Peter Gatrell, *The Making of the Modern Refugee* (Oxford: Oxford University Press, 2013), 283; Peter Loizos, "Misconceiving Refugees?," in *Therapeutic Care for Refugees: No Place Like Home*, ed. Renos K. Papadopoulos (London: Routledge, 2002), 45–48.

22. For an example by a prominent scholar, see Serhii Plokhy, *Yalta: The Price of Peace* (New York: Viking Penguin, 2010), 297–98.

23. Zemskov, *Vozvrashchenie sovetskikh peremeshchennykh lits*, 124.

24. Eugene Kulischer, *Europe on the Move: War and Population Changes, 1917–47* (New York: Columbia University Press, 1948), 282–94.

25. R. M. Douglas, *Orderly and Humane: The Expulsion of the Germans after the Second World War* (New Haven, CT: Yale University Press, 2012).

26. Gross, *Fear*; Grossmann, *Jew, Germans, and Allies*.

27. Lewis Siegelbaum and Leslie Page Moch, *Broad Is My Native Land: Repertoires and Regimes of Migration in Russia's Twentieth Century* (Ithaca, NY: Cornell University Press, 2014), 5.

28. James Harris, *The Great Urals: Regionalism and the Evolution of the Soviet System* (Ithaca, NY: Cornell University Press, 1999), 105–22; Lynne Viola, *Unknown Gulag: The Lost World of Stalin's Special Settlements* (Oxford: Oxford University Press, 2007). On the Gulag, see Oleg Khlevniuk, *The History of the Gulag: From Collectivization to the Great Terror* (New Haven, CT: Yale University Press, 2004), 332–38; Alan Barenberg, *Gulag Town, Company Town: Forced Labor and Its Legacy in Vorkuta* (New Haven, CT: Yale University Press, 2014); Wendy Goldman and Donald Filtzer, *Fortress Dark and Stern: The Soviet Home Front during World War II* (Oxford: Oxford University Press, 2021).

29. Polian, *Zhertvy dvukh diktatur*, 334.

30. Silvia Salvatici, "From Displaced Persons to Labourers: Allied Employment Policies in Post-war West Germany," in *The Disentanglement of Populations: Migration, Expulsion and Displacement in Post-war Europe, 1944–49*, ed. Jessica Reinisch and Elizabeth White (Basingstoke: Palgrave, 2011), 210–28; Salvatici, "'Help the People to Help Themselves': UNRRA Relief Workers and European Displaced Persons," *Journal of Refugee Studies* 25, no. 3 (2012): 428–51; Gregor Thum, *Uprooted: How Breslau Became Wroclaw during the Century of Expulsions* (Princeton, NJ: Princeton University Press, 2011), 53–104; Johannes-Dieter Steinert, "British Post-war Migration Policy and Displaced Persons in Europe," in *The Disentanglement of Populations: Migration, Expulsion and Displacement in Post-war Europe, 1944–49*, ed. Jessica Reinisch and Elizabeth White (Basingstoke: Palgrave, 2011), 229–47.

31. Holian, *Between National Socialism and Soviet Communism*, 47–48; Grossmann, *Jews, Germans, and Allies*, 148–49; Stephen Fritz, *Endkampf: Soldiers, Civilians, and the Death of the Third Reich* (Lexington: University of Kentucky Press, 2004), 250–51.

32. Voisin, "Retribute or Reintegrate?"

33. Zemskov, *Vozvrashchenie sovetskikh peremeshchennykh lits*, 127.

34. For an argument on the indiscriminate nature of Soviet justice before, during, and after the war, see Voisin, *L'URSS contre ses traîtres*.

35. On the terror of the 1930s, see David Shearer, *Policing Stalin's Socialism: Repression and Social Order in the Soviet Union, 1924–1953* (New Haven, CT: Yale University Press, 2009), 14.

36. Baron, "Remaking Soviet Society"; Voisin, "Retribute or Reintegrate?"

37. Golfo Alexopoulos, "Soviet Citizenship, More or Less: Rights, Emotions, and States of Civic Belonging," *Kritika* 7, no. 3 (2006): 487–88.

38. Sheila Fitzpatrick, *Tear Off the Masks! Identity and Imposture in Twentieth-Century Russia* (Princeton, NJ: Princeton University Press, 2005), 91–101.

39. Elena Zubkova, *Russia after the War: Hopes, Illusions and Disappointments, 1945–1957* (New York: M. E. Sharpe, 1998).

40. Henry Rousso, *The Vichy Syndrome: History and Memory in France since 1944* (Cambridge, MA: Harvard University Press, 1994); Jeffrey Herf, *Divided Memory: The Nazi Past in the Two Germanys* (Cambridge, MA: Harvard University Press, 1997); Richard Breitman and Norman Goda, *Hitler's Shadow: Nazi War Criminals, U.S. Intelligence, and the Cold War* (Washington, DC: National Archives, 2010).

41. Stuart Finkel, "Purging the Public Intellectual: The 1922 Expulsions from Soviet Russia," *Russian Review* 62, no. 4 (2003): 589–613.

42. Michael David-Fox, *Showcasing the Great Experiment: Cultural Diplomacy and Western Visitors to the Soviet Union, 1921–1941* (Oxford: Oxford University Press, 2012), 285–88.

43. Francine Hirsch, *Empire of Nations: Ethnographic Knowledge and the Making of the Soviet Union* (Ithaca, NY: Cornell University Press, 2005); Terry Martin, *The Affirmative Action Empire: Nations and Nationalism in the Soviet Union, 1923–1939* (Ithaca, NY: Cornell University Press, 2001); Yuri Slezkine, "The USSR as a Communal Apartment, or How a Socialist State Promoted Ethnic Particularism," *Slavic Review* 53, no. 2 (1994): 414–52.

44. David Brandenberger, *National Bolshevism: Stalinist Mass Culture and the Formation of Modern Russian National Identity, 1931–1956* (Cambridge, MA: Harvard University Press, 2002).

45. Brandon Schechter, *The Stuff of Soldiers: A History of the Red Army in World War II through Objects* (Ithaca, NY: Cornell University Press, 2019); Jonathan Brunstedt, *The Soviet Myth of World War II: Patriotic Memory and the Russian Question in the USSR* (Cambridge: Cambridge University Press, 2021), 5–6. On the growing importance of titular nationhood, see Krista Goff, *Nested Nationalism: Making and Unmaking Nations in the Soviet Caucasus* (Ithaca, NY: Cornell University Press, 2021).

46. Andrew Janco, "'Unwilling': The One-Word Revolution in Refugee Status, 1940–1951," *Contemporary European History* 23, no. 3 (2014): 429–46.

47. Sheila Fitzpatrick, "The Motherland Calls: 'Soft' Repatriation of Soviet Citizens from Europe, 1945–1953," *Journal of Modern History* 90, no. 2 (2018): 323–50.

48. Monica Kim, *The Interrogation Rooms of the Korean War: The Untold History* (Princeton, NJ: Princeton University Press, 2019).

49. Eric Lohr, *Russian Citizenship: From Empire to Soviet Union* (Cambridge, MA: Harvard University Press, 2012), 8; Tara Zahra, *The Lost Children: Reconstructing Europe's Families after World War II* (Cambridge, MA: Harvard University Press, 2011).

50. Alfred Rieber, "Civil Wars in the Soviet Union," *Kritika* 4, no. 1 (2003): 129–62; Jeffrey Burds, "The Early Cold War in Soviet West Ukraine, 1944–1948," no. 1505, in *The Carl Beck Papers in Russian and East European Studies* (Pittsburgh: University of Pittsburgh Press, 2001). On deportation from Ukraine and other border regions, see Tarik Amar, *The Paradox of Ukrainian Lviv: A Borderland City between Stalinists, Nazis, and Nationalists* (Ithaca, NY: Cornell University Press, 2015); Kate Brown, *A Biography of No Place: From Ethnic Borderland to Soviet Heartland* (Cambridge, MA: Harvard University Press, 2004); Alexander Statiev, *The Soviet Counterinsurgency in the Western Borderlands* (Cambridge: Cambridge University Press, 2010), 164–94.

51. Pamela Ballinger, *The World Refugees Made: Decolonization and the Foundation of Postwar Italy* (Ithaca, NY: Cornell University Press, 2020), 14–15; Lori Watt, *When Empire Comes Home: Repatriation and Reintegration in Postwar Japan* (Cambridge, MA: Harvard University Press, 2009).

1. WORKERS FROM THE EAST

1. The Soviet Repatriation Administration calculated that some 6.8 million people had been displaced from Soviet territories, including surviving prisoners of war but not

the unknown (but significant) number who died as laborers in the Third Reich. See table I.1 and table I.2.

2. Ulrich Herbert, *Hitler's Foreign Workers: Enforced Foreign Labor in Germany under the Third Reich* (Cambridge: Cambridge University Press, 1997), 2, 25.

3. Alex Kay, *Exploitation, Resettlement, Mass Murder: Political and Economic Planning for German Occupation Policy in the Soviet Union, 1940–1941* (New York: Berghahn, 2006), 47–67.

4. Oleg Khlevniuk, *Stalin: New Biography of a Dictator* (New Haven, CT: Yale University Press, 2015), 187–88, 199–200, 209.

5. David Stahel, *Operation Barbarossa and Germany's Defeat in the East* (Cambridge: Cambridge University Press, 2009), 3.

6. Herbert, *Hitler's Foreign Workers*, 143–44; G. D. Knat'ko and B. I. Adamushko, eds., *Belorusskie ostarbaitery: Ugon naseleniia Belarusi na prinuditel'nye raboty v Germaniiu (1941–1944): Dokumenty i materialy* (Minsk: NARB, 1996), 1:35.

7. Herbert, *Hitler's Foreign Workers*, 147.

8. Francine Hirsch, *Soviet Judgment at Nuremberg: A New History of the International Military Tribunal after World War II* (Oxford: Oxford University Press, 2020), 386.

9. Karel Berkhoff, *Harvest of Despair: Life and Death in Ukraine under Nazi Rule* (Cambridge, MA: Harvard University Press, 2004), 254.

10. Knat'ko and Adamushko, *Belorusskie ostarbaitery*, 1:10.

11. Berkhoff, *Harvest of Despair*, 256.

12. Berkhoff, *Harvest of Despair*, 171.

13. AUSBU MO, f. 5, spr. 8042, t. 2, ark. 126.

14. Knat'ko and Adamushko, *Belorusskie ostarbaitery*, 1:127–29; Herbert, *Hitler's Foreign Workers*, 174.

15. For these and other methods, see B. E. Chistova, *Preodolenie rabstva: Fol'klor i iazyk ostarbaiterov, 1942–1944* (Moscow: Zven'ia, 1998), 27, 28.

16. HDASBU, f. 1, spr. 692, ark. 271. See also Chistova, *Preodolenie rabstva*, 28.

17. Aleksandra A., ZA466, 99; Aleksandra Mikhaleva, *Gde vy, moi rodnye: Dnevnik ostarbaitera* (Moscow: AST, 2015), 166.

18. Polina E., ZA480, 85, 92–93.

19. Oleksandr I., ZA478, 8.

20. Anatolii A., ZA341, 9; Halyna K., ZA481, 28; Mariia Kh., ZA475, 68.

21. Marc Buggeln, *Slave Labor in Nazi Concentration Camps* (Oxford: Oxford University Press, 2014), 21.

22. Knat'ko and Adamushko, *Belorusskie ostarbaitery*, 2:218–20.

23. Anatolii A., ZA341, 11.

24. Petr A., ZA017, 3–4; Dina S., ZA338, 12.

25. Herbert, *Hitler's Foreign Workers*, 298.

26. Knat'ko and Adamushko, *Belorusskie ostarbaitery*, 1:149.

27. Mark Spoerer, *Zwangsarbeit unter dem Hakenkreuz: Ausländische Zivilarbeiter, Kriegsgefangene und Häftlinge im Deutschen Reich und im besetzten Europa 1939–1945* (Stuttgart: Deutsche Verlags-Anstalt, 2001) 186; Herbert, *Hitler's Foreign Workers*, 224.

28. Wendy Goldman and Donald Filtzer, introduction to *Hunger and War: Food Provisioning in the Soviet Union during World War II*, ed. Wendy Goldman and Donald Filtzer (Bloomington: Indiana University Press, 2015), 25.

29. Christian Streit (Shtrait), *"Oni nam ne tovarishchi": Vermakht i sovetskie voennoplennye v 1941–1945 gg.* (Moscow: ROSSPEN, 2009), 149–50.

30. Knat'ko and Adamushko, *Belorusskie ostarbaitery*, 2:374–78.

31. Mikhaleva, *Gde vy, moi rodnye*, 67–68. On a less successful wildcat strike where workers were punished with beatings, see Galina B., ZA468, 16–17.

32. Petr P., ZA021, 29, 32.

33. This coincides with the correlation between concentration camp size and mortality rates. The smaller the camp, the fewer deaths. Marc Buggeln, "Building to Death: Prisoner Forced Labour in the German War Economy—The Neuengamme Subcamps, 1942–1945," *European History Quarterly* 39, no. 4 (2009): 619.

34. Ivan S., ZA495, 53; Mikhaleva, *Gde vy, moi rodnye*, 148.

35. Serhyi K., ZA488, 93; Georgii T., ZA313, 17; Antonina S., ZA311, 29–30; Vadim N., ZA299, 23–25. See also Herbert, *Hitler's Foreign Workers*, 228–29.

36. Alfred Mierzejewski, *The Collapse of the German War Economy, 1944–1945: Allied Air Power and the German National Railway* (Chapel Hill: University of North Carolina Press, 1988), 123.

37. Mikhaleva, *Gde vy, moi rodnye*, 345, 362, 367; Mierzejewski, *Collapse of the German War Economy*, 134, 184.

38. Buggeln, *Slave Labor in Nazi Concentration Camps*, 22–23.

39. Vadim N., ZA299, 26–27.

40. A. N. Artizov and V. S. Khristoforov, eds., *General Vlasov: Istoriia predatel'stva* (Moscow: ROSSPEN, 2015), 1:886–87.

41. Valeriia F., ZA328, 64.

42. For instance, see GARF, f. 7021, op. 29, d. 1056.

43. GARF, f. 7021, op. 29, d. 1033, l. 50ob.

44. Vitalii Belikov, "Na dvukh arkhipelagakh," in *Skvoz' dve voiny, skvoz' dva arkhipelaga: Vospominaniia sovetskikh voennoplennikh i ostovtsev*, ed. P. M Polian and N. L. Pobol' (Moscow: ROSSPEN, 2007), 297.

45. Taisa T., ZA314, 43.

46. Stanislav K., ZA486, 17–18; Liudmila G., ZA349, 9–10; Mikhaleva, *Gde vy, moi rodnye*, 128.

47. Aleksandra A., ZA466, 99. See also Tet'iana B., ZA469, 59–60.

48. Mariia Kh., ZA475, 37.

49. Mikhail B., ZA033, 45–46. See also Nikolai G., ZA293, 71.

50. Pavel Polian, *Zhertvy dvukh diktatur: Zhizn', trud, unizheniia i smert' sovetskikh voennoplennykh i ostarbaiterov na chuzhbine i na rodine* (Moscow: ROSSPEN, 2002), 257–58; Adam Tooze, *The Wages of Destruction: The Making and Breaking of the Nazi Economy* (New York: Viking, 2007), 523.

51. Polian, *Zhertvy dvukh diktatur*, 261.

52. Antonina S., ZA311, 34.

53. Valeriia F., ZA328, 30–31.

54. USHMM, RG-14.070, reel 0552, VE_L 28496, frames 1187–212.

55. Herbert, *Hitler's Foreign Workers*, 180.

56. Knat'ko and Adamushko, *Belorusskie ostarbaitery*, 2:2, 65–69.

57. For an example of improvement, see Olga D., ZA011, 45. Taisa T. only left her camp on the eve of liberation in 1945 (see ZA314, 122).

58. This explanation appears in Herbert, *Hitler's Foreign Workers*, 319–23.

59. Uwe Danker, "Statuserhebung: Auslander im 'Arbeitseinsatz' in Schleswig–Holstein 1939 bis 1945" in *"Ausländereinsatz in der Nordmark": Zwangsarbeitende in Schleswig–Holstein 1939–1945*, ed. Robert Bohn, Uwe Danker, Nils Köhler, and Sebastian Lehmann (Bielefeld: Verlag für Regionalgeschichte, 2001), 58–59.

60. USHMM, RG-14.070, reel 2240, VE_L 10566, frames 1063–74.

61. Mierzejewski, *Collapse of the German War Economy*, 123.

62. Valentin Senger, *The Invisible Jew: The Story of One Man's Survival in Nazi Germany* (London: Sidgwick and Jackson, 1980), 172–73.

63. Jan Klussmann, *Zwangsarbeit in der Kriegsmarinestadt Kiel, 1939–1945* (Bielefeld: Verlag fur Regionalgeschichte, 2004), 109–10.

64. Herbert, *Hitler's Foreign Workers*, 319–20.

65. Nikolai Karpov, *Na zadvorkakh pobedy. Malen'kii ostarbaiter* (Moscow: ROSSPEN, 2008), 238–39.

66. Vadim N., ZA299, 35.

67. USHMM, RG-14.070, reel 2830, V E_L 74487, frames 481–511; reel 5704, VE_L 134709, frames 205–9; reel 2240, V E_L 10566, frames 1063–74.

68. Knat'ko and Adamushko, *Belorusskie ostarbaitery*, 1:54.

69. Geoffrey Giles, "Legislating Homophobia in the Third Reich: The Radicalization of Prosecution against Homosexuality by the Legal Profession," *German History* 23, no. 3 (2005): 339–54.

70. Knat'ko and Adamushko, *Belorusskie ostarbaitery*, 1:235–38.

71. RGVA, f. 1164, op. 1, d. 1, ll. 11–14 (USHMM, RG-11.001M, reel 394).

72. James Scott, *Domination and the Arts of Resistance: Hidden Transcripts* (New Haven, CT: Yale University Press, 1990), is the classic work on struggles between marginalized people and authorities.

73. RGVA, f. 1164, op. 1, d. 1, l. 2 (USHMM, RG-11.001M, reel 394).

74. Efim Brodskii, *Oni ne propali bez vesti: Ne slomlennye fashistskoi nevolei* (Moscow: Mysl', 1987), 283; Buggeln, *Slave Labor in Nazi Concentration Camps*, 55.

75. Ivan G., ZA002, 6–7, 61–62.

76. Nikolai G., ZA293, 9, 82; Iurii Kh., ZA348, 29–30.

77. Evdokiia P., ZA305, 18.

78. GARF, f. 9526, op. 6, d. 262, l. 136.

79. Halyna K., ZA481, 77.

80. Mariia Kh., ZA475, 55.

81. Anatolii Derevenets, "Skvoz' dve voiny. Zapiski soldata," in *Skvoz' dve voiny, skvoz' dva arkhipelaga: Vospominaniia sovetskikh voennoplennikh i ostovtsev*, ed. P. M Polian and N. L. Pobol' (Moscow: ROSSPEN, 2007), 260; Herbert, *Hitler's Foreign Workers*, 242.

82. Knat'ko and Adamushko, *Belorusskie ostarbaitery*, 1:165–69.

83. Polina E., ZA480, 4–5.

84. Waitman Beorn, *Marching into Darkness: The Wehrmacht and the Holocaust in Belarus* (Cambridge, MA: Harvard University Press, 2014), 71.

85. Ulrike Winkler, "'Hauswirtschaftliche Ostarbeiterinnen' Zwangsarbeit in deutschen Haushalten," in *Stiften gehen: NS-Zwangsarbeit und Entschadigungsdebatte*, ed. Ulrike Winkler (Cologne: PapyRossa, 2000), 152.

86. Zinaida B., ZA465, 9–10.

87. See his memoirs, Otto Wagener, *Hitler: Memoirs of a Confidant* (New Haven, CT: Yale University Press, 1985).

88. Halyna Ia., ZA479, 9–10, 14, 24, 27, 105–6.

89. Polina E., ZA480, 59–60.

90. Valentina S., ZA502, 5–8.

91. Here the comparison is meant with nonoccupied and nonbesieged areas of the USSR. In areas under occupation or under siege, the food situation was disastrous. See Alexis Peri, *The War Within: Diaries from the Siege of Leningrad* (Cambridge, MA: Harvard University Press, 2017); Richard Bidlack and Nikita Lomagin, *The Leningrad Blockade, 1941–1944: A New Documentary History from the Soviet Archives* (New Haven, CT: Yale University Press, 2012), 45–53; Berkhoff, *Harvest of Despair*, 164–87.

92. Rebecca Manley, *To the Tashkent Station: Evacuation and Survival in the Soviet Union at War* (Ithaca, NY: Cornell University Press, 2009), 172–80; Goldman and Filtzer, introduction to *Hunger and War*, 15.

93. Seth Bernstein, *Raised under Stalin: Young Communists and the Defense of Socialism* (Ithaca, NY: Cornell University Press, 2017), 207–10.

94. Olga Kucherenko, "State v. Danila Kuz'mich: Soviet Desertion Laws and Industrial Child Labor during World War II," *Russian Review* 71, no. 3 (2012): 409.

95. Knat'ko and Adamushko, *Belorusskie ostarbaitery*, 1:141.

2. FORCED LABOR EMPIRE

1. Viktor Zemskov, *Vozvrashchenie sovetskikh peremeshchennykh lits v SSSR. 1944–1952 gg.* (Moscow: Institut rossiiskoi istorii, 2016), 126.

2. For the case of privilege in the Lodz Ghetto, see Gordan Horwitz, *Ghettostadt: Lodz and the Making of a Nazi City* (Cambridge, MA: Harvard University Press, 2008), 242–46.

3. On the case of the Gulag, see Wilson Bell, "Sex, Pregnancy, and Power in the Late Stalinist Gulag," *Journal of the History of Sexuality* 24, no. 2 (2015): 198–224.

4. Anna Hajkova, "Sexual Barter in Times of Genocide: Negotiating the Sexual Economy of the Theresienstadt Ghetto," *Signs: Journal of Women in Culture and Society* 38, no. 3 (2013): 505.

5. G. D. Knat'ko and B. I. Adamushko, eds., *Belorusskie ostarbaitery: Ugon naseleniia Belarusi na prinuditel'nye raboty v Germaniiu (1941–1944): Dokumenty i materialy* (Minsk: NARB, 1996), 1:235–38.

6. Knat'ko and Adamushko, *Belorusskie ostarbaitery*, 2:299.

7. Vitalii Belikov, "Na dvukh arkhipelagakh," in *Skvoz' dve voiny, skvoz' dva arkhipelaga: Vospominaniia sovetskikh voennoplennikh i ostovtsev*, ed. P. M Polian and N. L. Pobol' (Moscow: ROSSPEN, 2007), 298–300, 305.

8. GARF, f. 7021, op. 29, d. 12, l. 5.

9. Jan Klussmann, *Zwangsarbeit in der Kriegsmarinestadt Kiel, 1939–1945* (Bielefeld: Verlag fur Regionalgeschichte, 2004), 98–99.

10. Camille Fauroux, "Shared Intimacies: Women's Sexuality in Foreign Workers' Camps 1940–1945," *German History* 39, no. 1 (2020): 41.

11. Anna P., ZA007, 10–11.

12. Vadim N., ZA299, 30.

13. Aleksandra Mikhaleva, *Gde vy, moi rodnye: Dnevnik ostarbaitera* (Moscow: AST, 2015), 125.

14. Yanina Karpenkina, "Sovetizatsiia evreiskogo naseleniia Zapadnoi Belorussii (1939–1941 gg.)" (PhD diss., Higher School of Economics, 2018), 79–91; Tetyana Lapan, "The Experience of Forced Labourers from Galician Ukraine," in *Hitler's Slaves: Life Stories of Forced Labourers in Nazi-Occupied Europe*, ed. Christoph Thonfeld, Almut Leh, and Alexander von Plato (New York: Berghahn, 2010), 242–43.

15. Anna M., ZA489, 19.

16. Ol'ga D., ZA011, 40–41, 61.

17. Ivan K., ZA485, 12. See also Pavel T., ZA505, 11.

18. Zemskov, *Vozrashchenie sovetskikh peremeshchennykh lits*, 126.

19. Mariia K., ZA482, 59.

20. Petr P., ZA021, 23.

21. Among many other letters in the same file from the city of Kursk, see GARF, f. 7021, op. 29, d. 12, l. 151.

22. Taisa T., ZA314, 41.

23. Knat'ko and Adamushko, *Belorusskie ostarbaitery*, 1:165–69; Mikhaleva, *Gde vy, moi rodnye*, 114.

24. Vadim N., ZA299, 35.

25. Aleksandra A., ZA466, 23.

26. Mikhail B., ZA033, 47–48.

27. See Malte Rolf, *Soviet Mass Festivals, 1917-1991* (Pittsburgh: University of Pittsburgh Press, 2013).

28. Mariia G., ZA473, 53; Mariia K., ZA482, 50; Anna M., ZA489, 26; Sof'ia T., ZA014, 29.

29. Mikhaleva, *Gde vy, moi rodnye*, 139.

30. Ulrich Herbert, *Hitler's Foreign Workers: Enforced Foreign Labor in Germany under the Third Reich* (Cambridge: Cambridge University Press, 1997), 316.

31. RGVA, f. 1164, op. 1, d. 32, ll. 5, 6, 11ob., 15.

32. Anatolii Derevenets, "Skvoz' dve voiny. Zapiski soldata," in *Skvoz' dve voiny, skvoz' dva arkhipelaga: Vospominaniia sovetskikh voennoplennikh i ostovtsev*, ed. P. M Polian and N. L. Pobol' (Moscow: ROSSPEN, 2007), 214.

33. Rolf, *Soviet Mass Festivals*, 134–36.

34. Mariia G., ZA473, 55.

35. Vitalii Semin, *Nagrudnyi znak "Ost"* (St. Petersburg: Amfora, 2015), 391–92.

36. Mikhaleva, *Gde vy, moi rodnye*, 194–95, 217.

37. On the Gulag, see Golfo Alexopoulos, *Illness and Inhumanity in Stalin's Gulag* (New Haven, CT: Yale University Press, 2017), 227; Wilson Bell, *Stalin's Gulag at War: Forced Labour, Mass Death, and Soviet Victory in the Second World War* (Toronto: University of Toronto Press, 2018), 58–60. On concentration camp specialists like *kapos*, prisoners who held administrative positions the camps, see Nikolaus Wachsmann, *KL: A History of the Nazi Concentration Camps* (Boston: Little, Brown, 2015), 512–27.

38. Semin, *Nagrudnyi znak "OST,"* 226.

39. On the Gulag, see Alexopoulos, *Illness and Inhumanity in Stalin's Gulag*, 174–78.

40. Derevenets, "Skvoz' dve voiny," 218.

41. Anna Sh., ZA312, 11–12, 67–68.

42. Petr. P., ZA021, 29.

43. One example is Mykolaiv arrestee Evgenii Kiselev, AUSBU MO, f. 5, spr. 8042, ark. 27–28.

44. Mikhaleva, *Gde vy, moi rodnye*, 182, 189.

45. Herbert, *Hitler's Foreign Workers*, 98–99, 214, 283.

46. Anna P., ZA007, 38.

47. Mikhaleva, *Gde vy, moi rodnye*, 39.

48. Antonina S., ZA311, 27–28. For another example, see HDASBU, f. 16, spr. 642, ark. 18–19.

49. See for example the chapter on German-Soviet resistance in Efim Brodskii, *Oni ne propali bez vesti: Ne slomlennye fashistskoi nevolei* (Moscow: Mysl', 1987), 144–71.

50. Oleksandr I., ZA478, 82.

51. Sergei B., ZA331, 11–12.

52. HDASBU, f. 1, spr. 692, ark. 253.

53. Mikhaleva, *Gde vy, moi rodnye*, 227–28.

54. Ivan S., ZA495, 51.

55. Herbert, *Hitler's Foreign Workers*, 327.

56. Ivan K., ZA485, 68; Sergei B., ZA331, 34; Aleksandra A., ZA466, 80; Andryi B., ZA467, 10.

57. Herbert, *Hitler's Foreign Workers*, 229.

58. Raisa B., ZA031, 27; Oleksandr I., ZA478, 36; Anna Sh., ZA312, 77; Mikhaleva, *Gde vy, moi rodnye*, 269, 270–71.

59. Valentin Senger, *The Invisible Jew: The Story of One Man's Survival in Nazi Germany* (London: Sidgwick & Jackson, 1980), 158–59.

60. Liudmila G., ZA349, 9–10.

61. Nina M., ZA038, 44.

62. Irina Scherbakowa, "Oral Testimonies from Russian Victims of Forced Labour," in *Hitler's Slaves: Life Stories of Forced Labourers in Nazi-Occupied Europe*, ed. Christoph Thonfeld, Almut Leh, and Alexander von Plato (New York: Berghahn, 2010), 272.

63. Oleksandr I., ZA478, 34–37.

64. GARF f. 9526, op. 6, d. 236, l. 128.

65. Mikhaleva, *Gde vy, moi rodnye*, 147.

66. IRI RAN, f. 2, r. 6, op. 22, d. 24, l. 23.

67. Mikhaleva, *Gde vy, moi rodnye*, 229.

68. Antonina V., ZA340, 41, 52–54.

69. Mikhaleva, *Gde vy, moi rodnye*, 300–301.

70. Mikhaleva, *Gde vy, moi rodnye*, 237, 322, 336, 338.

71. Iurii Kh. ZA348, 52–53.

72. Antonina S., ZA311, 39–41.

73. Ol'ga D., ZA011, 51.

74. Herbert, *Hitler's Foreign Workers*, 298.

75. Muza I., ZA035, 14–15; Valeriia F., ZA328, 60–63.

76. Hajkova, "Sexual Barter in Times of Genocide," 507.

77. Tet'iana B., ZA469, 63–64.

78. Galina G., ZA474, 13, 52–60.

79. Fauroux, "Shared Intimacies," 43.

80. Mikhaleva, *Gde vy, moi rodnye*, 248–50, 275.

81. On prostitution in concentration camps, see Robert Sommer, "Forced Sex Labour in Nazi Concentration Camps," in *Brutality and Desire: War and Sexuality in Europe's Twentieth Century*, ed. Dagmar Herzog (Basingstoke: Palgrave, 2009), 175.

82. Herbert, *Hitler's Foreign Workers*, 220, 322.

83. Evdokiia P., ZA305, 26; Muza I., ZA035, 12; Mariia V., ZA343, 36–45.

84. Christopher Browning, *Remembering Survival: Inside a Nazi Slave-Labor Camp* (New York: Norton, 2010), 9.

85. RGASPI, f. 1m, op. 4s, d. 97, l. 8. For an example of such a poem, see "Girls," in IRI RAN, f. 2, r. 6, op. 22, d. 7, ll. 22ob.–23, which criticizes deportee women for sexual treason and men for cowardice.

86. Regina Mühlhäuser, "Between 'Racial Awareness' and Fantasies of Potency: Nazi Sexual Politics in the Occupied Territories of the Soviet Union, 1942–1945," in *Brutality and Desire: War and Sexuality in Europe's Twentieth Century*, ed. Dagmar Herzog (Basingstoke: Palgrave, 2009), 199–203.

87. Mariia G., ZA473, 21–22.

88. See Anonymous, *A Woman in Berlin: Eight Weeks in the Conquered City: A Diary* (New York: Metropolitan, 2005). See also Atina Grossmann, *Jews, Germans, and Allies: Close Encounters in Occupied Germany* (Princeton, NJ: Princeton University Press, 2007), 54–55.

89. Muza I., ZA035, 14.

90. Birthe Kundrus, "Forbidden Company: Romantic Relationships between Germans and Foreigners, 1939 to 1945," *Journal of the History of Sexuality* 11, no. 1/2 (2002): 217; Christa Paul, *Zwangsprostitution: Staatlich errichtete Bordelle im Nationalsozialismus* (Berlin: Edition Hentrich, 1994), 117–27.

91. Mühlhäuser, "Between 'Racial Awareness' and Fantasies of Potency," 204–8; Maris Rowe-McCulloch, "Sexual Violence under Occupation during World War II: Soviet Women's Experiences Inside a German Military Brothel and Beyond," *Journal of the History of Sexuality* 31, no. 1 (2022): 1–27.

92. Mühlhäuser, "Between 'Racial Awareness' and Fantasies of Potency," 211.

93. Herbert, *Hitler's Foreign Workers*, 270.

94. Knat'ko and Adamushko, *Belorusskie ostarbaitery*, 2:182–83; "Memo on Pregnancies among Forced Laborers," in *Experiences of Forced Labor in Wartime Europe*, February 18, 1944, https://perspectives.ushmm.org/item/memo-on-pregnancies-among-forced-laborers/collection/experiences-of-forced-labor-in-wartime-europe.

95. Senger, *Invisible Jew*, 161–62.

96. *Krieg gegen Kinder*, http://www.birdstage.net/kgk/cgi-bin/pageview.cgi, accessed April 8, 2022.

97. Herbert, *Hitler's Foreign Workers*, 269; Nicholas Stargardt, "Wartime Occupation by Germany: Food and Sex," in *The Cambridge History of the Second World War*, vol. 2, *Politics and Ideology*, ed. Richard J. B. Bosworth and Joseph A. Maiolo (Cambridge: Cambridge University Press, 2015), 405–6.

98. One study suggests that the men may not have known about the laws against miscegenation. Cornelie Usborne, "Female Sexual Desire and Male Honor: German Women's Illicit Love Affairs with Prisoners of War during the Second World War," *Journal of the History of Sexuality* 26, no. 3 (2017): 460, 487.

99. Mariia G., ZA473, 28–30.

100. Laura Fahnenbruck, *Ein(ver)nehmen: Sexualität und Alltag von Wehrmachtsoldaten in den besetzten Niederlanden* (Göttingen: V & R Unipress, 2018), 378, 390–91.

101. As scholars of the Gulag have shown, though, recollections of Stalinist forced labor often criticized queer sexuality. Yet former Eastern Workers make seemingly no mentions of queer sexuality, critical or favorable, in oral history interviews. On the Gulag, see Dan Healey, *Russian Homophobia from Stalin to Sochi* (London: Bloomsbury, 2017), 80, 168.

102. Mikhaleva, *Gde vy, moi rodnye*, 421.

3. COLLABORATION AND RESISTANCE

1. For detailed discussion of these numbers, see Mark Edele, *Stalin's Defectors: How Red Army Soldiers Became Hitler's Collaborators, 1941–1945* (Oxford: Oxford University Press, 2017), 31, 132.

2. Efim Brodskii, *Zabveniiu ne podlezhit* (Moscow: Mysl', 1993), 111.

3. On the debates over resistance and *resistenz*, see Ian Kershaw, *The Nazi Dictatorship: Problems and Perspectives of Interpretation*, 4th ed. (London: Bloomsbury, 2015), 226–37.

4. Angelika Benz, *Handlanger der SS: Die Rolle der Trawniki-Männer im Holocaust* (Berlin: Metropol, 2014).

5. For those who have been more sympathetic to those designated as collaborators, see Benz, *Handlanger der SS*; Vanessa Voisin, *L'URSS contre ses traîtres: L'épuration soviétique: 1941–1955* (Paris: Publications de la Sorbonne, 2015). Among historians who largely agree with Soviet charges, see Aron Shneer, *Professiia—Smert': Uchebnyi lager' SS "Travniki": Prestupleniia i vozmezdie* (Moscow: Piatyi Rim, 2019); Iurii Arzamaskin, *Tainy sovetskoi repatriatsii* (Moscow: Veche, 2015); Lawrence Douglas, *Right Wrong Man: John Demjanjuk and the Last Great Nazi War Crimes Trial* (Princeton, NJ: Princeton University Press, 2016).

6. Philippe Burrin, *France under the Germans: Collaboration and Compromise* (New York: New Press, 1993), 461–62.

7. USHMM RG-38.001, d. 46256, t. 1, l. 21.

8. Kirill Aleksandrov, *Russkie soldaty Vermakhta: Geroi ili predateli* (Moscow: Eksmo, 2005), 142–68.

9. For a discussion of these numbers, which are incomplete and disputed, see Edele, *Stalin's Defectors*, 23; Alexander Dallin, *German Rule in Russia, 1941–1945: A Study of Occupation Policies* (Boulder, CO: Westview Press, 1981), 427.

10. For an account of the motivations of Soviet soldiers that balances these factors, see Roger Reese, *Why Stalin's Soldiers Fought: The Red Army's Military Effectiveness in World War II* (Lawrence: University Press of Kansas, 2011), especially 151–227. Matthew Lenoe, "Emotions and Psychological Survival in the Red Army, 1941–42," *Kritika* 22, no. 2 (2021): 313–44, emphasizes personal motivations and correspondence with loved ones as a means of emotional fortification. Jochen Hellbeck, *Stalingrad: The City That Defeated the Third Reich* (New York: Public Affairs, 2016), emphasizes ideological motivations.

11. Karel Berkhoff, *Motherland in Danger: Soviet Propaganda during World War II* (Cambridge, MA: Harvard University Press, 2012), 124–25.

12. Edele, *Stalin's Defectors*, 21, 119.

13. For various estimates and debates over numbers, Christian Streit (Shtrait),"*Oni nam ne tovarishchi*": Vermakht i sovetskie voennoplennye v 1941–1945 gg. (Moscow: ROSSPEN, 2009), 8; Edele, *Stalin's Defectors*, 124; Christian Hartmann, *Wehrmacht im Ostkrieg: Front und militärisches Hinterland 1941/42* (Munich: Oldenbourg, 2009), 568.

14. Karel Berkhoff, *Harvest of Despair: Life and Death in Ukraine under Nazi Rule* (Cambridge, MA: Harvard University Press, 2004), 91–93. On party members who survived to work under the Germans, see Jeffrey Burds, "'Turncoats, Traitors, and Provocateurs': Communist Collaborators, the German Occupation, and Stalin's NKVD, 1941–1943," *East European Politics and Societies and Cultures* 32, no. 3 (2018): 606–38.

15. Anatolii Derevenets, "Skvoz' dve voiny. Zapiski soldata," in *Skvoz' dve voiny, skvoz' dva arkhipelaga: Vospominaniia sovetskikh voennoplennikh i ostovtsev,* ed. P. M. Polian and N. L. Pobol' (Moscow: ROSSPEN, 2007), 162.

16. Streit, "*Oni nam ne tovarishchi,*" 148; Geoffrey Megargee, ed., *Encyclopedia of Camps and Ghettos, 1933–1945* (Bloomington: Indiana University Press, 2009), 1:210.

17. Martin Dean, *Collaboration in the Holocaust: Crimes of the Local Police in Belorussia and Ukraine, 1941–44* (Basingstoke: Palgrave, 1998), 25.

18. GARF, f. 7021, op. 87, d. 137, l. 10.

19. Brodskii, *Zabveniiu ne podlezhit*, 237.

20. "Letter to the Ruhr coal-mining authority concerning the use of Soviet prisoners, and typhus among them," *Nuremberg Trials Project*, February 3, 1942, https://nuremberg.law.harvard.edu/documents/786-letter-to-the-ruhr.

21. Georgii Timokhin, "'I fashizm iznuriaet menia . . .' Vospominaniia i pesni o plene" in *Skvoz' dve voiny, skvoz' dva arkhipelaga: Vospominaniia sovetskikh voennoplennikh i ostovtsev,* ed. P. M. Polian and N. L. Pobol' (Moscow: ROSSPEN, 2007), 258.

22. Hans Pfahlmann, *Fremdarbeiter und Kriegsgefangene in der Deutschen Kriegswirtschaft 1939–1945* (Darmstadt: Wehr und Wissen Verlagsges, 1968), 184.

23. Dean, *Collaboration in the Holocaust*, 55; Maris Rowe-McCulloch, "The Holocaust and Mass Violence in the German-Occupied City of Rostov-on-Don, 1941–1943" (PhD diss., University of Toronto, 2020), 111, 165.

24. A. A. Marinchenko, "'Vnesti razdory mezhdu narodami . . .' Rasovaia politika nemetskikh vlastei v otnoshenii sovetskikh voennoplennykh, 1941-nachalo 1942 goda," *Novaia i noveishaia istoriia,* no. 2 (2014): 81–87.

25. Mikhailo K., ZA487, 19.

26. For discussions of these figures, see Edele, *Stalin's Defectors*, 21, 123–24.

27. Charles Dick, *Builders of the Third Reich: The Organisation Todt and Nazi Forced Labour* (London: Bloomsbury, 2020), 122–23.

28. Aleksei R., ZA041, 31.

29. Nikolai Karpov, *Na zadvorkakh pobedy. Malen'kii ostarbaiter* (Moscow: ROSSPEN, 2008), 235; Derevenets, "Skvoz' dve voiny," 210.

30. Georgii T., ZA313, 31.

31. Dallin, *German Rule in Russia*, 536.

32. Matthew Cooper, *The Nazi War against Soviet Partisans, 1941–1944* (New York: Stein and Day, 1979), 145.

33. A. N. Artizov and V. S. Khristoforov, eds., *General Vlasov: Istoriia predatel'stva* (Moscow: ROSSPEN, 2015), 1:299–301.

34. A pro-German government in western Russia called the Lokot Autonomy formed under the command of local ethnic Russian Bronislav Kaminskii. See Igor' Ermolov, *Tri goda bez Stalina. Okkupatsiia: Sovetskie grazhdane mezhdu natsistami i bol'shevikami* (Moscow: Tsentrpoligraf, 2010). On Ukrainian Waffen-SS volunteers, see Jacek Andrzej Młynarczyk, Leonid Rein, Andrii Bolianovskyi, and Oleg Romanko, "Eastern Europe: Belarusian Auxiliaries, Ukrainian Waffen-SS Soldiers and the Special Case of the Polish 'Blue Police,'" in *The Waffen-SS: A European History*, ed. Jochen Böhler and Robert Gerwarth (Oxford: Oxford University Press, 2017), 198–206. On Muslim auxiliaries, see Xavier Bougarel, Alexander Korb, Stefan Petke, and Franziska Zaugg, "Muslim SS Units in the Balkans and the Soviet Union," 272–78, in the same volume. On the contemporary memory politics of wartime collaboration in Ukraine, see Per Anders Rudling, "'They Defended Ukraine': The 14. Waffen-Grenadier-Division der SS (Galizische Nr. 1) Revisited," *Journal of Slavic Military Studies* 25, no. 3 (2012): 329–68.

35. Alexander Statiev, *The Soviet Counterinsurgency in the Western Borderlands* (Cambridge: Cambridge University Press, 2010), 80–81.

36. A well-researched but overly sympathetic account of Vlasov's army is Aleksandrov, *Russkie soldaty Vermakhta*.

37. Cooper, *Nazi War against Soviet Partisans*, 145.

38. Dean, *Collaboration in the Holocaust*, 150–53.

39. Shneer, *Professiia—Smert'*, 11; Peter Black, "Foot Soldiers of the Final Solution: The Trawniki Training Camp and Operation Reinhard," *Holocaust and Genocide Studies* 25, no. 1 (2011): 7; Benz, *Handlanger der SS*.

40. Wendy Lower, *Nazi Empire-Building and the Holocaust in Ukraine* (Chapel Hill: University of North Carolina Press, 2005), 19, 99–100; Alex Kay, *Exploitation, Resettlement, Mass Murder: Political and Economic Planning for German Occupation Policy in the Soviet Union, 1940–1941* (New York: Berghahn, 2006), 79–80.

41. For a sample of volunteers, see Edele, *Stalin's Defectors*, 86.

42. For a description of such a commission, see V. D. Poremskii, "Wustrau," in *Memuary Vlasovtsev*, ed. A. V. Okorokov (Moscow: Veche, 2011), 200.

43. Petr Astakhov, *Zigzagi sud'by: Iz zhizni sovetskogo voennoplennogo i sovetskogo zeka* (Moscow: ROSSPEN, 2005), 80–81.

44. HDASBU, f. 6, spr. 71132fp, ark. 12–14, 24–25.

45. Benz, *Handlanger der SS*, 51.

46. AUSBU ChO, spr. 1009, ark. 181.

47. Benz, *Handlanger der SS*, 53.

48. On the Kielce pogrom, see Jan Gross, *Fear: Anti-Semitism in Poland after Auschwitz* (Princeton, NJ: Princeton University Press, 2006), 81–117.

49. AUSBU ChO, spr. 1009, ark. 109.

50. Poremskii, "Wustrau," 201.

51. AUSBU ChO, spr. 1009, ark. 15.

52. USHMM RG-38.001, d. 46206, t. 1, l. 10.

53. Frenzel appears in several documents but is never identified in more detail. Gerhard von Mende, an Eastern Ministry figure involved in recruiting Caucasian and Turkic nationalities from the USSR as auxiliaries, could not identify Frenzel's first name to the CIA. See "Gerhard von Mende," CIA Electronic Reading Room, accessed April 12, 2022, https://www.cia.gov/ readingroom/docs/MENDE,%20GERHARD%20VON_0002.pdf, 6.

54. USHMM RG-38.001, d. 46256, t. 1, l. 21.

55. Astakhov, *Zigzagi sud'by*, 124.

56. USHMM RG-38.001, d. 46256, t. 1, l. 21ob.

57. AUSBU ChO, spr. 1009, ark. 14ob., 112; USHMM RG-38.001, d. 46256, t. 1, l. 11ob.

58. AUSBU ChO, spr. 1009, ark. 127.

59. AUSBU ChO, spr. 1009, ark. 14ob.

60. Artizov and Khristoforov, *General Vlasov*, 1:932. On the Stalinist conservative turn, see Wendy Goldman, *Women, the State, and Revolution: Soviet Family Policy and Social Life, 1917–1936* (Cambridge: Cambridge University Press, 1993), 296–304, 326–31.

61. Erik Scott, *Familiar Strangers: The Georgian Diaspora and the Evolution of Soviet Empire* (Oxford: Oxford University Press, 2016), 127–35.

62. Igor' Obolenskii, "Uchitel' Stalina, gruzinskii 'Shindler' i 'Chernyi Abdulla,'" *Sputnik Gruziia*, May 9, 2016, https://sputnik-georgia.ru/columnists/20160509/231558885.html.

63. USHMM RG-38.001, d. 46206, t. 1, l. 453.

64. USHMM RG-38.001, d. 46206, t. 1, ll. 393–95.

65. The group appeared in the "UfA-Europawoche" newsreel, no. 52 from February 1944.

66. USHMM RG-38.001, d. 46185, t. 1, l. 89.

67. USHMM RG-38.001, d. 46256, t. 1, ll. 12, 218–19.

68. AUSBU ChO, spr. 1009, ark. 127; Astakhov, *Zigzagi sud'by*, 124.

69. AUSBU ChO, spr. 1009, ark. 40.

70. Astakhov, *Zigzagi sud'by*, 125.

71. Benz, *Handlanger der SS*, 88, 91.

72. AUSBU ChO, spr. 1009, ark. 16–18, 184–85.

73. AUSBU ChO, spr. 1009, ark. 190.

74. AUSBU ChO, spr. 1009, ark. 135, 136.

75. AUSBU ChO, spr. 1009, ark. 18ob.–19, 38.

76. USHMM RG-38.001, d. 46256, t. 1, ll. 20ob., 117–19.

77. USHMM RG-38.001, d. 46206, t. 1, ll. 395, 452.

78. Astakhov, *Zigzagi sud'by*, 127–35.

79. Astakhov, *Zigzagi sud'by*, 127.

80. USHMM RG-38.001, d. 46206, t. 1, l. 434.

81. Artizov and Khristoforov, *General Vlasov*, 1:318–21, 450–52.

82. USHMM RG-38.001, d. 46256, t. 1, ll. 86, 218–19; d. 4873, t. 1, l. 78.

83. USHMM RG-38.001, d. 46206, t. 1, ll. 151–53.

84. Astakhov, *Zigzagi sud'by*, 167–71.

85. For an intriguing oral history with an anonymous former Soviet spy who worked in deep cover in Germany, see Aron Shneer, *Iz NKVD v SS i obratno: Iz rasskazov shturmbannfiurera* (Moscow: Paralleli, 2005).

86. See Brodskii, *Zabveniiu ne podlezhit*, 111.

87. Secret police materials about the Leipzig group files are in HDASBU, f. 1, spr. 692–93, 695–96. Other groups' files are available in HDASBU, f. 1, spr. 694, 697–98, 738–39.

88. USHMM RG-38.001, d. 46256, t. 1, ll. 215–17.

89. HDASBU, f. 1, spr. 692, ark. 72–73.

90. HDASBU, f. 1, spr. 692, ark. 17–18, 52–53.

91. HDASBU, f. 1, spr. 694, ark. 291–92.

92. Brodskii, *Zabveniiu ne podlezhit*, 157.

93. Efim Brodskii, *Oni ne propali bez vesti: Ne slomlennye fashistskoi nevolei* (Moscow: Mysl', 1987), 264; HDASBU, f. 1, spr. 692, ark. 54.

94. HDASBU, f. 1, spr. 692, ark. 205.

95. Brodskii, *Zabveniiu ne podlezhit*, 163, 165.

96. HDASBU, f. 1, spr. 692, ark. 273.

97. Brodskii, *Zabveniiu ne podlezhit*, 165.

98. HDASBU, f. 1, spr. 692, ark. 54ob.–55.

99. Leipzig was disproportionately the destination of Eastern Workers deported from Pavlohrad according to questionnaires completed after return. GARF, f. 7021, op. 57, d. 321.

100. HDASBU, f. 1, spr. 692, ark. 46–48, 60.

101. Staatsarchiv Leipzig, 20793, Rud. Sack, Nr. 559 (Dsadsamia). Thanks to Anne Friebel for sharing this document.

102. Brodskii, *Zabveniiu ne podlezhit*, 227.

103. Brodskii, *Oni ne propali bez vesti*, 172.

104. A. A. Iskhak, *Poet-geroi Musa Dzhalil'* (Moscow: Znanie, 1956), 16–17.

105. Brodskii, *Oni ne propali bez vesti*, 129.

106. Brodskii, *Oni ne propali bez vesti*, 67.

107. Brodskii, *Oni ne propali bez vesti*, 108.

108. Brodskii, *Oni ne propali bez vesti*, 67.

109. USHMM RG-38.001, d. 46206, t. 1, ll. 100–101, 169, 184–85, 396, 453.

110. Georgii Tereshonkov, "'Vernut'sia na rodinu'. Zapiski begletsa iz Norvegii i iz vlasovskoi armii," *Skvoz' dve voiny, skvoz' dva arkhipelaga: Vospominaniia sovetskikh voennoplennikh i ostovtsev*, ed. P. M. Polian and N. L. Pobol' (Moscow: ROSSPEN, 2007), 286–87.

4. LIBERATED IN A FOREIGN LAND

1. On state preferences for legible populations, see James Scott, *Seeing Like a State: How Certain Schemes to Improve the Human Condition Have Failed* (New Haven, CT: Yale University Press, 1998). For an overview of the literature on fluid Eastern European national identities and the attempt to fix nationality, see Tara Zahra, "Imagined Noncommunities: National Indifference as a Category of Analysis," *Slavic Review* 69, no. 1 (2010): 99–102.

2. See Andrew Janco, "Soviet 'Displaced Persons' in Europe, 1941–1951" (PhD diss., University of Chicago, 2012).

3. Viktor Zemskov, *Vozvrashchenie sovetskikh peremeshchennykh lits v SSSR. 1944–1952 gg.* (Moscow: Institut rossiiskoi istorii, 2016), 141.

4. Here I am adapting the terms "wild purge" of perceived collaborators in postliberation France and "wild expulsion" of ethnic Germans from East-Central Europe. See Philippe Bourdrel, *L'épuration sauvage, 1944–1945* (Paris: Perrin, 1988); Benjamin Frommer, *National Cleansing: Retribution against Nazi Collaborators in Postwar Czechoslovakia* (Cambridge: Cambridge University Press, 2005), 33.

5. Ulrich Herbert, *Hitler's Foreign Workers: Enforced Foreign Labor in Germany under the Third Reich* (Cambridge: Cambridge University Press, 1997), 367, 373.

6. Fritz Bauer, ed., *Justiz und NS-Verbrechen: Sammlung deutscher Strafurteile wegen nationalsozialistischer Tötungsverbrechen 1945–1999* (Amsterdam: University Press Amsterdam, 1968), 14:458, 573–74, 597.

7. Bauer, *Justiz und NS-Verbrechen*, 14:568–71. Another typical case of summary execution is in vol. 11, 775–79.

8. AUSBU MO, f. 5, spr. 8042, t. 1, ark. 207–13.

9. Quoted in Herbert, *Hitler's Foreign Workers*, 357.

10. Anatolii A., ZA341, 24–26.

11. HDASBU, f. 1, spr. 739, ark. 92, 94.

12. Mariia G., ZA473, 31.

13. Wolfgang Jacobmeyer, *Vom Zwangsarbeiter zum heimatlosen Ausländer: Die Displaced Persons in Westdeutschland, 1945–1951* (Göttingen: Vandenhoeck & Ruprecht, 1985), 49. Panikos Panayi, "Return, Displacement and Revenge: Majorities and Minorities in Osnabrück at the End of the Second World War," in *The Disentanglement of Populations: Migration, Expulsion and Displacement in Post-war Europe, 1944–49*, ed. Jessica Reinisch and Elizabeth White (Basingstoke: Palgrave, 2011), 151–55, found some evidence of DP crime but based on a limited sample.

14. Herbert, *Hitler's Foreign Workers*, 380; Atina Grossmann, *Jews, Germans, and Allies: Close Encounters in Occupied Germany* (Princeton, NJ: Princeton University Press, 2007), 149.

15. Marvin Klemmé, *The Inside Story of UNRRA: An Experience in Internationalism* (New York: Lifetime Editions, 1949), 74.

16. Martin Dean, *Collaboration in the Holocaust: Crimes of the Local Police in Belorussia and Ukraine, 1941–44* (Basingstoke: Palgrave, 1998), 151–53; Sergei Drobiazko, *Pod znamenami vraga: Antisovetskie formirovaniia v sostave germanskikh vooruzhennykh sil 1941–1945 gg.* (Moscow: Eksmo, 2004), 225–29.

17. See a Vlasov army officer's report on a Russian unit's contribution to the ferocious German defense of Monte Cassino in Italy. A. N. Artizov and V. S. Khristoforov, eds., *General Vlasov: Istoriia predatel'stva*, vol. 2, pt. 2 (Moscow ROSSPEN, 2015), 376–79; Drobiazko, *Pod znamenami vraga*, 231–34.

18. GARF, f. 9526, op. 6, d. 45, l. 27.

19. International Committee of the Red Cross, *Geneva Convention Relative to the Treatment of Prisoners of War (Third Geneva Convention)*, July 27, 1929, https://en .wikisource.org/wiki/Geneva_Convention/Third_Geneva_Convention.

20. Jessica Reinisch, "Introduction: Relief in the Aftermath of War," *Journal of Contemporary History* 43, no. 3 (2008): 371–404.

21. Gerard Daniel Cohen, *In War's Wake: Europe's Displaced Persons in the Postwar Order* (Cambridge: Cambridge University Press, 2011), 35.

22. Nikolai Tolstoy, *Victims of Yalta: The Secret Betrayal of the Allies: 1944–1947* (1977; New York: Pegasus, 2013), 44. Charles de Gaulle and Stalin made a similar agreement for Franco-Soviet repatriation at the end of 1944. See Greg Burgess, "The Repatriation of Soviet Prisoners of War and Displaced Peoples from the Auvergne after the Second World War," *French History and Civilization* 7 (2017): 171.

23. See negotiations between Soviet and Western Allied officials over the implementation of repatriation from Halle in May 1945, GARF, 9526, op. 6, d. 42, ll. 123, 125; d. 44, ll. 46–52.

24. GARF, f. 9526, op. 6, d. 202, l. 33.

25. GARF, f. 9526, op. 6, d. 1124, ll. 156–57.

26. GARF, f. 9526, op. 6, d. 47, l. 77.

27. Malcolm Proudfoot, *European Refugees: 1939–52: A Study in Forced Population Movement* (Evanston, IL: Northwestern University Press, 1956), 107, 162–63.

28. April 16, 1945, SHAEF, Administrative Memorandum, No. 39, Repatriation of Soviet Citizens (RSC), Displaced Persons in Germany and Other Countries (DP), Prisoner

of War and Displaced Persons Branch (POW DP), Records of US Occupation Headquarters, World War II, RG 260, NACP; GARF, f. 9526, op. 1, d. 23a, l. 126.

29. July 31, 1945, Displaced Persons Conference, Russian Zone, Berlin District, RSC, DP, POW DP, RG 260, NACP; Zemskov, *Vozvrashchenie sovetskikh peremeshchennykh lits*, 141; GARF, f. 9526, op. 6, d. 58, l. 46.

30. AUSBU MO, f. 5, spr. 8042, t. 1, ark. 205.

31. Klemmé, *Inside Story of UNRRA*, 245; Janco, "Soviet 'Displaced Persons' in Europe, 1941–1951," 89, 105–7.

32. GARF, f. 9526, op. 6, d. 44, l. 50.

33. GARF, f. 9526, op. 1, d. 223, l. 55.

34. Viktor Sh., ZA308, 33.

35. Proudfoot, *European Refugees*, 172.

36. AUSBU MO, f. 5, spr. 8042, t. 2, envelop 2, July 30, 1946.

37. AUSBU MO, f. 5, spr. 8042, t. 1, ark. 72ob.

38. Aleksandra Mikhaleva, *Gde vy, moi rodnye: Dnevnik ostarbaitera* (Moscow: AST, 2015), 383.

39. Zinaida B., ZA465, 28–29.

40. GARF, f. 9526, op. 6, d. 49, l. 208. For similar vigilantism among liberated POWs in Norway, see d. 53, l. 139. On Vikhorev, see Mikhail Koriakov, *I'll Never Go Back: A Red Army Officer Talks* (London: Dutton, 1948), 184–85.

41. Amir Weiner, *Making Sense of War: The Second World War and the Fate of the Bolshevik Revolution* (Princeton, NJ: Princeton University Press, 2001), 182–83.

42. Surov-Kurov-Kin identified as an ethnic Russian from Kazakhstan. Asked about the odd surname by interrogators, Kiselev answered that he also was unsure of its provenance. AUSBU MO, f. 5, spr. 8042, t. 1, ark. 92ob.

43. On drinking and executions in the Holocaust, see Edward Westermann, *Drunk on Genocide: Alcohol and Mass Murder in Nazi Germany* (Ithaca, NY: Cornell University Press, 2021), who asserts that alcohol could loosen inhibitions about murder but also could serve a celebratory function. On the Great Terror, see Lynne Viola, *Stalinist Perpetrators on Trial: Scenes from the Great Terror in Soviet Ukraine* (Oxford: Oxford University Press, 2017), 113.

44. AUSBU MO, f. 5, spr. 8042, t. 2, ark. 106–7.

45. Fabrice Virgili, *Shorn Women: Gender and Punishment in Liberation France*, trans. John Flower (London: Berg Publishers, 2002); Mary Louise Roberts, *What Soldiers Do: Sex and the American GI in World War II France* (Chicago: University of Chicago Press, 2013). On Soviet policing of relationships with foreigners arriving with Lend-Lease goods, see Liudmila Novikova, "Criminalized Liaisons: Soviet Women and Allied Sailors in Wartime Arkhangel'sk," *Journal of Contemporary History* 55, no. 4 (2020): 745–63.

46. Anatolii A., ZA341, 27.

47. Mikhaleva, *Gde vy, moi rodnye*, 382, 389, 397, 401.

48. Mikhaleva, *Gde vy, moi rodnye*, 390.

49. AUSBU MO, f. 5, spr. 8042, t. 1, ark. 297.

50. On "field wives," see Catherine Merridale, *Ivan's War: Life and Death in the Red Army, 1939–1945* (New York: Metropolitan, 2006), 238–40; Roger Markwick and Euridice Cardona, *Soviet Women on the Frontline in the Second World War* (Basingstoke: Palgrave, 2012), 78–80.

51. HDASBU, f. 1, spr. 694, ark. 66–67.

52. On the Stalinist family, see Wendy Goldman, *Women, the State, and Revolution: Soviet Family Policy and Social Life, 1917–1936* (Cambridge: Cambridge University Press, 1993), 296–336.

53. Grossmann, *Jews, Germans, and Allies*, 186–88.

54. HDASBU, f. 16, spr. 642, ark. 18–19.

55. Jochen Hellbeck, *Revolution on My Mind: Writing a Diary under Stalin* (Cambridge, MA: Harvard University Press, 2006).

56. AUSBU MO, f. 5, spr. 8042, t. 2, ark. 28. This is the estimate of a German RROK member, Willy Gehlbach. Kiselev claimed, improbably, that as many as eight hundred people were at the meeting.

57. In Russian-language documents Gehlbach is usually called Gel'bik.

58. HDASBU, f. 1, spr. 692, ark. 19, 23, 55–56, 95, 260–62; spr. 694, ark. 18, 202–3; spr. 696, ark. 66.

59. HDASBU, f. 1, spr. 692, ark. 56.

60. HDASBU, f. 1, spr. 692, ark. 49ob., 61ob., 237, 239.

61. In 1948, Kyiv province secret police alone were investigating twenty-five groups. HDASBU, f. 1, spr. 52, ark. 267–78.

62. HDASBU, f. 1, spr. 692, ark. 50; AUSBU MO, f. 5, spr. 8042, t. 2, ark. 29.

63. Klemmé, *Inside Story of UNRRA*, 75, 126.

64. HDASBU, f. 6, spr. 68043fp., ark. 14–15, 131, 136, 156–57, 158–59, 166, 320.

65. GARF, f. 9526, op. 6, d. 48, ll. 62–64.

66. HDASBU, f. 16, spr. 661, ark. 202–5.

67. GARF, f. 9526, op. 6, d. 252, l. 291.

68. GARF, f. 9526, op. 6, d. 247, l. 11.

69. GARF, f. 9526, op. 6, d. 245, ll. 156–59.

70. GARF, f. 9526, op. 6, d. 245, l. 136.

71. Ivan K., ZA342, 9.

72. GARF, f. 9526, op. 1, d. 23a, l. 125.

73. July 11, 1945, Eisenhower to CG Seventh Army, RSC, DP, POW DP, RG 260, NACP.

74. GARF, f. 9526, op. 6, d. 274, l. 28.

75. GARF, f. 9526, op. 6, d. 266, ll. 1–3.

76. GARF, f. 9526, op. 6, d. 491, l. 151.

77. GARF, f. 9526, op. 6, d. 58, ll. 35–36.

78. Burgess, "Repatriation of Soviet Prisoners of War and Displaced Peoples," 177.

79. Antonina S., ZA311, 50, 54–55.

80. Lev Netto, ZA309, 30.

81. GARF, f. 9526, op. 6, d. 265, l. 100.

82. GARF, f. 9526, op. 6, d. 265, l. 90.

83. Valentina G., Memorial Ostarbeiter Archive, Moscow, 18.

84. HDASBU, f. 6, spr. 68043fp., ark. 2, 12, 20.

85. HDASBU f. 16, spr. 560, ark. 38.

86. GARF, f. 9526, op. 6, d. 266, ll. 4, 9–10, 50.

87. Antonina V., ZA340, 41–42, 52–54.

88. HDASBU, f. 6, spr. 68043fp., ark. 212–18.

89. Mikhaleva, *Gde vy, moi rodnye*, 391, 408.

90. Ivan Tvardovskii, *Rodina i chuzhbina: Kniga zhizni* (Smolensk: Posokh, 1996), 233–40.

91. GARF, f. 9526, op. 6, d. 192, l. 20.

92. GARF, f. 9526, op. 6, d. 368, ll. 2, 3.

93. A. R. L. Gurland, *Glimpses of Soviet Jewry: 1,000 Letters from the USSR and DP Camps* (New York: American Jewish Committee, 1948), 24.

94. Iosif A., ZA283, 106–9.

5. AMBIGUOUS HOMECOMING

1. GARF, f. 9526, op. 6, d. 51, ll. 325–36.

2. On notions of guilt for collaboration, see Karel Berkhoff, *Motherland in Danger: Soviet Propaganda during World War II* (Cambridge, MA: Harvard University Press, 2012), 236.

3. GARF, f. 9526, op. 6, d. 98, l. 32.

4. GARF, f. 9526, op. 6, d. 1, ll. 4–6.

5. GARF, f. 9526, op. 6, d. 3, l. 20; d. 4, l. 4.

6. GARF, f. 9526, op. 6, d. 103, ll. 7, 14.

7. GARF, f. 9526, op. 6, d. 98, ll. 115, 127; d. 103, ll. 42–43

8. GARF, f. 9526, op. 6, d. 34, l. 22.

9. GARF, f. 9526, op. 6, d. 103, l. 112.

10. Viktor Zemskov, *Vozvrashchenie sovetskikh peremeshchennykh lits v SSSR. 1944–1952 gg.* (Moscow: Institut rossiiskoi istorii, 2016), 124; GARF, f. 9526, op. 6, d. 48, l. 98.

11. GARF, f. 9526, op. 6, d. 100, l. 26.

12. GARF, f. 9526, op. 6, d. 103, ll. 126, 143.

13. GARF, f. 9526, op. 6, d. 283, ll. 301–2.

14. GARF, f. 9526, op. 6, d. 100, l. 26.

15. GARF, f. 9526, op. 6, d. 51, ll. 180, 221–22, 226; d. 106, ll. 9–12; d. 119, l. 17.

16. For similar incidents, see GARF, f. 9526, op. 6, d. 48, l. 2; d. 51, l. 57.

17. Aleksandra Mikhaleva, *Gde vy, moi rodnye: Dnevnik ostarbaitera* (Moscow: AST, 2015), 409–18.

18. GARF, f. 9526, op. 6, d. 110, l. 102.

19. Nikolai Karpov, *Na zadvorkakh pobedy. Malen'kii ostarbaiter* (Moscow: ROSSPEN, 2008), 251. For similar cases, see Anna P., ZA007, 12; Bronislava A., ZA020, 7.

20. GARF, f. 9526, op. 6, d. 119, l. 41; d. 278, ll. 219–20.

21. GARF, f. 9526, op. 6, d. 111, l. 259.

22. HDASBU, f. 16, spr. 560, ark. 37ob.

23. Calculations derived from numbers of returnees and lists of officers on GARF, f. 9408, op. 1, d. 19, ll. 1, 3–4.

24. Zinaida B., ZA465, 32, 39–40.

25. Aron Shneer, *Professiia—Smert': Uchebnyi lager' SS "Travniki": Prestupleniia i vozmezdie* (Moscow: Piatii Rim, 2019), 21.

26. AUSBU ChO, spr. 1009, ark. 88–89.

27. HDASBU, f. 16, spr. 578, ark. 72; spr. 580, ark. 309.

28. HDASBU, f. 6, spr. 68043fp, ark. 12, 20.

29. GARF, f. 9526, op. 6, d. 244, ll. 345–48.

30. See chapter 6 on the labor battalions and exiles.

31. GARF, f. 9526, op. 6, d. 278, l. 342.

32. Pavel Polian, *Zhertvy dvukh diktatur: Zhizn', trud, unizheniia i smert' sovetskikh voennoplennykh i ostarbaiterov na chuzhbine i na rodine* (Moscow: ROSSPEN, 2002), 537; Zemskov, *Vozvrashchenie sovetskikh peremeshchennykh lits*, 306–13.

33. Alexander Statiev, *The Soviet Counterinsurgency in the Western Borderlands* (Cambridge: Cambridge University Press, 2010), 277; Norman Naimark, *The Russians in Germany: A History of the Soviet Zone of Occupation, 1945–1949* (Cambridge, MA: Harvard University Press, 1995), 87, 160.

34. GARF, f. 9526, op. 6, d. 100, ll. 165–66.

35. GARF, f. 9526, op. 6, d. 100, l. 40.

36. Sergei B., ZA331, 41.

37. GARF, f. 9526, op. 6, d. 53, l. 79. Other recorded incidents: GARF, f. 9526, op. 6, d. 48, ll. 20, 69.

38. Katherine Jolluck, "Women in the Crosshairs: Violence against Women during the Second World War," *Australian Journal of Politics and History* 62, no. 4 (2016): 514–28.

39. GARF, f. 9526, op. 6, d. 50, ll. 173–74.

40. GARF, f. 9526, op. 6, d. 52, l. 263.

41. Polina E., ZA480, 107–9. For a similar story, see Galina Sh., Memorial Ostarbeiter Archive, Moscow, 9.

42. Atina Grossmann, "A Question of Silence: The Rape of German Women by Occupation Soldiers," *October* 72 (1995): 46. On Red Army rapes in Germany, see Atina Grossmann, *Jews, Germans, and Allies: Close Encounters in Occupied Germany* (Princeton, NJ: Princeton University Press, 2007), 49–68; Catherine Merridale, *Ivan's War: Life and Death in the Red Army, 1939–1945* (New York: Metropolitan, 2006), 317–20; Naimark, *Russians in Germany*, 69–140. On the comparative lack of Red Army sexual violence in Yugoslavia, see Vojin Majstorović, "The Red Army in Yugoslavia, 1944–1945," *Slavic Review* 75, no. 2 (2016): 396–421.

43. RGVA f. 32925, op. 1, d. 527, l. 175; d. 528, l. 2.

44. GARF, f. 9526, op. 6, d. 100, ll. 164–65.

45. GARF, f. 9526, op. 6, d. 281, l. 150; d. 283, l. 279.

46. Anonymous, *A Woman in Berlin: Eight Weeks in the Conquered City: A Diary* (New York: Metropolitan, 2005). See also Grossmann, *Jews, Germans, and Allies*, 54–55.

47. GARF, f. 9526, op. 6, d. 52, l. 1. For a similar case where a refusal resulted in arrest, see Mariia V., ZA343, 36–45.

48. GARF, f. 9526, op. 6, d. 51, l. 230.

49. GARF, f. 9526, op. 6, d. 100, l. 40.

50. On violence in the occupation regime, see Filip Slaveski, *The Soviet Occupation of Germany: Hunger, Mass Violence and the Struggle for Peace, 1945–1947* (Cambridge: Cambridge University Press, 2013).

51. Alfred Rieber, "Civil Wars in the Soviet Union," *Kritika* 4, no. 1 (2003): 129–62"; Statiev, *The Soviet Counterinsurgency in the Western Borderlands*.

52. Karel Berkhoff, *Harvest of Despair: Life and Death in Ukraine under Nazi Rule* (Cambridge, MA: Harvard University Press, 2004), 254–55; Polian, *Zhertvy dvukh diktatur*, 277–82.

53. Mark Edele, *Soviet Veterans of the Second World War: A Popular Movement in an Authoritarian Society, 1941–1991* (Oxford: Oxford University Press, 2008), 31–33; Brandon Schechter, *The Stuff of Soldiers: A History of the Red Army in World War II through Objects* (Ithaca, NY: Cornell University Press, 2019), 212–42.

54. GARF, f. 9526, op. 6, d. 279, ll. 30, 62.

55. Zinaida B., ZA465, 33.

56. GARF, f. 9526, op. 6, d. 104, l. 47.

57. GARF, f. 9526, op. 6, d. 111, l. 198.

58. GARF, f. 9526, op. 6, d. 51, l. 322.

59. GARF, f. 9526, op. 6, d. 104, ll. 46–47.

60. TsDAVO, f. 2, op. 2, spr. 2999, ark. 60–61.

61. TsDAVO, f. 2, op. 2, spr. 3020, ark. 14.

62. Franziska Exeler, *Ghosts of War: Nazi Occupation and Its Aftermath in Soviet Belarus* (Ithaca, NY: Cornell University Press, 2022), 194–202.

63. Rebecca Manley, *To the Tashkent Station: Evacuation and Survival in the Soviet Union at War* (Ithaca, NY: Cornell University Press, 2009), 256–64.

64. Robert Dale, *Demobilized Veterans in Late Stalinist Leningrad: Soldiers to Civilians* (London: Bloomsbury, 2015), 42–68.

65. GARF, f. 9526, op. 6, d. 111, ll. 198, 209.

66. GARF, f. 9526, op. 6, d. 283, l. 53.

67. GARF, f. 9526, op. 6, d. 278, l. 256.

68. GARF, f. 9526, op. 6, d. 283, ll. 196, 199.

69. GARF, f. 9526, op. 6, d. 51, l. 331.

70. GARF, f. 9526, op. 6, d. 104, l. 52. On the problem of resettlement to Kyiv, see Tetiana Pastushenko, *Ostarbaitery z Kyivshchyny: Verbuvannia, prymusova pratsia, repatriatsiia (1942–1953)* (Kyiv: Instytut istorii Ukrainy, 2009), 183–84.

71. GARF, f. 9526, op. 6, d. 48, l. 18.

72. GARF, f. 9526, op. 6, d. 104, l. 45.

73. GARF, f. 9526, op. 6, d. 278, ll. 343–44.

74. HDASBU, f. 6, spr. 68043fp, ark. 21.

75. Zemskov, *Vozvrashchenie sovetskikh peremeshchennykh lits*, 126.

76. TsDAHO, f. 1, op. 70, spr. 313, ark. 52. On "speaking Bolshevik," see Stephen Kotkin, *Magnetic Mountain: Stalinism as a Civilization* (Berkeley: University of California Press, 1995), 198–237.

77. DAKO, f. p-5, op. 2, spr. 1202-a, ark. 10–14.

78. Bronislava A., ZA020, 9.

79. HDASBU, f. 16, op. 1, spr. 576, ark. 255.

80. E. D. Voroshilova, and S. M. Zorina, eds., *Propaganda i agitatsiia v resheniiakh i dokumentakh VKP(b)* (Moscow: Gosudarstvennoe izdatel'stvo politicheskoi literatury, 1947), 486–87.

81. GARF, f. 9526, op. 6, d. 112, l. 137.

82. Golfo Alexopoulos, "Stalin and the Politics of Kinship: Practices of Collective Punishment, 1920s–1940s," *Comparative Studies in Society and History* 50, no. 1 (2008): 91–117.

83. GARF, f. 9526, op. 6, d. 111, l. 121.

84. Antonina M., Memorial Ostarbeiter Archive, 35.

85. On the treatment of people who lived under occupation, see Exeler, *Ghosts of War*, especially 133–40.

86. GARF, f. 9526, op. 6, d. 48, l. 17; d. 104, l. 51.

87. Mikhail B., ZA285, 13.

88. Lewis Siegelbaum, "The 'Flood' of 1945: Regimes and Repertoires of Migration in the Soviet Union at War's End," *Social History* 42, no. 1 (2017): 52–72, argues that postwar migrants used social networks to mitigate their disadvantageous position.

89. Raisa B., ZA031, 43–46.

90. Ol'ga G., Memorial Ostarbeiter Archive, Moscow, June 20, 2005, 16–18.

91. GARF, f. 9526, op. 6, d. 618, l. 22.

92. Liudmila G., ZA349, 20–22.

93. Andryi B., ZA467, 13–15, 48.

94. Nikolai G., ZA293, 16–17, 62–63.

95. Petr A., ZA017, 24.

96. Oleksandr I., ZA478, 60.

97. GARF, f. 9526. op. 6, d. 410, l. 161; d. 527, l. 96.

98. HDASBU, f. 16, spr. 541, ark. 115.

99. Zinaida B., ZA465, 45–47.

100. Antonina V., ZA340, 63–64.

101. Mikhaleva, *Gde vy, moi rodnye*, 465–67.

102. Antonina S., ZA311, 54–56.

103. Galina G., ZA474, 76–79.

104. Peter Gatrell, *A Whole Empire Walking: Refugees in Russia during World War I* (Oxford: Oxford University Press, 1999).

6. REPATRIATION AND THE ECONOMICS OF COERCED LABOR

1. Mark Harrison, "The Second World War," in *Economic Transformation of the Soviet Union, 1913–1945*, ed. R. W. Davies, M. Harrison, and S. G. Wheatcroft (Cambridge: Cambridge University Press, 2012), 265; Michael Haynes, "Counting Soviet Deaths in the Great Patriotic War: A Note," *Europe-Asia Studies* 55, no. 2 (2003): 303–9; Mark Harrison, "Counting Soviet Deaths in the Great Patriotic War: Comment," *Europe-Asia Studies* 55, no. 6 (2003): 939–44.

2. On restrictions on labor mobility in the postwar period, see Donald Filtzer, *Soviet Workers and Late Stalinism: Labour and the Restoration of the Stalinist System after World War II* (Cambridge: Cambridge University Press, 2009), 25–29.

3. James Harris, *The Great Urals: Regionalism and the Evolution of the Soviet System* (Ithaca, NY: Cornell University Press, 1999), 105–22; Lynne Viola, *Unknown Gulag: The Lost World of Stalin's Special Settlements* (Oxford: Oxford University Press, 2007).

4. Alan Barenberg, *Gulag Town, Company Town: Forced Labor and Its Legacy in Vorkuta* (New Haven, CT: Yale University Press, 2014).

5. Wendy Goldman and Donald Filtzer, *Fortress Dark and Stern: The Soviet Home Front during World War II* (Oxford: Oxford University Press, 2021), 190–94.

6. Mark Edele, *Soviet Veterans of the Second World War: A Popular Movement in an Authoritarian Society, 1941–1991* (Oxford: Oxford University Press, 2008), 102.

7. A. I. Barsukov, P. N. Bobylev, L. V. Dvoinykh, P. N. Dmitriev, Iu. N. Ivanova, Iu. N. Kupechatov, K. K. Mironova, and V. M. Mikhaleva, eds., *Russkii arkhiv: Velikaia Otechestvennaia: Prikazy narodnogo komissara oborony SSSR*, vol. 13, pt. 2 (Moscow: Terra, 1997), 58–60.

8. Artem Latyshev, "Sistema proverki voennosluzhashchikh Krasnoi armii, vernuvshikhsia iz plena i okruzheniia. 1941–1945 gg." (candidate [PhD] diss., Moscow State University, 2017), 76.

9. GAUMO, f. 4611, op. 6, d. 5, l. 27.

10. GAUMO, f. 4611, op. 6, d. 12, ll. 26–26ob., 27ob.

11. GAUMO, f. 4611, op. 7, d. 7, ll. 7, 8, 20. On the connections between Gulag prisoners and civilians, see Barenberg, *Gulag Town, Company Town*, 113–17; Wilson Bell, "Was the Gulag an Archipelago? De-convoyed Prisoners and Porous Borders in the Camps of Western Siberia," *Russian Review* 72, no. 1 (2013): 116–41.

12. GAUMO, f. 4611, op. 7, d. 16, ll. 28, 100, 101ob., 102; Latyshev, "Sistema proverki voennosluzhashchikh Krasnoi armii," 144.

13. Golfo Alexopoulos, *Illness and Inhumanity in Stalin's Gulag* (New Haven, CT: Yale University Press, 2017), 147.

14. Viktor Zemskov, *Vozvrashchenie sovetskikh peremeshchennykh lits v SSSR. 1944–1952 gg.* (Moscow: Institut rossiiskoi istorii, 2016), 314–16.

15. Zemskov, *Vozvrashchenie sovetskikh peremeshchennykh lits*, 364–66.

16. GARF, f. 9479, op. 1, d. 372, l. 110.

17. Mark Elliott, *Pawns of Yalta: Soviet Refugees and America's Role in Their Repatriation* (Champaign: University of Illinois Press, 1982), 87–90.

18. GARF, f. 9479, op. 1, d. 328, l. 299.

19. GARF, f. 9479, op. 1, d. 372, l. 160.

20. GARF, f. 9479, op. 1, d. 372, ll. 148–49.

21. GARF, f. 9526, op. 6, d. 117, ll. 11–13, 23–25.

22. Vitalii Belikov, "Na dvukh arkhipelagakh," in *Skvoz' dve voiny, skvoz' dva arkhipelaga: Vospominaniia sovetskikh voennoplennikh i ostovtsev*, ed. P. M Polian and N. L. Pobol' (Moscow: ROSSPEN, 2007), 301–2.

23. Zemskov, *Vozvrashchenie sovetskikh peremeshchennykh lits*, 30–31.

24. GARF, f. 9526, op. 6, d. 351, l. 47.

25. For a full text of the resolution, see Zemskov, *Vozvrashchenie sovetskikh peremeshchennykh lits*, 235–38.

26. GARF, f. 9526, op. 6, d. 239, l. 292.

27. HDASBU, f. 16, spr. 568, ark. 19–20.

28. Filtzer, *Soviet Workers and Late Stalinism*, 24.

29. Zemskov, *Vozvrashchenie sovetskikh peremeshchennykh lits*, 267.

30. HDASBU, f. 16, spr. 568, ark. 27, 71.

31. GARF, f. 9526, op. 6, d. 281, l. 176.

32. GARF, f. 9526, op. 6, d. 281, l. 14.

33. GARF, f. 9526, op. 6, d. 281, ll. 37–40, 99–100.

34. GARF, f. 9526, op. 6, d. 281, ll. 119–20, 164–69, 172–76.

35. GARF, f. 9526, op. 6, d. 414, l. 91.

36. Zemskov, *Vozvrashchenie sovetskikh peremeshchennykh lits*, 262–63, 268.

37. GARF, f. 9526, op. 6, d. 417, ll. 219–20.

38. See, for example, Oleg Khlevniuk, "The Pavlenko Construction Enterprise: Large-Scale Private Entrepreneurialism in Stalin's USSR," *Europe-Asia Studies* 71, no. 6 (2019): 892–906.

39. GARF, f. 9526, op. 6, d. 617, ll. 110–12, 115.

40. Filtzer, *Soviet Workers and Late Stalinism*, 159–64, 166.

41. GARF, f. 9526, op. 6, d. 412, ll. 77, 78.

42. Iosif A., ZA283, 20–21, 112.

43. HDASBU, f. 16, spr. 640, ark. 58–59. For a similar case, see spr. 609, ark. 211–14.

44. Kiril Feferman, "Soviet Investigation of Nazi Crimes in the USSR: Documenting the Holocaust," *Journal of Genocide Research* 5, no. 4 (2003): 587–602.

45. AUSBU ZO, spr. s-1746, t. 4, ark. 184.

46. Oleksandr I., ZA478, 51–56.

47. GARF, f. 9526, op. 6, d. 414, l. 92.

48. GARF, f. 9526, op. 6, d. 411, ll. 88–89.

49. GARF, f. 9526, op. 6, d. 528, l. 47.

50. Norman Naimark, *The Russians in Germany: A History of the Soviet Zone of Occupation, 1945–1949* (Cambridge, MA: Harvard University Press, 1995), 169.

51. GARF, f. 9526, op. 6, d. 107, l. 128.

52. GARF, f. 9526, op. 6, d. 118, l. 166.

53. On local provisioning during wartime, see Brandon Schechter, *The Stuff of Soldiers: A History of the Red Army in World War II through Objects* (Ithaca, NY: Cornell University Press, 2019), 83–84.

54. GARF, f. 9526, op. 6, d. 99, ll. 160–61, 177–78.

55. GARF, f. 9526, op. 6, d. 276, l. 114.

56. GARF, f. 9526, op. 6, d. 275, ll. 13–14.

57. GARF, f. 9526, op. 6, d. 276, l. 48.

58. GARF, f. 7317, op. 20, d. 42, ll. 2, 4.

59. GARF, f. 9526, op. 6, d. 275, l. 41.

60. GARF, f. 9526, op. 6, d. 283, l. 279.

61. GARF, f. 9526, op. 6, d. 275, ll. 63–64.

62. GARF, f. 9526, op. 6, d. 118, ll. 167–68.

63. GARF, f. 9526, op. 6, d. 48, l. 59.

64. GARF, f. 9526, op. 6, d. 281, ll. 149–50.

65. GARF, f. 9526, op. 6, d. 281, l. 203.

66. GARF, f. 9526, op. 6, d. 281, l. 110.

67. GARF, f. 9526, op. 6, d. 118, ll. 156–57.

68. GARF, f. 9526, op. 6, d. 280, l. 390.

69. GARF, f. 9526, op. 6, d. 277, ll. 131–37.

70. GARF, f. 9526, op. 6, d. 280, l. 391.

71. GARF, f. 9526, op. 6, d. 277, ll. 131–37.

72. Michael Ellman, "The 1947 Soviet Famine and the Entitlement Approach to Famines," *Cambridge Journal of Economics* 24, no. 5 (2000): 611–12.

73. HDASBU, f. 16, spr. 578, ark. 40.

74. HDASBU, f. 16, spr. 578, ark. 19.

75. GARF, f. 9526, op. 6, d. 236, l. 175.

76. GARF, f. 9526, op. 6, d. 277, ll. 11–14.

77. GARF, f. 9526, op. 6, d. 283, l. 276.

78. Johannes-Dieter Steinert, "British Post-war Migration Policy and Displaced Persons in Europe," in *The Disentanglement of Populations: Migration, Expulsion and Displacement in Post-war Europe, 1944–49*, ed. Jessica Reinisch and Elizabeth White (Basingstoke: Palgrave, 2011), 229–47.

79. Pavel Polian, *Zhertvy dvukh diktatur: Zhizn', trud, unizheniia i smert' sovetskikh voennoplennykh i ostarbaiterov na chuzhbine i na rodine* (Moscow: ROSSPEN, 2002), 334.

80. Tara Zahra, *The Great Departure: Mass Migration from Eastern Europe and the Making of the Free World* (New York: Norton, 2016), 193; Silvia Salvatici, "From Displaced Persons to Labourers: Allied Employment Policies in Post-war West Germany," in *The Disentanglement of Populations: Migration, Expulsion and Displacement in Post-war Europe, 1944–49*, ed. Jessica Reinisch and Elizabeth White (Basingstoke: Palgrave, 2011), 210–28.

7. A RETURN TO POLICING

1. David Shearer, *Policing Stalin's Socialism: Repression and Social Order in the Soviet Union, 1924–1953* (New Haven, CT: Yale University Press, 2009), 14; Oleg Budnitskii, "The Great Terror of 1941: Toward a History of Wartime Stalinist Criminal Justice," *Kritika* 20, no. 3 (2019): 447–80.

2. An exception is members of German formations that redefected to Soviet partisans and received lesser sentences based on these mitigating circumstances. See Franziska Exeler, *Ghosts of War: Nazi Occupation and Its Aftermath in Soviet Belarus* (Ithaca, NY: Cornell University Press, 2022), 165–66.

3. For an account that focuses on the arbitrary nature of collaborator investigations, see Vanessa Voisin, *L'URSS contre ses traîtres: L'épuration soviétique: 1941–1955* (Paris: Publications de la Sorbonne, 2015).

4. On France, see Megan Koreman, *The Expectation of Justice: France 1944–1946* (Durham, NC: Duke University Press, 1999), 92–147; Henry Rousso, *The Vichy Syndrome: History and Memory in France since 1944* (Cambridge, MA: Harvard University Press, 1994). On Germany, see Jeffrey Herf, *Divided Memory: The Nazi Past in the Two Germanys* (Cambridge, MA: Harvard University Press, 1997); Robert Moeller, *War Stories: The Search for a Usable Past in the Federal Republic of Germany* (Berkeley: University of California Press, 2003). On Yugoslavia and the Baltic states, see Jelena Subotić, *Yellow Star, Red Star: Holocaust Remembrance after Communism* (Ithaca, NY: Cornell University Press, 2019).

5. Johannes Due Enstad, *Soviet Russians under Nazi Occupation: Fragile Loyalties in World War II* (Cambridge: Cambridge University Press, 2018), 214; Exeler, *Ghosts of War*, 185–86.

6. HDASBU, f. 16, spr. 539, ark. 155–63, 251–56.

7. The most numerous examples of Soviet leniency involved pro-German auxiliaries who defected in the thousands to partisans. See A. N. Artizov and V. S. Khristoforov, eds., *General Vlasov: Istoriia predatel'stva* (Moscow: ROSSPEN, 2015), 1:318–21, 450–52.

8. HDASBU, f. 16, spr. 560, ark. 26–27.

9. Irina Makhalova, "Heroes or Perpetrators? How Soviet Collaborators Received Red Army Medals," *Journal of Slavic Military Studies* 32, no. 2 (2019): 280–88.

10. HDASBU, f. 9, spr. 17-sp, ark. 322; spr. 223-sp, ark. 194–95.

11. Angelika Benz, *Handlanger der SS: Die Rolle der Trawniki-Männer im Holocaust* (Berlin: Metropol, 2014); Peter Black, "Foot Soldiers of the Final Solution: The Trawniki Training Camp and Operation Reinhard," *Holocaust and Genocide Studies* 25, no. 1 (2011): 1–99.

12. Aron Shneer, *Professiia—Smert': Uchebnyi lager' SS "Travniki": Prestupleniia i vozmezdie* (Moscow: Piatii Rim, 2019), 11.

13. Lawrence Douglas, *Right Wrong Man: John Demjanjuk and the Last Great Nazi War Crimes Trial* (Princeton, NJ: Princeton University Press, 2016), 52–53; Benz, *Handlanger der SS*, 258–71.

14. On the passport system, see David Shearer, "Elements Near and Alien: Passportization, Policing, and Identity in the Stalinist State, 1932–1952," *Journal of Modern History* 76, no. 4 (2004): 835–81.

15. In many cases, authorities transferred these files to local archives. Access varies by province. A large collection of filtration files from the State Archive of Kyiv Province has been digitized and is available on microfilm in various repositories (for example, at the United States Holocaust Memorial Museum) in World War II Documents, pt. 3, The Long Road Home: Documents of Ukrainian Forced Labor Workers Detained in Soviet Filtration Camps in Germany from the State Archive of Kiev Oblast.

16. Nick Baron, "Remaking Soviet Society: The Filtration of Returnees from Nazi Germany, 1944–49," in *Warlands: Population Resettlement and State Reconstruction in the Soviet-East European Borderlands, 1945–50*, ed. Nick Baron and Peter Gatrell (Basingstoke: Palgrave, 2009), 109.

17. On autobiographical practices, see Sheila Fitzpatrick, *Tear Off the Masks! Identity and Imposture in Twentieth-Century Russia* (Princeton, NJ: Princeton University Press, 2005).

18. HDASBU, f. 16, spr. 608, ark. 1–2; spr. 642, ark. 1–2. Available records do not provide a complete accounting of the number of investigations. Data from 1948 include only Ukrainian secret police (MGB) investigations. To that point, MGB officers in the republic had made 9,291 arrests. The final available report with criminal police (MVD) data is from June 1947. In this report, MVD officers were recorded as arresting 4,582 returnees. Data from previous months' reports suggest that MVD arrests in the months between June 1947 and February 1948 might have numbered as many as an additional 500. Under this assumption, arrests of returnees in Ukraine totaled some 14,000 in February 1948. The number of returnees registered in Ukraine in February 1948 was 1,212,237.

19. HDASBU, f. 9, spr. 240-sp, ark. 43.

20. Tanja Penter, "Local Collaborators on Trial: Soviet War Crimes Trials under Stalin (1943–1953)," *Cahiers du Monde russe* 49, no. 2/3 (2008): 342.

21. Alfred Rieber, "Civil Wars in the Soviet Union," *Kritika* 4, no. 1 (2003): 129–62.

22. Alexander Statiev, *The Soviet Counterinsurgency in the Western Borderlands* (Cambridge: Cambridge University Press, 2010), 96.

23. HDASBU, f. 16, spr. 568, ark. 58–59, 229.

24. On Lviv, see GARF, f. 9526, op. 6, d. 416, l. 2. On Ukraine, see HDASBU, f. 16, spr. 608, ark. 1–2; GARF, f. 9526, op. 6, d. 278, l. 342.

25. Koreman, *Expectation of Justice*, 85.

26. Mark Elliot, *Pawns of Yalta: Soviet Refugees and America's Role in Their Repatriation* (Champaign: University of Illinois Press, 1982), 193; Nikolai Tolstoy, *Victims of Yalta: The Secret Betrayal of the Allies: 1944–1947* (1977; New York: Pegasus, 2013), 409.

27. HDASBU, f. 16, spr. 642, ark. 1–2; spr. 608, ark. 1–2.

28. GARF, f. 9526, op. 6, d. 278, ll. 201–2.

29. HDASBU, f. 16, spr. 608, ark. 1–2.

30. GARF, f. 9526, op. 6, d. 527, l. 84.

31. Long Road Home, reel 172, d. 113071.

32. HDASBU, f. 16, spr. 578, ark. 72.

33. HDASBU, f. 1, spr. 52, ark. 34, 218; spr. 39, ark. 30.

34. HDASBU, f. 1, spr. 52, ark. 35.

35. For information on other informants, see HDASBU, f. 1, spr. 52, ark. 137, 176; f. 16, spr. 569, ark. 157. For a report on a case based on these materials, see HDASBU, f. 1, spr. 52, ark. 117–19.

36. Mariia S., ZA347, 41–44.

37. HDASBU, f. 1, spr. 52, ark. 6–9; spr. 39, ark. 94.

38. HDASBU, f. 1, spr. 39, ark. 12–13.

39. HDASBU, f. 16, spr. 611, ark. 115–23.

40. USHMM RG-31.018M reel 21, images 2596–625. On postwar denunciations, see Exeler, Ghosts of War, 188–94.

41. Aleksandr Kashia, the head of the Wustrau propaganda camp's Georgian barracks, attracted enough attention that the second volume of his arrest file included some thirty accusations from other cases. See USHMM RG-38.001, d. 46256, folder 2.

42. HDASBU, f. 16, spr. 652, ark. 146–47.

43. See, for example, Alexander Vatlin, Agents of Terror: Ordinary Men and Extraordinary Violence in Stalin's Secret Police (Madison: University of Wisconsin Press, 2016), 99, 109.

44. E. A. Zaitsev, ed., Sbornik zakonodatel'nykh i normativnykh aktov o repressiiakh i reabilitatsii zhertv politicheskikh repressii (Moscow: Respublika, 1993), 43–45.

45. For a detailed discussion of the distinctions introduced by the decree of April 1943 and the continuation of arbitrary judgment, see Voisin, L'URSS contre ses traîtres, especially 247. On these trials, see also Seth Bernstein and Irina Makhalova, "Aggregate Treason: A Quantitative Analysis of Collaborator Trials in Soviet Ukraine and Crimea," Soviet and Post-Soviet Review 46, no. 1 (2019): 36; Exeler, Ghosts of War, 144–52.

46. Seth Bernstein, Raised under Stalin: Young Communists and the Defense of Socialism (Ithaca, NY: Cornell University Press, 2017), 218.

47. V. P. Iampol'skii, V. S. Antonov, I. K. Belik, V. K. Vinogradov, N. M. Emel'ianova, S. S. Konokotov, V. I. Kochanov, V. D. Krivets, O. B. Mozokhin, E. V. Shumilova, eds., Organy gosudarstvennoi bezopasnosti SSSR v Velikoi Otechestvennoi voine, vol. 4, no. 1 (Moscow: Rus', 2008), 104.

48. USHMM RG-38.001, d. 46256, folder 1, l. 178.

49. USHMM RG-38.001, d. 46256, folder 1, ll. 133–35. For other Wustrau cases available in the Georgian police archive, see USHMM RG-38.001, d. 4839, 4865, 4873, 4929, 46118, 46206, 46261, 46262, 46263, 46270, 46273, 46275, 46278, 46293, 46294, 46296, 46301, 46306, 46312, 48177.

50. USHMM RG-38.001, d. 46256, folder 1, ll. 614, 659.

51. AUSBU ChO, spr. 1009, ark. 197–98.

52. USHMM RG-38.001, d. 46256, folder 1, ll. 156–57, 197, 228; AUSBU ChO, spr. 1009, ark. 251–53.

53. USHMM RG-38.001, d. 46256, folder 2, l. 126.

54. USHMM RG-38.001, d. 46256, folder 1, ll. 192ob.–193, 198–219.

55. USHMM RG-38.001, d. 46256, folder 1, l. 185.

56. USHMM RG-38.001, d. 46256, folder 1, ll. 209ob., 213ob., 218ob.

57. HDASBU, f. 6, spr. 71132fp, ark. 19, 38–39, 41, 44–46.

58. HDASBU, f. 6, spr. 71132fp, ark. 77.

59. HDASBU, f. 6, spr. 38840fp, ark. 11, 20, 28, 55–56, 79, 129.

60. HDASBU, f. 6, spr. 38840fp, ark. 141–42.

61. HDASBU, f. 6, spr. 38840fp, ark. 158.

62. In other collaboration cases, appeals to extenuating circumstances had some impact on sentencing, although not on conviction. Diana Dumitru, "The Gordian Knot of Justice: Prosecuting Jewish Holocaust Survivors in Stalinist Courts for 'Collaboration' with the Enemy," *Kritika* 22, no. 4 (2021): 729–56; Exeler, *Ghosts of War*, 160–66.

63. HDASBU, f. 16, spr. 568, ark. 58–59.

64. Oleg Khlevniuk, *Stalin: New Biography of a Dictator* (New Haven, CT: Yale University Press, 2015), 267.

65. Khlevniuk, *Stalin*, 265.

66. "O zhurnalakh 'Zvezda' i 'Leningrad,'" *Pravda*, August 21, 1946.

67. For a documentary history of the trial of the Jewish Anti-Fascist Committee, see Joshua Rubenstein and Vladimir Naumov, *Stalin's Secret Pogrom: The Postwar Inquisition of the Jewish Anti-Fascist Committee* (New Haven, CT: Yale University Press, 2001). Gennadii Kostyrchenko, *Tainaia politika Stalina*, vol. 2, *Na fone kholodnoi voiny* (Moscow: Mezhdunarodnye otnosheniia, 2015), is a current account of the postwar anti-Jewish campaign in Russian.

68. Jeffrey Burds, "The Early Cold War in Soviet West Ukraine, 1944–1948," no. 1505, in *The Carl Beck Papers in Russian and East European Studies* (Pittsburgh: University of Pittsburgh Press, 2001), 11–18; Richard Breitman and Norman Goda, *Hitler's Shadow: Nazi War Criminals, U.S. Intelligence, and the Cold War* (Washington, DC: National Archives, 2010), 73–97.

69. Benjamin Tromly, *Cold War Exiles and the CIA: Plotting to Free Russia* (Oxford: Oxford University Press, 2019).

70. Vatlin, *Agents of Terror*, 40–41.

71. HDASBU, f. 16, spr. 576, ark. 270–72.

72. HDASBU, f. 16, spr. 642, ark. 1–2.

73. On opposition to the collective farm system, see Elena Zubkova, *Russia after the War: Hopes, Illusions and Disappointments, 1945–1957* (New York: M. E. Sharpe, 1998), 59–67.

74. For a sampling of these cases, see their summaries here; HDASBU, f. 16, spr. 576, ark. 107, 108, 279, 282; spr. 577, ark. 16–17, 100–103, 107, 320–23; spr. 578, ark. 67–68; spr. 580, ark. 304–5; spr. 611, ark. 113–16; spr. 655, ark. 48–50; spr. 663, ark. 163–66; spr. 666, ark. 67–70; f. 1, spr. 52, ark. 202.

75. HDASBU, f. 16, spr. 642, ark. 1–2.

76. HDASBU, f. 16, spr. 663, ark. 11–14.

77. HDASBU, f. 6, spr. 5295fp, ark. 24–26.

78. HDASBU, f. 6, spr. 37516fp, ark. 298.

79. HDASBU, f. 6, spr. 5295fp, ark. 58, 60, 84–90, 276ob., 278ob.

80. HDASBU, f. 6, spr. 5295fp, ark. 269–70, 279ob., 285.

81. HDASBU, f. 6, spr. 5295fp, ark. 87.

82. On prophylactic policing methods in the Khrushchev period, see Edward Cohn, "Coercion, Reeducation, and the Prophylactic Chat: *Profilaktika* and the KGB's Struggle with Political Unrest in Lithuania, 1953–64," *Russian Review* 76, no. 2 (2017): 272–93.

83. HDASBU, f. 6, spr. 37516fp, ark. 14–15, 87–88ob., 278ob.

84. For a sampling of summary reports involving returnees who claimed to help the Allies find and punish war criminals, see HDASBU, f. 16, spr. 568, ark. 67, 68; spr. 569, ark. 152, 153; spr. 576, ark. 276, 286, 287; spr. 577, ark. 107–8; spr. 579, ark. 60–61; spr. 580, ark. 26; spr. 608, ark. 198–200; spr. 610, ark. 26; f. 1, spr. 39, ark. 81, 111; spr. 52, ark. 18.

85. A sampling of summary reports involving returnees who worked in DP camps can be found in HDASBU, f. 16, spr. 560, ark. 190, 191; spr. 568, ark. 66, 67; spr. 569, ark. 152; spr. 580, ark. 307; f. 1, spr. 39, ark. 15, 227, 228; spr. 52, ark. 220.

86. HDASBU, f. 9, spr. 240-sp, ark. 61ob.

87. HDASBU, f. 6, spr. 37516fp, ark. 239, 303.

88. HDASBU, f. 16, spr. 576, ark. 62.

89. HDASBU, f. 6, spr. 37243fp, ark. 15–25.

90. HDASBU, f. 6, spr. 37516fp, ark. 317, 346.

91. Shearer, *Policing Stalin's Socialism*, 180; Vatlin, *Agents of Terror*, 21–22.

92. On white-collar Gulag labor, see Golfo Alexopoulos, *Illness and Inhumanity in Stalin's Gulag* (New Haven, CT: Yale University Press, 2017), 50.

93. Petr Astakhov, *Zigzagi sud'by: Iz zhizni sovetskogo voennoplennogo i sovetsk-ogo zeka* (Moscow: ROSSPEN, 2005), 234, 273–74, appendix of photographs ("Spravka o reabilitatsii P. P. Astakhova [1982]").

94. This split reversal was true in the case of Aleksandr Kovalenko, the pro-German police officer accused of being a spy; HDASBU, f. 6, spr. 37243fp, ark. 250–51.

8. UNHEROIC RETURNS

1. HDASBU, f. 1, spr. 692, ark. 291.

2. Frederick Corney, *Telling October: Memory and the Making of the Bolshevik Revolution* (Ithaca, NY: Cornell University Press, 2004); Jochen Hellbeck, *Revolution on My Mind: Writing a Diary under Stalin* (Cambridge, MA: Harvard University Press, 2006), 43–46; Elaine MacKinnon, "Writing History for Stalin: Isaak Izrailevich Mints and the *Istoriia grazhdanskoi voiny*," *Kritika* 6, no. 1 (2005): 5–54; Sergei Zhuravlev, *Fenomen "Istorii fabrik i zavodov": Gor'kovskoe nachinanie v kontekste epokhi 1930-kh godov* (Moscow: Institut rossiiskoi istorii, 1997).

3. See Sheila Fitzpatrick, *Tear Off the Masks! Identity and Imposture in Twentieth-Century Russia* (Princeton, NJ: Princeton University Press, 2005), 91–101.

4. HDASBU, f. 1, spr. 52, ark. 267–78.

5. See, for example, Oleksandr Melnyk, "Rezidentura 'Maksim': Soviet Intelligence Operations in the Nazi Occupied Kyiv. History and Memory" (unpublished manuscript, July 26, 2020), 36–43.

6. "Otechestvennaia voina," *Pravda*, June 23, 1941. On the use of the Napoleonic Wars in Soviet propaganda, see Oleg Budnitskii, "Izobretaia Otechestvo: Istoriia voiny s Napoleonom v sovetskoi propagande 1941–1945 godov," *Rossiiskaia istoriia*, no. 6 (2012): 157–69; Karel Berkhoff, *Motherland in Danger: Soviet Propaganda during World War II* (Cambridge, MA: Harvard University Press, 2012), 11.

7. Oleg Budnitskii, "A Harvard Project in Reverse: Materials of the Commission of the USSR Academy of Sciences on the History of the Great Patriotic War," *Kritika* 19, no. 1 (2018): 176.

8. NA IRI RAN, f. 2, r. 6, op. 22, d. 28, ll. 2–3; HDASBU, f. 1, spr. 739, ark. 40, 111–17.

9. On German POWs in Soviet captivity, see Mark Edele, "Take (No) Prisoners! The Red Army and German POWs, 1941–1943," *Journal of Modern History* 88, no. 2 (2016): 342–79.

10. Efim Brodskii, *Eto izvestno nemnogim: Vospominaniia politrabotnika RKKA* (Krasnogorsk: Memorial'nyi muzei nemetskikh antifashistov, 1996), 15, 39–44, 136–37.

11. Efim Brodskii, *Zabveniiu ne podlezhit* (Moscow: Mysl', 1993), 25.

12. Efim Brodskii, "Iz arkhivov Miunkhenskogo Gestapo," *Novyi Mir*, no. 6 (1964): 258–76.

13. Brodskii, *Zabveniiu ne podlezhit*, 35.

14. Brodskii, *Zabveniiu ne podlezhit*, 27.

15. Brodskii, *Zabveniiu ne podlezhit*, 28–29.

16. GARF, f. 9526, op. 6, d. 844, l. 56.

17. Efim Brodskii, *Oni ne propali bez vesti: Ne slomlennye fashistskoi nevolei* (Moscow: Mysl', 1987), 108–9.

18. GARF, f. 9526, op. 6, d. 844, l. 55.

19. On Stalin's consolidation of power, see Oleg Khlevniuk, *Master of the House: Stalin and His Inner Circle* (New Haven, CT: Yale University Press, 2008). On decentralization during the war, see Oleg Khlevniuk, "Decentralizing Dictatorship: Soviet Local Governance during World War II," *Russian Review* 77, no. 3 (2018): 470–84; Kenneth Slepyan, *Stalin's Guerrillas: Soviet Partisans in World War II* (Lawrence: University Press of Kansas, 2006), 279–80.

20. Brodskii, *Zabveniiu ne podlezhit*, 29.

21. Brodskii, *Zabveniiu ne podlezhit*, 31.

22. Mark Edele, *Soviet Veterans of the Second World War: A Popular Movement in an Authoritarian Society, 1941–1991* (Oxford: Oxford University Press, 2008), 44–47, 133; Brandon Schechter, *The Stuff of Soldiers: A History of the Red Army in World War II through Objects* (Ithaca, NY: Cornell University Press, 2019), 65–72.

23. HDASBU, f. 1, spr. 739, ark. 13, 35–48.

24. NA IRI RAN, f. 2, r. 6, op. 22, d. 7, l. 22ob.

25. HDASBU, f. 1, spr. 739, ark. 9, 189–90.

26. "Explosion," *Mista Pameti Naroda*, accessed April 15, 2022, http://www.mistapametinaroda.cz/?lc=en&id=1120.

27. HDASBU, f. 1, spr. 739, ark. 81–82, 87–88.

28. HDASBU, f. 1, spr. 739, ark. 99.

29. Oleksandr Melnyk, "Historical Politics, Legitimacy Contests, and the (Re)construction of Political Communities in Ukraine during the Second World War" (PhD diss., University of Toronto, 2016), 194–200; Franziska Exeler, *Ghosts of War: Nazi Occupation and Its Aftermath in Soviet Belarus* (Ithaca, NY: Cornell University Press, 2022), 222–33.

30. Vladimir Solonari, *A Satellite Empire: Romanian Rule in Southwestern Ukraine, 1941–1944* (Ithaca, NY: Cornell University Press, 2019), 206–8.

31. Seth Bernstein, *Raised under Stalin: Young Communists and the Defense of Socialism* (Ithaca, NY: Cornell University Press, 2017), 216.

32. HDASBU, f. 1, spr. 739, ark. 7, 43, 44.

33. HDASBU, f. 1, spr. 739, 187–88; AUSBU ChO, spr. R-15980, ark. 400.

34. HDASBU, f. 1, spr. 739, ark. 202.

35. HDASBU, f. 1, spr. 739, ark. 43.

36. HDASBU, f. 1, spr. 739, ark. 110.

37. HDASBU, f. 1, spr. 739, ark. 148.

38. AUSBU ChO, spr. R-15980, ark. 3.

39. AUSBU ChO, spr. R-15980, ark. 398ob, 400ob.

40. GARF, f. 8131, op. 30, d. 67636, l. 7.

41. AUSBU MO, f. 5, spr. 8042, t. 1, ark. 85ob.–86.

42. AUSBU MO, f. 5, spr. 8042, t. 1, ark. 88; GARF, f. 9526, op. 6, d. 103, l. 143.

43. AUSBU MO, f. 5, spr. 8042, t. 1, ark. 84ob., 217; t. 2, ark. 37, 46–48.

44. AUSBU MO, f. 5, spr. 8042, t. 2, ark. 111–16, 201–2, 231, 278–79.

45. AUSBU MO, f. 5, spr. 8042, t. 1, ark. 28, 310; t. 2, ark. 289, 294, 297, 322.

46. AUSBU MO, f. 5, spr. 8042, t. 2, ark. 82ob., 94–95.

47. AUSBU MO, f. 5, spr. 8042, t. 2, ark. 104.

48. S. S. Makarchuk, *Reabilitirovani istorieiu: Mykolaivs'ka oblast'* (Kyiv: Svitohliad, 2010), 5:138.

49. AUSBU MO, f. 5, spr. 8042, t. 2, ark. 8, 69–70.

50. AUSBU MO, f. 5, spr. 8042, t. 2, ark. 122.

51. AUSBU MO, f. 5, spr. 8042, t. 2, envelope 2, unnumbered letter from Surov-Kurov-Kin to Kiselev, March 6, 1946.

52. AUSBU MO, f. 5, spr. 8042, t. 2, ark. 145–48.

53. Golfo Alexopoulos, "Portrait of a Con Artist as a Soviet Man," *Slavic Review*, 57, no. 4 (1998): 774–90; Sheila Fitzpatrick, "The World of Ostap Bender: Soviet Confidence Men in the Stalin Period," *Slavic Review* 61, no. 3 (2002): 535–37; David Shearer, *Policing Stalin's Socialism: Repression and Social Order in the Soviet Union, 1924–1953* (New Haven, CT: Yale University Press, 2009), 371–404.

54. AUSBU MO, f. 5, spr. 8042, t. 2, ark. 115.

55. AUSBU MO, f. 5, spr. 8042, t. 1, ark. 41.

56. AUSBU MO, f. 5, spr. 8042, t. 2, ark. 35–37.

57. AUSBU MO, f. 5, spr. 8042, t. 2, ark. 294.

58. AUSBU MO, f. 5, spr. 8042, t. 2, ark. 322.

59. GARF, f. 8131, op. 31, d. 67636, l. 7.

60. AUSBU MO, f. 5, spr. 8042, t. 2, ark. 322–23, 329–31, 335–36, 349ob., 352.

61. AUSBU MO, f. 5, spr. 8042, t. 2., ark. 355, 361–62.

62. AUSBU ChO, spr. 15980, ark. 416, 421, 427, 451, 456, 460.

63. AUSBU ChO, spr. 15980, ark. 455.

64. HDASBU, f. 1, spr. 692, ark. 16, 35–39, 56ob.; spr. 694, ark. 32, 47–48, 66–67, 261ob.

65. HDASBU, f. 1, spr. 696, ark. 101.

66. USHMM RG-38.001, d. 46185, folder 1, l. 92.

67. HDASBU, f. 1, spr. 692, ark. 72–73, 75–76, 77–79.

68. HDASBU, f. 1, spr. 692, ark. 45–51, 52–57, 58–62, 97–98.

69. HDASBU, f. 1, spr. 694, ark. 42–43.

70. HDASBU, f. 1, spr. 694, ark. 40.

71. HDASBU, f. 1, spr. 692, ark. 142–43.

72. HDASBU, f. 1, spr. 694, ark. 219.

73. HDASBU, f. 1, spr. 692, ark. 114, 126, 127–29.

74. HDASBU, f. 1, spr. 693.

75. HDASBU, f. 1, spr. 692, ark. 135–36, 156–57.

76. HDASBU, f. 1, spr. 694, ark. 54–57, 261–62.

77. HDASBU, f. 1, spr. 694, ark. 55, 160, 261.

78. HDASBU, f. 1, spr. 694, ark. 170–72.

79. HDASBU, f. 1, spr. 696, ark. 80, 115–17.

80. HDASBU, f. 1, spr. 694, ark. 291–92.

81. HDASBU, f. 1, spr. 696, ark. 184–87.

82. HDASBU, f. 1, spr. 694, ark. 227.

83. Aleksandr Pecherskii, *Vosstanie v Sobiburovskom lagere* (Rostov-na-Donu: Rostizdat, 1945). On his return to the USSR, see the foreword to Nikolai Svanidze and Il'ia Vasil'ev, *Sobibor: Vozvrashchenie podviga Aleksandra Pecherskogo* (Moscow: Eksmo, 2018), 5.

84. Nataliia Bespalova, "Pamiatnik Deviataevu," *Rossiiskaia gazeta*, December 16, 2003, https://rg.ru/2003/12/16/devyataev.html.

85. Efim Brodskii, "Osvoboditel'naia bor'ba sovetskikh liudei v fashistskoi Germanii (1943–1945 gody)," *Voprosy istorii*, no. 3 (1957): 85–99; Brodskii, "Imeni Rumiantseva," *Novyi mir*, no. 10 (1961): 303–7; Brodskii, "Iz arkhivov Miunkhenskogo Gestapo."

86. See, for example, customer reviews of Mary Louise Roberts, *What Soldiers Do: Sex and the American GI in World War II France* (Chicago: University of Chicago Press, 2013);

GI Joe, "I Was There," *Amazon*, June 16, 2013, https://www.amazon.com/gp/customer
-reviews/RRVO46XH0Z7HR/. On mythmaking after war in general, see Alexander
Statiev, "'La Garde meurt mais ne se rend pas!': Once Again on the 28 Panfilov Heroes,"
Kritika 13, no. 4 (2012): 796.

87. Henry Rousso, *The Vichy Syndrome: History and Memory in France since 1944*
(Cambridge, MA: Harvard University Press, 1994), 37–38, 52–53, 59.

9. WAYWARD CHILDREN OF THE MOTHERLAND

1. Anna Holian, *Between National Socialism and Soviet Communism: Displaced Persons in Postwar Germany* (Ann Arbor: University of Michigan Press, 2011), 134–49.

2. On displaced children as an object of early Cold War politics, see Tara Zahra, *The Lost Children: Reconstructing Europe's Families after World War II* (Cambridge, MA: Harvard University Press, 2011), especially 198–221.

3. January 8, 1946, Report of 4 December 1945, Subversive Activities of USSR Officers, Intelligence and Investigative Dossiers Impersonal Files (IIDIF), Records of the Army Staff, RG 319, NACP.

4. Viktor Zemskov, *Vozvrashchenie sovetskikh peremeshchennykh lits v SSSR. 1944–1952 gg.* (Moscow: Institut rossiiskoi istorii, 2016), 142–43.

5. Gerard Daniel Cohen, *In War's Wake: Europe's Displaced Persons in the Postwar Order* (Cambridge: Cambridge University Press, 2011), 35.

6. GARF, f. 9526, op. 6, d. 358, l. 16.

7. GARF, f. 9526, op. 6, d. 240, ll. 100–102.

8. GARF, f. 9526, op. 6, d. 96, l. 9.

9. GARF, f. 9526, op. 6, d. 239, l. 73.

10. Vladislav Zubok, *Failed Empire: The Soviet Union in the Cold War from Stalin to Gorbachev* (Chapel Hill: University of North Carolina Press, 2007), 49.

11. February 16, 1946, Subversive activities of USSR officers, Subversive Activities of USSR Officers, IIDIF, RG 319, NACP.

12. GARF, f. 9526, op. 6, d. 252, l. 180; Zemskov, *Vozvrashchenie sovetskikh peremeshchennykh lits*, 124.

13. GARF, f. 9526, op. 6, d. 246, l. 82.

14. GARF, f. 9526, op. 6, d. 244, l. 301.

15. GARF, f. 9526, op. 6, d. 245, ll. 255, 256–57.

16. GARF, f. 9526, op. 6, d. 247, l. 52.

17. Holian, *Between National Socialism and Soviet Communism*, 82.

18. Cohen, *In War's Wake*, 21. All the American occupation internal policy directives I saw ruled out forced repatriation for people from the annexed Western territories. See, for example, December 1945, Joint Chiefs to McNarney and Clark (WX-89544), Repatriation or Resettlement of Soviet Citizens, Displaced Persons in Germany and Other Countries, 1945–1949 (DP), Records of US Occupation Headquarters, RG 260, NACP.

19. GARF, f. 9526, op. 6, d. 248, ll. 31–33, 43–45, 46–51, 52, 55–56.

20. GARF, f. 9526, op. 6, d. 245, ll. 253–54.

21. The earliest report in the records of the US National Archives is from February 18, 1946, although the operation had clearly begun earlier. February 18, 1946, Progress Report on Operation Bingo, Operation Bingo, IIDIF, RG 319, NACP.

22. GARF, f. 9526, op. 6, d. 250, ll. 8–21.

23. GARF, f. 9526, op. 6, d. 251, l. 284.

24. "Refugees and Displaced Persons 62 (I)," United Nations High Commissioner for Refugees, December 15, 1946, https://www.unhcr.org/en-us/excom/bgares/3ae69ef14/refugees-displaced-persons.html; Cohen, *In War's Wake*, 26–28, quotations on 26.

25. EUCOM [United States European Command] signed Huebner to CINCEUR SX2139, August 16, 1947, Repatriation and Resettlement Missions, DP, POW DP, RG 260, NACP.

26. GARF, f. 9526, op. 6, d. 248, ll. 110, 245; d. 358, l. 5.

27. April 2, 1946, Spot Report, Operation Bingo, IIDIF, RG 319, NACP. For similar incidents of kidnapping in France, see Greg Burgess, "The Repatriation of Soviet Prisoners of War and Displaced Peoples from the Auvergne after the Second World War," *French History and Civilization* 7 (2017): 177.

28. Mark Clark, *Calculated Risk* (1950; New York: Enigma, 2007), 694.

29. GARF, f. 9526, op. 6, d. 252, l. 5.

30. GARF, f. 9526, op. 6, d. 252, ll. 3–5, 7–9, 10, 12, 14, 34, 49.

31. GARF, f. 9526, op. 6, d. 258, l. 98.

32. GARF, f. 9526, op. 6, d. 252, l. 275.

33. GARF, f. 9526, op. 6, d. 245, ll. 252–53.

34. GARF, f. 9526, op. 6, d. 252, l. 309. See Andrew Janco, "'Unwilling': The One-Word Revolution in Refugee Status, 1940–1951," *Contemporary European History* 23, no. 3 (2014): 438.

35. GARF, f. 9526, op. 6, d. 244, l. 387.

36. GARF, f. 9526, op. 6, d. 261, l. 42; d. 262, l. 186; d. 363, l. 22.

37. Terry Martin, *Affirmative Action Empire: Nations and Nationalism in the Soviet Union, 1923–1939* (Ithaca, NY: Cornell University Press, 2001).

38. David Brandenberger, *National Bolshevism: Stalinist Mass Culture and the Formation of Modern Russian National Identity, 1931–1956* (Cambridge, MA: Harvard University Press, 2002); Seth Bernstein, "Valedictorians of the Soviet School: Professionalization and the Impact of War in Soviet Chess," *Kritika* 13, no. 2 (2012): 412.

39. Krista Goff, *Nested Nationalism: Making and Unmaking Nations in the Soviet Caucasus* (Ithaca, NY: Cornell University Press, 2021).

40. GARF, f. 9526, op. 6, d. 242, l. 34.

41. GARF, f. 9526, op. 6, d. 262, ll. 132–33.

42. GARF, f. 9526, op. 6, d. 263, l. 238.

43. GARF, f. 9526, op. 6, d. 261, ll. 47–49.

44. GARF, f. 9526, op. 6, d. 262, l. 70.

45. GARF, f. 9526, op. 6, d. 261, l. 254.

46. GARF, f. 9526, op. 6, d. 261, ll. 50–52, 55, 65, 68–73.

47. GARF, f. 9526, op. 6, d. 261, ll. 217–19.

48. GARF, f. 9526, op. 6, d. 261, ll. 331–33.

49. USHMM RG-67.049M, reel 1, pt. 10. "Incident at Blomberg Camp," December 17, 1946.

50. GARF, f. 9526, op. 6, d. 261, l. 61.

51. GARF, f. 9526, op. 6, d. 363, l. 299.

52. See, for instance, GARF, f. 9526, op. 6, d. 258, ll. 101, 103.

53. GARF, f. 9526, op. 6, d. 358, l. 130.

54. FO 1032/1225, Soviet Repatriation Mission, "Colonel Brukhanov—Soviet Military Mission for Repatriation," April 19, 1947.

55. GARF, f. 9526, op. 6, d. 359, l. 132.

56. GARF, f. 9526, op. 6, d. 360, ll. 20–22.

57. FO 1052/424, Soviet Repatriation Mission, "Soviet Missions—Policy in the British Zone."

58. GARF, f. 9526, op. 6, d. 359, ll. 215–17, 258, 261; d. 360, ll. 106–7, 116, 128–30; d. 378, ll. 271–73.

59. GARF, f. 9526, op. 6, d. 363, ll. 246, 247, 250–51; Mark Wyman, *DPs: Europe's Displaced Persons, 1945–1951* (1989; Ithaca, NY: Cornell University Press, 1998), 186.

60. Harry Truman, "Special Message to the Congress on Admission of Displaced Persons," American Presidency Project, July 7, 1947, https://www.presidency.ucsb.edu/documents/special-message-the-congress-admission-displaced-persons. On resettlement as a way of reducing "surplus population," see Cohen, *In War's Wake*, 100–125.

61. Tara Zahra, *The Great Departure: Mass Migration from Eastern Europe and the Making of the Free World* (New York: Norton, 2016), 194–204.

62. GARF, f. 9526, op. 6, d. 358, l. 151; May 15, 1951, List of Male DP's from the USSR and Soviet Satellites Eligible for Induction into the Armed Services, Operation Aerodynamic Operations Volume 9, NACP.

63. On US intelligence and Russian émigrés, see Benjamin Tromly, *Cold War Exiles and the CIA: Plotting to Free Russia* (Oxford: Oxford University Press, 2019).

64. Zahra, *Lost Children*, esp. 118–46.

65. GARF, f. 9526, op. 6, d. 526, l. 194.

66. GARF, f. 9526, op. 6, d. 281, ll. 217–19; d. 280, ll. 178, 226.

67. GARF, f. 9526, op. 6, d. 365, l. 15.

68. GARF, f. 9526, op. 6, d. 263, ll. 261–63, 266.

69. FO 1006/523, Liaison Soviet, "Report on Visit to Children's Home, Haffkrug"; GARF, f. 9526, op. 6, d. 360, ll. 88–99.

70. GARF, f. 9526, op. 6, d. 360, l. 182.

71. GARF, f. 9526, op. 6, d. 1124, l. 11.

72. GARF, f. 9526, op. 6, d. 378, l. 61.

73. GARF, f. 9526, op. 6, d. 467, ll. 363, 394–95.

74. HDASBU, f. 16, spr. 652, ark. 67–68.

75. HDASBU, f. 16, spr. 641, ark. 47.

76. GARF, f. 9526, op. 6, d. 527, ll. 5–6.

77. GARF, f. 9526, op. 6, d. 1124, l. 156.

78. HDASBU, f. 1, spr. 373, ark. 23.

79. GARF, f. 9526, op. 6, d. 250, l. 46; d. 252, l. 162; d. 363, l. 288.

80. GARF, f. 9526, op. 6, d. 358, ll. 122, 123, 126.

81. GARF, f. 9526, op. 6, d. 360, l. 184. For a report on the use of repatriate informants by the military intelligence agency SMERSH, see a report forwarded to Soviet leaders in V. N. Khaustov, V. P. Naumov, and N. S. Plotnikova, eds., *Lubianka: Stalin i NKVD-NKGB-GUKR "Smersh": 1939–mart 1946* (Moscow: Mezhdunarodnyi fond "Demokratiia," 2006), 550–52. (Citing GARF, f. 9401, op. 2, d. 134, ll. 265–68.)

82. March 30, 1946, recruiting methods for Soviet agents, Operation Bingo, IIDIF, NACP.

83. GARF, f. 9526, op. 6, d. 262, ll. 136, 138.

84. GARF, f. 9526, op. 6, d. 262, l. 10.

85. GARF, f. 9526, op. 6, d. 363, ll. 67–74.

86. GARF, f. 9526, op. 6, d. 358, l. 208; d. 462, l. 52.

87. GARF, f. 9526, op. 6, d. 373, l. 59.

88. GARF, f. 9526, op. 6, d. 377, ll. 153–55, 160–68.

89. GARF, f. 9526, op. 6, d. 487, l. 80.

90. Christopher Simpson, *Blowback: America's Recruitment of Nazis and Its Destructive Impact on Our Domestic and Foreign Policy* (London: Weidenfeld and Nicolson, 1988), 27–29, 156–75; Richard Breitman and Norman Goda, *Hitler's Shadow: Nazi War Criminals, U.S. Intelligence, and the Cold War* (Washington, DC: National Archives, 2010), 73–97.

91. Melissa Feinberg, *Curtain of Lies: The Battle over Truth in Stalinist Eastern Europe* (Oxford: Oxford University Press, 2017).

92. Francine Hirsch, *Soviet Judgment at Nuremberg: A New History of the International Military Tribunal after World War II* (Oxford: Oxford University Press, 2020), 82–83.

93. October 16, 1945, Lt. Colonel Alexander K. Oreshkin, USSR Liaison Officer, Operation Bingo, IIDIF, RG 319, NACP; FO 1013/2109 Russian Liaison, "Russian Los," February 18, 1946; GARF, f. 9526, op. 6, d. 470, l. 139.

94. GARF, f. 9526, op. 6, d. 358, l. 412.

95. HDASBU, f. 1, spr. 694, ark. 191-93.

96. GARF, f. 9526, op. 6, d. 263, ll. 225-27.

97. GARF, f. 9526, op. 6, d. 263, ll. 226, 284-85.

98. GARF, f. 9526, op. 6, d. 263, l. 281.

99. GARF, f. 9526, op. 6, d. 96, l. 51.

100. GARF, f. 9526, op. 6, d. 249, ll. 139-42; d. 258, l. 250.

101. For the story of one successful escape, see Mikhail Koriakov, *I'll Never Go Back: A Red Army Officer Talks* (London: Dutton, 1948), 232-35; GARF, f. 9526, op. 6, d. 265, ll. 21-22.

102. GARF, f. 9526, op. 6, d. 466, ll. 54-57, 60-61.

103. Norman Naimark, *The Russians in Germany: A History of the Soviet Zone of Occupation, 1945-1949* (Cambridge, MA: Harvard University Press, 1995), 144; Filip Slaveski, *The Soviet Occupation of Germany: Hunger, Mass Violence and the Struggle for Peace, 1945-1947* (Cambridge: Cambridge University Press, 2013), 19-20.

104. GARF, f. 9526, op. 6, d. 360, l. 35.

105. GARF, f. 9526, op. 6, d. 360, ll. 15-16, 32-34.

106. GARF, f. 9526, op. 6, d. 380, ll. 104-5, 117-21.

107. GARF, f. 9526, op. 6, d. 380, ll. 168-72.

108. GARF, f. 9526, op. 6, d. 416, l. 9.

109. GARF, f. 9526, op. 6, d. 380, l. 212.

110. GARF, f. 9526, op. 6, d. 784, l. 26.

111. GARF, f. 9526, op. 6, d. 470, l. 142.

112. GARF, f. 9526, op. 6, d. 476, l. 251. Briukhanov would also write an argumentative memoir about his experiences. Aleksei Briukhanov, *Vot kak eto bylo: O rabote missii po repatriatsii sovetskikh grazhdan* (Moscow: Gospolitizdat, 1958).

113. Seth Bernstein, "Burying the Alliance: Interment, Repatriation and the Politics of the Sacred in Occupied Germany," *Journal of Contemporary History* 52, no. 3 (2017): 727-28.

114. For this argument, see Sheila Fitzpatrick, "The Motherland Calls: 'Soft' Repatriation of Soviet Citizens from Europe, 1945-1953," *Journal of Modern History* 90, no. 2 (2018): 350.

10. RETURN AFTER STALIN

1. Sheila Fitzpatrick, "Soviet Repatriation Efforts among 'Displaced Persons' Resettled in Australia, 1950-53," *Australian Journal of Politics and History* 63, no. 1 (2017): 45-61.

2. Lists of migrants compiled by the KGB are available in four files: HDASBU, f. 1, spr. 772, 773, 774, 775.

3. Tara Zahra, *The Great Departure: Mass Migration from Eastern Europe and the Making of the Free World* (New York: Norton, 2016), 105-42.

4. Alexander Statiev, *The Soviet Counterinsurgency in the Western Borderlands* (Cambridge: Cambridge University Press, 2010).

5. On Ukrainians working for American intelligence, see Richard Breitman and Norman Goda, *Hitler's Shadow: Nazi War Criminals, U.S. Intelligence, and the Cold War* (Washington, DC: National Archives, 2010), 73-91. On ethnic Russian émigrés, see Benjamin Tromly, *Cold War Exiles and the CIA: Plotting to Free Russia* (Oxford: Oxford University Press, 2019).

6. Susan Reid, "Cold War in the Kitchen: Gender and the De-Stalinization of Consumer Taste in the Soviet Union under Khrushchev," *Slavic Review* 61, no. 2 (2002): 211–52.

7. On this dynamic in Stalinist elections, see Serhy Yekelchyk, *Stalin's Citizens: Everyday Politics in the Wake of Total War* (Oxford: Oxford University Press, 2014), 141–78.

8. R. M. Douglas, *Orderly and Humane: The Expulsion of the Germans after the Second World War* (New Haven, CT: Yale University Press, 2012); Benjamin Frommer, *National Cleansing: Retribution against Nazi Collaborators in Postwar Czechoslovakia* (Cambridge: Cambridge University Press, 2005); Gregor Thum, *Uprooted: How Breslau Became Wroclaw during the Century of Expulsions* (Princeton, NJ: Princeton University Press, 2011).

9. Pamela Ballinger, *The World Refugees Made: Decolonization and the Foundation of Postwar Italy* (Ithaca, NY: Cornell University Press, 2020), 135.

10. Krista Goff, *Nested Nationalism: Making and Unmaking Nations in the Soviet Caucasus* (Ithaca, NY: Cornell University Press, 2021).

11. Catherine Gousseff, "Evacuation versus Repatriation: The Polish-Ukrainian Population Exchange, 1944–6," in *The Disentanglement of Populations: Migration, Expulsion and Displacement in Postwar Europe, 1944–49*, ed. Jessica Reinisch and Elizabeth White (Basingstoke: Palgrave, 2011), 93.

12. Joanne Laycock, "Belongings: People and Possessions in the Armenian Repatriations, 1945–49," *Kritika* 18, no. 3 (2017): 511.

13. Laurie Manchester, "Fusing Russian Nationalism with Soviet Patriotism: Changing Conceptions of Homeland and the Mass Repatriation of Manchurian Russians after Stalin's Death," *Kritika* 20, no. 3 (2019): 529.

14. GARF, f. 9526, op. 6, d. 236, ll. 124–25; d. 242, l. 1.

15. V. F. Zima, *Golod v SSSR 1946–1947 godov: Proiskhozhdenie i posledstviia* (Moscow: Institut rossiiskoi istorii, 1996), 37.

16. GARF, f. 9526, op. 6, d. 283, l. 15.

17. GARF, f. 9526, op. 6, d. 279, ll. 146, 149, 151.

18. Mikhail Koriakov, *I'll Never Go Back: A Red Army Officer Talks* (London: Dutton, 1948), 204.

19. GARF, f. 9526, op. 6, d. 372, l. 8.

20. GARF, f. 9526, op. 6, d. 266, ll. 165–67.

21. GARF, f. 9526, op. 6, d. 279, ll. 150–51.

22. GARF, f. 9526, op. 6, d. 279, ll. 167–68.

23. GARF, f. 9526, op. 6, d. 372, l. 407; d. 418, l. 13; d. 458, l. 15.

24. GARF, f. 9526, op. 6, d. 279, ll. 150–51.

25. Gerard Daniel Cohen, *In War's Wake: Europe's Displaced Persons in the Postwar Order* (Cambridge: Cambridge University Press, 2011), 101.

26. GARF, f. 9526, op. 6, d. 1124, ll. 3, 11.

27. Gennadii Kostyrchenko, *Tainaia politika Stalina*, vol. 2, *Na fone kholodnoi voiny* (Moscow: Mezhdunarodnye otnosheniia, 2015), 604–5.

28. A. N. Artizov, Iu. V. Sigachev, V. G. Khlopov, and I. N. Shevchuk eds., *Reabilitatsiia: Kak eto bylo*, vol. 1, *Mart 1953–fevral' 1956* (Moscow: Demokratiia, 2000), 259–60.

29. HDASBU, f. 1, spr. 613, ark. 85–86.

30. Edward A. Morrow, "780 in Argentina Heed Soviet Call: Boatload of Refugees Sail for Home," *New York Times*, April 17, 1956, 12.

31. Tromly, *Cold War Exiles and the CIA*, 264–65.

32. HDASBU, f. 1, spr. 613, ark. 9–10, 88–91.

33. HDASBU, f. 1, spr. 786, ark. 3–4, 26–27.

34. Tromly, *Cold War Exiles and the CIA*, 249.

35. For police instructions on cataloging nonreturners and a sample list, see HDASBU, f. 1, spr. 383, ark. 75–76, 78–81.

36. HDASBU, f. 1, spr. 786, ark. 9.

37. Serge Cipko, *Ukrainians in Argentina, 1897–1950: The Making of a Community* (Toronto: Canadian Institute of Ukrainian Studies Press, 2011), xviii, 56–57.

38. Elena Osokina, *Our Daily Bread: Socialist Distribution and the Art of Survival in Stalin's Russia, 1927–1941* (New York: M. E. Sharpe, 2001), xii–xiii. On Stalinist promises of prosperity, see Kristy Ironside, *A Full-Value Ruble: The Promise of Prosperity in the Postwar Soviet Union* (Cambridge, MA: Harvard University Press, 2021), 3.

39. Elena Zubkova, *Russia after the War: Hopes, Illusions and Disappointments, 1945–1957* (New York: M. E. Sharpe, 1998), 34.

40. Reid, "Cold War in the Kitchen"; Aaron Hale-Dorrell, *Corn Crusade: Khrushchev's Farming Revolution in the Post-Stalin Soviet Union* (Oxford: Oxford University Press, 2018); Steven Harris, *Communism on Tomorrow Street: Mass Housing and Everyday Life after Stalin* (Baltimore: Johns Hopkins University Press, 2013).

41. On cars as status symbols, see Lewis Siegelbaum, *Cars for Comrades: The Life of the Soviet Automobile* (Ithaca, NY: Cornell University Press, 2008), 238–41.

42. "Vesti s rodiny," *Za vozvrashchenie na Rodinu*, no. 1 (1956): 2.

43. A. Pushka, "Chem my bogaty," *Za vozvrashchenie na Rodinu*, no. 17 (1960): 3–4.

44. "V Ministerstve inostrannykh del," *Pravda*, August 30, 1956, 2.

45. Tobias Rupprecht, *Soviet Internationalism after Stalin: Interaction and Exchange between the USSR and Latin America during the Cold War* (Cambridge: Cambridge University Press, 2015), 44–47.

46. Iurii Slepukhin, "V chem ia obviniaiu glavarei NTS," *Za vozvrashchenie na Rodinu*, no. 46 (1959): 2–3.

47. Iurii Slepukhin, *Kimmeriiskoe leto. Iuzhnyi krest* (Leningrad: Sovetskii pisatel', 1983), 425.

48. HDASBU, f. 1, spr. 767, ark. 3–5.

49. HDASBU, f. 1, spr. 765, ark. 74.

50. Slepukhin, *Kimmeriiskoe leto. Iuzhnyi krest*, 433.

51. Database derived from HDASBU, f. 1, spr. 772, 773, 774, 775.

52. HDASBU, f. 1, spr. 1262, ark. 3; spr. 765, ark. 46–47.

53. HDASBU, f. 1, spr. 765 ark. 280.

54. HDASBU, f. 1, spr. 1262, ark. 179–80.

55. HDASBU, f. 1, spr. 1262, ark. 61.

56. Victoria Smolkin, *A Sacred Space Is Never Empty: A History of Soviet Atheism* (Princeton, NJ: Princeton University Press, 2018).

57. HDASBU, f. 1, spr. 798, ark. 123, 125.

58. HDASBU, f. 1, spr. 766, ark. 42.

59. HDASBU, f. 1, spr. 1262, ark. 179ob.

60. HDASBU, f. 1, spr. 767, ark. 6–7.

61. HDASBU, f. 1, spr. 769, ark. 57; spr. 767, ark. 7.

62. On allocation of apartments, see Harris, *Communism on Tomorrow Street*, 121–34.

63. HDASBU, f. 1, spr. 766, ark. 57.

64. Kate Brown, *A Biography of No Place: From Ethnic Borderland to Soviet Heartland* (Cambridge, MA: Harvard University Press, 2004), 192–225; Tarik Amar, *The Paradox of Ukrainian Lviv: A Borderland City between Stalinists, Nazis, and Nationalists* (Ithaca, NY: Cornell University Press, 2015); Catherine Gousseff, *Échanger les peuples: Le déplacement des minorités aux confins polono-soviétiques (1944–1947)* (Paris: Fayard Histoire, 2015). On the homogenization of Ukrainian official culture, see Serhy Yekelchyk, *Stalin's Empire of Memory: Russian-Ukrainian Relations in the Soviet Historical Imagi-

nation (Toronto: University of Toronto Press, 2004). On the Ukrainian Communist Party and the construction of a unified "Ukrainian imaginary space" along the western borderlands, see Alexandr Voronovici, "'Communist Ukrainian International'" (draft paper presented at the Higher School of Economics, Moscow, January 25, 2019).

65. Glenna Roberts and Serge Cipko, *One-Way Ticket: The Soviet Return-to-the-Homeland Campaign, 1955–1960* (Manotick, ON: Penumbra Press, 2008), 91.

66. HDASBU, f. 1, spr. 1262, ark. 23, 101.

67. Roberts and Cipko, *One-Way Ticket*, 83

68. HDASBU, f. 1, spr. 1262, ark. 43–48.

69. Roberts and Cipko, *One-Way Ticket*, 95–96.

70. HDASBU, f. 1, spr. 1262, ark. 102.

71. A characteristic case: HDASBU, f. 1, spr. 769, ark. 110–11.

72. HDASBU, f. 1, spr. 1262, ark. 173, 174–75, 176.

73. HDASBU, f. 1, spr. 772, ark. 157; spr. 1262, ark. 67, 92, 219–24, 247.

74. HDASBU, f. 1, spr. 1251, ark. 5–6. See also Edward Cohn, "Coercion, Reeducation, and the Prophylactic Chat: *Profilaktika* and the KGB's Struggle with Political Unrest in Lithuania, 1953–64," *Russian Review* 76, no. 2 (2017): 272–93.

75. HDASBU, f. 1, spr. 1263, ark. 266–72.

76. HDASBU, f. 1, spr. 769, ark. 177–79.

77. HDASBU, f. 1, spr. 1467, ark. 240.

78. HDASBU, f. 1, spr. 1467, ark. 236–37.

79. Roberts and Cipko, *One-Way Ticket*, 158–60.

80. HDASBU, f. 1, spr. 769, ark. 115–17.

81. HDASBU, f. 1, spr. 769, ark. 192.

82. HDASBU, f. 1, spr. 1456, ark. 266–67.

83. S. V. Shabel'tsev, "Ukrains'ki reemigranty z Arhentyny (1950-1960-ti rr.)," *Ukrains'kyi istorychnyi zhurnal*, no. 5 (2002): 103; HDASBU, f. 1, spr. 1467, ark. 316.

84. Roberts and Cipko, *One-Way Ticket*, 131–32.

85. HDASBU, f. 1, spr. 1467, ark. 319–22.

86. For these letters, see S. Borisoglebskaia, "Moi pozhelaniia," *Za vozvrashchenie na Rodinu*, no. 89 (November 1959): 3; "'Golos Rodiny'. Slovo v khode odnoi diskusii," *Za vozvrashchenie na Rodinu*, no. 2 (January 1960): 3.

CONCLUSION

1. GARF, f. 9526, op. 6, d. 52, l. 248. The literal phrasing in the pamphlet ("We will not forget anything. We will not forgive anyone.") is not as pithy as the Berggolts poem.

2. Michael Jansen, Günter Saathoff, and Kai Hennig, eds., "Final Report on the Compensation Programs Carried Out by the 'Remembrance, Responsibility and Future' Foundation," in *"A Mutual Responsibility and a Moral Obligation": The Final Report on Germany's Compensation Programs for Forced Labor and Other Personal Injuries*, ed. Michael Jansen, and Günter Saathoff (Basingstoke: Palgrave, 2009), 102, 118.

3. Mikhailo K., ZA487, 88.

4. Alexander Statiev, "'La Garde meurt mais ne se rend pas!': Once Again on the 28 Panfilov Heroes," *Kritika* 13, no. 4 (2012): 786–88.

5. Gelinada Grinchenko, "The Ostarbeiter of Nazi Germany in Soviet and Post-Soviet Ukrainian Historical Memory," *Canadian Slavonic Papers* 54, no. 3–4 (2012): 423.

NOTE ON SOURCES

1. Peter Holquist, "'Information Is the Alpha and Omega of Our Work': Bolshevik Surveillance in Its Pan-European Context," *Journal of Modern History* 69, no. 3 (1997): 448–49.

2. There are dozens, if not hundreds, of works on forced laborers in various regions of Germany and the Reich. For general accounts, see Ulrich Herbert, *Hitler's Foreign Workers: Enforced Foreign Labor in Germany under the Third Reich* (Cambridge: Cambridge University Press, 1997); Mark Spoerer, *Zwangsarbeit unter dem Hakenkreuz. Ausländische Zivilarbeiter, Kriegsgefangene und Häftlinge im Deutschen Reich und im besetzten Europa 1939–1945* (Munich: Deutsche Verlagsanstalt, 2001).

Note on Sources

The research for this book mostly comes from three sets of materials. The first is the published diaries, memoirs, and interviews of displaced persons. Most come from the hundred-plus interviews Soviet returnees gave with researchers in or around 2005, part of a collective effort by researchers in 2005–7 in the German-based project "Forced Labor 1939–1945. Memory and History." Oral historians from across Europe collected remembrances of forced laborers and prisoners of war under German rule.

These interviews have unavoidable flaws, despite the good work of the interviewers. Most interviewees were in their teens or early twenties during the war, young enough to have survived to tell their stories in the first years of the new millennium. This age-group made up most Eastern Workers in Germany. There were older Eastern Workers, though, and their stories are probably underrepresented in the sources. Almost all the recordings took place when the interviewees were in their late seventies or older, and their fading memory was apparent in many cases.

Like all oral history interviews, the responses were shaped by contemporary outlooks. The interviewees rarely or never broached topics like sexual violence and homosexuality, for example. Despite the problems with these interviews, they are perhaps the best source available about social life among forced laborers in Germany. Archives seldom record the views of marginalized peoples, as the forced laborers were in Germany and as repatriates were in the USSR. The interviews offer a unique social perspective on events that are otherwise accessible only through the reports of state actors.

The second source base is the archive of the Soviet Repatriation Administration, held at the State Archive of the Russian Federation. These materials provide the institutional history of repatriation from a variety of state actors in the Communist Party, the secret police, the Repatriation Administration, and others. They also are a key source for understanding the interactions between displaced persons, Soviet officials, and the Western Allies in occupied Germany. The collection includes reports from officials about the progress of repatriation, stenographic records of meetings between Soviet officials and their counterparts among the Western Allies, and materials from officers working in repatriation missions in Allied-occupied Europe.

Third, I used secret police materials from Ukraine and Georgia. These include thousands of pages of investigations of individual returnees, collective dossiers about suspect groups, and reports about migrants overall. The arrest files include a variety of documents: summary information about the arrestee's biography; stenographic records of interrogations with the arrestee and witnesses; supplementary evidence found by the investigation or seized from the arrestee, such as German documents, letters, or personal photographs; a record of the trial; and posttrial appellate documents, including appeals and reviews that extend into the 1990s. These materials are uniquely able to provide contemporaneous information about life under German rule, repatriation, postwar Stalinism, and the rehabilitation process for Soviet people convicted of collaboration. They also help us to understand the policies and attitudes of the police toward repatriates.

Soviet police documents have shortcomings as sources. Historians have rightfully cautioned against using police reports as a source of representative popular opinion; the police were not interested in gathering an accurate picture of people's beliefs but in finding and excising anti-Soviet attitudes.[1] For this reason, police reports on popular opinion often say more about the regime's policies than about the public mood. Stalinist arrest files are also notorious for falsifications. Interrogators were particularly willing to fabricate confessions during the years 1937–38, when quotas set by Stalin forced them to fulfill their "plan" by any means possible, including violence. With some notable exceptions, I have found that the investigators of the postwar period, though they infused cases with their own Stalinist conclusions, sought an accurate account of events. After Stalin's death, Khrushchev's government commuted the sentences of many convicted repatriates and offered them the opportunity to appeal their cases. In their petitions, repatriates largely confirmed the accounts given to Stalinist interrogators about their lives, even as they contested obvious falsifications and the investigators' assertions that their wartime actions had been crimes. We should not underestimate the pressure—psychological and sometimes physical—that arrestees faced. Nonetheless, it is possible to read the interrogations as an adversarial oral history, written in tandem by the investigator and arrestee.

This book brings the history of Soviet-born displaced people closer to the history of population politics in wartime and postwar Europe. Although I explore a transnational topic, the perspective is largely Soviet. Instead of focusing on nonreturners, I have made people who returned to the USSR the main subjects. The primary revelations about state policies are from the Soviet side as well. The political history of foreign labor under Nazism has been investigated, and it is not my goal to revise it.[2]

Index

Page numbers in *italics* indicate illustrations.

Abakumov, Viktor, 131
agricultural and domestic labor, 27–31, *29*
Akhmatova, Anna, 159
alcohol and drunkenness, 24, 39, 63, 67, 90, 209, 211, 212, 257n43
Aleksandra A., 38
Alexopoulos, Golfo, 10
Aliferenko, Vasilii, 89, 95
Altshuler, Isaak, 185–86
ambivalence/suspicion: of late returners and repatriation mission members, 191, 212–13; of POWs, 128, 134; remembrance/forgiveness and, 235–39; of repatriates, 104–5, 111, 114–20, *119*, 124–25, 159, 194, 235
America. *See* United States
American Jewish Joint Distribution Committee, 102
Anatolii A., 20, 83–84, 91
Andreichuk, Khariton, 224
Anna M., 36
Anna P., 35
Anna Sh., 41
annexations 1939–45 by Soviets, *xviii*, 2, 7–8, 12, 36, 87, 97, 103, 190. *See also specific states*
anticommunism, 3, 6, 11, 12, 69
Antilucci, Brosildo, 96, 97
antisemitism. *See* Jews
Antonina M., 119
Antonina S., xvii, 42–43, 46–47, 99, 124
Antonina V., 45, 101, 123
Archer, Ernest, 86
Argentina, re-émigrés from, 215, 220–26, 228–33
arrests of repatriates, 110, 143, 147–48, 158, 159, 229, 230, 265n18
Arteniuk, Aleksei ("Dmitruk"), 230, 233
Article 58, 151–52
Astakhov, Petr, xvii, 61–62, 69, 72–73, 80, 164
Astashina, Klavdia, 177
Auschwitz-Birkenau, 58, 102
auxiliaries, 7, 52, 54, 56, 60, 78, 86, 109, 127, 128, 145

Baltic republics, 2, 12, 59, 61, 102, 108, 137, 190, 194, 199, 208. *See also* Estonia/Estonians; Latvia/Latvians; Lithuania/Lithuanians
Baron, Nick, 10
Basilov, Iakov, 212
Belarus/Belarusians, 2, 30, 36, 38, 47, 56, 59, 61, 93, 102, 108, 115, 118, 121, 148, 190, 197, 199, 217, 218
Belashov, Anatolii, 210
Belikov, Vitalii, 35, 131–32
Belov, Senior Lieutenant, 139
Berggolts, Olga, 235
Beria, Lavrentii, 130, 134, 137, 181
Berkun, Natalia, xvii, 77, 183, 186–87
Beznos, Leonid/Lev, 150
Bishop, Alec, 201
Black Allied soldiers, racism against, 91
Blonskii (repatriate and labor battalion member), 136
Bondarenko, Vsevolod, 180
Bormatov (peat processing plant dispatcher), 119–20
Breisler (Alimov), Mikhail, 58
Britain: émigré community working with Anglo-American intelligence in Cold War, 216; monument to displaced in, 3, *4*; postwar concerns about spies from, 158–65
Briukhanov, Aleksei, 197–202, 207, 210–13, 274n112
Brodskii, Efim, xvii, 78, 167, 169–72, 188–89, 238
Bronislava A., 117
BSV (Brotherly Union of Prisoners of War), 77–78
Buchenwald, 82–83, *84*, 89, 176, 179, 180, 182
Bulganin, Nikolai, 138, 140, 217

Canada, emigration to/re-émigrés from, 100, 227–29, 231–33
capitalism, 100, 114, 143, 158, 164, 191, 193, 203, 204, 208, 214, 216, 222, 228, 230, 232, 234, 237

liberation); methodological approach, 5–6; nationalist state, emergence of Soviet Union as, 11–12; nonreturners, 2, 7, 10, 190–214, 237 (*See also* nonreturners); numbers, classification, and outcomes of, *2*; remembering/forgiving, 235–39; repatriation of, 2–4, 7–11, 236–37 (*See also* repatriation; social tensions in repatriation); Return to the Motherland campaign, 13, 215–34, 237 (*See also* Return to the Motherland campaign); secret police and, 14, 143–65, 236 (*See also* secret police); source materials, 5, 279–80; Ukraine and, 13 (*See also* Ukraine); youth of, 37, 90, 116, 117

Doctors' Plot, 219

DP camps: anti-Soviet activity, believed to be hotbeds of, 214; Leipzig theater troupe in, *193*; Lesnichenko as camp coordinator after liberation, 89, 94; liberation and, 81, *85*, 87–89; nonreturners remaining in (*See* nonreturners); POWs as leaders of, 88; resistance, leaders claiming involvement in, 88

DPs (displaced persons). *See* displaced Soviets in WWII and Cold War

Dragun, Vasilii, 88, 89

Druz, Petr, 175

Dunchevskii, Aleksei, xvii, 63, *65*, *66*, 69–71, 73, 153

Dzadzamia, Aleksandr, xvii, 74, 77–79, 94, 95, 183–84, *185*, 187–88

Dzhalil, Musa (Cälil), 77–78, 188

Eastern Workers, 15–53, 235–36; adaptation to life in Germany, 37–38; agricultural and domestic labor, 27–31, *29*; alcohol and drunkenness, 24, 39; barracks/room supervisors (*starosta*), 41; bombing raids and, 22, 24–25; Brodskii on, 188–89; city/factory work, 20–27; communities established by, 33–42; cooperation with mobilization, 19, 20; criminality, German fears of, 25–27, 40; deportation and displacement of, 2, 16–20; Eastern Workers (Ostarbeiter), concept of, 15–16; executions of, near end of war, 83, 91; food rations, housing, and living conditions, 20–21, 23, 24, 27–28, 38, 39; German reparations for, 238–39; holidays, celebration of, 38–39; as informants, 40; as kitchen workers, 41–42; labor conditions and discipline, 22–23, 28; letters home, 17–19, 37; medical examina-

tions and treatment, 20, 24, 40–41; mortality rates of, 24, 246n33; numbers of, 244–45n1; OST badge, 15, 23–24, 84–85, *85*; POWs as, 17, 59–60; propaganda about, 17, *18*, 50, *51*; protests by, 21, 26–27, 36, 245n31; religion and, 34–35, 38; repatriation process for, 106, *107*; sex lives of, 33–34, 45–53, *51*; Slavic inferiority, German notions of, 15, 16, 22, 31–32, 33, 34, 53; source materials for, 15–16; Soviet mobilized workers compared, 31–32, 247n91; from Soviet-annexed regions, 36; time off, 21, 23, 28, 37–38, 39; translators and interpreters for, 41; transnational relationships of, 33, 34, 42–44; volunteers versus, 17–19; youth of, 37. *See also* collaboration, resistance, and agency; liberation; nonreturners; repatriation

Eden, Anthony, 86, 87

education, efforts of repatriates to resume, 116, 117

Eisenhower, Dwight, 83, 99

émigré community: Cold War, working with Anglo-American intelligence in, 216; collaboration/resistance/agency and, 61, 63, 67, 68, 70, 71, 72; early Soviet attitudes toward, 11; Eastern Workers and, 30, 34, 35, 41, 42; late returnees and, 208; liberation and, 98, 99, 100, 103; nonreturners in DP camps and, 207; Return to the Motherland campaign and, 216, 217–18, 220–21, 223–24; secret police investigations and, 152–53, 159; Soviet repatriation mission and, 197; Union of Soviet Patriots, 208; war orphans from, 203

Emil (French boyfriend/husband of Galina G.), 47–48, 124

Eremenko, Nikolai, 221

escapes: by labor battalion members, 135–37; by POWs, 58–59; self-liberations, 82–84, 176; from special camps/settlements, 129–30

Estonia/Estonians, 97, 99, 121, 137, 199, 200. *See also* Baltic republics

ethnic belonging, Soviet conceptions of, 102

ethnic Estonians, 99, 199

ethnic exchanges/cleansing, 217, 227

ethnic Germans, 8, 16, 50, 53, 59, 61, 67, 106, 111, 175, 217, 227

ethnic homogenization of Soviet Republics, 13, 216–17, 227

ethnic identities, beliefs about stability of, 229

ethnic Italians, 217

prostitution, 48–49

Protsenko, Vladimir, 100–101

Putin, Vladimir, 239

racial ideology of Nazis: concerns about racial mixing, 23, 49–50, 251n98; Orientalist prejudices, 52, 60; POW release program and, 59; Slavic inferiority, German notions of, 15, 16, 22, 31–32, 33, 34, 53, 83; Westarbeiter (Western Europeans), 33, 42

racism against Black Allied soldiers, 91

Raisa B., 121

rape and sexual violence, 48, 49, 52, 112–13, 209

Ravensbrück, 39, 121

Razumov, A. A., 106, 107, 113

Red Army: E. Brodskii in, 169; collaboration/resistance and, 68, 69, 70, 71, 72, 74, 76, 78; Eastern Workers joining, post-WWII, 131–32; film treatments of, 118, 119; former German auxiliary troops joining, 145; *Krasnaia Zvezda*, 67, 170; liberation and DPs, 86, 87, 89, 91, 92–93, 95, 98, 102; management of repatriation by, 9, 102, 105, 106; partisan operations dovetailing with, 175; rape and sexual predation by, 1, 8, 49, 92–93; reintegration of POWs into, 128–29, 130, 131, 132; retribution following arrival of, 144–45; violence against/exploitation of DPs, 111–14; in WWII, 15, 16, 19, 37, 71, 72. *See also* prisoners of war

re-émigrés, concept of, 215. *See also* Return to the Motherland campaign

refugees, UN resolution on (1946), 195, 198

registration records, 146, 148–49

religion: Eastern Workers and, 34–35, 38; Orthodox Church, 35, 38, 131, 195, 225–26

repatriation, 2–4, 7–11, 236–37; agreements to repatriate all Soviet subjects, 3, 81, 86–87, 256n22; arrests of repatriates, 110, 143, 147–48, 158, 159, 229, 230, 265n18; circumvention of official means of, 108; desire of most displaced persons to return, 7, 96, 103, 237–38; end of, 219; family, desire to reunite with, 101–2; forced, 3, 7, 190, 194, 195, 198, 206, 213, 271n18; Geneva Convention of 1929 on, 86; of Jews, 102; late returners, 191, 206–13; mixed marriages and, 99–100; numbers of people seeking, 106–7, 206; post-filtration outcomes, 3–4, 5, 110; process of, 105; Western attitudes toward, 12, 81, 86–87, 97, 98–100, 103, 190, 192, 194–96, 198; Western POWs and, 87.

See also Return to the Motherland campaign; social tensions in repatriation

Repatriation Administration, 8–9, 104–5; abuses of repatriates, investigating, 104, 116; on Brodskii, 171; closing of, 13; closure of (1953), 219; collaboration, report on post-liberation vigilante trials for, 90; establishment of, 106; labor battalion members, petitions from, 133; nonreturners, on detentions of, 195, 196; petitions to, 101; repurposed as recruiting office for Soviet diaspora, 217, 218; source documents from, 242n11; Soviet repatriation missions in Germany, 191–97, 199, 209–13; Soviet-occupied Europe, labor demand in, 138–41; suspicion of repatriates from, 118; on war orphans, 203

Repshis, Captain, 199

resistance. *See* collaboration, resistance, and agency; returnee-resisters

Return to the Motherland campaign (1950s), 13, 215–34, 237; affinity between diaspora and motherland, morphing into promotion of, 233–34; arrests/interrogations of re-émigrés, 229, 230; children returning under, 224–25; émigré community and, 216, 217–18, 220–21, 223–24; exiting the USSR from, 228–34; KGB and, 215, 220–21, 224, 225, 228–34; lives/living conditions of re-émigrés, 222–28, 231, 232, 233; reasons for appeal to Soviet diaspora, 215–16; reasons of re-émigrés for returning, 223–26; recruitment techniques and goals, 216–22

returnee-resisters, 166–89; after death of Stalin, 188; exaggerated or falsified claims of, 168, 172–82; P. Lesnichenko as, 166, *167*, 176, 179, 182–87, 189; POWs as, 182–83, 184; RROK, postwar suspicions about, 166, 182–88; writing history of, 166–67, 168–72, 188–89

returnees. *See* filtration; repatriation

ROA (Russian Liberation Army/Vlasovites), 22, 55, 56, 57, 60, 67, 79, 111, 126, 130, 131, 139, 157, 169

Romanov, Mikhail, 150

Romm, Mikhail, 118, 184

Roosevelt, Franklin, 3, 86

Rosenberg, Alfred, 56, 61

RROK (Russian Workers Liberation Committee): Dzadzamia's RROK card, *185*; Kiselev and, 94–95, 176, 179, 181; in Leipzig, *75*, 94–96; Lesnichenko and, 94–96, 166, 176, 179, 182–87, 189; postwar suspicions about, 166, 182–88

CPSIA information can be obtained
at www.ICGtesting.com
Printed in the USA
LVHW101913050123
736514LV00016B/287/J